Windows 98® One Step at a Time

Windows 98®
One Step at a Time

Brian Underdahl

IDG Books Worldwide, Inc.

An International Data Group Company

FOSTER CITY, CA · CHICAGO, IL · INDIANAPOLIS, IN · NEW YORK, NY · SOUTHLAKE, TX

Windows 98® One Step at a Time
Published by
IDG Books Worldwide, Inc.
An International Data Group Company
919 E. Hillsdale Blvd., Suite 400
Foster City, CA 94404
www.idgbooks.com (IDG Books Worldwide Web site)

Library of Congress Catalog Card No.: 97-78217

ISBN: 0-7645-3184-0

Printed in the United States of America

10 9 8 7 6 5 4 3 2 1

1E/RV/QV/ZY/FC

Distributed in the United States by IDG Books Worldwide, Inc.

Distributed by Macmillan Canada for Canada; by Transworld Publishers Limited in the United Kingdom; by IDG Norge Books for Norway; by IDG Sweden Books for Sweden; by Woodslane Pty. Ltd. for Australia; by Woodslane New Zealand Ltd. for New Zealand; by Addison-Wesley Longman Singapore Pte Ltd. for Singapore, Malaysia, Thailand, and Indonesia; by Distribuidora Norma S.A.-Colombia for Colombia; by Intersoft for South Africa; by International Thompson Publishing for Germany, Austria, and Switzerland; by Toppan Company Ltd. for Japan; by Distribuidora Cuspide for Argentina; by Livraria Cultura for Brazil; by Ediciencia S.A. for Ecuador; by Addison-Wesley Publishing Company for Korea; by Ediciones ZETA S.C.R. Ltda. for Peru; by WS Computer Publishing Corporation, Inc., for the Philippines; by Unalis Corporation for Taiwan; by Contemporanea de Ediciones for Venezuela; by Computer Book & Magazine Store for Puerto Rico; by Express Computer Distributors for the Caribbean and West Indies. Authorized Sales Agent: Anthony Rudkin Associates for the Middle East and North Africa.

For general information on IDG Books Worldwide's books in the U.S., please call our Consumer Customer Service department at 800-762-2974. For reseller information, including discounts and premium sales, please call our Reseller Customer Service department at 800-434-3422.

For information on where to purchase IDG Books Worldwide's books outside the U.S., please contact our International Sales department at 650-655-3200 or fax 650-655-3297.

For information on foreign language translations, please contact our Foreign & Subsidiary Rights department at 650-655-3021 or fax 650-655-3281.

For sales inquiries and special prices for bulk quantities, please contact our Sales department at 650-655-3200 or write to the address above.

For information on using IDG Books Worldwide's books in the classroom or for ordering examination copies, please contact our Educational Sales department at 800-434-2086 or fax 817-421-5012.

For press review copies, author interviews, or other publicity information, please contact our Public Relations department at 650-655-3000 or fax 650-655-3299.

For authorization to photocopy items for corporate, personal, or educational use, please contact Copyright Clearance Center, 222 Rosewood Drive, Danvers, MA 01923, or fax 978-750-4470.

is a trademark under exclusive license to IDG Books Worldwide, Inc., from International Data Group, Inc.

ABOUT IDG BOOKS WORLDWIDE

Welcome to the world of IDG Books Worldwide.

IDG Books Worldwide, Inc., is a subsidiary of International Data Group, the world's largest publisher of computer-related information and the leading global provider of information services on information technology. IDG was founded more than 25 years ago and now employs more than 8,500 people worldwide. IDG publishes more than 275 computer publications in over 75 countries (see listing below). More than 60 million people read one or more IDG publications each month.

Launched in 1990, IDG Books Worldwide is today the #1 publisher of best-selling computer books in the United States. We are proud to have received eight awards from the Computer Press Association in recognition of editorial excellence and three from *Computer Currents*' First Annual Readers' Choice Awards. Our best-selling *...For Dummies*® series has more than 30 million copies in print with translations in 30 languages. IDG Books Worldwide, through a joint venture with IDG's Hi-Tech Beijing, became the first U.S. publisher to publish a computer book in the People's Republic of China. In record time, IDG Books Worldwide has become the first choice for millions of readers around the world who want to learn how to better manage their businesses.

Our mission is simple: Every one of our books is designed to bring extra value and skill-building instructions to the reader. Our books are written by experts who understand and care about our readers. The knowledge base of our editorial staff comes from years of experience in publishing, education, and journalism — experience we use to produce books for the '90s. In short, we care about books, so we attract the best people. We devote special attention to details such as audience, interior design, use of icons, and illustrations. And because we use an efficient process of authoring, editing, and desktop publishing our books electronically, we can spend more time ensuring superior content and spend less time on the technicalities of making books.

You can count on our commitment to deliver high-quality books at competitive prices on topics you want to read about. At IDG Books Worldwide, we continue in the IDG tradition of delivering quality for more than 25 years. You'll find no better book on a subject than one from IDG Books Worldwide.

John J. Kilcullen
John Kilcullen
CEO
IDG Books Worldwide, Inc.

Steven Berkowitz
Steven Berkowitz
President and Publisher
IDG Books Worldwide, Inc.

*Eighth Annual
Computer Press
Awards ≥1992*

*Ninth Annual
Computer Press
Awards ≥1993*

*Tenth Annual
Computer Press
Awards ≥1994*

*Eleventh Annual
Computer Press
Awards ≥1995*

IDG Books Worldwide, Inc., is a subsidiary of International Data Group, the world's largest publisher of computer-related information and the leading global provider of information services on information technology. International Data Group publishes over 275 computer publications in over 75 countries. Sixty million people read one or more International Data Group publications each month. International Data Group's publications include: **ARGENTINA:** Buyer's Guide, Computerworld Argentina, PC World Argentina; **AUSTRALIA:** Australian Macworld, Australian PC World, Australian Reseller News, Computerworld, IT Casebook, Network World, Publish, Webmaster; **AUSTRIA:** Computerwelt Oesterreich, Networks Austria, PC Tip Austria; **BANGLADESH:** PC World Bangladesh; **BELARUS:** PC World Belarus; **BELGIUM:** Data News; **BRAZIL:** Annuario de Informatica, Computerworld, Connections, Macworld, PC Player, PC World, Publish, Reseller News, Supergamepower; **BULGARIA:** Computerworld Bulgaria, Network World Bulgaria, PC & MacWorld Bulgaria; **CANADA:** CIO Canada, Client/Server World, ComputerWorld Canada, InfoWorld Canada, NetworkWorld Canada, WebWorld; **CHILE:** Computerworld Chile, PC World Chile; **COLOMBIA:** Computerworld Colombia, PC World Colombia; **COSTA RICA:** PC World Centro America; **THE CZECH AND SLOVAK REPUBLICS:** Computerworld Czechoslovakia, Macworld Czech Republic, PC World Czechoslovakia; **DENMARK:** Communications World Danmark, Computerworld Danmark, Macworld Danmark, PC World Danmark, Techworld Denmark; **DOMINICAN REPUBLIC:** PC World Republica Dominicana; **ECUADOR:** PC World Ecuador; **EGYPT:** Computerworld Middle East, PC World Middle East; **EL SALVADOR:** PC World Centro America; **FINLAND:** MikroPC, Tietoverkko, Tietoviikko; **FRANCE:** Distributique, Hebdo, Info PC, Le Monde Informatique, Macworld, Reseaux & Telecoms, WebMaster France; **GERMANY:** Computer Partner, Computerwoche, Computerwoche Extra, Computerwoche FOCUS, Global Online, Macwelt, PC Welt; **GREECE:** Amiga Computing, GamePro Greece, Multimedia World; **GUATEMALA:** PC World Centro America; **HONDURAS:** PC World Centro America; **HONG KONG:** Computerworld Hong Kong, PC World Hong Kong, Publish in Asia; **HUNGARY:** ABCD CD-ROM, Computerworld Szamitastechnika, Internetto online Magazine, PC World Hungary, PC-X Magazin Hungary; **ICELAND:** Tolvuheimur PC World Island; **INDIA:** Information Communications World, Information Systems Computerworld, PC World India, Publish in Asia; **INDONESIA:** InfoKomputer PC World, Komputek Computerworld, Publish in Asia; **IRELAND:** ComputerScope, PC Live!; **ISRAEL:** Macworld Israel, People & Computers/Computerworld; **ITALY:** Computerworld Italia, Macworld Italia, Networking Italia, PC World Italia; **JAPAN:** DTP World, Macworld Japan, Nikkei Personal Computing, OS/2 World Japan, SunWorld Japan, Windows NT World, Windows World Japan; **KENYA:** PC World East African; **KOREA:** Hi-Tech Information, Macworld Korea, PC World Korea; **MACEDONIA:** PC World Macedonia; **MALAYSIA:** Computerworld Malaysia, PC World Malaysia, Publish in Asia; **MALTA:** PC World Malta; **MEXICO:** Computerworld Mexico, PC World Mexico; **MYANMAR:** PC World Myanmar; **NETHERLANDS:** Computer! Totaal, LAN Internetworking Magazine, LAN World Buyers Guide, Macworld Netherlands, Net, WebWereld; **NEW ZEALAND:** Absolute Beginners Guide and Plain & Simple Series, Computer Buyer, Computer Industry Directory, Computerworld New Zealand, MTB, Network World, PC World New Zealand; **NICARAGUA:** PC World Centro America; **NORWAY:** Computerworld Norge, CW Rapport, Datamagasinet, Financial Rapport, Kursguide Norge, Macworld Norge, Multimediaworld Norge, PC World Ekspress Norge, PC World Nettverk, PC World Norge, PC World ProduktGuide Norge, PC World Norge, **PAKISTAN:** Computerworld Pakistan; **PANAMA:** PC World Panama; **PEOPLE'S REPUBLIC OF CHINA:** China Computer Users, China Computerworld, China InfoWorld, China Telecom World Weekly, Computer & Communication, Electronic Design China, Electronics Today, Electronics Weekly, Game Software, PC World China, Popular Computer Week, Software Weekly, Software World, Telecom World; **PERU:** Computerworld Peru, PC World Profesional Peru, PC World SoHo Peru; **PHILIPPINES:** Click!, Computerworld Philippines, PC World Philippines, Publish in Asia; **POLAND:** Computerworld Poland, Computerworld Special Report Poland, Cyber, Macworld Poland, Networld Poland, PC World Komputer; **PORTUGAL:** Cerebro/PC World, Computerworld/Correio Informático, Dealer World Portugal, Mac*In/PC*In Portugal, Multimedia World; **PUERTO RICO:** PC World Puerto Rico; **ROMANIA:** Computerworld Romania, PC World Romania, Telecom Romania; **RUSSIA:** Computerworld Russia, Mir PK, Publish, Seti; **SINGAPORE:** Computerworld Singapore, PC World Singapore, Publish in Asia; **SLOVENIA:** Monitor; **SOUTH AFRICA:** Computing SA, Network World SA, Software World SA; **SPAIN:** Communicaciones World España, Computerworld España, Computerworld España, Computerworld España, Dealer World España, Macworld España, PC World España; **SRI LANKA:** Infolink PC World; **SWEDEN:** CAP&Design, Computer Sweden, Corporate Computing Sweden, Internetworld Sweden, it.branschen, Macworld Sweden, MaxiData Sweden, MikroDatorn, Nätverk & Kommunikation, PC World Sweden, PCaktiv, Windows World Sweden; **SWITZERLAND:** Computerworld Schweiz, Macworld Schweiz, PCtip; **TAIWAN:** Computerworld Taiwan, Macworld Taiwan, NEW ViSiON/Publish, PC World Taiwan, Windows World Taiwan; **THAILAND:** Publish in Asia, Thai Computerworld; **TURKEY:** Computerworld Turkiye, Macworld Turkiye, Network World Turkiye, PC World Turkiye; **UKRAINE:** Computerworld Kiev, Multimedia World Ukraine, PC World Ukraine; **UNITED KINGDOM:** Acorn User UK, Amiga Action UK, Amiga Computing UK, Apple Talk UK, Computing, Macworld, Patents and Computers UK, PC Advisor, PC Home, PSX Pro, The WEB; **UNITED STATES:** Cable in the Classroom, CIO Magazine, Computerworld, DOS World, Federal Computer Week, GamePro Magazine, InfoWorld, I-Way, Macworld, Network World, PC Games, PC World, Publish, Video Event, THE WEB Magazine, and WebMaster; online webzines: JavaWorld, NetscapeWorld, and SunWorld Online; **URUGUAY:** InfoWorld Uruguay; **VENEZUELA:** Computerworld Venezuela, PC World Venezuela; and **VIETNAM:** PC World Vietnam.

3/24/97

CREDITS

Acquisitions Editor
Andy Cummings

Development Editor
Katharine Dvorak

Technical Editors
John Preisach
Keith Underdahl

Copy Editors
Kyle Looper
Nate Holdread
Suki Gear

Production Coordinator
Ritchie Durdin

Book Designer
seventeenth street studios

Graphics & Production Specialists
Vincent F. Burns
Dina F Quan

Graphics Technicians
Hector Mendoza
Trevor Wilson
Linda Marousek

Quality Control Specialists
Mick Arellano
Mark Schumann

Proofreader
Annie Sheldon

Indexer
Richard Shrout

ABOUT THE AUTHOR

Brian Underdahl has been a full-time author since 1989. During that time he has authored or co-authored about 40 titles covering a broad range of computer-related subjects. He has also written articles for several publications, including *PC World* and several computer newsletters.

WELCOME TO ONE STEP AT A TIME!

The book you are holding is very special. It's just the tool you need for learning software quickly and easily. More than a book, it offers a *unique learning experience*. Along with our text, the dynamic *One Step at a Time On-Demand* software included on the bonus CD-ROM in this book coaches you through the tutorials at *your own pace*. You'll never feel lost!

See examples of how to accomplish specific tasks. Listen to clear explanations of how to solve your problems.

Use the *One Step at a Time On-Demand* software in these ways:

- **Demo mode** shows you how to perform a task in movie-style fashion — in sound and color! Just sit back and watch the *One Step* software demonstrate the correct sequence of steps on-screen. Seeing is understanding!

- **Teacher mode** simulates the software environment so you can practice completing a task without worrying about making a mistake. The *One Step* software guides you every step of the way. Trying is learning!

Our goal is for you to learn the features of a software application by guiding you painlessly through valuable and helpful tutorials. Our *One Step at a Time On-Demand* software — combined with the step-by-step tutorials in our One Step at a Time series — will make your learning experience fast-paced and fun.

See it. Try it. Do it.

To the wolves who thought I'd never realize there was a better place for me.

"Be content. You have put your head inside a Wolf's mouth and take it out again in safety; that ought to be reward enough for you."

Aesop

My thanks to those who helped me take my head out of the Wolf's mouth!

FOREWORD

Even with its improved interface, Windows 98 is still a complex operating system. Using it effectively means much more than simply knowing how to drag and drop files or launch applications. To really get the most from Windows 98, you need a deeper understanding of the capabilities and features in the operating system. So, you need a book that treats those topics in sufficient depth to get you up to speed.

Brian Underdahl brings that type of depth to Windows 98 in *Windows 98 One Step at a Time*. This book will bring you up to speed on the most important features of Windows 98 whether you are a novice or expert. You'll find complete coverage of the types of topics you'll run into on a daily basis, as well as those you'll deal with only once in a blue moon.

Over the years I've worked with Brian on several books, primarily covering the topics of DOS, Windows 3.x, Windows 95, and most recently, Windows NT. As I did, Brian started his experience with computers back in the good old days when a computer with 256K of RAM was a wonder machine. Since then, Brian has had extensive experience in using, programming, and supporting PCs with a wide variety of applications. He brings to this subject the background and knowledge to do the topic justice and bring you an information-packed but very readable book.

On a personal note, Brian and I seem to be competing to determine who can write or contribute to the most books before he dies. This is Brian's 38th book as author or co-author. He is a few ahead of me, but I think he has a few years on me, so I have hopes of catching up. Unfortunately, Brian has the advantage of living in a climate where, unlike where I live, the ground doesn't freeze solid before Labor Day and the populace is forced to hibernate for much of the year. In exchange for writing this foreword, I get to camp in his backyard next winter. Brian has to supply the tent — I'll bring the bug spray.

Jim Boyce
Contributing Editor
WINDOWS Magazine

PREFACE

Chances are, if you use a computer, that computer runs either Windows 95 or Windows 98. As the most common operating system on modern PCs, Windows 95 is everywhere. Windows 98 is the upgrade for Windows 95-based PCs. This book tells you all about the important changes Windows 98 will bring to your desktop, and it shows you how to learn to use Windows 98 as quickly and painlessly as possible.

In this book I teach you all the essentials so that you can quickly learn everything you need to know about Windows 98 in a few simple lessons. I won't waste your time, either. I've created a series of focused, hands-on lessons that will help you become comfortable with using Windows 98. In these lessons I focus on the needs of the new Windows 98 user. I want to make certain you learn what you need to learn without being swamped by a lot of extra information that you don't need.

As an experienced author and trainer, I've had the opportunity to learn what real people want when learning about a topic such as Windows 98. I've seen the frustration of both new and experienced PC users who just wanted to know how to get a job done with the least amount of fuss and aggravation. In writing this book I distilled the knowledge I've gained through these experiences into the essence of Windows 98 training. I'm certain you'll learn more in less time and with far less aggravation from my book than you can from any other method.

Who This Book Is For

I've written this book for you, a beginning to intermediate PC user. You don't want a lot of technical jargon — you want to learn how to use your PC and Windows 98 as quickly and painlessly as possible. You also want a book that's straightforward, and one that doesn't make you feel stupid and confused just because you don't already know all those strange little buzz words computer people tend to throw around. I understand how you feel, and I'll make certain you'll learn what you really need to know.

How This Book Is Organized

You'll find this book broken down into a series of easy-to-follow lessons, with each lesson building on the knowledge you've gained in the earlier lessons. Each lesson focuses on a number of related topics to help you easily learn Windows 98.

JUMP START

This section gives you a warm-up by showing you some of the basics, including a look at the Windows 98 desktop and the Windows 98 Explorer. It also shows you how to run your programs and how to open your documents. If using a mouse is a little foreign to you, you'll find out how to become comfortable with that tethered rodent, too.

LESSON 1: GETTING STARTED WITH WINDOWS 98

In this first full-blown lesson I expand on what you learned in the warm-up section and show you how you can find files, use shortcuts, get help right from Windows 98, and automatically run your favorite programs.

LESSON 2: CHANGING THE APPEARANCE OF WINDOWS 98

In this lesson I show you how to have some fun with Windows 98 by customizing its appearance. This lesson is more than just fun, though, because you learn how to make some simple changes that will actually make Windows 98 easier to use.

LESSON 3: WORKING WITH FILES

Here you learn how to manage your files and organize your folders. You see how long filenames can be a real help in keeping track of your work, and you see what you can do if you accidentally erase a file.

LESSON 4: WORKING WITH DISKS

This lesson shows you how to work with both your diskettes and your hard disks. You learn how to format diskettes so you can use them to store data, how to make certain your disks don't contain errors that could destroy your data, and how to improve performance. You even see how you can increase the capacity of your disks using tools built into Windows 98.

LESSON 5: LIGHTS, ACTION, MULTIMEDIA!

Working all the time is no fun, so this lesson gives you a chance to play around with multimedia a bit. You see how to use both the sound and video capabilities of Windows 98 to make your PC a bit more exciting.

LESSON 6: INSTALLING AND UNINSTALLING PROGRAMS

In this lesson you see how you can add new programs to your PC as well as remove old ones you no longer need. In addition, you see that there are interesting pieces of Windows 98 itself that probably aren't installed on your system, and you learn how you can add or remove DOS programs, too.

LESSON 7: CREATING A LETTER WITH WORDPAD

You don't need a lot of fancy software just to create a simple letter in Windows 98. This lesson shows you how to use WordPad, one of the accessory programs included free with Windows 98, to create, format, and print letters. You'll even see that you can use WordPad for other creative purposes, too.

LESSON 8: CREATING A MASTERPIECE WITH WINDOWS PAINT

This lesson covers another of the Windows 98 accessory programs, Paint, which you can use to create colorful graphics. Even if you aren't much of an artist, I'm sure you'll have fun with this lesson.

LESSON 9: WORKING WITH FONTS

Nothing dresses up your documents more than using a good-looking font. In this lesson you see how you can determine which typefaces you have, how you can install new fonts, and even how you can use Wingdings and Dingbats. Want to know more? This lesson is right up your alley.

LESSON 10: DON'T BE STINGY; SHARE YOUR DATA

If you're tired of wasting time re-entering the same information time after time, you'll really enjoy this lesson. I show you how to reuse information without going through the hassles of retyping. You can even create links between programs so your final data is automatically updated whenever new information becomes available!

LESSON 11: WORKING WITH WINDOWS 98 APPLICATIONS

Your computer should work for you — not the other way around. In this lesson you see how to take advantage of your Windows 98 applications and do less of the work yourself.

LESSON 12: LET'S GET CONNECTED TO THE INTERNET

If it seems like the whole world but you is on the Internet, here's your chance to see what all the fuss is about. You'll be surfing in no time!

LESSON 13: JUST THE MAIL, PLEASE

You need to communicate to stay current, and this lesson shows you how to set up and use both email and fax with the Windows 98 Messaging System. You see how to organize all your mail in one central location, and you learn how to create and send e-mail over the Internet.

LESSON 14: HYPER HYPERTERMINAL

Although the Internet seems to get all the publicity, many computer users communicate directly without ever using the Internet. In this lesson you see how you can use the Windows 98 HyperTerminal program to connect two computers directly, and how you can use this connection to exchange files right over your phone line.

To conclude this book, I provided information that will help you install Windows 98, answers to the bonus study questions included with each lesson, and a glossary of Windows 98 terms.

How To Use This Book

This series is designed for the way people in the real world learn. Every lesson has a consistent structure, so you can quickly become comfortable using all the following elements:

- **Stopwatch.** It is best if you can complete each lesson without interruption, so look for the stopwatch symbol at the beginning of each lesson. This stopwatch tells you approximately how much time to set aside to work through the lesson.

- **Goals.** The goals of each lesson are clearly identified, so you can anticipate what skills you will acquire.

- **Get Ready.** Here you find out what files you need to complete the steps in the lessons, and you see an illustration of the worksheet you will create by completing the exercises.

- **Visual Bonus.** This is a one- or two-page illustration with labels to help you more clearly understand a special procedure or element of Microsoft Office.

- **Skills Challenge.** Every lesson ends with a comprehensive Skills Challenge exercise incorporating the skills you've learned in the individual exercises. The steps in the Skills Challenge are less explicit than those in the exercises, so you have a chance to practice and reinforce your Office skills.

- **Bonus Questions.** Sprinkled throughout the Skills Challenge exercise are bonus questions. Check Appendix B for the answers to these questions to see if you got them right.

- **Troubleshooting.** Near the end of each lesson is a series of useful tips and tricks to avoid the traps and pitfalls that many new Office 97 users experience. Look over the troubleshooting tips even if you don't have problems so you can avoid potential problems in the future.

- **Wrap Up.** Here you get an overview of the skills you learned, as well as a brief preview of the next lesson.

The One Step at a Time CD-ROM

The CD-ROM that accompanies this book includes the exclusive *One Step at a Time On-Demand* interactive tutorial. This software coaches you through the exercises in the book while you work on your computer at your own pace. You can use the software on its own or concurrently with the book. In addition, the software includes the entire text of the book so that you can search for information on how to perform a function, learn how to complete a task, or make use of the software itself.

The Conventions Used In This Book

We've tried to make it easy for you to use this book by including several easy-to-understand features. For example, when you see:

You'll know that the text that follows is a special tip intended to give you some "inside information" that can save you some time or frustration.

When you see:

The text that follows explains a special note about the subject. Notes tend to be a bit more technically oriented than the rest of the text, but the information they contain is important if you want to know "why" rather than simply "what."

Another special element you'll see is the command arrow (➤) separating a series of menu selections you'll need to choose in order to complete a command. For example, File ➤ Open means, click the File menu and select the Open command.

Speaking of commands, text that you need to type appears in **bold** characters. You should type the exact characters shown in bold text.

Text messages that appear on your screen are shown in a special font like this: `This is a message from your computer.`

We've also made certain to include the figures immediately after they're referenced in the text. You won't have to flip pages back and forth to compare a figure with the text.

Finally, the *Windows 98 One Step at a Time* CD-ROM also includes the text files used in the exercises so you don't have to do a lot of extra typing.

Feedback

Please feel free to let us know what you think about this book, and whether you have any suggestions for improvements. You can send your questions and comments to me and the rest of the *Windows 98 One Step at a Time* team on the IDG Books Worldwide Web site at `www.idgbooks.com`.

ACKNOWLEDGMENTS

An author is but one part of a whole team of people who create a book. Without all the members of that team, the book would never be finished. I'd like to thank the following special people who helped so much on this project:

Ellen Camm, senior acquisitions editor; **Andy Cummings**, acquisitions editor; **Walt Bruce**, vice president and associate publisher; **Katharine Dvorak**, development editor; **Nate Holdread**, copy editor; **John Preisach**, technical editor; **Ritchie Durdin**, production coordinator; and the rest of the wonderful production staff.

Special thanks to **Jim Boyce**, Contributing Editor, *WINDOWS Magazine*.

CONTENTS AT A GLANCE

CONTENTS

Jump Start

GOALS

This Jump Start is intended to get you off to a fast start with Windows 98 by covering the following topics:

- Starting Windows 98

- Starting programs and documents

- Using the mouse

- Finding help

Get ready

GET READY

Because this book is about Windows 98, you should make certain you have Windows 98 installed and ready to use before you begin. If you don't already have Windows 98 installed on your PC, you probably want to take a short detour to Appendix A, "Installing Windows 98," near the back of this book. When you have Windows 98 running, come back here and get started learning what Windows 98 is all about.

WHAT AM I LOOKING AT?

Did you know that computers can actually be easy and fun to use? It's true, and believe it or not, they don't bite, either! Follow along in this book, and I'll show you that in no time at all you can learn how to use Windows 98 to do a lot of the fun things you've heard people talk about. It doesn't matter whether you're new to personal computers or already have some experience using another computer and are looking for a way to get started with Windows 98. I'll act as your personal trainer and show you the important things you need to know about Windows 98. Just like any good coach, though, I don't want you to waste a lot of your time worrying about unimportant things. You've got too much to do already without trying to become another computer nerd (that's my job).

A hands-on approach is the best way to learn almost anything, but especially when you're learning something as complex as using a computer. When you work through the steps, you learn faster and remember more than if you just read about something. That's why in this book I use the hands-on approach to help you get going with Windows 98 as quickly as possible. I feel it's best for you to be sitting at your computer so you can follow through the lessons. Now, let's get started.

STARTING WINDOWS 98

Windows 98 is an *operating system*, which is just a fancy way of saying it's the software your PC needs to load before it can do anything. Without Windows 98 (or another operating system) your computer doesn't know how to do anything except sit there and take up desk space. That's because computers are not very smart all by themselves — they're just a bunch of electronic parts with no one to tell them what to do. Windows 98 acts as a director, telling your computer what it needs to know so you can run your favorite software, such as a word processor, a spreadsheet, or a game.

Because Windows 98 is so important to your PC, it is also easy to start. In fact, Windows 98 probably starts up automatically a few moments after you turn on the power switch. First you hear a few beeps and probably some other strange noises, and then you see a screen that has clouds in the background and says "Windows 98" somewhere near the middle. This screen is just there to hide the technical things your computer is doing and to let you know that something is still happening — that's why there's a moving band along the bottom of the screen. Wait for another minute or so, and finally you see the Windows 98 desktop, which looks something like the figure on the right. Don't worry if your Windows 98 desktop doesn't look exactly like the figure. As you use your PC and add programs, your desktop changes from time to time, too.

You may find that one extra step is required before you can see the Windows 98 desktop, especially if you use Windows 98 at work or are connected to a network. You may have to *log on* to your PC by entering your name and possibly a password. Logging on enables Windows 98 to identify you and allows you to access your files. If a user name and password are required on your system, someone has probably already told you what to enter. Be sure to type your user name and password correctly — and don't write them down on a note taped to the side of your monitor!

If you are using your own computer and aren't connected to a network, you may not need to worry about using a password or even entering your name when you start Windows 98. It won't hurt anything if you do have a password and user name, but they're optional for most home PC users. If you customize the appearance of the Windows 98 desktop, though, you may decide that entering a user name is a good idea. Windows 98 can remember the custom settings for several different users, so each user can pick his or her own preferences without affecting others who share the same PC. In Lesson 2 you learn how to change the appearance of Windows 98 to suit your preferences.

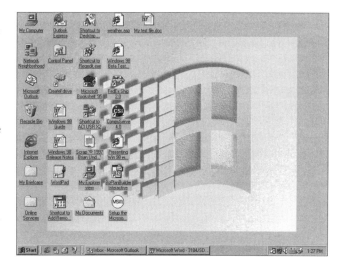

Starting programs and documents

STARTING PROGRAMS AND DOCUMENTS

As interesting as the Windows 98 desktop may be at first, you probably want to do more than simply sit and stare at your computer screen. Eventually you want to explore and learn what you can accomplish with your PC. First, however, you need to understand a couple computer terms:

- **Programs** (also known as *software*) are the sets of instructions that tell your PC how to accomplish something. For example, a word-processing program tells your computer how to work with words so you can create letters. A game program tells your computer what pictures to display, which sounds to make, and everything else it needs to know to let you play a game.

- **Documents** are the files and reports produced by a program. When you write a letter with your word-processing program, you create a file containing your letter, and you probably print a copy, too. Although you probably think the printed copy of the document is more important, your computer needs the electronic version of the document — the file — to do its work. The electronic version of the document holds the information your computer uses to display your letter on the screen, and the electronic version enables your computer to print the paper copy for your use.

Windows 98 knows a lot about programs and documents. In fact, it usually knows which program you used to create a document, so you can generally open the correct program simply by opening the document you want to use. This helps make your computer a bit easier to use because you can use whichever method you prefer and still get the same result. Windows 98 offers many such options.

■ What's this Start button?

You may already have noticed at the lower left of your screen a button labeled with the word "Start" and a Windows 98 flag emblem. Quite logically, that button is called the Start button. This button is used to run programs, open documents, change some settings, locate different things on your computer, find help, and prepare your PC to be shut down. That's an awful lot for one button to do, but it's not magic. When you move the mouse pointer to the Start button and click the left mouse button, you display the Start menu, which enables you to select the action you want to perform. In the figure on the right, I clicked the Start button and then moved the mouse up until Documents was selected. In this case it looks like I'd better get to work and create some documents, because my list of documents is empty. Just to the right of the Start button is the Quick Launch toolbar. You can click the icons on the Quick Launch toolbar to open Internet Explorer or Outlook Express, view your desktop, or visit special Web sites.

Notice that five of the items on the Start menu have a small, solid triangle displayed to their right. That triangle is a clue telling you that another menu with more selections is available. When you move the mouse up or down in the Start menu and select different options, different menus appear to the right of the Start menu. Select the different items on the Start menu, and here is what you see:

- **Programs** includes many of the programs installed on your system. You may also see additional items marked with a small solid triangle indicating that these items contain even more choices. Some programs won't appear on the Programs list, especially if those programs weren't designed for Windows 98.

- **Favorites** shows folders and places on the Internet you visit often. You can click items in this list to quickly return to documents or Web sites you've opened before.

- **Documents** shows a list of the documents used most recently. You can use this list as a shortcut to help you reopen documents you've been working on. Because the list is limited to about fifteen documents, older documents drop off the list as you work on newer ones.

- **Settings** enables you to access the Control Panel, the Printers folder, and the Taskbar. These options give you the chance to exercise a lot of control over Windows 98, but you can create serious problems for yourself if you don't understand what you're doing. For now, I suggest leaving the options under Settings alone until you learn about them later in this book.

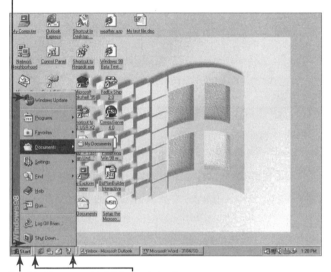

Start menu

Start button   Quick Launch toolbar

- **Find** provides you the tools to help you locate files you've saved on your PC. If you can't remember where you put your files or even what you named them, Find can be a real lifesaver! I use the Find tool quite often myself, and I'm certain you'll also find it useful.

■ How do I open programs and documents?

You need to open programs and documents to work with them, so it's important to know the best ways to do so. Windows 98 is pretty versatile; you can accomplish tasks such as opening programs and files in several ways. Which way is the best way? That depends on several things, including which method seems most comfortable to you. The following sections show you some of the most common methods of starting programs and opening documents.

STARTING PROGRAMS AND DOCUMENTS FROM THE START MENU

Follow these steps to open WordPad — a mini word processor included with Windows 98 — using the Start menu:

① Click the Start button. The Start menu pops up.

② Move the mouse pointer over the Programs selection. (The list of installed programs appears to the right of the Start menu.)

③ Select Accessories. (Move the mouse pointer over the list of programs to the right.)

NOTE *Be careful to keep the mouse pointer inside the menu box as you move the mouse — you can only select Accessories if the mouse pointer remains in the box.*

④ Select WordPad. (Move the mouse into the list of Accessories to the right.)

⑤ Click the left mouse button to start WordPad.

WordPad is one of the extra programs that comes with Windows 98. You can use it to create simple documents or letters. You can also use WordPad to open documents created in Microsoft Word. For this example, follow these steps:

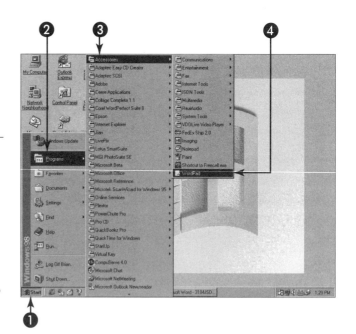

1. Type your name in the empty WordPad document.

2. Click File.

3. Click Save.

4. Type **My test file** as the name of your document.

5. Click Save to store a copy of the file on disk.

6. Click File.

7. Click Exit to exit WordPad.

When you leave WordPad, you return to the Windows 98 desktop. Now you can open your document without first opening WordPad.

STARTING PROGRAMS AND DOCUMENTS FROM THEIR FILES

After you've created documents, it's easy to open them without first opening the program you used to create the document and then opening your document. Because Windows 98 remembers which program created most documents, you can simply open the document and the correct program opens, too. To try this out with your newly created file, follow these steps:

1. Click the Start button to pop up the Start menu.

2. Select Documents.

3. Choose My test file.doc from the list of documents.

4. Click the left mouse button to open your document and start WordPad.

Don't worry if your document opens in a program other than WordPad. Although Windows 98 tries to remember which program you used to create a document, sometimes it's hard to tell the correct program to use. If you have Microsoft Word installed on your PC, Windows 98 probably tries to use Word in place of WordPad to open documents such as My test file.doc. That's not a problem because WordPad is really just a simple version of Word, without all the bells and whistles.

When you're finished admiring your handiwork, click File ➤ Exit to leave WordPad (or Word).

Using Explorer to start programs

So far the only part of Windows 98 displayed on your screen has been the desktop. There's another view of Windows 98 that's quite useful, too — the Explorer. The Windows 98 Explorer enables you to view (or explore) all your *folders* and their contents as well as sites on the Internet (see Lesson 12 for more information on using the Internet-related features). Folders are the Windows 98 term for directories; they are simply the places where you store your files on your computer's disks. You can use folders to organize your work so that it's easier to find things when you need them — instead of everything being lumped together in one big pile, you can keep related items together.

To try out the Explorer, follow these steps:

1 Right-click the Start button (be sure to click the right, not the left, button on the mouse).

2 Select Explore from the pop-up menu to display the Explorer window.

3 Click the Desktop folder in the left-hand pane to open the Desktop folder and display its contents in the right-hand pane.

4 Quickly click twice (double-click) on the icon to the left of My test file.doc in the right-hand pane to open your document and start WordPad.

In Windows 98 you have the option of choosing whether you single- or double-click to open items. In Lesson 2 you learn how you can make this choice. For consistency, I tell you to double-click to open programs and documents. If your system is configured so that a single-click opens programs and documents, remember that your PC will respond to a single-click when the text tells you to double-click.

When you open the Desktop folder in the Explorer window, your screen will look something like the figure on the right. In this case I've already selected My test file.doc in the right-hand pane, but I haven't double-clicked the icon to open the document. Your screen may not show the files in quite the same way as this figure because Explorer has several optional views you can select. For now,

Open desktop folder   Document selected in right-hand pane

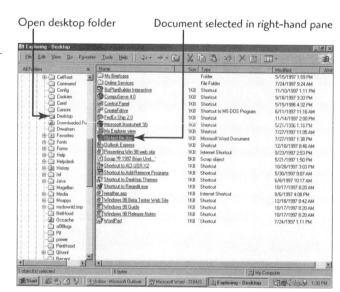

don't worry about which view is displayed; what is important is that you find your document and double-click the left mouse button to open the document.

If you opened My test file.doc, click File ➤ Exit to leave WordPad. Then click File ➤ Close to close the Explorer window.

USING THE DESKTOP TO START PROGRAMS AND OPEN DOCUMENTS

The Desktop folder you opened in the Explorer window probably looked a little familiar. There's a good reason for that — the Desktop folder contains the items you see on the Windows 98 desktop. It makes sense that if you can open things in the Desktop folder by double-clicking them, then the same should work on the Windows 98 desktop, too. You probably won't be too surprised to find out that this is exactly how the Windows 98 desktop works. To open your document, double-click the My test file.doc icon.

If you can open documents and programs on the Windows 98 desktop just like you can in the Explorer windows, why would you want to go through the extra steps necessary to use the Explorer window? Simply because the Windows 98 desktop just doesn't have room for everything. The Windows 98 desktop is just one of many folders on your computer and, like the top of your real desk, would soon become too cluttered for working if you kept everything there. Use your Windows 98 desktop for things you need to access quickly, and keep everything else organized in folders.

USING MY COMPUTER TO START PROGRAMS AND OPEN DOCUMENTS

If your PC has several disk drives, such as a CD-ROM drive in addition to one or more hard drives, you may find it a little hard to narrow your view in the Explorer window. It's often difficult to access the right place when you're trying to find a document or program that isn't on your main hard disk (which is always drive C). That's especially true if you have quite a few folders on drive C, because most of the Explorer window is filled with drive C's folders. The My Computer icon in the upper-left corner of the Windows 98 desktop provides a shortcut method for looking at the folders on any of your disks.

Double-click the My Computer icon to display a window similar to the one in the figure on the right. This window has separate icons for each disk drive, and when you double-click any of them, you

Jumping with the Taskbar

open an Explorer window that shows only the folders on the single drive you selected. You can continue to double-click folders until you reach the one you want, and then double-click the program or document you want to start. When you've finished with the windows, click File ➤ Close to close each window (you learn some shortcut methods later).

■ Jumping to other programs with the Taskbar

The Start button isn't the only useful part of the *Taskbar* — the gray band that stretches across the bottom of your Windows 98 screen. The Taskbar also holds the Quick Launch toolbar and buttons for every program currently open. You can easily switch from one program to another by moving the mouse pointer onto the button for the program you want to use and clicking the left mouse button. In the figure on the right, I have four programs open at the same time, and I can select any one of them with a single click.

As you learn more about Windows 98, you'll find that the Taskbar makes your life a lot easier because you can keep several programs open and available for instant use. If you need to use your spreadsheet, you don't have to close your word processor first. Just click the right button on the Taskbar and you're soon using whichever program you need. Click another button and you're right back where you were. There's no need to waste time closing and reloading programs just because you need to work with more than one program during the day. You can get more done in less time because your PC and Windows 98 are helping you to be more efficient.

There is a limit, however, to the number of programs you can really run at the same time. Because each running program uses some of your computer's power, trying to run too many programs at the same time can make your PC slow down. How many is too many? It's impossible to answer that question without knowing more about your computer and the programs you want to run. In general, almost any PC can run three or four programs at the same time, and many PCs can run quite a few more. The best way to find the answer is to try running the programs you need. If you don't notice your system running quite a bit slower than normal, you're probably okay.

HOW DO I USE A MOUSE?

There's a famous scene in one of the Star Trek movies where the crew
has been transported back into the twentieth century. Scottie, the
engineer, is trying to use someone's computer, and he starts talking
into the mouse as if it were a microphone. If you've never used a
mouse before, you may well feel that Scottie was on the right track!
At first it may seem a little awkward to use a mouse to control a
computer, but you soon find it's not half bad. If you want, you can
even get a fancy mouse pad to make it even more fun.

■ Clicking and double-clicking

The Windows 98 environment is a highly visual place. There are
buttons to click, menu items to select, and many places to go.
Although it's possible to do many of these things just using the
keyboard, it's almost always easier to just accept that the mouse
works better. Remember when you started WordPad the first time?
A few mouse clicks and you were there. Sure, you can start WordPad
using the keyboard, but here's what you need to do:

1 Press Ctrl+Esc to display the Start menu.

2 Press the up-arrow key nine times to reach the Programs item.

3 Press the right-arrow key twice to reach the list of accessory
programs (and you may have to use the up-arrow or down-
arrow key to reach the Accessories item).

4 Press the down-arrow key several times to reach WordPad.

5 Press Enter to start WordPad.

Even if you don't think you want to use a mouse, it's hard to
argue that having to press at least six different keys is easier than
moving the mouse and clicking the mouse button!

Okay, so the mouse may be easier, but why do you sometimes
have to click the button once and other times twice? Why can't it
always be the same? What's the difference, anyway?

If you have your PC configured the traditional way:

■ Clicking the left mouse button once selects whatever is under the
mouse pointer. After the program or document is selected, you

can choose a menu option or perform some other action on the selection. You might, for example, choose to open a document in your word processor or copy a file to another location.

■ Double-clicking an item first selects the item and then performs a default action. That's why you can double-click your document My test file.doc and it opens in WordPad — opening is the *default* action for a document.

■ You have to click the left mouse button twice fairly quickly for Windows 98 to recognize your actions as a double-click. If you click twice but nothing happens, you probably didn't click the second time quite soon enough. Later you learn how to adjust this response time, but for now, practice double-clicking My test file.doc on your Windows 98 desktop a few times. If the document opens in WordPad (or Word), you double-clicked fast enough. If the document didn't open, you need to click more quickly.

If you have your PC configured for single-clicking:

■ Moving the mouse pointer over an item selects the item under the mouse pointer. You can then choose a menu option or perform another action on the selection.

■ Clicking an item selects the item and performs the default action. If your system is configured for single-clicking, you can click My test file.doc and it opens in WordPad.

■ Selecting more than one thing at a time

I bet that you don't go to the grocery store every time you need one item; rather, you probably make your trip more productive by getting several items in a single trip. You can do the same thing in Windows 98. Instead of selecting one file to copy, move, or delete, you can select several related files and use one command to process all the files at the same time.

To see how you can select several files at the same time, try this:

❶ Right-click the Start button.

❷ Select Explore from the pop-up menu.

❸ Click the Desktop folder in the left-hand pane.

4 Hold down Ctrl while you click (or highlight if your system is configured for single clicks) several files. Make certain you click several files that aren't next to each other—skip some of the files.

5 Hold down Shift.

6 Click one file near the beginning of the files, and then click one near the end.

Did you notice anything different between what happened when you held down Ctrl and when you held down Shift? If not, try again, selecting different groups of files. Notice that when you hold down Ctrl and click on files, you select only those files you actually click. When you hold down Shift, you select the first file you clicked, the last file you clicked, and all files between the two. Any files you select remain selected after you release Ctrl or Shift, too. When you want to do the same thing to several files at once, be sure to remember Ctrl and Shift—they're real time savers!

■ Finally, there's use for the right mouse button!

Most PC mice have two buttons, but until Windows 98 came along, only the left mouse button was used very much. A few programs used the right mouse button, but Windows pretty much ignored it. You've already learned that you can use the right mouse button to quickly access the Explorer, but there are other uses for this button, too.

`DISPLAYING PROPERTIES`

Objects have *properties*—characteristics that help describe the object. For example, a car may be red or white, may have two or four doors, and may have four or six cylinders in its engine. Windows 98 treats almost everything—programs, documents, disk drives, printers, modems, and so on—as objects with properties. These properties can tell you a lot about an object, such as whether a document file has been backed up, when a program file was created, and the current printing quality setting for your printer.

You can use the right mouse button to view and change many of the properties for the various objects on your PC. To see an example, try this:

Displaying file previews with Quick View

1 Right-click a blank area of the Taskbar (make certain the mouse pointer is in the Taskbar but not on one of the buttons before you click the right mouse button).

2 Click Properties on the menu that pops up.

This displays the Taskbar Properties dialog box shown in the figure on the right. Notice that there are four checkboxes you can check or uncheck to control how the Taskbar works. Don't change any of the settings right now—you could accidentally hide the Taskbar.

3 Click Cancel to close the dialog box.

You find a Properties choice at the bottom of most of the right-click pop-up menus. Of course, different types of objects have different selections of properties you can view and, in some cases, change. Try right-clicking several other objects and choosing the Properties option. One interesting object to right-click is your desktop. You may be surprised how many properties your desktop has.

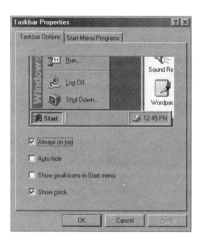

DISPLAYING FILE PREVIEWS WITH QUICK VIEW

There's one more interesting thing you can do with the right mouse button—view the contents of documents even if you don't have the software that created the document. As an example of how useful this might be, suppose someone gave you a spreadsheet they created using Excel, but you don't have Excel on your PC. With *Quick View* you can have a look at the spreadsheet without buying and installing Excel. Just right-click the spreadsheet file in Explorer, choose Quick View, and you're looking at the spreadsheet. Give it a try with some of the files on your PC.

Your right-click menu may show Quick View Plus rather than Quick View, especially if you have one of the office suites installed on your system. Quick View Plus is simply a more capable version of Quick View, and it's able to display the contents of many additional types of files.

I NEED HELP!

Everyone needs a little extra help now and then. You can get answers to some of your Windows 98 questions using Windows 98's online help system. Just click the Start button and select Help from the Start menu to see the Help window shown in the figure on the right. Click a topic to see more information. Click the Close button (the button with the X in the upper-right corner of the window) when you're finished.

END OF THE WARM UP

This warm up has given you a quick "jump start" to Windows 98. There's quite a bit more to learn, but now that you know some of the basics, Windows 98 shouldn't seem quite so intimidating. I'm quite certain you managed to get all the way through the exercises without ever once having the computer bite you, and I'm also sure you've learned that Windows 98 has some interesting things to learn about. In the lessons that follow, you'll have fun learning about them.

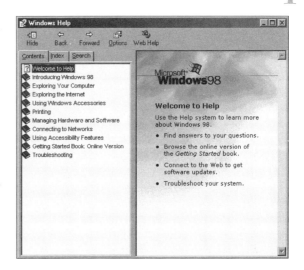

Getting Started with Windows 98

50 MINUTES

GOALS

The goals of Lesson 1 reinforce many of the skills you already have, but they also go well beyond what you learned in the Jump Start. The major goals of Lesson 1 include the following:

- Learning how to explore your computer
- Using shortcuts and icons
- Starting programs with the Start menu
- Getting help when you need it

Get ready

GET READY

The most important things you need to do to prepare for Lesson 1 are to be at your PC and to make certain the system is on and Windows 98 is started. To print help topics, you also need to have a printer attached to your system and powered on. Finally, you need one formatted diskette that has enough space for a small file.

When you finish the exercises, you will have learned how to do the following tasks: open Windows Explorer using two different methods; find your files and delete old ones; create shortcuts; edit a shortcut name; choose an icon for your shortcuts; run programs with the Start menu; use the Start menu document list; change the Start menu; use the Send To command; use pop-up help; use the help window; and finally, print a help topic.

If you're ready, it's time to begin with the exercises.

EXPLORING YOUR COMPUTER

To work effectively and efficiently, you really need to know how to find files on your computer. Both program and document files can be buried quite deeply in the folders on your hard disk, and if you can't find them, you can't use them. Old, unneeded files may be even worse than lost files. You need to know how to remove files you no longer need to make room for newer files and to prevent your PC from slowing to a crawl while Windows 98 struggles to write to a hard disk bloated with obsolete data. Finally, you need to know what to do when you accidentally delete the wrong file.

Windows 98 is a very graphical operating environment, and this makes it much easier to explore your computer than if you were using a nongraphical operating system such as MS-DOS. In fact, Windows 98 is often called a *Graphical User Interface* or *GUI* ("gooey"). In contrast, MS-DOS uses a *command line interface* or *prompt*. What this means to you is pretty simple — a computer running Windows 98 is much easier to use than a computer that just displays a DOS prompt.

Your Windows 98 screen shows you a lot more information than you would see in any nongraphical operating system. Windows 98 also provides you easy access to a whole range of tools through simple mouse clicks. When you combine these two benefits, you realize one of the great advantages of Windows 98 — you don't have to remember a lot of commands to use Windows 98. In fact, you could use Windows 98 for years and never type a single command. As the following exercises illustrate, however, a few simple commands can often be quite useful.

The tool you use to explore your Windows 98 computer is the Windows Explorer. If you've used an older version of Windows, you probably used the File Manager on occasion. Windows Explorer is probably best described as File Manager on steroids. Even though Windows Explorer is very powerful, it's also very easy to use.

There are several ways to start the Windows Explorer; each method produces slightly different results. You can use these differences to help you accomplish different goals.

Using right-click to open Windows Explorer

To use the first method for opening the Windows Explorer, follow these steps:

❶ Right-click the Start button.

❷ Click Explore.

When Windows Explorer opens, it displays the contents of the Start Menu folder.

TIP

When you are using a menu that you displayed by right-clicking something, you can use either mouse button to make selections from the menu. You can click Explore with either the left or right mouse button.

When you take a close look at the Windows Explorer window, you notice that a lot of information is displayed. At the top of the screen is the *title bar,* which says `Exploring - Start Menu`, telling you exactly which folder is open. At the far right side of the title bar is a button with an ✕ on the face — the Close button. If you click the Close button, you close Windows Explorer.

The menu bar (below the title bar) contains several menus that drop down and display their commands when you click one of

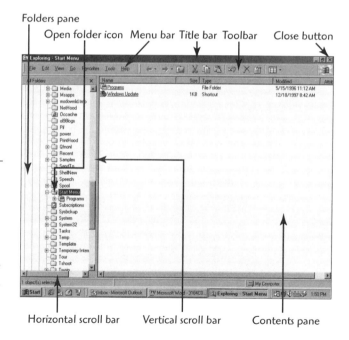

Folders pane

Open folder icon   Menu bar   Title bar   Toolbar   Close button

Horizontal scroll bar   Vertical scroll bar   Contents pane

the menu bar choices. The toolbar buttons are shortcuts to some of those commands. Hold the mouse pointer over the toolbar buttons for a bit without clicking, and Windows 98 pops up a short description of the button.

The Windows Explorer window has two panes. The left-hand pane displays the folders, and the right-hand pane displays the contents of the open folder. You can tell which folder is open by looking at the icons in the left-hand pane — the open folder has an icon that looks like an open folder, while all the other folder icons look like closed folders. Notice the little square boxes to the left of some of the folder icons. If no square box is shown, the folder doesn't contain any additional folders. If there is a square box that contains a plus sign (+), the folder contains additional folders you can't see right now because the folder is collapsed. The plus sign changes to a minus sign (–) when the folder's contents are completely visible.

3 Click the plus sign next to the Programs folder to expand the Programs folder display.

Each computer is likely to have different items in the Programs folder, so you probably won't see the same items that are shown in the figure — unless you're using my computer!

If you select View ➤ Explorer Bar, you can add a different pane to the Windows Explorer window to replace the All Folders pane. This new pane can include buttons to connect to your favorite Web sites, channels, search options, or your favorite folders on your PC. The figure on the next page shows the Favorites Explorer Bar added to the Windows Explorer window.

To view the contents of a different folder, click the icon of the folder you want to view. If necessary, click the arrows at the ends of the scrollbars to bring the folder you want into view.

4 Click the Programs folder icon to display the contents of the Programs folder.

The Programs folder contains all the items you see when you choose Programs from the Start menu. Later, you learn how to use this information to modify the Start menu.

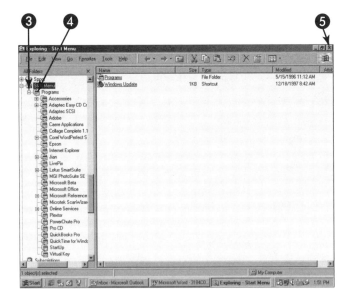

5 Click the Close button at the upper-right corner of the Windows Explorer window to close Explorer.

Using the Start menu to open Windows Explorer

You can also start Windows Explorer using the Start menu.

1 Click the Start button to display the Start menu.

2 Click Programs.

3 Select Windows Explorer to display the Windows Explorer window.

Can you distinguish the difference between opening Windows Explorer by right-clicking the Start button and by using the Start menu? When you use the Start menu to open Windows Explorer, the window displays the contents of drive C rather than the contents of the Start Menu folder. This view is more useful most of the time because you can more easily see all the folders on your hard drive when you start from the *root directory* — the ultimate parent of all the folders on a disk.

There's one more way to open Windows Explorer, but before you have a look at it, close the Windows Explorer by clicking the Close button at the upper-right corner of the Windows Explorer window.

Opening Windows Explorer where you want

Wouldn't it be handy if you could tell Windows Explorer which folder to open so you wouldn't have to search through the list of folders each time? Guess what? It's pretty easy to do, and after you learn how, you'll know something that most Windows users don't know! Here you are in your first Windows 98 lesson, and already you're becoming an expert.

The key to controlling Windows Explorer is to create a shortcut that tells Windows Explorer just what you want to do. In this exercise you tell Windows Explorer to open the Windows folder automatically.

1 Right-click an empty place on your desktop.

2 Select New in the menu that appears.

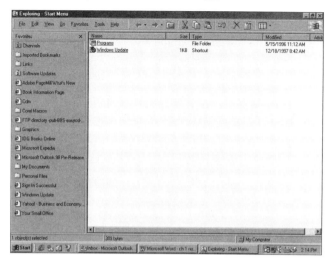

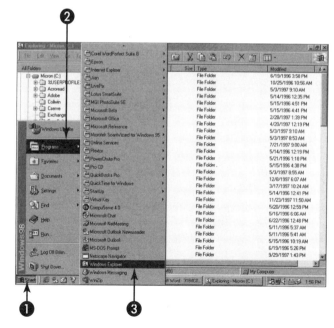

3 Select Shortcut. The Create Shortcut dialog box appears.

4 Type this text in the Command line text box: **explorer /e, \windows**. (If your Windows folder happens to have a different name than `Windows`, you have to substitute the correct name in the command.)

5 Click Next to continue.

6 Type this text in the Select a name for the shortcut text box: **My Explorer view**.

7 Click Finish to place the shortcut on your desktop.

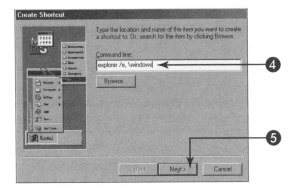

Test your shortcut by double-clicking the new My Explorer view icon on your desktop. If you see a message like the one shown in the figure on the lower right, your Windows directory probably isn't named windows. Use the Windows Explorer to find the correct name and then start over with Step 1.

If you did everything correctly, double-clicking your shortcut should produce results similar to the figure on the next page. Notice that because my Windows directory is called Win95, in Step 4 I had to enter the command as **explorer /e,\win95**. It doesn't matter whether you use upper- or lowercase letters when you enter the command; Windows 98 ignores any differences in the case of the letters.

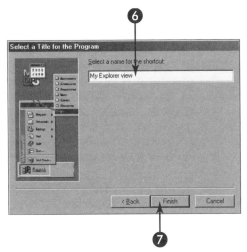

 NOTE

Yes, it's true. My Windows 98 folder is called Win95. The reason for this is really pretty simple — I upgraded my PC from Windows 95 to Windows 98, but renaming the Windows folder isn't an easy task. If you simply rename the Windows folder, most of your programs and possibly Windows itself will stop functioning. Even if your Windows folder has an outdated name, it's better to leave the old name than deal with the major problems involved in making a change.

TIP

*To enter a folder name that contains spaces, enclose the entire name in quotation marks. For example, type **explorer /e,"\windows\start menu"** to create a shortcut that works just like right-clicking the Start button and choosing Explore.*

Finding your files

Your hard disk holds hundreds if not thousands of files. Finding specific files in all the chaos of folders on a typical PC can be frustrating — unless you know what you're doing, of course. Fortunately Windows 98 has a powerful file-finding tool to help you out. In this exercise you learn how to take advantage of this tool.

Before Windows 98 came along, PC users were limited in how they could name their files. Filenames used a maximum of 11 characters, which were split into an eight character name and a three character extension. Because the extensions were normally used to indicate a file's type, you really only had eight characters available for naming any file. This restriction often led to some creative file naming, and also meant that filenames were often so cryptic that it took a real genius to remember what each file contained. Was that letter to the bank named LT2B626.DOC or was it BK011796.DOC? Windows 98 changed all that by allowing you to use up to 255 characters in a filename. Now you can name the letter to your bank "Letter to bank regarding loan 6-26-97.DOC" or something similar.

In practical terms, filenames are usually limited to fewer than 255 characters because the complete name of the file (which includes the drive letter, the names of the folders containing the file, and the extension) is limited to 260 characters.

■ Use filenames to find your files

Although long filenames make it a lot easier for you to recognize your files, they also add a major complication to working with your files. If

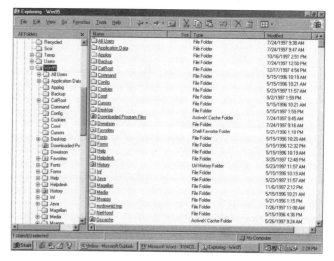

Getting Started with Windows 98

Use filenames to find your files

you use spaces in a filename, Windows 98 can have a difficult time determining just what you mean when you try to find the file.

NOTE

Several of the following examples assume you have a file named My test file.doc on your desktop. You can create such a file by right-clicking a blank area of your desktop and selecting New ➤ Text Document. Type **My test file.doc** *as the name of the document, and click Yes to change the file type.*

As an example to illustrate this, try the following exercise.

❶ Click the Start button to display the Start menu.

❷ Select Find.

❸ Select Files or Folders to display the Find dialog box.

❹ Type the following text in the Named text box: **my test file.doc**.

❺ Click Find Now to search for files that match.

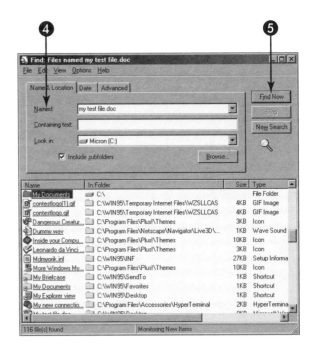

On my system the search found 116 files. How many did it find on yours? Although Windows 98 actually found the file you specified, it also found quite a few files that really didn't seem to match what you were trying to find. That's because Windows 98 really couldn't tell if the name you typed was a complete filename or a group of names — any of which it should match. In other words, Windows 98 looked for files with any of the words you typed in their filenames. Can you determine why Windows 98 found all the files shown in the figure? At least one of the words you typed is contained in each of the filenames (yes, even Mdmyorik.inf has one of the words — just look a little closer and you see it).

Now try a new search that focuses more directly on just what you want to find. This time, give Windows 98 a little help by telling it that you're entering a complete filename, not a series of names.

❶ Click New Search to clear your old results.

❷ Click OK to confirm that you want to begin a new search.

❸ Type this text in the Named text box: **"my test file.doc"** (be sure to include the quotation marks).

Use dates to find your files

4 Click Find Now.

By enclosing the filename in quotation marks, you told Windows 98 to find only the files that matched exactly. In this case Windows 98 found only one file, but if you had more files with the same name in different folders, those files would appear in the results list, too.

You can further limit the search by carefully using some of the Find dialog box options. For example, if you remove the check from the Include subfolders checkbox, Windows 98 looks only in the current location shown in the Look in text box. Usually, though, you want to leave this checkbox selected so your searches aren't limited to the current folder. You can also click the Browse button and then select where to begin the search. Use this option only if you have a pretty good idea where you want to locate a specific copy of a file when you know several copies exist.

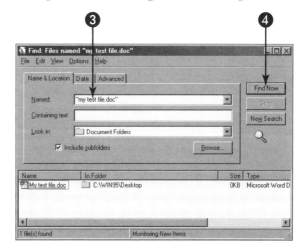

■ Use dates to find your files

You can also find files based on when they were created or last modified. In this exercise, you search for files created or modified on a specified date — June 24, 1997.

1 Click the Date tab in the Find dialog box to see the date options.

2 Click New Search to clear your old results.

NOTE

If you don't clear your old search, Windows 98 tries to find all files that match the old search and your new search conditions — you want to use only the new conditions in this case.

3 Click the Find all files created or modified radio button.

4 Click the between radio button.

5 Type **6/24/97** in both boxes.

6 Click Find Now. Your screen should look similar to the figure on the right when the search is complete.

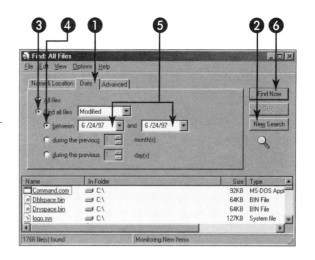

Use advanced techniques to find files

The number of files dated 6/24/97 that Windows 98 finds depends on a number of factors, including how much you've used your system and the programs you have installed.

TIP

If your searches don't seem to produce the desired results, make certain you select the correct location in the Look in list box on the Name & Location tab. By default, Windows searches only document folders.

You can also find files that were recently created or modified by clicking either the during the previous month(s) button or the during the previous day(s) button and specifying the number of months or days.

■ Use advanced techniques to find your files

If none of the filename, location, or date options pin down your search well enough, Windows 98 still has more useful tricks to offer. You can look for files by type, by searching them for specific text messages, or even by size. By itself, Windows 98 knows about a lot of file types, but when you install new programs, it learns even more file types. You can search for things like applications (programs), help files, sound files, animated cursors, or a whole raft of other types. In this exercise you find all the application files on your PC.

❶ Click New Search to clear your old results.

❷ Click the Advanced tab in the Find dialog box to see the advanced options.

❸ Click the arrow next to the Of type list box.

❹ Select Application.

❺ Click Find Now. Windows 98 displays results similar to the figure on the right.

Although Windows 98 lists a large number of your files as applications, don't make the assumption that you can simply double-click any of them and have a new, undiscovered program to play with. Quite a few of the files listed as applications really aren't programs you can run. Many of them are there to help another

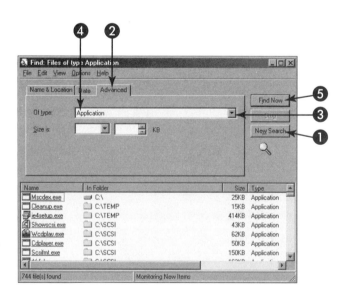

program, and some of them could cause damage if you're not careful. If you're not sure about one of these files, don't try to run it!

You can also search for files by entering text in the Containing text box on the Name & Location tab, but don't be too surprised if you don't find just what you expect. If you specify a fairly common word, many files among the hundreds on your hard disk probably match. Also, files are often stored in a format other than plain text, so you might not find a file using a text search even if the file exists. If a text search doesn't produce the results you want, try a different type of search.

Deleting old files

There's an old axiom in the computer world: "Data expands to fill the available space." Even though the size of hard drives in PCs today is larger than ever before, you'll eventually run out of room if you don't remove old files you no longer need. Long before you run out of room on your hard disk, however, you encounter degraded system performance due to the clutter of old files. Do your house cleaning to keep your computer running efficiently.

Before you simply delete old files, you should consider whether there's a chance you may need them in the future. Sometimes it makes more sense to move old files to diskettes and store them away rather than simply deleting them. That way you can always recover your data if it suddenly becomes important again. Notice, though, that I said *your* data. I didn't say program files. Data is the information you created through hard work. You can always restore your program files using the original distribution diskettes or CD-ROM, so there's really no reason to waste your time saving those types of files, is there?

Okay, you've decided to get rid of an old file you no longer need. In this exercise you delete that file.

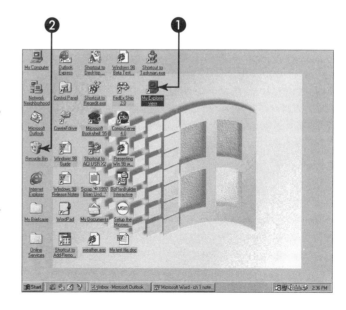

❶ Move the mouse pointer to the icon on your desktop labeled My Explorer view.

❷ Hold down the left mouse button and move the mouse pointer to the icon labeled Recycle Bin.

❸ Release the left mouse button.

Recovering files from the Recycle Bin

Holding down the left mouse button while you move a selected object as you did in Step 2 is called *dragging*. Releasing the object as you did in Step 3 is called *dropping*. In this exercise you dragged and dropped the My Explorer view icon from your desktop into the Recycle Bin. This is the easiest way to remove files you don't need from your desktop, but most files aren't on your desktop; you need a way to delete those other files, too. In the following exercise, you use Windows Explorer to delete files.

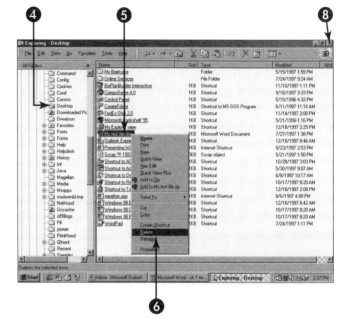

1. Click the Start button to display the Start menu.

2. Click Programs.

3. Select Windows Explorer to display the Windows Explorer.

4. Click the Desktop folder to display its contents in the right pane.

5. Right-click the My test file.doc icon to display the pop-up menu.

6. Click Delete in the pop-up menu to display the Confirm File Delete dialog box.

7. Select Yes to delete the file.

8. Click the Close button at the upper-right corner of the Windows Explorer window to close Explorer.

Windows 98 almost always gives you choices, so it should come as no surprise that there are alternate ways to delete files, too. You can click the Delete button on the Windows Explorer toolbar to delete any files you've selected, or you can use the File ➢ Delete command to do the same thing. You can even drag and drop files to the Recycle Bin folder, but this may not be easy if the Recycle Bin folder isn't visible.

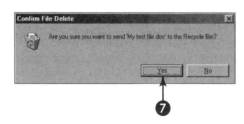

▶ Oops, recovering files from the Recycle Bin

I bet you wonder why it was called the Recycle Bin, don't you? Why not just call it a trash can? The Recycle Bin is named that way to let you know that sending files to the Recycle Bin isn't just a one-way street. Everyone makes mistakes, and deleting the wrong file could be very costly. The Recycle Bin is there to save you from these types of mistakes.

Recovering files from the Recycle Bin

In Windows 98 you can choose to use a double-click or a single-click to select and activate items on your desktop and in the Windows Explorer. To switch between the two options, open My Computer and select View ➢ Options. Select Web Style to use a single click or Classic Style to use double-clicks. You can also choose Custom to select a combination of options. Click OK and then the Close button to activate your changes and close My Computer.

■ Getting your files back

In this exercise you recover the two files you just deleted.

① Double-click the Recycle Bin icon to display the Recycle Bin contents. (You may want to drag the edges of the Recycle Bin window to see the contents more easily.)

② Hold down Ctrl while you select the My Explorer view and My test file.doc icons. (If these two icons are the only items in the Recycle Bin, you can use Ctrl+A as a shortcut to select everything in the Recycle Bin.)

③ Click File.

④ Select Restore to move the two files from the Recycle Bin back to their original location on your desktop.

⑤ Click File.

⑥ Click the Close button to close the Recycle Bin.

You safely restored your two files back to your desktop and didn't lose the work it took to create them. These two small files wouldn't be difficult to reproduce, of course, but at some point you'll probably accidentally delete a file that would be a lot of work to redo. Fortunately, the Windows 98 Recycle Bin is there to help.

TIP

Files you delete at the Windows 98 DOS prompt aren't placed in the Recycle Bin and cannot be recovered once deleted. Always delete files using Windows Explorer so that you have a second chance.

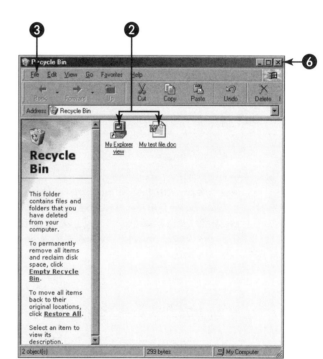

Taking out the trash

■ Taking out the trash

Eventually, even the Recycle Bin can get too full. When that happens, it's difficult to find the things you want to restore amid all the trash. In extreme cases you could even lose files you really wanted to restore, because when the Recycle Bin gets full, Windows 98 automatically throws out the oldest items to make room for more deleted files. To save yourself from these problems, all you need to do is take out the trash by emptying the Recycle Bin now and then.

❶ Restore any files currently in the Recycle Bin that you want to save. Remember, after you empty the Recycle Bin, there's no going back!

❷ Right-click the Recycle Bin icon to display the pop-up menu shown in the figure on the right.

❸ Select Empty Recycle Bin.

❹ Click Yes to confirm that you want to delete the files remaining in the Recycle Bin.

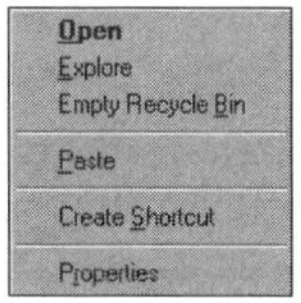

> **Open**
> Explore
> Empty Recycle Bin
> Paste
> Create Shortcut
> Properties

TIP 👍
You can prevent files from filling up the Recycle Bin by holding down Shift while you delete them. This prevents these files from being placed in the Recycle Bin, but it also prevents you from recovering them, so use this tip with extreme caution!

USING SHORTCUTS AND ICONS

There's probably nothing worse than doing something the hard way time after time when you know there's probably a shortcut that can save you a lot of time. In Windows 98 you can take advantage of many existing shortcuts, and you can create your own shortcuts, too. Why wade through several levels of menus or dig through a whole series of nested folders when you can easily create a shortcut right on your Windows 98 desktop?

Shortcuts and icons really make life with Windows 98 a lot easier. Instead of typing a command to start a program or open a document, you can simply double-click the mouse button. *Icons* are small pictures that represent a program or document. The Trash Can icon, for example, is used for the Recycle Bin. You can think of *shortcuts* as copies of those icons you use to access a program or document. Shortcut icons have a small arrow in their lower-left corner to remind you that they're shortcuts, while icons that are not shortcuts don't have the arrow. There's an important difference between shortcut icons and normal icons—you can delete shortcut icons without deleting the program or document, but *if* you delete a normal icon, you do delete the program or document.

Creating shortcuts to programs or documents

It's a good idea to create shortcuts to some of your favorite programs and maybe even to documents you use often. One woman I know keeps shortcuts to forms she frequently uses on her desktop so she can always open the form with just a double-click. I keep shortcuts to programs rather than shortcuts to documents on my desktop because I don't reuse the same documents very often, but I do use the same programs quite a bit. You may find that a mix of program and document shortcuts works best for you.

There are two primary ways to create desktop shortcuts. Earlier you created a shortcut to Windows Explorer by right-clicking the desktop, selecting New ➢ Shortcut, and then entering the command to start Windows Explorer where you preferred. Although this method certainly works—your shortcut ran Windows Explorer just as you expected—it has one major shortcoming. Before you can create a shortcut manually, you already have to know the correct command necessary to run the program you want. As bad as this sounds, it's even harder to create a shortcut to a document. A document shortcut not only has to start the correct program, but it has to load the document, too. Fortunately, there's a much simpler way to create shortcuts—your old friend drag and drop.

In this exercise you create a shortcut to WordPad using drag & drop.

❶ Click the Start button.

❷ Click Programs.

❸ Select Windows Explorer.

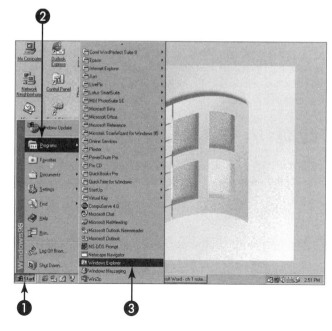

4 Click the plus sign (+) to the left of the Windows folder to expand the view of the folders.

5 Expand the Start Menu folder.

6 Expand the Programs folders.

7 Click the Accessories folder to display its contents in the right-hand pane.

8 Click the Restore button, the second button from the right in the Windows Explorer title bar, to reduce the size of the Windows Explorer window so you can also see your desktop. The Restore button changes appearance slightly when the window size is reduced, and it is then called the Maximize button.

9 Point to the WordPad icon and hold down the right mouse button.

10 Drag the pointer onto your desktop. A small pop-up menu appears on the screen.

11 Click Create Shortcut(s) Here.

12 Click the Windows Explorer Close button.

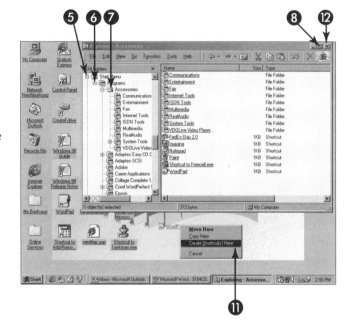

Now that you've created a desktop shortcut to WordPad, you can start WordPad without going through several levels of the Start menu. It's certainly much easier to double-click the WordPad shortcut icon on your desktop than to wade through the menus, isn't it? Your WordPad shortcut icon isn't just a one-trick pony, though. Try this to see what I mean:

1 Point to the icon for My test file.doc.

2 Hold down the left mouse button and drag the icon onto the Shortcut to WordPad icon.

3 Release the mouse button to drop the document onto the Shortcut to WordPad icon.

When you drop the document onto the WordPad icon, you're telling Windows 98 to open the document using WordPad. You can use this same trick to open any text document or Microsoft Word document.

Creating shortcuts to your frequently used folders

You can make opening your most frequently used folders just as easy as running your favorite programs by creating shortcuts to those folders. After you have created shortcuts to your folders, a quick double-click shows you everything in the folder, giving you quick access to the programs and documents in the folder. You've opened the Accessories folder pretty often in the exercises, so that folder seems like a good candidate for a desktop shortcut. In this exercise you create a shortcut for the Accessories folder.

❶ Click the Start button.

❷ Click Programs.

❸ Select Windows Explorer.

❹ Click the plus sign (+) to the left of the Windows folder.

❺ Click the plus sign (+) to the left of the Start Menu folder.

❻ Click the plus sign (+) to the left of the Programs folder.

❼ Click the Restore button to reduce the size of the Windows Explorer window if the Windows Explorer window is covering the entire pane.

❽ Point to the Accessories folder icon in the left pane and hold down the right mouse button.

❾ Drag the pointer onto your desktop.

❿ Click Create Shortcut(s) Here.

⓫ Click the Windows Explorer Close button.

To test your new folder shortcut, double-click the Shortcut to Accessories icon. Open the Accessories folder as shown in the figure on the right. You may have different items in your Accessories folder than appear in mine, but your shortcut still provides you with quick access to anything in the folder.

Editing a shortcut name

Editing a shortcut name

When you create a shortcut, Windows 98 automatically creates a name that begins with `Shortcut to` and ends with the program, document, or folder name. You're probably more creative than that and can probably think of names you'd rather use. The name doesn't have to say `Shortcut to` and it doesn't even have to use the real name of the program, document, or folder, either. You can use whatever name you prefer. Crowded desktops especially benefit from short, to-the-point names.

Here's how you can rename the Shortcut to Accessories icon to My stuff:

1 Right-click the Shortcut to Accessories icon.

2 Click Rename.

3 Type **My stuff**.

4 Press Enter.

There's another slightly trickier way to rename icons that you should try, too. Click the label Shortcut to Accessories once, pause, and click the label again. You can then type the new label and press Enter. This method is a little harder to master than the right-click method, because clicking the second time too quickly opens the program, document, or folder instead of editing the name.

Choosing your own shortcut icon

You don't have to accept the default icon that Windows 98 uses when you create a shortcut. Although the default icon is intended to provide visual feedback about the purpose of the shortcut, you can have some fun by customizing shortcuts to use a different icon. Here's how you can choose a different icon for the My Stuff shortcut:

1 Right-click the My Stuff icon.

2 Select Properties to display the My Stuff Properties dialog box.

The General tab shows you basic information about the shortcut and enables you to change the attributes for the shortcut — don't change any of these settings!

Choosing your own shortcut icon

3 Click the Shortcut tab.

4 Click the Change Icon button to display the Change Icon dialog box.

5 Click the icon that shows a desktop, located in the third row of the Current icon list box.

6 Click OK in the Change Icon dialog box.

7 Click OK in the My Stuff Properties dialog box to change the icon (there is a slight delay before the icon changes).

You won't find as many optional icons for some shortcuts as you did for the My Stuff shortcut. Shortcuts to programs and documents use icons built into the program rather than Windows 98's set of icons. Still, some programmers do have a sense of humor and include optional icons that are more fun than the default icons. One database program, for example, pokes a little fun at its name with optional icons, including one with a pair of ducks and another with a pair of docks.

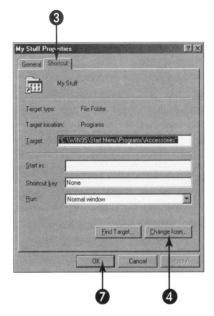

USING THE START MENU

By now you should be pretty accustomed to accessing the Start menu. You've used it several times in previous exercises, so in the following exercises you learn a few tricks you haven't seen before, as well as reinforce some of the things you've already learned. The Windows 98 Start menu has a major advantage over desktop shortcuts — the Start menu is often much easier to access than the desktop. Even when you're running a program that covers the whole screen, you can usually get to the Start menu with a single click of the mouse. You can also use the Start menu to automatically start programs whenever you start Windows 98, and to ease the task of editing many types of files.

TIP

If you can't see the Start button, you can still open the Start menu by pressing Ctrl+Esc. Some newer PCs also have a Windows key ▦ that displays the Start menu.

Getting Started with Windows 98

Running a program from the Start menu

Running a program from the Start menu

You probably won't find all of your programs on the Start menu. There just isn't room for everything, and you probably have some programs that you don't use often enough to want to have them on the Start menu. But just because a program doesn't appear on the Start menu doesn't mean you can't easily run the program. In this exercise you learn to use the Run command that appears on the Start menu.

The Run command also provides you added flexibility compared to selecting a program icon from the Start menu or the desktop. When you use the Run command, you can add additional information — known as *arguments* or *parameters* — to control how the program runs. For example, you can run a program and specify which document to open in a single command. In this exercise you see how you can use the Run command to open Windows Explorer and display a slightly different view than you've seen before.

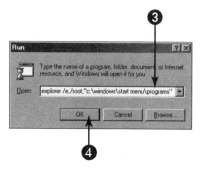

❶ Click the Start button.

❷ Click Run.

❸ Type this text in the Run text box (remember to use the correct name if your Windows directory has a different name than `Windows`): **explorer /e,/root,"c:\windows\start menu\programs"**

❹ Click OK to run the Windows Explorer. Your screen should look something like the figure on the right.

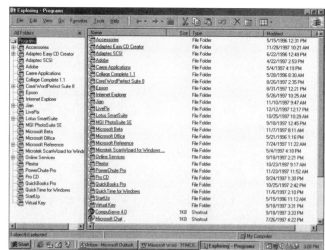

Can you see how this Windows Explorer view is different from the ones you've seen before? By adding the `/root` argument, you told Windows Explorer to treat c:\windows\start menu\programs as the *root* or parent of the view. None of the folders on drive C are visible except those branching off c:\windows\start menu\programs. In this example you entered the command to run Windows Explorer, `explorer`, and then three arguments that told Windows Explorer how you wanted the program to run: `/e`, `/root`, and `"c:\windows\start menu\programs"`.

Using the Start menu document list

1

> *Use the Run command when you need to specify additional arguments you don't normally use — for example, when you need to specify a special command-line argument to enter an administrative mode in an application program so you can access commands not available to ordinary users.*
>
> *The Run command remembers the last 25 or so commands you entered. To see the History list, click the down arrow at the right side of the Open text box. You can then select any of the listed commands to repeat.*

Using the Start menu document list

The Start Menu document list is a handy listing of the documents you've used most recently. You can use the list to gain quick access to any of the documents.

■ Opening a document from the list

In this exercise you open one of the documents you've recently used.

1 Click the Start button.

2 Click Documents.

3 Select My test file.doc. (Your documents list probably has different documents than those shown in the figure on the right simply because the list changes every time you open new documents.)

■ Removing documents from the list

Unfortunately, you're not the only one who can look at your Start Menu document list to see your list of recently used documents. Do you really want your boss to know you've been working on your resume? Sometimes it's simply not a good idea to have certain documents appear on the Start Menu document list. Following are two ways to remove documents from the list.

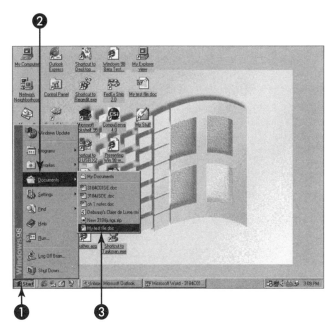

Using the Start menu document list

1 Right-click a blank space in the Taskbar (at the bottom edge of your screen).

2 Click Properties.

3 Click the Start Menu Programs tab.

4 Click Clear to remove everything from the Start Menu document list.

5 Click the OK button to close the dialog box.

Although this method of clearing the Start Menu document list is effective, it has one shortcoming — everything is removed from the list, even those items you'd rather keep for easy access. Perhaps a selective method of removing documents from the list would be more useful.

Here's a way you can remove some of the items from the Start Menu document list without removing everything:

1 Double-click the My test file.doc icon to open the file.

2 Click the Close button to close WordPad so My test file.doc once again appears in the list of documents.

3 Right-click the Start button.

4 Click Explore.

5 Click the Recent folder (which is a bit above the open Start Menu folder).

6 Click My test file.doc.

7 Click the Delete button.

8 Click Yes to confirm the deletion.

9 Click the Close button.

You can select as many documents as you like in Step 4 by holding down Ctrl as you select each document.

Changing your Start Menu

You probably use the Programs section on your Start menu more than almost any other component of Windows 98, so it only makes

Changing your Start Menu

sense to customize this section for your needs. Your Start menu Programs section begins with a collection of items added automatically when you install Windows 98. When you install new programs, they probably end up there, too. Pretty soon you can have a real mess, and your Start menu is hard to use because it contains so much junk while it lacks some things that would be quite useful.

You can modify the Programs section by adding new items or removing ones you don't want. The layout of this section is predetermined — folders are arranged alphabetically at the top with programs arranged alphabetically below the folders.

TIP

Because numbered items sort above items starting with letters, you can control the layout of items in the Programs section by renaming them with numbers before the names.

In this exercise you learn how to add a program to the Programs section. The program you add — Program Manager — isn't too useful in Windows 98, but you can have a little fun with it making your friends think you have a strange version of Windows installed. Program Manager makes Windows 98 look almost like Windows 3.x.

1 Right-click a blank space on the Taskbar.

2 Click Properties.

3 Click the Start Menu Programs tab.

4 Click Add.

5 Type this text in the Command line text box: **c:\windows\ progman.exe**. (Don't forget to use the correct name for your Windows directory.)

6 Click Next to continue.

7 Select the Programs folder in the Select Program Folder dialog box.

8 Click Next to continue.

9 Type this text in the Select a name for the shortcut text box: **Program Manager**.

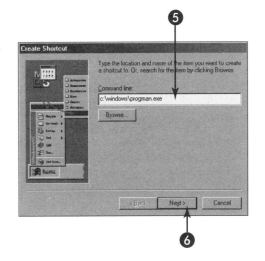

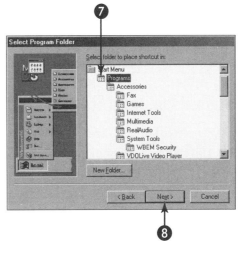

Getting Started with Windows 98

1

Running applications at startup

TIP

You could leave the name as progman.exe, but a descriptive name helps you remember what the entry actually is.

⑩ Click Finish to place the new entry on your Start menu. (You don't need to close the Taskbar Properties dialog box right now.)

To test your work, click the new Program Manager item on the Programs section of your Start menu. You should see the Windows 3.x-style Program Manager window with each of the Start menu folders in a separate window. Click the Program Manager window Close button to close Program Manager.

Removing an item from the Start menu is just as easy. In this exercise you remove Program Manager from your Start menu — you can always add it back later if you want to.

❶ If the Taskbar Properties dialog box is not still open, right-click a blank space on the Taskbar and select Properties to reopen it.

❷ Click Remove to display the Remove Shortcuts/Folders dialog box.

❸ If necessary, use the vertical scrollbar to scroll down until you can click Program Manager.

❹ Click Remove. If the Remove button is grayed out, you haven't selected an item you can remove.

❺ Click the Close button on the Remove Shortcuts/Folders dialog box.

❻ Click the Close button on the Taskbar Properties dialog box.

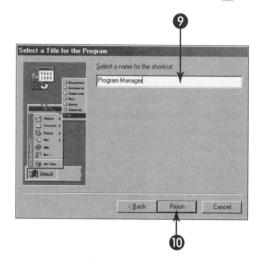

Running applications at startup

You've probably noticed that the Start menu Programs section includes a folder called StartUp. Anything you place in this folder automatically runs whenever you start Windows 98. You might use this feature to make certain your word processing software automatically starts if word processing is your main use of your PC, for example. Some programs, like Microsoft Office, place items in the StartUp folder without even asking you.

Running applications at startup

Use the same procedure for adding an item to the StartUp folder as you did to add Program Manager to the Start menu. The only step you need to change is the step where you select the location for the shortcut — it should be in the StartUp folder rather than in the Programs folder.

In this exercise you place Program Manager in the StartUp folder.

1 Right-click a blank space on the Taskbar.

2 Click Properties.

3 Click the Start Menu Programs tab.

4 Click Add.

5 Type this text in the Command line text box:
c:\windows\progman.exe.

6 Click Next to continue.

7 Select the StartUp folder in the Select Program Folder dialog box.

8 Click Next to continue.

9 Type this text in the Select a name for the shortcut text box:
Program Manager.

10 Click Finish to place the new entry on your Start menu. (You don't need to close the Taskbar Properties dialog box right now.)

Using the Send To command

It's always nice when something you have to do often is pretty easy, isn't it? In Windows 98 there are a lot of little helpers just waiting to make your life easier. In this exercise, you learn how one often-overlooked technique can save you a bit of time copying files to a diskette. You should develop the habit of saving copies of your critical files to diskettes to protect yourself from losing data in the event something goes wrong with your computer. This exercise shows you just how easy it can be to make a quick backup of an important file. The technique works equally well on the Windows 98 desktop or in Windows Explorer.

Using the Send To command

1 Insert a formatted diskette into drive A. You need to make certain the small plastic write-protect slider is pushed toward the center of the diskette so the hole is covered — otherwise your PC won't be able to copy anything to the diskette.

2 Right-click My test file.doc.

3 Click Send To.

4 Select 3 ½ Floppy (A) to copy the file to the diskette.

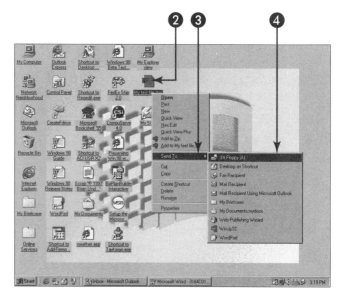

It couldn't get much easier than that, could it? A couple of clicks and you've got a backup copy of your document.

By the way, if you try this exercise a second time, you see a message similar to the message in the figure on the right. In this case it's pretty clear that both the existing file, the one already on the diskette, and the new file are the same. They have the same size, date, and time, so you can be pretty sure they're identical. If any of the information differed, you'd have to decide whether you wanted to replace your backup with the new file. You might even want to keep your existing backup copy and copy the new file to a different diskette.

You can make the Send To command even more useful by creating additional shortcuts in the SendTo folder (which you can find under the Windows folder). These shortcuts can point to programs or folders.

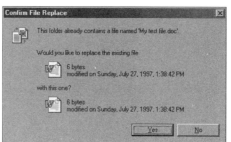

USING WINDOWS HELP

Using a computer is frustrating sometimes, isn't it? You know what you want to do, so why doesn't the stupid machine let you do it? Usually the problem is pretty simple — you just don't know how to tell your PC exactly what you want it to do in terms it can understand. Sometimes it's hard to remember that computers are, after all, just machines, and they really don't think. That's why Windows 98 has online help available — to teach you the language your computer understands.

Unless you have a photographic memory, you probably need to look up information from time to time. When you know how to look up information in the Windows 98 online help system, you can access help with just a few keystrokes and mouse clicks. You can even print some of the more complex help topics to use as a constant reference while you work with Windows 98.

Using pop-up help

Often all you need is a quick reminder rather than a complete explanation. That's why Windows 98 often displays a little pop-up help window when you point to one of the toolbar buttons. In this short exercise you see how these *tooltips* work as you try out several Windows Explorer toolbar buttons.

1 Click the Start button.

2 Click Programs.

3 Select Windows Explorer.

4 Point to the button at the right end on the Standard Buttons toolbar until the word `Views` appears below the mouse pointer, and then click the button. The display changes to a listing of filenames without details, a listing of large or small icons, or a listing with full details, depending on the current view.

5 Click the down arrow to the right of the Views button.

6 Find List and click it.

7 Click Details.

8 Click the Close button.

Using the Help window

When you need more than just a quick reminder of a button's purpose, it's time to turn to the Help window. In this exercise you open the Help window and find topics.

1 Click the Start button.

2 Click Help to display the Help window.

3 Click the closed book icon next to Using Windows Accessories. This opens the book and shows you what's inside.

4 Click the closed book icon next to Words and Pictures.

Printing a Help topic

⑤ Click the icon next to WordPad. Each question mark icon represents a help document you can jump to by double-clicking the icon.

⑥ Click the Index tab to display the Index pane.

⑦ Type this text in the blank text box below the tabs: **ani**.

As you type, the list of topics scrolls up until your screen looks like the figure on the lower right. You can display any topic by double-clicking the topic or by selecting the topic and clicking Display.

⑧ Click the Close button to close the Help window.

Printing a Help topic

There are times when onscreen help is just a little too hard to use. If you have to perform a number of steps to solve a problem or perhaps even restart your computer, a printed copy of the Help information is the only way to go. In this exercise you print the instructions for adding a new folder to the Programs section of the Start menu.

① Click the Start button.

② Click Help.

③ If the Index pane is not displayed, click the Index tab.

④ Type this text in the blank text box below the tabs: **adding**.

⑤ Double-click `submenus to the Start menu` (you may have to scroll down some to find this item).

⑥ Click Display.

⑦ Click Options.

⑧ Click Print.

⑨ Click OK to print the help topic.

⑩ Click the Close button to close the Help window.

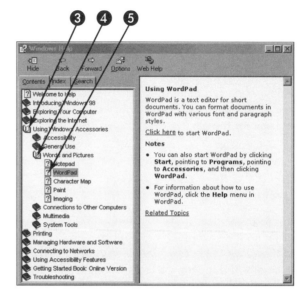

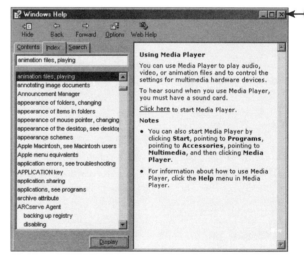

SKILLS CHALLENGE: PUTTING YOUR WINDOWS EXPLORER KNOWLEDGE TO THE TEST

It's time to see if you remember what you've learned in Lesson 1. I give you some tasks here, but I don't tell you the steps you need to take to accomplish them.

1 Open Windows Explorer.

 How would you create a shortcut that opens Windows Explorer with the C:\Windows\Start Menu\Programs\Accessories folder visible in the contents pane?

 How would you create a shortcut that opens Windows Explorer with the contents of your CD-ROM drive visible?

2 Open the Desktop folder.

3 Rename the My Explorer view shortcut to Special Explorer.

4 Add a copy of the Special Explorer shortcut to a diskette in drive A.

 How can you add WordPad as an option to the Send To command?

 What could you do to make it easy to copy files to a specified folder using the right-click menu?

5 Use the Run command to open a Windows Explorer window that has c:\windows as its root.

 What would you do to make Windows Explorer run automatically whenever you start Windows 98?

 How would you find files created during June, 1997?

Skills challenge

 7 *How can you find out which files were created or modified by a program you installed today?*

 8 *How can you find a document file someone created on your computer yesterday if you don't know the name or location of the file?*

6 Check to see whether the Recycle Bin is empty.

7 Find out what's new in Windows 98 by looking on the Help window Contents tab.

 9 *How would you find and open the help file called Backup.hlp?*

8 Find out what the Help window Index tab says about scraps.

9 Remove My test file.doc from the list of recently used documents.

10 Add My test file.doc back to the list of recently used documents without using Windows Explorer.

How did you do? Some of these tasks were a little harder than others, but you should have been able to figure out how to complete each one using the skills you've learned.

TROUBLESHOOTING

If you encounter problems while trying to work through the exercises, here are some ideas that might help you correct the problems and keep going.

Problem	Solution
I don't see the Toolbar and buttons in my Windows Explorer window	Click View ➤ Toolbar to display the Toolbar.
My Taskbar is missing	Move the mouse pointer to the bottom of the screen. When the Taskbar appears, right-click a blank space, click Properties, uncheck Auto hide, and then click OK.
When I try to use Send To, I see an error message that says something like `Cannot create file.`	Make certain the write-protect tab on the diskette is blocking the hole.
My Windows Explorer window shows icons instead of the full listing shown in the figures.	Click the Details button at the right side of the Windows Explorer Toolbar.

WRAP UP

This lesson covered a lot of ground, didn't it? Along the way you've become familiar with Windows Explorer, your desktop, the Start menu, and Windows 98 help. You've learned some of the basics of how to use Windows 98. I'm sure Windows 98 seems quite a bit easier to understand and use now that you're comfortable and know your way around.

The next lesson is a lot of fun. You learn how to customize the appearance of Windows 98 so your PC won't look just like everyone else's. But don't worry, it isn't all play and no work—you also learn how to make Windows 98 easier to use.

Changing the Appearance of Windows 98

45 MINUTES

GOALS

"One size fits all" rarely works for anyone. That's why restaurants always have more than one item on their menus, why clothing stores sell shirts in different colors, and why you need to know how to customize Windows 98. The simple modifications you learn in this lesson can boost your enjoyment while working with Windows 98 and increase your productivity, too. The major goals for Lesson 2 include:

- Customizing your desktop

- Having fun with the screen saver

- Customizing your Taskbar

- Customizing Send To

- Customizing the mouse

- Customizing the keyboard

- Using the Taskbar clock

- Using the new Windows 98 utilities

Get ready

GET READY

You don't need too much to complete Lesson 2. You need to have
Windows 98 completely installed, of course. To change the resolution
of your screen, you need at least a Super VGA monitor and adapter—
one that supports at least 800 × 600 resolution. Unless you're working
on a laptop PC (personal computer), this isn't likely to be a problem.
If you are working on a laptop PC, you may not be able to complete
one of the exercises because some laptop PCs have a fixed-screen
resolution. If your laptop PC can't change screen resolutions, you have
my permission to skip that exercise—just don't make a habit of it! To
complete some of the lessons, you will also need your *Windows 98 One
Step at a Time* CD-ROM to access sample images in the Images folder.

When you finish the exercises in this lesson, you will have
changed the appearance of Windows 98 in the following ways: the
screen resolution, the number of colors shown on your monitor, the
size of your desktop fonts, and the wallpaper and background
pattern of your desktop. You will have also set up a screen saver;
moved, hidden, and resized the Taskbar; added an item to the Send
To menu; created a "lefty" mouse; and adjusted your double-click
speed, pointer speed, keyboard settings, and the system clock.

Okay, time to begin. Make certain you're sitting at your PC with
the Windows 98 desktop on your screen. Close any programs you may
be running—we don't want any unnecessary distractions.

CUSTOMIZING YOUR DESKTOP

I bet you've added some of your own touches to your home,
apartment, or office. No matter what the efficiency experts might
have to say, not everyone can do their best work without some little
personal touches.

You can make quite a few changes to Windows 98 by starting with
your desktop. You're just a few clicks away from seeing more on your
screen (or less, if you prefer), changing the number of colors on your
screen, changing the size of the fonts, selecting your own color scheme,
adding some wallpaper, or displaying a pattern on the desktop.

In a highly visual environment like Windows 98, the amount of
information displayed on the screen can be pretty incredible, can't it?

Changing the screen resolution

That's one reason for one of the biggest trends in PCs over the last several years — bigger monitors. With all the title bars, toolbars, menus, status lines, scrollbars, and so on, you need more room just to do your work. Buying a new, larger monitor, however, doesn't automatically let you see more on the screen. Unless you know how to adjust the display, your larger monitor simply displays the same information in a large size — probably not just what you expected. In the following exercises, you learn how to adjust several different display properties so your screen suits your needs.

Changing the screen resolution

Screen resolution is measured using a rather funny-sounding unit of measure — the *pixel* — which is short for a picture element. One pixel is the smallest amount of space, either horizontal or vertical, that can be controlled by your PC. If your display is set for the standard VGA setting of 640 × 480 (most people drop the word pixel when talking about screen resolution), there are 480 rows each containing 640 columns on your display. If you don't believe me, start counting the dots — you should get to 307,200 by the time you've counted them all!

 NOTE *The screen resolution settings available on your PC are highly dependent on the type of display adapter installed in your system as well as the capabilities of your monitor. Older PCs generally have fewer options available than do the newer systems.*

Although 640 × 480 sounds like a lot of dots, most monitors can display even more. There are two additional common settings, 800 × 600 and 1024 × 768. Your PC may have additional options, but these three settings are the most common.

In this exercise you examine your current display settings and try out one of the optional settings. You change the screen resolution using the standard Windows 98 method. Although it's possible that your system includes other tools for changing the screen resolution — for example, a screen-resolution changer provided by your display adapter's manufacturer — we ignore those for now so you can learn how to use the method built into Windows 98.

1 Right-click a blank space on your desktop.

Changing the screen resolution

② Select Properties from the pop-up menu to display the Display Properties dialog box.

③ Click the Settings tab. If your screen is set to 640 × 480, your display is probably pretty similar to the figure on the right.

④ Drag the resolution slider (in the Screen area box) to the right until the setting shows as 800 × 600 pixels.

⑤ Click Apply.

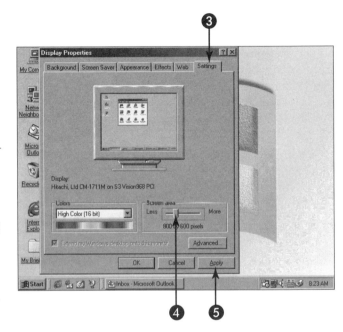

NOTE *After you click Apply, you probably see the message shown in the figure on the right; it tells you that Windows 98 intends to test the new setting. If so, click OK. If you see a message telling you that you have to restart Windows 98 before the new settings can be used, go ahead and let Windows 98 restart.*

⑥ After your desktop is resized, click Yes within 15 seconds to keep the new setting. If you don't click Yes within 15 seconds, Windows 98 restores your old desktop size. (If your display never shows the new desktop setting you selected, or if your display seems quite distorted at the new setting, your monitor may not be capable of properly displaying the selected resolution.)

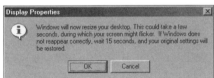

NOTE *If your display seems distorted when you switch to a new resolution, you may be able to adjust your monitor for the new setting. You may need to look in the monitor user's manual to see how to adjust your particular monitor.*

The figure on the next page shows how the screen appears at the new 800 × 600 pixel setting. Compare this figure to the earlier 640 × 480 figure to see how much more you can see at the higher resolution.

⑦ Click OK to close the dialog box.

Changing the colors on your monitor

NOTE

Click the Show settings icon on task bar checkbox to include the resolution settings icon on your Taskbar. You can use this icon to select a new screen resolution without first displaying the Display Properties dialog box.

When you compare the 640 × 480 and 800 × 600 screens, you can see that everything is a little smaller at 800 × 600. That's because Windows 98 is packing more dots into the same space — the display area of your monitor. This isn't a problem on larger monitors, but you probably don't want to use anything higher than 800 × 600 unless you have at least a 17-inch monitor. It's up to you, of course, but if you set the resolution too high on a small monitor, you may strain your eyes trying to read the display.

TIP

*If your monitor seems to flicker at higher resolutions, change back to a lower resolution setting. Some monitors cannot display higher resolutions properly, and the flickering can quickly tire your eyes or even cause headaches. You can usually find out about your monitor's capabilities in the user manual — make certain you use a resolution setting that allows your monitor to use a **vertical refresh rate** of at least 72 Hz if possible. The vertical refresh rate refers to the number of times per second your screen is redrawn, and too low a rate causes flickering.*

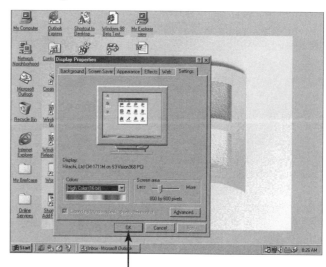

Changing the number of colors on your monitor

How many colors do you need on your computer screen? That's not an easy question to answer, because the answer depends on how you use your PC. The first computer displays had only two colors, black and white, which certainly wouldn't work too well for the graphical environment of Windows 98. In fact, Windows 98 requires a minimum of 16 colors, but it can use a whole lot more.

More colors allow pictures to be more realistic. Imagine how much more true-to-life a photo of a rainbow would appear if the photo had several-hundred color variations instead of 16, for example. Now imagine that the number of colors available jumped into the thousands or even millions. With each jump the picture would look more like a real rainbow and less like a child's drawing. Increasing the number of colors shown on your monitor has the same effect — up to a point. A photo that contains 256 colors doesn't look any better if you set your display to 16 million colors than if you set the display to 256 colors.

Unfortunately, your computer has to move more data and work harder to display more colors. You may not notice the difference on a fast computer, but you might if your PC already seems slow. It takes twice as much information to display a picture in 256 colors as it does to display the same picture in 16 colors; therefore, the number of bits of data required to display different color settings often distinguishes the resolution rather than the number of colors displayed. The following table shows the most common color settings:

Bits of Data	# of Colors
4	16
8	256
15	32,768
16	65,536
24	16,777,216
32	4,294,967,296

Because I don't know your current color setting, I want you to set the display to 16 colors to start the exercise. To do so, follow these steps:

1 Right-click a blank space on your desktop.

2 Select Properties from the pop-up menu that appears to display the Display Properties dialog box.

3 Click the Settings tab.

4 Click the down arrow at the right edge of the Color palette list box to display the list of color options. (The available options are determined by your display adapter and may not include all the choices shown in this figure.)

5 Choose 16 Colors as the new color setting.

6 Click Apply.

7 Depending on your display adapter, Windows 98 may either offer to test the setting or ask if you want to restart Windows 98. Click OK or Yes as appropriate to continue.

8 Click OK to close the dialog box.

You probably won't notice too much difference on your desktop, but you will if you try to view any pictures that use more than 16 colors. Instead of looking like a normal picture, any image you view while Windows 98 is set to 16 colors looks like a poster. You might try some of the images in the Images folder on the CD-ROM that accompanies this book to see the difference.

Repeat the exercise, this time setting your display to 256 colors. When your display is set to 256 colors, you can continue on to the next exercise.

Changing font sizes

When you set your display for higher resolution, everything on the screen becomes a bit smaller, including the descriptive text in dialog boxes, under icons, and in menus. If you choose a very high-resolution setting or use a fairly small monitor, you may find yourself straining to read the text on your screen. In this exercise, you learn how to adjust the font size so the text is easy to read.

1 Right-click a blank space on your desktop.

2 Select Properties from the pop-up menu.

3 Click the Settings tab.

4 Click the Advanced button.

5 Click the down arrow at the right end of the Font size list box to see the two standard options — Small Fonts and Large Fonts. In most cases, one of these options should work well.

6 Click Other to display the Custom Font Size dialog box. You can use the settings in this dialog box to reduce or increase the font size by a factor of five.

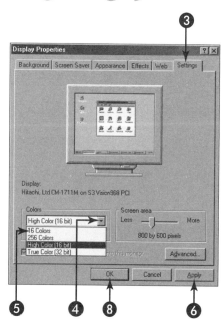

2

Changing the Appearance of Windows 98

Choosing Windows colors

⑦ Drag one of the ruler markings left to decrease the font size to 50% of normal. (The current size is shown in the Scale fonts to be x% of normal size box.)

⑧ Release the mouse button to see how the sample text appears below the ruler.

⑨ Drag a ruler marking right to increase the font size to 150% of normal.

⑩ Release the mouse button to see the change in the sample text.

⑪ Return the font size to 100%.

⑫ Click OK to close the Custom Font Size dialog box.

⑬ Click Cancel to close the Display Properties dialog box. This prevents Windows 98 from applying any changes you made to the font size.

Changing the font size does not affect the size of text in most programs. Your word processing program, for example, continues to use its own settings.

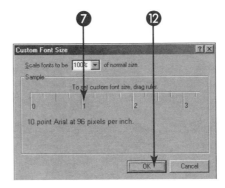

Choosing Windows colors

Want to add some color to your desktop? You can change the colors of virtually every part of your Windows 98 display using the settings on the Appearance tab of the Display Properties dialog box. You can also select from a list of predefined color schemes if you're not feeling quite artistic enough to choose your own colors.

❶ Right-click a blank space on your desktop.

❷ Select Properties from the pop-up menu.

❸ Click the Appearance tab. The window in the top half of this tab shows the effects of any color selections you make and can also be used to select individual items so you can change their appearances.

Click an object in this window to select it in the Item list box

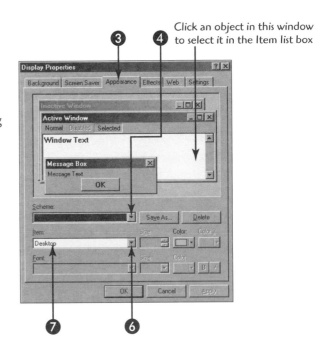

Choosing Windows colors

4 Click the down arrow at the right side of the Scheme list box to display the list of predefined color schemes. (Use the down-arrow key to scroll through the choices. As you choose each color scheme, you see how the color scheme appears in the sample window.)

5 Choose Windows Standard to return the colors to the normal settings.

6 Click the down arrow at the right side of the Item list box to display the list of items that have colors you can change individually.

You can click an item in the sample window to select it if you're not certain of the item's name. For example, click the text `Inactive Window` to see that the object is called the `Inactive Title Bar`. When you select an object like a title bar that contains text, the font options become available, and you can choose how you'd like the object's text to appear.

A few items, such as Icon Spacing (Horizontal) and Icon Spacing (Vertical), can only be selected by choosing them from the list box. You can use these two settings to control how far apart your desktop icons are spaced.

7 Choose Desktop.

8 Click the Color box to display the color palette. You can choose a color for your desktop from this palette by clicking one of the boxes.

9 Select fluorescent green, the third box down in the left column.

10 Click OK to close the dialog box.

TIP *You can use the Save As button in the Display Properties dialog box to save your special color schemes under their own names. It's a good idea to save your favorite color scheme so you can quickly restore your settings if someone changes your colors.*

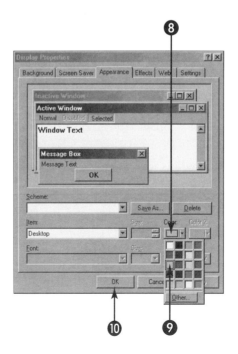

Changing the Appearance of Windows 98

2

Hanging some wallpaper

Hanging some wallpaper

To make your Windows 98 desktop even more interesting, you can display a picture under the icons. You might want to use a sunny scene to brighten your mood during stormy weather or even a scanned photo of your dog to make your desktop unique. (For this lesson you need to insert your *Windows 98 One Step at a Time* CD-ROM into your CD-ROM drive.) In this exercise you add wallpaper to your Windows 98 desktop.

1 Right-click a blank space on your desktop.

2 Select Properties from the pop-up menu to display the Display Properties dialog box.

3 Click the Background tab.

4 Click Browse.

5 Choose SierraSn.bmp from the Images folder on the *Windows 98 One Step at a Time* CD-ROM. (You have to select your CD-ROM drive in the Look in list box to view the image files available in this folder.)

6 Select Center in the Display list box. This places a single copy of the image in the center of your desktop. If you select Tile, the image is repeated several times to cover the entire desktop.

7 Click OK to add the wallpaper to your desktop and close the dialog box.

You can use any Windows bitmap image as your desktop wallpaper. Select None to remove the current wallpaper. You can find several other interesting images in the Images folder on the *Windows 98 One Step at a Time* CD-ROM.

Using a background pattern

Background patterns change the texture of the desktop background. In this exercise you add a background pattern.

1 Right-click a blank space on your desktop.

Using a background pattern

2 Select Properties from the pop-up menu to display the Display Properties dialog box.

3 Click the Background tab.

4 Click the Pattern button.

5 Choose Waffle's Revenge from the Pattern list box.

6 Click OK.

7 Click OK again. If you've been following along with the exercises, your screen probably looks just about as bad as mine does in the figure on the right.

Feel free to restore your original desktop color, remove the wallpaper, and remove the pattern. While the selections you made in these exercises didn't really do much to improve the appearance of your desktop, they did show you your options.

Changing the Monitor Refresh Rate

Windows has the capability to set the refresh rate for many monitors. A higher refresh rate reduces flicker and eyestrain. If your display adapter and monitor are able to support variable refresh rates, and Windows 98 includes support for making this setting with your adapter and monitor, then you may be able to select a higher refresh rate.

NOTE
If you select a refresh rate that is too high, you may damage your monitor. The only safe way to determine the highest refresh rate for your monitor is to look in your monitor owner's manual. This is one area where you can cause expensive damage by not taking the time to make certain you know what you're doing before you experiment. The author and publisher take no responsibility if you damage your monitor because you set your refresh rate too high!

In this exercise you check whether your monitor refresh rate can be adjusted.

1 Right-click a blank space on your desktop.

2

Changing the Appearance of Windows 98

Changing the Monitor Refresh Rate

2 Select Properties from the pop-up menu to display the Display Properties dialog box.

3 Select the Settings tab.

4 Select Advanced.

5 Click the Adapter tab.

6 If your display adapter and monitor are adjustable, then the Refresh rate list box shows the available options. Select Optimal to choose the preferred setting. Do not select a setting higher than what is listed in your monitor's owner's manual.

7 Click OK to close the dialog box.

Many popular (and expensive) display adapters have faulty display drivers that result in flickering. Unfortunately, display adapter manufacturers generally deny that any problems exist, so PC users in the past have been forced to endure poor display quality. Now that Windows 98 gives you the ability to override the refresh rate setting, you are able to reduce the eyestrain and headaches often associated with PC use.

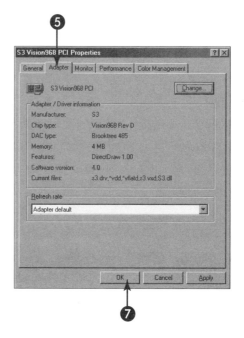

► Using the Effects tab

In Windows 98, a new tab called Effects appears in the Display Properties dialog box. This new tab gives you several options that were available in Windows 95 only if you spent extra for the Plus! add-on. You can change the icons for My Computer, Network Neighborhood, and the Recycle Bin. You can also change several other visual settings, as you learn in this exercise.

1 Right-click a blank space on your desktop.

2 Choose Properties to display the Display Properties dialog box.

3 Click the Effects tab.

4 To change one of the icons, select the icon you want to change.

5 Click the Change Icon button to display the Change Icon dialog box.

6 Choose an icon.

7 Click OK.

8 Select the Use large icons checkbox if you want your desktop icons to be larger. This option is especially useful if you use one of the higher resolution settings for your screen display. You may want to experiment with this setting to see whether you prefer normal or large icons.

9 Select the Show window contents while dragging checkbox to show the contents of a window rather than just a dotted outline while you're dragging a window on your desktop. You may prefer to deselect this option if the slightly jumpy appearance of a window that is being dragged bothers you.

10 Select the Smooth edges of screen fonts checkbox to improve the appearance of larger-size fonts. You probably won't notice much difference when you choose this option, but your Windows 98 display is a little easier to read when this option is selected. Choosing to smooth the edges of screen fonts won't affect how fonts print — printed TrueType fonts always have smooth edges. The Smooth edges option will work only if the Color palette on the Settings tab is on High color or True color.

11 Select the Show icons using all possible colors checkbox to make certain desktop icons have the best possible appearance. This setting probably won't have much visual effect, but you may want to deselect this option if your system uses a 486 processor.

12 Select Use menu animations to make menus a bit livelier. You may not notice too much difference if this is selected, but you may want to deselect it if your system seems slow.

13 Click Apply to see your changes.

14 Click OK to close the Display Properties dialog box.

Although you probably won't notice much difference, the visual enhancements you can apply using the Effects tab of the Display Properties dialog box may decrease your system performance by a small amount. If your PC has a slow processor or less than 16MB of memory and you want top performance, then you may want to avoid using these enhancements. Or you may want to test each of the options individually to see if you notice a difference and then decide whether the visual improvement outweighs any slight performance degradation.

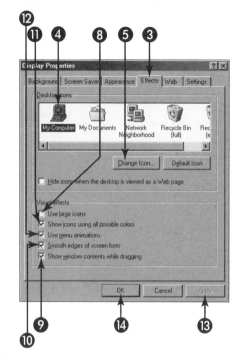

Changing the Appearance of Windows 98

2

Using the Active Desktop

Using the Active Desktop

The most fundamental change in Windows 98 is something Microsoft calls the *Active Desktop*. The Active Desktop essentially makes your Windows 98 desktop similar to a Web page. Icons on the Active Desktop function like the links you see on a Web page — you can activate an icon using a single mouse click rather than by double-clicking the icon.

The Active Desktop can also contain additional items that have direct links to the Internet. For example, you can add a stock ticker or a scrolling news window to your desktop. In this exercise you add an active weather map to your Active Desktop.

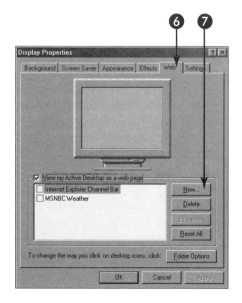

❶ Right-click a blank space on your Windows 98 desktop.

❷ Select Active Desktop.

❸ Check the View as Web Page checkbox.

❹ Right-click a blank space on the desktop.

❺ Select Properties to display the Display Properties dialog box.

❻ Click the Web tab.

❼ Select New to display the New Active Desktop Item dialog box.

❽ Click Yes to connect to the Internet and visit the Active Desktop gallery. (You can also click No, but you'll have to enter the correct address yourself rather than having it added automatically.)

❾ Confirm that you want to connect to the Internet, if necessary. After you've connected to the Active Desktop Gallery Web site, your screen should look similar to the figure on the right. You'll probably see different choices because Microsoft is constantly adding new objects for the Active Desktop.

❿ Click Weather.

⓫ Click MSNBC Weather Map as the item you want to add to your desktop. The Weather Map from the MSNBC Web page loads.

⓬ Click the Add to Active Desktop button to add the item to your desktop.

⑬ Click OK. This displays the Add Item to Active Desktop dialog box.

⑭ Select OK to add the item to your desktop.

⑮ Click the Close button to close Internet Explorer when the download is complete.

If the weather map does not automatically appear on your desktop, right-click a blank space on the desktop and choose Refresh. The figure on the lower right shows how the weather map appears. If you like, you can drag the corners or edges of the weather map to resize the map.

Items you add to the Active Desktop need to be updated from time to time if they're going to be of any value to you. The update method you use depends on the type of Internet connection you have. If you connect to the Internet using a modem, you probably want to update the items manually. To update the weather map manually, move the mouse pointer into the weather map title bar. When the gray bar appears at the top of the map, click the down arrow at the left edge of the gray bar. Choose Properties and then click the Schedule tab. Click Update Now to retrieve the latest weather data. The Schedule tab also includes additional options you can use to schedule automatic updates.

To remove items from the desktop, remove the check from the item's checkbox on the Web tab of the Display Properties dialog box.

HAVING FUN WITH THE SCREEN SAVER

Screen savers don't really save your screen from anything simply because modern monitors are designed so that they don't suffer damage from what's displayed on the screen. Still, screen savers can be fun, and if you use a password, they can protect you from snoops when you leave your desk for a few minutes.

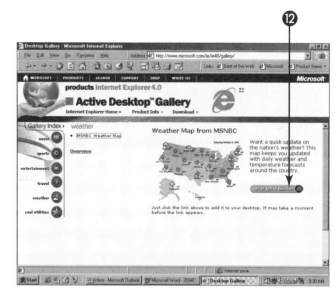

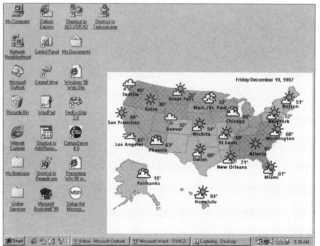

Setting up a screen saver

Setting up a screen saver

In this exercise you learn how you can display moving text as a screen saver whenever you stop using your PC for a few minutes. You also learn how to add a password so no one else can see what's on your screen under the screen saver.

❶ Right-click a blank space on your desktop.

❷ Select Properties from the pop-up menu to display the Display Properties dialog box.

❸ Select the Screen Saver tab.

❹ Click the down arrow on the Screen Saver list box.

❺ Choose Scrolling Marquee.

❻ Select Settings to display the Options for Scrolling Marquee dialog box.

❼ Type this text in the Text box: **Windows 98 is fun!**

Your screen should now look like the figure on the right (I moved the Options for Scrolling Marquee dialog box to the side so you could see the screen a little better).

❽ Click OK to close the Options for Scrolling Marquee dialog box.

❾ Click Preview to see how your screen saver appears. Be careful not to bump your mouse or touch any of the keys — as soon as you do, the screen saver disappears. This is also the way to restore your screen when the screen saver is displayed later.

❿ Select the Password protected checkbox.

⓫ Click Change to display the Change Password dialog box.

⓬ Type this text in both text boxes: **idg**.

This is your screen saver password, and it is very important that you remember it exactly. Unless you know your password, you can't restore your screen after the screen saver appears.

⓭ Click OK to close the Change Password dialog box.

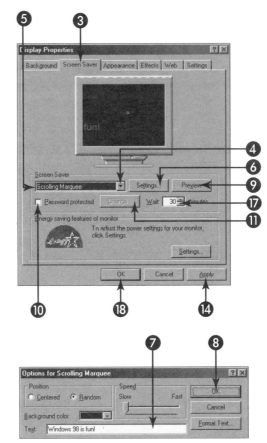

⓮ Click Apply and then sit back and wait for the screen saver to appear.

⓯ Press a key or move your mouse after the screen server appears and you've enjoyed reading the message several times.

⓰ Type this text to restore your screen: **idg**.

⓱ Click the up arrow at the right side of the Wait box until the time is set to 30 minutes.

⓲ Click OK to confirm your changes and close the Display Properties dialog box.

TIP

*To instantly activate your screen saver just before you leave your desk, click the Start button, select Run, and enter the text **Scrolling Marquee.scr** in the Open text box. Click OK to run the screen saver.*

▶ *Using your display's energy-saving feature*

Many monitors made in the past few years incorporate energy saving features that allow them to go into a low-power mode when they receive a special signal from the computer. If your monitor has this feature, you can configure Windows 98 to send the power down signal to your monitor after a specified period of time. Some energy-saving monitors have two low-power modes, but for most monitors the two energy-saving modes are identical. You have to read your owner's manual to see which energy-saving modes apply to your monitor. In this exercise you activate the energy saving features of your monitor.

❶ Right-click a blank space on your desktop.

❷ Select Properties from the pop-up menu to display the Display Properties dialog box.

❸ Select the Screen Saver tab.

❹ Click Settings to configure the monitor power settings.

❺ Select a scheme from the Power schemes list box.

6 Select the time in the Turn off monitor list box.

7 Click OK to close the dialog box.

After your monitor has gone into low-power-standby mode, you can reactivate the monitor by pressing a key or moving the mouse. This usually works to reactivate the monitor when it enters shut off mode, too, but your owner's manual tells you if you need to do anything else to reactivate the monitor in case that doesn't work.

The Display Properties Dialog Box

The Display Properties dialog box contains quite a few settings, so I've gathered them all into one place so you can more easily see the various options.

Use the Background tab to set desktop wallpaper or a pattern.

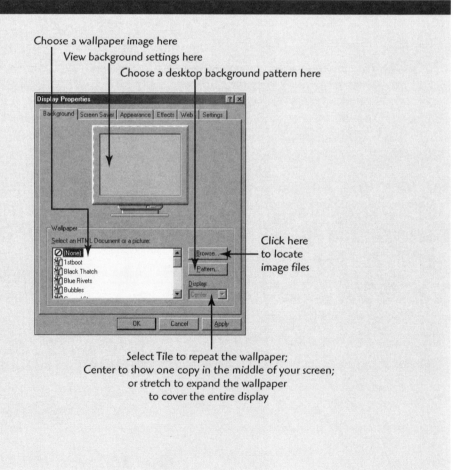

Choose a wallpaper image here

View background settings here

Choose a desktop background pattern here

Click here to locate image files

Select Tile to repeat the wallpaper; Center to show one copy in the middle of your screen; or stretch to expand the wallpaper to cover the entire display

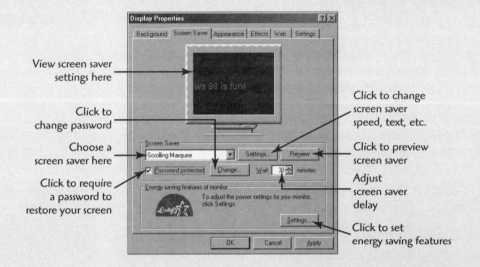

View screen saver settings here

Click to change password

Choose a screen saver here

Click to require a password to restore your screen

Click to change screen saver speed, text, etc.

Click to preview screen saver

Adjust screen saver delay

Click to set energy saving features

Use the Screen Saver tab to set up a screen saver.

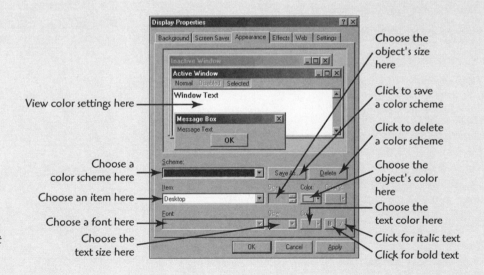

View color settings here

Choose a color scheme here

Choose an item here

Choose a font here

Choose the text size here

Choose the object's size here

Click to save a color scheme

Click to delete a color scheme

Choose the object's color here

Choose the text color here

Click for italic text

Click for bold text

Use the Appearance tab to set display colors.

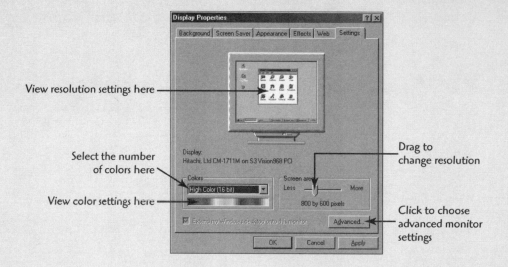

View resolution settings here

Select the number of colors here

View color settings here

Drag to change resolution

Click to choose advanced monitor settings

Use the Settings tab to set resolution and color level.

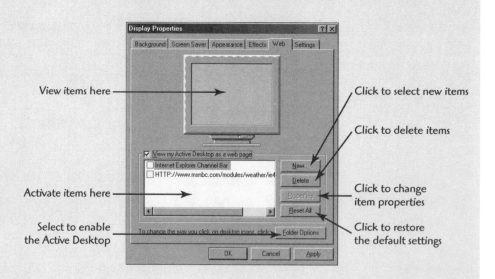

View items here

Click to select new items

Click to delete items

Activate items here

Click to change item properties

Select to enable the Active Desktop

Click to restore the default settings

Use the Web tab to select items for the Active Desktop.

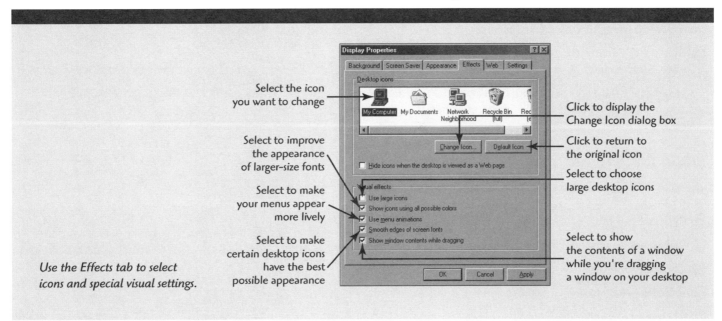

Select the icon
you want to change

Click to display the
Change Icon dialog box

Click to return to
the original icon

Select to improve
the appearance
of larger-size fonts

Select to choose
large desktop icons

Select to make
your menus appear
more lively

Select to make
certain desktop icons
have the best
possible appearance

Select to show
the contents of a window
while you're dragging
a window on your desktop

*Use the Effects tab to select
icons and special visual settings.*

CUSTOMIZING YOUR TASKBAR

The Windows 98 Taskbar is pretty useful without any changes, but
why let that stop you from playing with it a little? There's no harm
in having a little fun, especially when you might end up with a
more useful Taskbar.

Moving the Taskbar

Your Taskbar doesn't have to be at the bottom of your screen. If you
prefer, you can move the Taskbar to the top or to either side of your
screen. In this exercise you move the Taskbar.

1 Point to an empty area of the Taskbar.

2 Drag it to the right edge of the screen.

As you drag the Taskbar, you see a gray line indicating where
the Taskbar will appear when you release the mouse button.

Hiding the Taskbar

The figure on the right shows how the Taskbar appears when moved to the right edge of the screen.

3 Drag the Taskbar to the top of the screen, and then to the left edge, and finally back to the bottom of the screen.

No matter where you place your Taskbar, I refer to it as being at the bottom of your screen. If you've left it somewhere else, keep that in mind as you follow along in the exercises.

Hiding the Taskbar

There are times when you need all of the screen space you can get, and the Taskbar just seems to get in the way. In those cases, you can hide the Taskbar — just be sure to remember where you hid it!

1 Right-click an empty place on the Taskbar.

2 Choose Properties.

3 Select the Auto hide checkbox.

4 Click Apply to make the Taskbar disappear.

5 To view the Taskbar, move the mouse pointer just below the bottom edge of the screen. The Taskbar remains visible until you move the mouse pointer up above the Taskbar.

6 Deselect Auto hide by clicking in the checkbox.

7 Click OK to close the dialog box.

TIP

You can display the Taskbar and the Start menu by pressing Ctrl+Esc even when the Taskbar is hidden.

Resizing the Taskbar

When you only have a few programs running, the Taskbar has plenty of room to show a button with descriptive text for each program. This may not be the case if you have quite a few programs running together. In this exercise you resize the Taskbar to give each program button more room.

Resizing the Taskbar

❶ Point to the top edge of the Taskbar. When the mouse pointer changes to a double-headed arrow, you're in the correct position.

❷ Drag the top edge of the Taskbar up. You see a gray line appear above the Taskbar to indicate where the top edge of the Taskbar will be when it's resized.

❸ Release the mouse button when the Taskbar is approximately triple its original height, as shown in the figure on the right. You don't have to worry about precisely sizing the Taskbar; it automatically jumps to the correct height for the program buttons.

❹ Return the Taskbar to its original size — just high enough for one row of program buttons.

If you move the Taskbar to either side of your screen, you find that resizing the Taskbar isn't quite the same because the Taskbar size doesn't change in predefined increments. If the Taskbar is on either side of the screen, you can resize the Taskbar to any size you like — up to the limit of one half the screen.

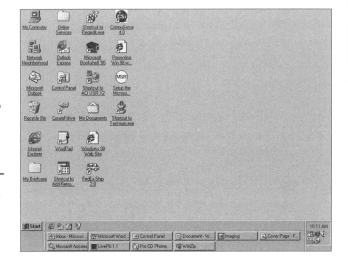

CUSTOMIZING SEND TO

In Lesson 1 you learned how to use the Send To command to quickly copy files to a diskette. There's no reason to limit this useful command to the built-in options, though. You can add other useful items to the Send To command so you can have instant shortcuts available whenever you need them.

Adding an item to the Send To menu

To add an item to the Send To menu, you must create a shortcut to it in the \Windows\SendTo folder. This can be a shortcut to a program or a folder, but if you create a shortcut to a program, the program should be able to correctly handle any files or documents you send to the program. That's one reason WordPad is a pretty good choice for adding to Send To — WordPad can open most types of files.

In this exercise you add WordPad to the Send To menu.

❶ Right-click the Start button.

Adding an item to the Send To menu

2 Select Explore.

3 Open the \Windows\Start Menu\Programs\Accessories folder.

4 Point to the shortcut to WordPad, hold down the right mouse button, drag the shortcut to the SendTo folder, and release the mouse button.

5 Select Create Shortcut(s) Here.

You may be tempted to add shortcuts to all of your favorite programs in the SendTo folder so they appear on the Send To menu, but there's really no reason to do so. Most of the time you use your favorite programs to open one type of document file, such as a spreadsheet or a word processor file. When you install programs on your PC, the installation programs tell Windows 98 which types of document files they can open. That's why Windows Explorer shows you a document is a Word document, an Excel Spreadsheet, or an Access database. Because Windows 98 already knows which program to use to open those types of files, there's no reason to clutter your Send To menu with shortcuts to the programs.

CUSTOMIZING THE MOUSE

Are you comfortable with your mouse? Do you ever get frustrated when you try to open something and Windows 98 doesn't do anything? Do you ever lose track of where the mouse pointer is on your screen? Would you rather the two buttons were swapped? If so, this is the right place to find the answers.

Adjusting your double-click and pointer speed

Learning to double-click correctly is probably one of the hardest things for a new mouse user to master. Either you don't get the two clicks quite fast enough, or you accidentally double-click when you just meant to single-click. In this exercise you adjust the double-click setting for your mouse and end that frustration forever.

1 Click the Start button.

2 Select Settings.

③ Select Control Panel.

④ Double-click Mouse to display the Mouse Properties dialog box.

NOTE
Your Mouse Properties dialog box may differ from the one shown in the figure on the right, depending on the type of mouse you have. If so, you may need to look on more than one tab to find all the settings. You use this dialog box to do all of your mouse customizing.

⑤ Double-click in the Test area to see whether your double-clicking is fast enough. If the umbrella pops up, Windows 98 recognized your double-click.

⑥ Double-click the Set box to change the double click speed. If your Mouse Properties dialog box uses a slider to set the speed, drag the double-click setting pointer to the right to make the speed setting faster (you must double-click faster), or drag the pointer to the left to make the speed setting slower (you have more time between clicks).

⑦ Drag the Pointer speed selector to the left end of the setting.

⑧ Click Apply.

⑨ Test this setting by moving the mouse around. Notice that you must move the mouse quite some distance to move the mouse pointer.

⑩ Drag the Pointer speed selector to the right end of the setting.

⑪ Click Apply.

⑫ Move the mouse around to test this setting. Now the mouse pointer moves faster than the mouse. Choose a setting that feels comfortable.

If you set the speed too fast, Windows 98 doesn't recognize double-clicks. If you set the speed too slow, Windows 98 assumes that mouse clicks as much as a second apart are a double-click.

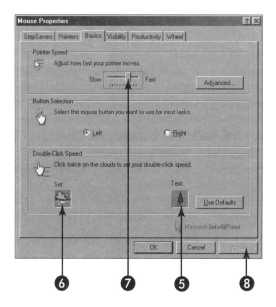

Creating a lefty mouse

Creating a lefty mouse

In the middle of the Mouse Properties dialog box, shown in the previous figure, you find two radio buttons. You can select Left for normal mouse operations or Right if you want to swap the functions of the mouse buttons. If you're left-handed, placing the mouse at the left side of the keyboard may feel more natural. Swapping the functions of the mouse buttons allows you to more comfortably use your left index finger to click the buttons. If you do swap the mouse buttons, you need to remember that you've done so as you complete the rest of the lessons: Use the correct button based on your mouse setting. That is, when the text says `right-click`, you have to remember this means left-click on your PC.

1. Click the Start button.
2. Select Settings.
3. Select Control Panel.
4. Double-click Mouse to display the Mouse Properties dialog box.
5. Click the Basics tab.
6. Click the Right radio button.
7. Click OK to close the Mouse Properties dialog box.

Adding trails

In this exercise you see how you can get used to the mouse by getting a better idea where your mouse is pointing. This setting is quite useful on some low-contrast laptop PC screens, too.

1. Click the Start button.
2. Select Settings.
3. Select Control Panel.
4. Double-click Mouse to display the Mouse Properties dialog box.
5. Click the Visibility tab (some Mouse Properties dialog boxes have this setting on the Motion tab).

Adding trails

6 Click the Display pointer trails checkbox.

7 Move the mouse around to see the effect of this setting.

8 Click Settings to display the Settings for Trails dialog box. Try moving the slider to various points between Short and Long to see which setting you prefer.

9 Click OK to close the Settings for Trails dialog box.

10 When you are satisfied with your settings, click OK to close the Mouse Properties dialog box.

You may want to test your mouse settings and fine-tune your adjustments to make your mouse function the way you like. If you share a PC with other users, make certain all users enter their own names when they start Windows 98. Because Windows 98 keeps track of the settings for each user name entered, all users can have their own custom settings.

Configuring for single clicking

If you've ever wondered why you have to double-click items on your desktop but single-click items on the Internet, you don't have to wonder any longer. In Windows 98 you can configure your PC so that a single mouse click selects and activates objects. In this exercise you learn how to adjust how your desktop responds to mouse clicks.

1 Double-click My Computer.

2 Select View.

3 Select Folder Options to display the Folder Options dialog box.

4 Click the Web style radio button to enable single-click selection and activation of desktop items.

5 Click the Classic style radio button to use double-clicking to activate desktop items.

6 Click the Custom radio button to use a combination of the old and new styles.

7 Click Settings to display the Custom Settings dialog box.

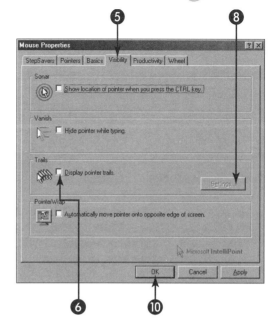

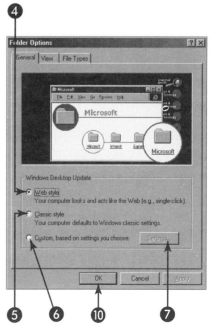

2

Changing the Appearance of Windows 98

Configuring for single clicking

⑧ Choose Single-click to open an item (point to select) or Double-click to open an item (single-click to select), depending on whether you prefer to single- or double-click.

⑨ Click OK to close the dialog box.

⑩ Click OK again to confirm your changes.

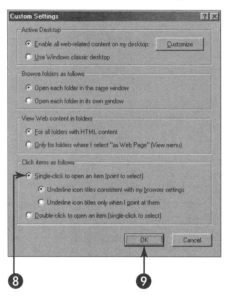

 NOTE *If you choose the Custom setting and later decide to return to either Web style or Classic style, make certain your choices in the Web Integration Settings dialog box match the style radio button you choose in the Options dialog box. Otherwise, you may find that the mouse does not always work quite as you expect.*

CUSTOMIZING YOUR KEYBOARD

You can also change the way your keyboard responds to your keystrokes. If you're a slow typist, you may find keys repeating because the delay before keys repeat is too short or the repeat rate is too high. If you're a fast typist, you may want to set a shorter delay or a faster repeat rate so your keyboard doesn't feel so sluggish. Either way, there's help available. You can also change the rate the cursor blinks.

Adjusting keyboard settings

In this exercise you customize your keyboard to match your typing style.

❶ Click the Start button.

❷ Select Settings.

❸ Select Control Panel.

❹ Double-click Keyboard to display the Keyboard Properties dialog box. (All of the settings you adjust in this lesson are on the Speed tab, which is displayed automatically when you open the dialog box.)

❺ Drag the Repeat delay slider to the left.

Adjusting keyboard settings

6 Click the test area.

7 Hold down a key. Notice the length of time before the key repeats.

8 Drag the Repeat delay slider to the right and test the length of time before the key repeats. Choose a setting that seems right for your typing style.

9 Drag the Repeat rate slider left and right to test the different settings. Here, too, you should select a setting that feels comfortable.

10 Drag the Cursor blink rate slider left or right to find a setting you like.

11 Click OK to save your settings and close the Keyboard Properties dialog box.

You may need to test your new keyboard settings in several of your favorite programs to determine the most comfortable combination. What works well in your spreadsheet may not be the best for your word processor, but, because you can change your settings anytime, you can find out what's right for you with a little experimentation.

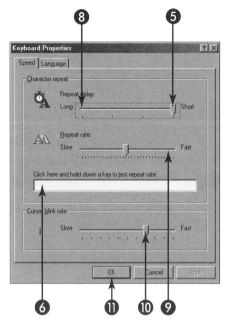

USING THE TASKBAR CLOCK

That little time display in the lower-right corner of your Windows 98 desktop is actually your connection to your PC's internal clock and calendar. The correct date and time are quite important. Every time you save a new file or modify an existing one, Windows 98 records the exact date and time as part of the file information. You can then use this information to locate the newest versions of files, find files you worked with on a specific date, or even determine how much time has passed since you last backed up your files.

Adjusting the system clock

You can make several adjustments to the system clock. Not only can you correct the time, but you can also set the date, your time zone, and even whether you want automatic adjustments for daylight savings time. In this exercise you adjust your PC's clock.

Changing the Appearance of Windows 98

2

CHANGING THE APPEARANCE OF WINDOWS 98   **77**

Adjusting the system clock

1 Double-click the time display at the right edge of the Taskbar to display the Date/Time Properties dialog box.

2 Click the down arrow to the right of the month list box to select a different month.

3 Click the up or down arrows at the right side of the year box to select a different year.

4 Click a date in the calendar display to change the date.

5 To adjust the time, click the digital time display to select the portion of the time you want to change. (To change the hour, click the hour portion of the time. Use the up or down arrow to the right of the time display to make the adjustment.)

6 Click the Time Zone tab to display the time zone options.

7 To change the time zone, choose the correct time zone from the list box.

8 Select the Automatically adjust clock for daylight saving changes checkbox if you are in a location that uses daylight savings time. Windows 98 then changes your PC's clock for you when you go on or off daylight savings time.

9 Click OK to confirm your changes and close the Date/Time Properties dialog box.

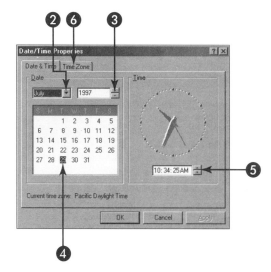

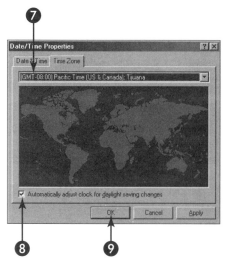

NOTE
Be careful when setting your calendar so you don't choose a date in the future. If you have any trial versions of software installed, choosing a future date could disable that software. Setting the date back to the correct date probably doesn't reenable the software, either.

USING THE NEW WINDOWS 98 UTILITIES

Windows 98 includes several new utilities you'll find quite useful. These utilities can help you maintain your computer and ensure that it is running as efficiently as possible. The following exercises cover three of the new utilities.

Using the System Information Utility

Using the System Information Utility

The System Information Utility provides a wealth of interesting information about your PC. Much of this information can be quite valuable for troubleshooting purposes. You probably won't have much need for this troubleshooting information, but if your system experiences problems, then you'll be able to provide the technical support person with information that may help him or her solve the problem more quickly.

1 Click the Start button.

2 Select Programs.

3 Select Accessories.

4 Select System Tools.

5 Select System Information.

6 Select the information category you want to examine. In the figure on the right, the Printing category information is displayed.

7 Click the Print button to create a printed record of the selected category.

8 Click the Close button to close the System Information Utility.

You may find the System Information Utility especially useful if you add or change hardware or system driver files. You can print a copy of the information about a category both before and after you make any changes. Then if something doesn't work correctly after the upgrade, you can examine the two printed reports to see what was changed.

Using the System File Checker

The System File Checker checks important Windows 98 system files to make certain they haven't been damaged or improperly overwritten. Files can be damaged if your system crashes. In addition, poorly written software installation programs can replace important system files with out-of-date versions that may cause your computer to malfunction. In this exercise you verify that your system files are okay.

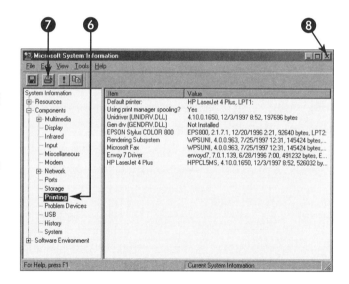

2

Changing the Appearance of Windows 98

Using the System File Checker

1. Click the Start button.

2. Select Programs.

3. Select Accessories.

4. Select System Tools.

5. Select System Information.

6. Select Tools.

7. Select System File Checker to open the System File Checker.

8. Click Start to begin checking the errors.

9. If System File Checker finds system files that have changed, you see a dialog box similar to the one shown in the figure on the right.

10. Choose Update if you know the file has been updated.

11. Choose Restore if you want to revert to the original Windows 98 file.

12. Choose Ignore if you're not certain but want to try the changed file.

13. Choose Update verification for all changed files if you've applied an update to Windows 98.

14. Click OK to continue.

15. Select Close to close the System File Checker.

If Microsoft supplies a *Service Pack* — an update for Windows 98 — be sure to run System File Checker before you apply the update. You should then run System File Checker and choose Update verification for all changed files to update the System File Checker database.

Using the Windows Tune-Up Wizard

Your PC probably isn't running quite as fast as it could. In this exercise you use the Windows Tune-Up Wizard, which is intended to help you get the most out of your system by making your favorite programs run faster, making certain your hard disk doesn't contain errors, and that disk space isn't being wasted on unnecessary files.

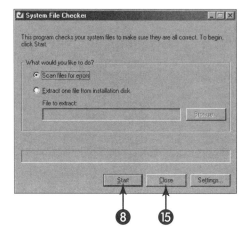

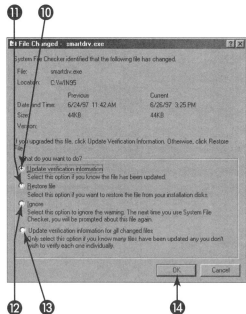

Using the Windows Tune-Up Wizard

1 Click the Start button.

2 Select Programs.

3 Select Accessories.

4 Select System Tools.

5 Select Windows Tune Up to open the Windows Tune-Up Wizard dialog box. If you've run the Windows Tune-Up Wizard in the past, you may need to select the Change my tune-up settings or schedule radio button and click OK to open this dialog box.

6 Select the Custom radio button.

7 Click Next to begin.

8 Select the time to run the tune-ups. In this case, select Custom.

9 Click Next to continue.

10 Click Next again to see the schedule for speeding up programs.

11 To change a task schedule, click the Reschedule button to display the Reschedule dialog box. (You may want to reschedule any tasks scheduled for times when you normally use your PC.)

12 After you have adjusted the schedule, click OK to close the Reschedule dialog box.

13 Click Next to continue. The Windows Tune-Up Wizard then shows the schedule for scanning the hard disk for errors.

14 Click Next to continue.

15 Click Next again. The Windows Tune-Up Wizard then confirms the schedule.

16 Click Finish to close the Windows Tune-Up Wizard dialog box.

Make certain you don't turn off your PC during the time scheduled for Windows Tune-Up Wizard tasks. You can turn off your monitor to save energy, but your system must be running for the tasks to complete.

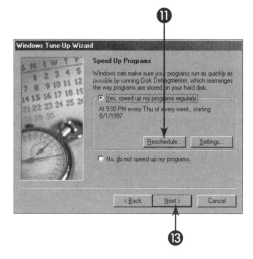

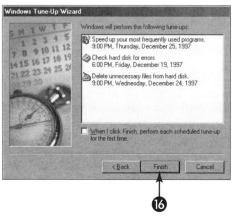

SKILLS CHALLENGE: CUSTOMIZING WINDOWS 98

It's time to see if you remember what you've learned in Lesson 2. This is a quick run through the exercises without giving you every step along the way.

1 Find your current display resolution setting.

2 Determine how many colors your monitor can display at the current settings.

3 Change the desktop background color to gray.

> **1** *How would you change to the High Contrast White (Extra Large) color scheme?*

4 Change the font used to display icon titles to Large Fonts.

> **2** *How would you increase the size of the onscreen text to five times normal so a vision-impaired user could read the Windows 98 screen?*

5 Change the desktop pattern to Buttons.

6 Check to see how your wallpaper looks when tiled, and then set it back to centered.

> **3** *How do you make a picture into wallpaper that covers your entire desktop?*

7 Preview your screen saver.

8 Change the screen saver delay time to ten minutes.

> **4** *What can you do to protect your privacy when you step away from your desk?*

9 Determine the font name and size for text displayed in the inactive title bar.

> **5** *How can you hide the title bar text?*

10 Move the Taskbar to the top of the screen.

Hide the Taskbar.

6 *How would you find out where someone hid the Taskbar?*

 Restore the Taskbar, move it to the bottom of the screen, and increase the Taskbar height so two rows of program buttons can be displayed.

 Determine whether your mouse is set to right- or left-handed.

7 *How would you make it easier for someone with limited physical abilities to double-click the mouse?*

8 *What would you do to make the mouse pointer easier to find for someone who's never used a mouse before?*

 Increase the cursor blink rate by one notch.

9 *What two settings can you use to make the keyboard easier to use for someone who's just learning to type?*

⑮ Determine whether your clock is set to automatically adjust for daylight savings time.

⑯ Open the System Information Utility and view your system information.

⑰ Reschedule one of the Windows Tune-Up Wizard tasks.

Troubleshooting

TROUBLESHOOTING

If you encounter problems while trying to work through the exercises, here are some ideas that may help you correct the problems and keep going.

Problem	Solution
I can't increase my resolution setting above 640 × 480 pixels.	Your display adapter is set as a standard VGA adapter. You need to check your owner's manual to see if you really have a different adapter that can use higher settings. If your display adapter can use higher settings, click the Change Display Type button on the Display Properties dialog box Settings tab, choose Change, and then select the correct adapter type.
I can't set my display to more than 16 colors.	This problem is caused by having your display adapter set as standard VGA. See the previous problem to determine if you can overcome this problem.
My Display Properties dialog box looks different than the one in the figures.	Some display adapters have their own special drivers that modify the appearance of the Display Properties dialog box. You should still be able to find the settings used in the exercises, and you can ignore the extra settings for now.
When I try to set up a screen saver, I can't find any screen savers listed in the Screen Saver list box.	You need to install the screen savers using your Windows 98 disks or CD–ROM. Click the Start button, select Settings ➤ Control Panel, and double-click Add/Remove Programs. Click the Windows Setup tab, select Accessories, and click Details. Select Screen Savers and then OK. Click Apply and follow the prompts to install the screen savers.

WRAP UP

In this lesson you've learned how you can customize the appearance of Windows 98 so it's a bit more fun to use. You've also seen how you can protect your privacy so people aren't snooping around your computer when you walk away from your desk.

You may want to consider how you can apply what you've learned in Lesson 2 to help other people use a PC. What changes would help a young learner or a visually impaired user, for example?

In the next lesson you learn more about working with files in Windows 98. Because your files contain your work, it's pretty important to know where your files are and how you can protect yourself from the disaster of losing your work.

2

Changing the Appearance of Windows 98

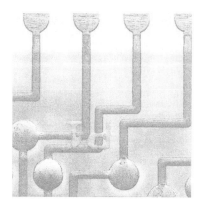

Working with Files

GOALS

You've already worked with some files in Lessons 1 and 2; you simply can't get around using files when you use your PC. This lesson takes you several steps farther down the path toward really understanding the Windows 98 file management system by covering the following topics:

- Managing your files and folders
- Working with long filenames
- Changing the view
- Starting programs by opening documents
- Scheduling events

Get ready

GET READY

You can't do any real work on your PC without working with files. Everything you store on your computer — your databases, your letters, your spreadsheets — is stored in files. If you lose your files, your data goes with them. If you're like most people, your data files are worth more to you than the entire cost of your computer. Just think for a minute about all the work you have tied up in your data files, and you see what I mean. That's why this lesson is so important — your files are a valuable asset you can't afford to lose.

In this lesson you use a number of files, but to keep the lesson easy to follow, most are files already on your PC and files included on the *Windows 98 One Step at a Time* CD-ROM in the Lesson 3 folder. You also create some very small files as you go through the exercises. If you've completed Lessons 1 and 2, you should be ready to start this lesson without any additional items.

When you have completed the exercises in this lesson, you will have learned how to do the following: find lost files; create new folders; move, copy, delete, and sort files and folders; work with long filenames; change the width of panes and columns in Windows Explorer; display and hide different file types; register a new file type; and edit an existing file type.

If you're ready, it's on to Lesson 3. Make certain you're sitting at your PC and the Windows 98 desktop is on your screen.

MANAGING YOUR FILES AND FOLDERS

In this set of exercises you learn how to find, select, rename, copy, and move files. You also learn how to make the Recycle Bin work as your safety net, preventing you from the disaster of losing files because you accidentally deleted them.

Some of the tasks you practice in this lesson may seem familiar because you've already learned some of the relevant skills in Lesson 1. Here, however, you learn how to make Windows 98 do more of the work for you. You also learn some new techniques I didn't cover earlier because I didn't want to hit you with too much at one time.

Finding your lost files

Lost files sometimes seem like lost sheep — they never seem to be where you're sure you left them. Windows 98 sometimes contributes to this phenomenon by offering to save your files either on your desktop or in the last folder you used. The problem with this is simple — the computer is doing what you're telling it to do, not what you're thinking it should do. Unfortunately, we still don't have computers that understand "do what I mean, not what I say." Until we do, you may find yourself looking for your lost files occasionally.

In Lesson 1 you learned that you can use the Find command in a number of ways. For example, you can find files by looking for them by name or even part of the name, by the type of file, by the date the file was created or modified, or even by searching for files containing specified text. As useful as all these options are, you're likely to use just a few of the options repeatedly. You might, for example, want to find all word processing document files containing references to a specific project. Rather than re-enter the same search parameters each time, why not have Windows 98 remember what you wanted last time, and do the same search again?

In this exercise you create a useful search and then tell Windows 98 to save the parameters so you can perform the same search in the future with just a few clicks. In this case, the search is for all files created in the past week that have .doc as the file extension. The .doc file extension is used by both WordPad and Word to indicate word processing document files.

① Click the Start button.

② Select Find.

③ Select Files or Folders.

④ Type the following text in the Named text box: ***.doc**.

⑤ Click the Date tab.

⑥ Select the During the previous x days radio button.

⑦ Click the up arrow until the number of days is 7.

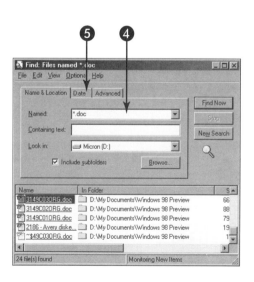

Finding your lost files

8 Select Options and make certain that a check appears in front of Save Results. (This command is a *toggle* — each time you select the command, it changes states from selected to deselected, or from deselected to selected.)

9 Select Find Now to start the search.

10 When Windows 98 has completed the search, select File.

11 Select Save Search to place an icon named Files named @.doc.fnd on your desktop.

12 Click the Close button to close the Find window.

13 Double-click the Files named @.doc.fnd icon to redisplay the saved search results.

14 Select Find Now to begin a new search for documents created or modified within the past week. You have to do a new search, because when you double-click the Files named @.doc.fnd icon, the results shown in the Find window are the saved results, not the results of a new search.

15 Click the Close button to close the Find window.

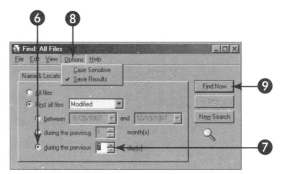

There is a potential "gotcha" you may encounter in trying to save a file search for future use. I carefully steered you around the problem, but now that you've successfully completed the exercise, I'll explain what could have gone wrong.

TIP

Whenever you click the New Search button, be sure to check the Look in list box to make certain Windows 98 hasn't replaced your selection with Document Folders.

You must make certain that you've selected Options ➤ Save Results and clicked Find Now *before* you select File ➤ Save Search. Oh sure, Windows 98 is perfectly happy to save the Files named @.doc.fnd icon on your desktop before you've completed Steps 7 and 8, but something important is missing — the setting on the Date tab that limits the search to files created or modified in the past seven days. In fact, Windows 98 totally forgets that you wanted to

only one small detail — you don't bother to find the matching files before you save the search.

1 Click the Start button.

2 Select Find.

3 Select Files or Folders.

4 Type the following text in the Named text box: ***.doc**.

5 Click the Date tab.

6 Select the During the previous *x* days radio button.

7 Click the up arrow until the number of days is 7.

8 Select Options and make certain that a check appears in front of Save Results. (Again, this command is a *toggle* — each time you select the command, it changes states from selected to deselected, or from deselected to selected, as the case may be.)

9 Select File.

10 Select Save Search to place an icon named Files named @.doc (2).fnd on your desktop.

11 Click the Close button to close the Find window.

12 Double-click the Files named @.doc (2).fnd icon to redisplay the saved search.

13 Click the Date tab and you see that the All files radio button is selected rather than the During the previous 7 days radio button. From this, you can probably guess that Windows 98 isn't going to limit its search as you intended.

14 Click Find Now to begin a new search. This time the search finds all files with a .doc extension, not just those created or modified in the past week. The accompanying figure shows that Windows 98 found over 200 files on my computer because the search wasn't limited to files from the past week.

15 Click the Close button to close the Find window.

This exercise has shown you something few Windows 98 "experts" know — if you want to save a search that finds files modified

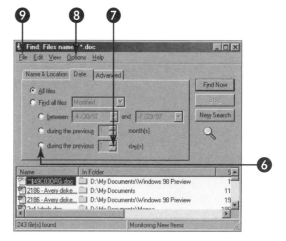

Selecting files and folders

within a specified number of days or months before today, you must actually perform the search before you save it. I don't mind if you tease your local Windows 98 expert with this one!

Selecting files and folders

You can only work with files and folders that you've selected. That's true whether you're trying to open a document, run a program, delete old files, or copy files to a diskette. In this exercise you learn a few tricks that make navigating folders and selecting files a little easier.

1 Click the Start button.

2 Select Programs.

3 Select Windows Explorer.

4 Click the Windows folder to display its contents in the contents pane.

5 Press Tab to move the selector into the contents pane and highlight the item at the top of the listing. Remember that Windows 98 displays folders at the top of the listing, with files following the folders.

6 Press Ctrl+A to select all the files and folders in the Windows folder. (Ctrl+A is a keyboard shortcut for the Edit ➢ Select All command.)

7 Press End to move the selector to the last item in the Windows folder.

8 Press Home to move the selector to the first item in the Windows folder.

9 Press the letter *F* to move the selector to the first item in the list that begins with the letter *F*. This is likely to be a folder rather than a file, because Windows 98 normally has several folders under the Windows folder that begin with F.

10 Press F again to move the selector to the next item that begins with F.

11 Continue pressing F until the selector jumps back to the first item that begins with F. When there are no more folders beginning with F, the selector jumps back to the first file that begins with F.

⑫ Press Shift+Home to select all items between the selector and the top of the list. (This shortcut enables you to select a group of items between the item you've currently selected and the top of the list.)

⑬ Press Shift+End to select all items between the selector and the end of the list. (Like Shift+Home, this shortcut enables you to select a group of items quickly.)

⑭ Press *W* to select the first item that starts with *W*.

⑮ Hold down Shift while you press the down-arrow key four times. (Because you're holding down Shift, Windows 98 extends the selection to include all items from the first selected to the last selected.)

⑯ Continue to hold down Shift and click an item several rows below the last selected item. (Shift also extends your selection when you use the mouse.)

⑰ Release Shift.

⑱ Hold down Ctrl while you click another item several rows below the current selection. (Ctrl also extends your selection but without selecting items between the current selection and your new addition.)

⑲ Continue to hold down Ctrl and click one of the items in the middle of the selected items. (As long as you hold down Ctrl, you can click items to add them to the selection, or click selected items to remove them from the selection.)

⑳ Release Ctrl.

㉑ Click one of the items in the list. This selects only the item you click and removes all other items from the selection.

These same selection techniques work in the folders pane, too.

Selecting files and folders

NOTE

If you have enabled the Active Desktop, you need only point to files to select them. For example, to select a range of files, point to the first file, hold down Shift, and move the pointer to the last file you want to select without clicking the mouse button. Move the mouse pointer off the list of selected files to stop expanding the selection. You may want to practice this until you're comfortable with the new way your mouse works in Windows 98 — it's easy to select and open a file accidentally when you only intended to select it.

VISUAL BONUS

Selecting Files and Folders

It may be a little easier for you to visualize how to select folders and files by looking at the accompanying figure.

You can select items using a combination of keystrokes and your mouse.

Press a letter to move the selector to the next item starting with that letter

The current folder is listed here

Hold down Shift to extend a selection to include all items between the first and the last selected items

Use the scrollbar to see items not currently visible

The status line shows how many objects are selected and their size

Hold down Ctrl while you click a selected item to remove it from the selection

Hold down Ctrl to add an item to a selection without including items you don't click

Press Home to move to the top of the list, End to move to the bottom

Creating new folders

In Windows 98 you use folders to organize your files. You can create new folders inside existing folders, and then create new folders inside those new folders. You aren't limited to a specific number of levels of nested folders, although the complete name of a file, including all its parent folders, can't be longer than 260 characters. It's not likely that you'll ever have a problem with this limit.

Because you can nest folders within folders, it's pretty easy to use separate folders for different projects. These separate project folders are an excellent organizational tool because they make it so much easier to keep track of all the documents related to a project. You might start out with a folder called My Documents and then add new folders within that folder for each different job. I always create a new folder for each book project. Each chapter of the book, all screen captures, and any auxiliary files for the book go into this folder. Once I've completed a book, I can simply move all the files from the folder onto diskettes to create a complete backup for a single project. Organizing your files this way makes it far less likely to lose a stray file that's hiding somewhere on your hard disk.

In this exercise you begin by opening the My Documents folder and then creating a new folder nested within the My Documents folder. If you don't already have a My Documents folder, creating it is one of your first tasks.

1 Click the Start button.

2 Select Programs.

3 Select Windows Explorer.

4 If the My Documents folder already exists, click it to open the folder and then skip to Step 11.

5 If you don't already have a My Documents folder, click the drive icon for drive C in the folders pane.

6 Select File.

7 Select New.

8 Select Folder to create a new folder named New Folder.

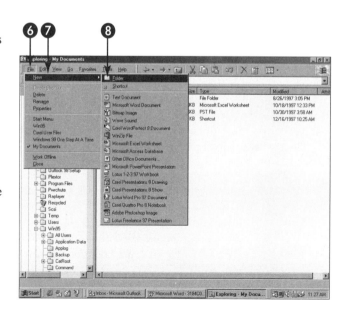

Moving and copying files and folders

⑨ Type the following text to name the new folder: **My Documents**.

⑩ Click the My Documents folder in the folders pane to open the folder.

⑪ Select File.

⑫ Select New.

⑬ Select Folder to create a new folder named New Folder.

⑭ Type the following text to name the new folder: **Windows 98 One Step at a Time**.

⑮ Click the Windows 98 One Step at a Time folder in the folders pane to open the folder.

If you want to create additional new folders, make certain you start from the correct location. The exercise ended with the Windows 98 One Step at a Time folder open. If you were again to select File ➢ New ➢ Folder to create a new folder, the new folder would be nested within the Windows 98 One Step at a Time folder—which is nested within the My Documents folder. To create a new folder nested within the My Documents folder but not nested within the Windows 98 One Step at a Time folder, make certain you select the My Documents folder before you create the new folder.

Moving and copying files and folders

You've probably noticed that Windows 98 treats files and folders almost identically. It should come as little surprise that this similar treatment extends to moving and copying, too. The only real difference you may notice is that when you move or copy a folder, any files contained in the folder are moved or copied also.

There's one important rule you need to remember for successful moving or copying—you can't have two folders or files with the same name. You can have slight variations on the same name, such as file1.txt and file2.txt, or file1.txt and copy of file1.txt. You can use the same name for two files if they're in different folders; the two names are

actually different because the folder name is part of each file's name. The full name of file1.txt in folder1 on drive C would be C:\folder1\file1.txt, while the full name of file1.txt in folder2 on drive C would be C:\folder2\file1.txt. That's why you can have a file1.txt in both folders.

In this exercise you first copy a file from one folder to another and then move the copied file to a different folder. You also learn what happens when you try to make a copy of the file in the same folder.

1 Click the Start button.

2 Select Programs.

3 Select Windows Explorer.

4 Click the plus sign to open the *Windows 98 One Step At a Time* CD-ROM.

5 Click the Lesson 3 folder to display the contents of the Lesson 3 folder in the contents pane.

6 Right-click 3Horses.bmp to display the pop-up menu.

7 Select Copy to copy the 3Horses.bmp file to the Windows 98 Clipboard — an area in memory where Windows 98 temporarily holds items you've copied.

8 Right-click the My Documents folder.

9 Select Paste to copy the 3Horses.bmp file to the My Documents folder. (Notice that copying the file doesn't open the My Documents folder.)

10 Open the My Documents folder and verify that it now contains the 3Horses.bmp file.

11 Right-click the 3Horses.bmp file.

12 Select Properties.

13 Remove the check from the Read-only checkbox.

14 Click OK.

3

Working with Files

Deleting files and folders

⑮ Expand the My Documents folder to see the Windows 98 One Step at a Time folder.

⑯ Drag 3Horses.bmp to the Windows 98 One Step at a Time folder and release the mouse button, moving the file from the My Documents folder to the Windows 98 One Step at a Time folder.

It doesn't matter whether you drop the file on the Windows 98 One Step at a Time folder in the folder pane or the contents pane — either one works.

⑰ Open the Windows 98 One Step at a Time folder.

⑱ Drag 3Horses.bmp to the Windows 98 One Step at a Time folder in the folder pane. (When you release the left mouse button, Windows 98 displays the error message shown in the figure on the right. Click OK.)

⑲ Hold down Ctrl.

⑳ Drag 3Horses.bmp to the Windows 98 One Step at a Time folder.

㉑ Release the mouse button to create a copy of 3Horses.bmp in the Windows 98 One Step at a Time folder.

㉒ Release Ctrl after the copy is complete.

By holding down Ctrl, you told Windows 98 you wanted to make a copy of the file rather than move the file. Because the original file already existed in the folder, Windows 98 added *Copy of* to the filename. If you copy the 3Horses.bmp file to a different folder that doesn't already contain the 3Horses.bmp file, Windows 98 doesn't add *Copy of* to the filename.

Deleting files and folders

Your hard disk soon fills up if you keep making extra copies of files you don't need. Rather than let that happen, in this exercise you learn how to use the Recycle Bin effectively. The copies of 3Horses.bmp you created in the last exercise seem like good candidates for recycling, don't they?

❶ Click the Start button.

2 Select Programs.

3 Select Windows Explorer.

4 Click the Windows 98 One Step at a Time folder to display the contents of the folder.

5 Right-click 3Horses.bmp.

6 Select Delete. Windows 98 displays the Confirm File Delete message shown in the figure on the right.

7 Click Yes to send the file to the Recycle Bin.

 NOTE *Items you delete from a diskette don't go to the Recycle Bin — they're permanently deleted.*

8 Right-click Copy of 3Horses.bmp.

9 Hold down Shift.

10 Select Delete. Windows 98 displays the Confirm File Delete message shown in the figure on the right. Do you see the difference between this message and the previous one? By holding down Shift, you tell Windows 98 to skip the Recycle Bin.

11 Click Yes to delete the file.

12 Open the Recycled (or Recycle Bin) folder. When you do, notice that the icon for this folder looks like a miniature version of the waste basket icon on your desktop. You can work with the Recycle Bin either by double-clicking the Recycle Bin icon on your desktop or by opening the Recycled folder in Windows Explorer.

13 Right-click 3Horses.bmp.

14 Select Restore to move the file back to its original location in the Windows 98 One Step at a Time folder.

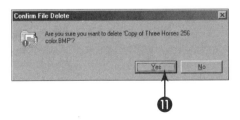

Because you deleted Copy of 3Horses.bmp without sending it to the Recycle Bin, you can't restore the Copy of 3Horses.bmp file. If Copy of 3Horses.bmp had been an important file you

Deleting files and folders

accidentally deleted, you'd be out of luck because you bypassed the Recycle Bin.

15 Right-click the Recycled folder in the folders pane.

16 Select Empty Recycle Bin. (You can't select this if the Recycle Bin is already empty.)

17 Click Yes to confirm that you want to empty the Recycle Bin and permanently delete the files. Remember, however, that once you delete the files from the Recycle Bin, you can't restore them — there's no Recycle Bin for the Recycle Bin!

If you don't empty the Recycle Bin yourself, the Recycle Bin will eventually reach its capacity. When the Recycle Bin is full, the oldest files in the Recycle Bin are deleted to make room for newer files. Depending on the size of your Recycle Bin and the files you delete, it may take weeks or months before old files disappear from the Recycle Bin. But if your Recycle Bin is quite small and you delete large files, you may lose the chance to restore accidentally deleted files much sooner than you expect.

Unfortunately, simply making the Recycle Bin larger isn't always the best choice. Space you allocate to the Recycle Bin is lost to other uses. If you're running short on disk space, you may want to adjust the Recycle Bin size downward to free up additional room on your hard drive.

Follow these steps to adjust the Recycle Bin size up or down:

1 Right-click the Recycle Bin icon on your desktop or the Recycled folder in Windows Explorer.

2 Select Properties to display the Recycle Bin Properties (or the Recycled Properties) dialog box.

3 If the Recycled Properties dialog box is displayed, click the Global tab.

The figure on the next page shows the Recycle Bin Properties dialog box for my system, which has two hard drives. If your PC has a different number of hard drives, or if you clicked the Recycled folder in Windows Explorer, the other dialog box tabs are a little different than shown in the figure.

4 Drag the slider to the left to reduce the maximum size of the Recycle Bin, or to the right to increase the size. Because the size is shown as a percentage of the disk size, a setting of 10% would allocate about 120MB of space on a 1.2GB drive.

5 Deselect the Display delete confirmation dialog box by clicking the checkbox. This prevents Windows 98 from always asking if you really want to delete files.

6 Uncheck the Do not move files to the Recycle Bin checkbox, if it is selected. If this checkbox is selected, you can't recover files you accidentally delete.

7 Click OK to close the dialog box.

If you have more than one hard drive, you can configure the Recycle Bin settings differently for each drive. You should probably use the same settings for all drives — unless you really feel the need to tinker!

WORKING WITH LONG FILENAMES

What are long filenames? That seems like a strange question, doesn't it? Long filenames aren't the names of long files, they're a wonderful improvement introduced to the PC with the introduction of Windows 95.

Before Windows 95, PC users struggled along with a really tough limitation on how they could name their files. You could use from one to eight characters for a filename, and up to three characters for an extension. In Windows 98 you can use up to 255 characters in a filename. Now that you can use truly descriptive names for your files, confusion over which file is which should be a thing of the past. (But if you use any old applications that weren't designed for Windows 98, or if you need to access your Windows 98 files in DOS, you may be in for a surprise if you don't know that Windows 98 has two names for every file. See "Working with long filenames in MS-DOS" later in this chapter for more information.)

Working with long filenames

Although Windows 98 allows up to 255 characters in a filename, there's another limit that generally prevents filenames from being that long. The complete name of a file, including the drive letter and any folder names, is limited to 260 characters, as described in "Creating new folders" earlier in this chapter. Still, you'd have to try pretty hard to create filenames that were too long for Windows 98.

If the old, short-style filenames could only include eight characters in the name and three characters in the extension, then any filename with more than 8.3 characters must be a long filename, right? As a matter of fact, yes, but there are other factors that can make even the old 8.3-style names into long filenames, too.

Any filename that includes special characters, such as spaces or commas, is a long filename regardless of the length of the name. Any filename that contains both uppercase and lowercase letters is also considered a long filename. Both TEST 1.TXT and Test.txt are long filenames, but TEST1.TXT is not.

There's really only one time when you need to be concerned about long filenames. Windows 98 can only store 512 names in the root directory (C:\) on your hard drive — unless you are using the FAT32 file system. (See Lesson 4 for more information on FAT32.) But it takes two or more of those 512 entries to store each long filename, depending on the length of the name. This effectively cuts you down to a maximum of 256 entries in the root, and maybe even fewer. There is no limit to the number of files and folders you can store in a folder, however, so you can use long filenames as often as you want, provided you store your files in folders rather than in the root directory.

Although Windows 98 has no problem with long filenames, you may be restricted to using shorter names if you're on a network with computers that aren't using Windows 98 and are restricted to using the 8.3 file-naming convention. Your network administrator can tell you whether there are any restrictions on naming files on your network.

Naming files and folders

You can use almost any character in a filename. In fact, the only characters on your keyboard you can't use are these:

\ / : * ? " < > |

Each of these prohibited characters has a special meaning at the command line, which is why you can't use them in filenames — doing so would confuse Windows 98.

There's one other character you can use (but may want to avoid) — the space character you create by pressing the spacebar. Windows 98 enables you to include spaces in filenames, but those spaces can cause confusion. In this exercise you learn how to work around the problem.

1 Right-click a blank space on the desktop.

2 Select New.

3 Select Text Document to create New Text Document.txt on your desktop.

4 Click the Start button.

5 Select Find.

6 Select Files or Folders.

7 Type this text in the Named text box: **New Text Document.txt**.

8 Click Find Now to search for your new file.

9 Now type this text in the Named text box: **"New Text Document.txt"**. (Make certain you include the quotation marks.)

10 Again click Find Now, and your results probably look more like the figure on the right.

11 Right-click a blank space on the desktop.

12 Select New.

13 Select Text Document to create another text document.

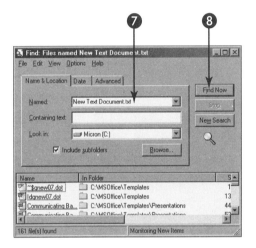

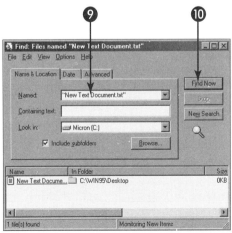

Long filenames in MS-DOS

14 Type the following text to rename the new file:
New_Text_Document.txt.

Make certain you don't include any spaces in the name, but use the underscore (_) to connect the words in the name.

15 Now type this text in the Named text box of the Find dialog box: **New_Text_Document.txt**.

16 Click Find Now again. Your results should be similar to the figure on the right.

If you include spaces in a filename, you must always remember to enclose the name in quotes when you use the filename in a command, such as the Find command. When you use an underscore in place of a space in a filename, Windows 98 knows that the filename is one name, rather than a series of names separated by spaces. It's your choice whether you substitute an underscore (or some other character) for a space in a filename — both are acceptable to Windows 98.

Working with long filenames in MS-DOS

You may never have to use the MS-DOS prompt, especially if you only use programs designed for Windows 98. If you do use the MS-DOS prompt, you soon find that Windows 98 creates a rather funny-looking short name to go along with the long filename.

Follow these steps to view both sets of names for the items on your desktop:

1 Click the Start button.

2 Select Programs.

3 Select MS-DOS Prompt.

4 Type the following text to change to the desktop folder and press Enter: **cd desktop**.

5 Type the following text and press Enter: **dir**.

Windows 98 creates the short filenames by using the first six characters of the filename, converting them to uppercase, dropping any spaces, and then adding a tilde (~) and a sequential number. If more than nine files result in names similar enough that the first six

The short filename is shown in the first column   The long filename is shown in the last column

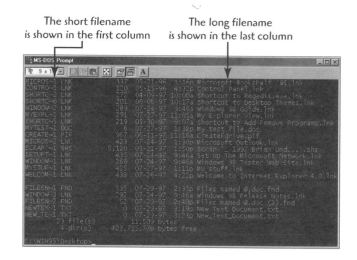

characters are the same, Windows 98 uses the first five characters and
keeps on incrementing the numbers at the ends of the names.

CHANGING THE VIEW

Windows Explorer has quite a few different ways of showing you your
files. You want to learn how to control the view and use Windows
Explorer to its fullest.

You don't have to accept the default Windows Explorer view of
your files and folders. Sometimes a different view may be handier.
You might want to see the files sorted in a different order, see more
or less information, or maybe hide certain types of files. You can
choose the options that work best for you.

▶ *Sorting files and folders*

Have you ever tried to find something but weren't quite sure where
to look? When you're looking for files on your PC, the problem can
be even worse because you might not even know the name of the
file you're trying to find. Sorting the Windows Explorer file list may
help you locate the file. In this exercise you change the Windows
Explorer sort order.

❶ Right-click the Start button.

❷ Select Explore. (If necessary, click the Views button and select
Details.)

❸ Open the Command folder.

TIP

*Regardless of the sort order you select, Windows
Explorer adds new files to the end of the file listing
unless you refresh the view. The quickest way to refresh
the view is to press F5.*

❹ Select View.

❺ Select Arrange Icons.

Sorting files and folders

6 Select by Type to sort the file listing according to the file type as shown in the figure on the right. This view is useful if you know what kind of file you're seeking but aren't sure of the name. Notice that Windows Explorer sorts the listing first by file type, and then by name within each type.

7 Select View.

8 Select Arrange Icons.

9 Select by Size to sort the file listing according to the size of the files, as shown in the figure on the right.

This view is handy when you're cleaning up your hard disk. Scroll down to the bottom of the list to see which files are using the most space.

10 Select View.

11 Select Arrange Icons.

12 Select by Date to view the file listing sorted by their last creation or modification date, as shown in the figure on the right.

You can use this view to find files you've created most recently at the top of the listing, and files you haven't used for a long time at the bottom of the listing.

13 Select View.

14 Select Arrange Icons.

15 Select by Name to once again view the file listing sorted by filename. (You can leave the Windows Explorer window open because you use it again in the following exercises.)

There's another way to sort the files in Windows Explorer even faster than selecting options from the View menu. In Windows 98 you can click the column title (Name, Size, Type, or Modified) to sort the files in ascending order by the selected column. Click the column title again to sort the view in descending order.

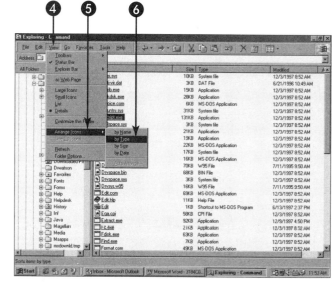

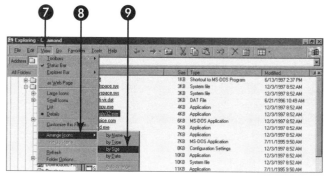

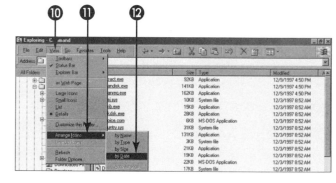

Changing the detail level

I'm the kind of person who likes to have as much information as possible, so I prefer the full-detail view in the Windows Explorer file listing. You may find all this information distracting, or you may just prefer to see icons instead of the file information. If you skip the file details, more files can be shown in the same space and you don't have to use the scrollbars as often. In this exercise you change the level of detail shown in the Windows Explorer window.

1 Click the down arrow to the right of the Views button.

2 Choose Large Icons to change the file view to large icons. This view uses file icons similar in size to those you see on your desktop.

3 Click the down arrow to the right of the Views button.

4 Choose Small Icons to change the view to the smaller file icons you normally see in Windows Explorer. In this view the file icons are arranged across the top of the contents pane.

5 Click the down arrow to the right of the Views button.

6 Choose List to change the view once again. The list view uses the same small file icons as the small icon view, but displays the files in columns rather than in rows.

7 Finally, click the down arrow to the right of the Views button.

8 Choose Details to return the listing to the full-detail view.

You can also use the View ➢ Large Icons, View ➢ Small Icons, View ➢ List, or View ➢ Details commands to change the level of detail, but I think clicking a button is easier and faster than using a menu command.

Changing the width of panes and columns

You may be pleasantly surprised to discover that you aren't stuck with the sometimes crowded way Windows Explorer displays file listings. If you have deeply nested folders, for example, the folder pane may be too narrow to show all the folders. If your filenames are quite long, the names may be cut off in the contents pane. In this exercise you adjust the width of panes and columns to show all the folders and filenames.

1 Right-click the Start button.

2 Select Explore.

3 Select View.

4 Select Details.

5 Move the mouse pointer onto the separator between the folders pane and the contents pane.

When the mouse pointer changes to a double-headed arrow, hold down the left mouse button and drag the separator left or right to adjust the width of the panes. The vertical gray line shows where the separator will appear when you release the button.

6 Drag the vertical bar between the Name and Size columns of the contents pane left or right to adjust the width of the Name column.

The vertical bar is at the top of the contents pane. You can adjust each column by dragging the bar at the right edge of the column.

Double-click the vertical bar between columns in the contents pane to size the column to fit the widest entry automatically. For example, double-click the vertical bar between the Name and Size columns to resize the Name column to display the longest filename completely.

The best compromise is first to adjust the column widths just a little wider than necessary to view all the information in the columns, and then adjust the width of the contents pane so all the file details are just visible. This makes the folders pane wide enough so you're able to see most nested folders without using the horizontal scrollbar at the bottom of the folders pane.

Displaying or hiding different file types

The Windows Explorer file display can be a little overwhelming with all the different types of files it shows. Worse yet, many of the files you can see in Windows Explorer are needed by Windows 98; if you move or delete the wrong files, you may not be able to launch Windows 98.

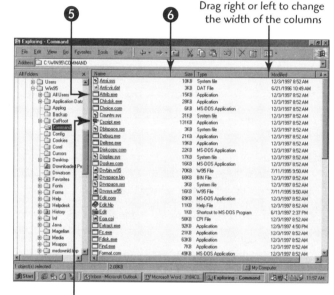

Drag right or left to change the width of the columns

Drag right or left to change the width of the panes

Displaying or hiding different file types

Follow these steps to protect yourself from the hazard of deleting important files accidentally and, at the same time, clean up your display:

1 Right-click the Start button.

2 Select Explore.

3 Select View.

4 Select Folder Options to display the Folder Options dialog box.

5 Click the View tab.

6 Select Do not show hidden or system files to remove the listed file types from the Windows Explorer file display. (The files still remain on your hard disk, but they don't appear in the file listings. This prevents you from accidentally choosing any of these files.)

7 Select the Hide file extensions for known file types checkbox if you don't want to see the three character file extensions. This only changes the filename display for file types that Windows 98 knows, such as text files and applications. If Windows 98 can't determine the file type from the extension, Windows Explorer still shows the file extension.

8 Select Display the full path in title bar if you want to see the complete path name to the selected folder rather than just the name of the folder. You may find this option especially useful if you're on a network and sometimes forget whether you've opened a local folder or one on the network.

9 Click OK to confirm your changes and close the dialog box.

If you choose to hide some types of files rather than showing all file types, the Windows Explorer status line at the bottom of the Windows Explorer window tells you if a folder contains any hidden files that aren't being displayed. Be sure to look at the status line before you delete any folders that appear empty. If the folder contains hidden files, it's usually best to leave the folder alone — otherwise you run the risk of disabling some of your programs or even Windows 98 itself.

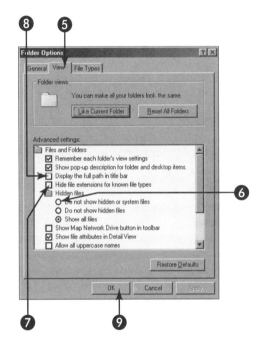

Registering a new file type

In Windows 98 you can open most documents directly without opening a program first. By learning a few tricks, you can make this feature even more useful. You can, for example, tell Windows 98 which program to use to open new file types, or tell Windows 98 to use a different program than it normally would to open certain types of files.

By now you've started programs by opening documents several times. You may wonder how Windows 98 knows which program to use to open a document. The answer is the file extension — the one to three characters that follow a period at the end of the filename. When you install programs, the programs register the types of files they can open with Windows 98. For example, Microsoft Word registers the .doc extension for its document files, while Microsoft Excel registers the .xls extension for its spreadsheet files.

Once a file extension is registered, Windows 98 knows which application program to use to open any files with that extension. You can use this to your advantage by adding new file types or adjusting existing ones to suit your needs.

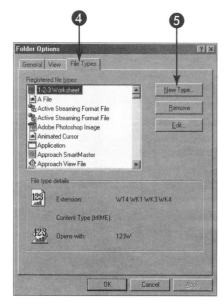

Registering a new file type

Why would you want to register a new file type? I can give you an example from experience, showing one reason why I registered my own file type: A magazine publisher I sometimes write for wants authors to use their initials as the file extension on the document files they submit. In my case this means I use .bju as the file extension. But because Windows 98 doesn't have an application registered to open files with a .bju extension, I can't tell my word processor to start and open my .bju files automatically when I double-click those files. The solution is to register .bju files as a new file type, which is what you do in this exercise.

① Open Windows Explorer.

② Select View.

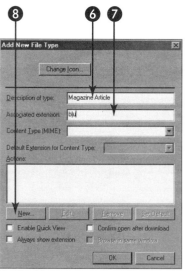

❸ Select Options to display the Options dialog box.

❹ Click the File Types tab. This tab shows each of the registered file types and their associated applications.

❺ Select New Type to display the Add New File Type dialog box. You use this dialog box to begin adding the new type.

❻ Type the following text in the Description of type text box: **Magazine Article**.

❼ Type the following text in the Associated extension text box: **bju**.

❽ Click New to display the New Action dialog box.

❾ Type the following text in the Action text box: **Open with WordPad**.

❿ Type the following text in the Application used to perform action text box: **"C:\Program Files\Accessories\Wordpad.exe"**.

⓫ Click OK to close the New Action dialog box.

⓬ Click Close to close the Add New File Type dialog box. The Options dialog box should now have your new registered file type.

⓭ Click Close to close the Options dialog box.

Now that you've added the Magazine Article file type with the .bju file extension, all you need to do is double-click any files with a .bju extension to open them in WordPad. (To see for yourself, open TheFox.bju, located in the Lesson 3 folder on the CD-ROM that accompanies this book. Double-click to launch the file.) Of course, you probably want to use your own initials for the file extension. You can also create other file types that open with different applications. Just specify the correct application program in the New Action dialog box. If you don't know the correct command line necessary to start the program, use the Browse button to search for the program.

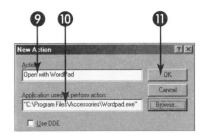

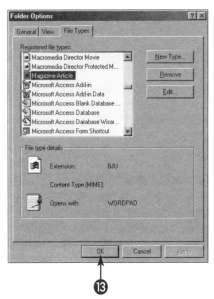

Editing an existing file type

Editing an existing file type

You may occasionally need to change the action associated with a registered file type. You might, for example, upgrade to a new word processor and want to use the new program to edit files with the .bju extension. Or perhaps you want the option to open the .bju files with either WordPad or your new word processor. In this exercise you edit an existing file type.

1 Open Windows Explorer.

2 Select View.

3 Select Options.

4 Click the File Types tab.

5 Choose the file type you wish to edit; in this case, Magazine Article.

6 Click Edit to display the Edit File Type dialog box.

7 To change the existing action, click Edit.

8 Correct the entry in the Application used to perform action text box, and then click OK.

9 To add an additional action, click New.

10 Fill in the Action text box and the Application used to perform action text box.

11 Click OK (or Cancel if you didn't add an additional action).

12 Click OK twice more to close the dialog boxes.

If you have more than one action associated with a file type, you can select the action you prefer from the pop-up menu when you right-click the file in Windows Explorer.

USING THE TASK SCHEDULER

The Task Scheduler program helps you keep your Windows 98 system in good shape by performing some of the routine maintenance chores you may not perform as often as you should. Two examples of these chores are defragmenting your hard disk and checking your hard disk for errors. Both of these tasks are important in keeping your files safe and your system performance at an acceptable level, but both are also tasks people tend to forget. In the following exercise you learn how to use the Task Scheduler to schedule these types of tasks.

NOTE *If you upgraded to Windows 98 from Windows 95 and had the Plus! add-on for Windows 95 installed, the Task Scheduler may seem familiar. The Task Scheduler is an updated version of the System Agent that was part of the Plus! add-on.*

Viewing the Task Scheduler schedule

When you install Windows 98, certain events are automatically added to the Task Scheduler schedule. Depending on your personal schedule, you may want to adjust events on the Task Scheduler schedule to better suit your needs. In this exercise you learn how to view and adjust events that appear on the Task Scheduler schedule.

TIP *The Windows Tune-Up Wizard adds events to the Task Scheduler schedule. (See Lesson 2 for more information on using the Windows Tune-Up Wizard.)*

❶ Click the Start button.

❷ Select Programs.

❸ Select Accessories.

❹ Select System Tools.

❺ Select Scheduled Tasks to open the Task Scheduler's Scheduled Tasks folder. If you have items scheduled, you can also double-click the Task Scheduler icon on the Taskbar to open the Task Scheduler.

❻ Double-click ScanDisk for Windows (Standard test) to display the Properties dialog box for this event.

Viewing the Task Scheduler schedule

7 Click the Schedule tab, as shown in the accompanying figure. This tab box provides the most important scheduling options for an event.

8 To change the time when the selected program is run, select one of the options in the Schedule Task list box. It's not a good idea to select Once, because the event will only run one time rather than at scheduled intervals. Likewise, the At System Startup option is generally a poor choice because this would run events every time you started your PC rather than when you weren't using your system.

9 Type the time you want the event to begin in the Start time box.

10 Click the Settings tab.

11 Select the Only start the scheduled task if computer is idle for checkbox. This ensures that the event won't disrupt your work if you happen to be using your PC when an event is scheduled to run.

12 Click OK to close the Change Schedule dialog box.

It's important to remember that the Task Scheduler can only run scheduled events if your PC is running. Modern PCs take very little power, especially if you turn off your monitor or if you use the screen saver options to power down your monitor automatically. If you prefer not to leave your PC running, you can schedule events for times when your system is on, such as during lunch.

NOTE *The Task Scheduler can cause problems for you if you use your PC for certain types of tasks, such as recording a CD-ROM. If you have a CD-R drive in your PC and intend to record a CD-ROM, open the Task Scheduler window and select Advanced ➢ Stop Using Task Scheduler, and then click Yes to remove the Task Scheduler before you attempt to record the CD-ROM. You can restart Task Scheduler by selecting Scheduled Task from the Programs ➢ Accessories ➢ System Tools menu.*

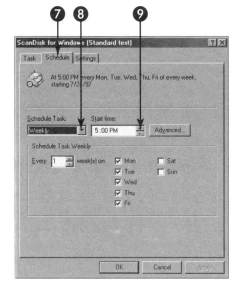

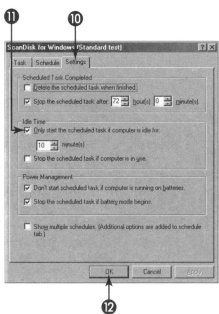

Skills challenge

SKILLS CHALLENGE: MASTERING YOUR FILES

Here's a chance for you to practice what you've learned in this lesson.

1 Find all the text files with a .txt file extension on your hard drive.

What is the one step you must always remember to do before saving a Find Files search if you want Windows 98 to remember any date specification you entered?

2 Select the first text file that has a filename starting with M.

What is the fastest way to find the first item that starts with W in the Windows Explorer contents pane?

3 Select all files between the currently selected file and the end of the list.

How can you remove one item from a selection?

4 Move the newest text file to the desktop.

5 Delete the text file you just moved to the desktop.

6 Restore the text file you just deleted.

7 View the Desktop folder, but change the sort order to show the files by date.

8 Add an action that opens a file with a .tmp extension using WordPad.

How can you add an option to open the Text Document file type with WordPad in addition to keeping the default action?

9 Adjust the schedule for one of the Task Scheduler events.

Troubleshooting

TROUBLESHOOTING

If you encounter problems while trying to work through the exercises, here are some ideas that might help you correct the problems and keep going.

Problem	Solution
There are no buttons to click in my Windows Explorer window.	Select View ➢ Toolbar to display the buttons.
I can't find a folder called Windows.	Right-click the Start button and select Explore to open the Start Menu folder. Your Windows 98 folder is in the next column of dotted lines to the left of the column containing the Start Menu folder. The Windows folder is above the Start Menu folder.

WRAP UP

You've learned quite a bit about managing your files in this lesson. Not only did you learn how to find, copy, and move files and folders, you also practiced with long filenames and saw how you can change the Windows Explorer view. You also learned how to teach Windows 98 a little about yourself, enabling you to use your own file extensions.

In the next lesson you play around with disks and see how to prepare disks for use. You also see how you can use disk compression to make more room for your files, how you can make your computer run a little faster, and how to back up your files.

Working with Disks

GOALS

Almost everything you do on your PC requires working with your disk drives. You can't save a file, load a program, or view a document without using your disks. Even though you've worked with disks a little in some of the earlier lessons, this lesson takes you beyond the basics to show you how to use your disks more effectively so you can store more information and get better performance at the same time. In this lesson you learn about the following topics:

45 MINUTES

- Formatting a floppy disk

- Copying a file to a disk

- Copying a disk

- Compressing files

- Improving disk performance

Get ready

GET READY

To complete this lesson, you need at least two blank diskettes. The diskettes don't have to be empty, but any files on the diskettes will be destroyed. Don't use diskettes that contain any files you may need.

This lesson also uses several Windows 98 disk tools that may or may not already be installed on your PC. DriveSpace, Defrag, and ScanDisk are all on your Windows 98 installation disks and must be installed before you can complete this lesson. You can wait until you reach the point in the exercises where a tool is needed before worrying about whether each tool is installed. If a tool is missing, you can select the Add/Remove Programs icon in Control Panel and use the Disk Tools option on the Windows Setup tab to add any missing tools.

When you complete the exercises, you will have learned how to do the following: format a diskette, copy files to a diskette, copy a diskette, compress a drive and adjust the size of the free space on the compressed drive, convert your disks to the new FAT32 format, defragment your disks, use ScanDisk, and back up and restore your files.

 Working with disks can be hazardous to the health of your programs and data files. In this lesson you practice using some tools that can cause you to lose data or destroy your programs if you don't follow the directions carefully. To lessen the danger, the exercises use diskettes whenever possible. Please be careful not to substitute different drive letters for the ones shown in the exercises!

PREPARING TO USE YOUR DISKS

Disks are one of the few mechanical parts of your PC. Because disks are a mechanical component, they need some preparation before they're ready to use. In the following exercises, you learn the basics you need to know in order to use your disks.

▶ Formatting a diskette

If you've ever watched young children learning to print, you know that they need some help to get the job done. You may do quite well writing on blank paper, but young children need those lines on the paper if they are to have any hope of creating characters anyone else can understand. In many ways, your PC is similar to a young child — without some extra help, your PC simply can't write anything useful on a disk.

The extra help your PC needs to be able to write on a disk is called *formatting* — the process of creating the electronic marks that enable your disk drives to write in the correct places on a disk. When you format a disk, any existing information on the disk is wiped out. That's why you should never format a disk that contains data or program files you may need — you can't get the data or programs back after you format the disk!

TIP *You can often buy preformatted diskettes for about the same price as unformatted diskettes, and you save the time and trouble of formatting the diskettes yourself. If you buy preformatted diskettes, make certain they are formatted in IBM PC format.*

Follow these steps to format a diskette:

1 Place a blank diskette in drive A.

NOTE *If you need to reuse a diskette you've already used, be certain you choose one that does not contain any important files — use Windows Explorer to verify this before you continue! Be sure to close Windows Explorer before you continue to Step 2.*

2 Click the My Computer icon on your desktop to display the My Computer window. Your My Computer window may not show as many objects as the figure on the next page, but it includes an icon for each of your disk drives, the Control Panel, and Printers.

Formatting a diskette

3 Right-click the icon for drive A. On my computer, drive A is listed as 3½ Floppy (A:), which is probably the way it is shown on your computer, too. If your PC is a bit older, it's possible that your drive A is shown as 5¼ Floppy (A:).

4 Select Format from the pop-up menu that appears to display the Format dialog box. The Capacity list box may show a different size depending on the diskette you placed in drive A.

5 Verify that the correct diskette capacity shows in the Capacity list box. The most common sizes are 1.44MB or 720K for 3½-inch diskettes, and 1.2MB or 360K for 5¼-inch diskettes. Although 3½-inch disk drives can automatically sense whether the diskette can be formatted at the greater 1.44MB capacity, 5¼-inch drives cannot automatically determine the diskette's capacity. Generally, you want to use the highest capacity supported by your drive.

6 Select the type of format to perform:

Full format takes the longest but has the advantage of checking the entire disk surface for any errors. If the diskette is unformatted, you can only select Full format. Always use Full format if you seem to be having problems with your diskettes. Select Full format for this exercise.

TIP *Choose Full format to verify whether a diskette has any errors before saving data you can't afford to lose. If formatting uncovers errors on the diskette, throw away the diskette rather than trust the diskette not to fail further.*

Quick format simply erases any files that may already be on the disk by marking the entire diskette as available and doesn't check for errors. Quick format doesn't use any areas already marked as damaged, but it also doesn't find any new errors that may have appeared. Quick format is considerably faster than Full format.

Copy system files adds only the files necessary to create a *boot disk* — a disk you can use to start Windows 98 — to a diskette that's already formatted. You seldom use this option.

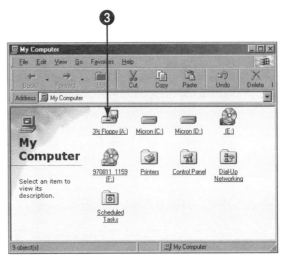

Select type of format here

Select formatted capacity here

Click here to skip the disk label

Enter a name for the disk here

Click here to make a boot disk

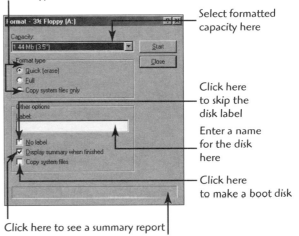

Click here to see a summary report

This band shows the progress as the disk is being formatted

7 Type the following text in the Label text box to name the diskette: **w98onestep**. You can use up to 11 characters to name a disk, and Windows 98 automatically changes the label to all uppercase letters.

NOTE *Make certain the No label checkbox is not selected. If you select this option, Windows 98 ignores any name you type in the Label text box.*

Make certain the Display summary when finished checkbox is selected so you can see the summary report after the diskette has been formatted. This report shows the final formatted capacity of the diskette, and it tells you whether any errors were found. It's a good idea to discard diskettes that contain errors, because you can't be certain more errors won't occur later.

Select the Copy system files checkbox only if you want to make a boot disk. Boot disks have less room available for your files because part of the space is used up by the system files.

8 Click Start to begin formatting the diskette. The progress band at the bottom of the dialog box shows how far along the format is at any time during the format. When the format is complete, the Format Results dialog box shown in the figure on the right shows you a summary of the format process.

9 Click Close to return to the Format dialog box.

10 Click Close to return to the My Computer window.

11 Click the Close button to close My Computer.

Although a full format is a little safer because the diskette is checked for errors, quick formats are useful, too. A quick format is the fastest way to erase any files and folders on a diskette, especially if the diskette contains a large number of files and folders.

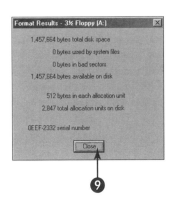

4

Working with Disks

Copying files to a diskette

Copying files to a diskette

Now that your diskette has been formatted, it's ready to use. There are several methods you can use to copy files to diskettes, and in this exercise you try a few of them.

1. Place your newly formatted diskette into drive A.
2. Right-click the Start button.
3. Select Explore.
4. Choose the Command folder by clicking it to open the folder and display its contents in the contents pane.
5. Right-click Ansi.sys.
6. Select Send To.
7. Select 3½ Floppy (A:) to copy the file to drive A. (If your A drive is a 5¼-inch drive, select 5¼ Floppy (A:).)
8. Right-click Attrib.exe.
9. Select Copy.
10. Right-click drive A in the folders pane.
11. Select Paste to copy Attrib.exe to drive A.
12. Point to Chkdsk.exe in the contents pane and hold down the left mouse button.
13. Drag the file to drive A. When the mouse pointer changes from a shortcut arrow to a plus sign, release the mouse button to copy the file.
14. Click the icon for drive A in the folders pane to display the contents of drive A. The three files you just copied should appear in the contents pane.

Each of the three methods of copying a file works quite well, and you can choose the method that seems the most comfortable. You aren't limited to copying a single file at a time, either. You may notice, however, that the drag & drop method can be a little tricky, especially if you're copying a number of files at the same time. It can

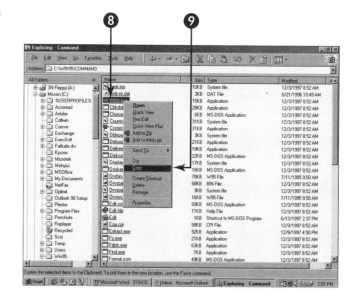

be difficult to drop the files in the correct location. If you make a mistake, choose Edit ➤ Undo Copy immediately — you can only undo the copy if you do so before you copy or move any more files.

Copying a diskette

Even though the 3½-inch diskettes, which are most commonly used in PCs today, are a lot more rugged than the older 5¼-inch diskettes, it's still possible to damage or lose a diskette. Needless to say, the one diskette you do manage to destroy will be the one containing your only copy of some important file. Backup copies of your important diskettes provide some of the best insurance against disaster, especially when you can quickly and easily make those copies.

NOTE   *There are some diskettes you cannot easily copy. The diskettes Microsoft uses to distribute software, for example, are specially formatted to prevent you from copying all except disk 1. This special format, **DMF** (**Distribution Media Format**) can only be copied using special tools that are not part of Windows 98. A **shareware** program called Winimage is designed to copy DMF formatted diskettes, but the program can be tricky to use and may not work on all PCs.*

When you copy diskettes, you'll probably have to use the same disk drive to read the original, or *source* disk, and to write to the copy, or *destination* disk. It's extremely important to make certain you insert the correct diskette when you change disks. If you don't watch carefully, you can lose the files you're trying to copy.

TIP   *You can only copy a diskette to another diskette of the same size.*

The following steps outline how to copy a diskette. Before you begin, however, turn over the source diskette so you can see the little plastic write-protect slider. Move the slider towards the edge of the diskette so you can see through the hole. This prevents your PC from writing anything on this diskette until you move the slider back to cover the hole. (If you're copying a 5¼-inch diskette, place a piece

Copying a diskette

of dark tape over the notch in the side of the diskette to write-protect the diskette.)

1 Place the source diskette in drive A.

2 Open Windows Explorer if it is not already open.

3 Right-click drive A and select Copy Disk from the pop-up menu to display the Copy Disk dialog box.

NOTE *Unless you have two identical diskette drives, the Copy from and Copy to drive are the same. If you have two diskette drives, make certain the correct drive is selected.*

4 Click Start to begin the copy.

When the source diskette has been completely read, Windows 98 displays the message shown in the figure on the right. When you see this message, remove your source diskette from drive A and insert the destination diskette.

5 Click OK to continue.

6 Once the copy is complete, click Close to return to Windows Explorer.

7 Remove the diskette copy from drive A. Be sure to mark the diskette label so you know what is on the diskette.

Don't forget that you moved the slider to write-protect the source diskette. If you need to place additional files on the source diskette or change any of the files already on the source diskette, you need to move the slider back to the closed position to allow writing on the diskette.

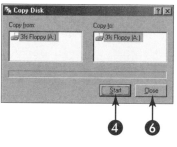

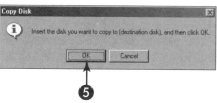

MAKING MORE ROOM AT THE INN

It seems like there's never enough room for everything. That huge hard disk that came inside your PC can start to look pretty small once you start loading your favorite programs, can't it? Fortunately, Windows 98 includes a tool, DriveSpace, that can help create more free space on your disks by compressing your files into less space. If you've ever ridden a subway train at rush hour, you probably already know about how compression can fit more people into less space — everyone just gets packed a bit tighter together so there's room for more people in each car.

 NOTE *Windows 98 DriveSpace disk compression isn't compatible with other operating systems such as Windows NT, OS/2, or UNIX. If your PC sometimes has to run another operating system in addition to Windows 98, don't use DriveSpace to compress your hard disks — the other operating system won't be able to access the hard drive. You can follow along with the DriveSpace exercises even if you don't want to use DriveSpace on your hard disk because the exercises use diskettes rather than your hard drive.*

Windows 98 introduces a new disk format called FAT32 that uses the available space on disk drives larger than 512MB more efficiently. Unfortunately, FAT32 and DriveSpace are not compatible — you can choose to use FAT32 or DriveSpace, but you can't choose both. How do you decide whether to use FAT32 or DriveSpace? The answer isn't always easy to determine, but here are some guidelines you can use:

- If your hard disk is larger than 2GB and you want to use the entire disk as a single drive, your only choice is FAT32. No other format will enable you to have more than 2GB on one drive letter.

- If your hard disk is smaller than 512MB, FAT32 offers no advantage. DriveSpace is the only way to increase the efficiency of disk space usage on drives under 512MB.

- If you store many compressed files, such as Zip files, on your hard drive, use FAT32 because DriveSpace cannot compress files that are already compressed.

- If you need to dual boot your system so you can run another operating system, don't use DriveSpace or FAT32 — neither one is currently compatible with other operating systems. There are indications that Windows NT 5 may support FAT32, but there's no guarantee until Windows NT 5 is actually released.

Compressing a drive with DriveSpace

- Both DriveSpace and FAT32 can cause slight performance losses, although you probably won't notice the difference.

See the exercise "Using FAT32" later in this chapter for more information on FAT32.

Compressing a drive with DriveSpace

In this exercise you use DriveSpace to compress a diskette, resulting in more free space for storing additional files. Once you compress the diskette, you can only use the diskette on a PC that is running Windows 95 or Windows 98 and has DriveSpace loaded. You can use the same diskette you used as the destination diskette in the last exercise.

① Place the diskette you want to compress in drive A.

② Click the Start button.

③ Select Programs.

④ Select Accessories.

⑤ Select System Tools.

⑥ Select DriveSpace to display the DriveSpace dialog box. This dialog box shows each disk drive on your system, so you may have slightly different options than in the figure on the right.

⑦ Choose the icon for drive A to select the drive.

⑧ Select Drive.

⑨ Select Compress to display the Compress a Drive dialog box. This dialog box shows the current status of the drive and an estimate of how much room will be available after the drive is compressed.

⑩ Click Options to display the Compression Options dialog box.

Normally you want to accept the default settings, but you can change the drive letter of the host drive or the amount of free space left on the host drive, if necessary. (Windows 98 creates a *host* drive for each compressed drive — this is the drive letter used to access the physical rather than the compressed drive. You don't really need to worry about host drives.)

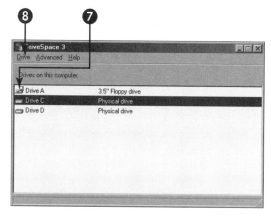

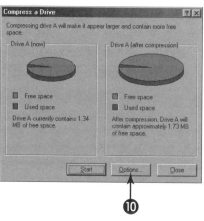

⑪ Click OK to continue.

⑫ You may see a caution message like the one shown in the figure on the right. Because you're only compressing a diskette and not a hard drive, you can click OK to continue.

TIP

If you want to compress a large hard disk that contains many files, plan to start the process at a time when you can let DriveSpace work by itself, such as during lunch or at night when you don't need to use your system.

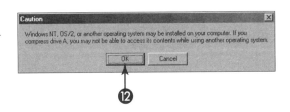

⑬ Compressing a disk can take a long time, so Windows 98 warns you with a message that asks you if you are sure you want to compress drive A. It's much faster to compress disks that don't already contain a lot of files. Click Compress Now to continue.

⑭ Once DriveSpace has compressed the drive, the Compress a Drive dialog box reappears and shows more accurate information than the earlier estimate. Click Close to return to the DriveSpace dialog box.

The DriveSpace dialog box includes a new drive, the host drive for drive A. You don't need to worry about the host drive, however, because all your files are on drive A, the compressed drive.

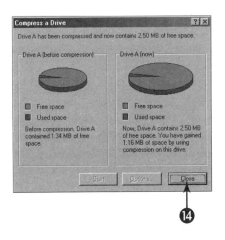

The free space that DriveSpace reports as available on a compressed drive can be a little confusing. While it's true you can store more files on a compressed drive, different types of files compress differently. As a result, you may not be able to store quite as much on a compressed disk as it would appear by looking at the available free space. The only way to find out how much you can add to a disk is to try copying the files to the compressed drive — if you don't get an out-of-disk-space message, you're in luck!

▶ Adjusting compressed drive free space

DriveSpace creates additional space on a disk by storing the files in a special file called a *compressed volume file* or CVF. The files stored in the CVF are compressed and are only accessible once DriveSpace is

Adjusting compressed drive free space

loaded into memory. This means that Windows 98 has to be able to read some system files — notably the DriveSpace program files — before it can read the compressed files. These important system files must be stored as normal files, not compressed files, which means they must be stored on an uncompressed drive. That's the point of having a host drive for a compressed drive — the host drive contains both the compressed volume file and any system files needed to access DriveSpace volumes. Any space reserved for system files on the host drive reduces the available free space on the compressed drive.

The system files needed to start your PC and read compressed disks take up much more room than is available on a diskette and are normally stored on your hard disk. When you compress a diskette, you usually use all the available space for the CVF, because there's generally no reason to leave part of the diskette uncompressed. (The files necessary to read a compressed disk generally already reside on your hard disk.) However, because you're compressing a diskette rather than your hard disk for these exercises, you need to adjust the free space on your compressed diskette. If you later compress your hard disk, you can use the same methods to adjust the free space on it, too.

There are actually two different ways to adjust the apparent free space on a compressed disk. The first, which I just mentioned, changes the allocation of the space on the host drive so the CVF uses more or less of the physical space. The second method doesn't actually change the amount of available space, but it does change the estimate of the extent to which files can be compressed when they're stored on the compressed drive. Because some files can be compressed more than others, changing the estimated compression ratio is more an art than a science, but it's an option you get to practice in this exercise.

1. Place the compressed diskette in drive A.

2. Click the Start button.

3. Select Programs.

4. Select Accessories.

5. Select System Tools.

6. Select DriveSpace to display the DriveSpace dialog box.

7 Choose the icon for drive A.

8 Select Drive.

9 Select Adjust Free Space to display the Adjust Free Space dialog box.

10 You can enter an exact value in either the compressed drive or the host drive Free space text box, or you can drag the slider right or left to adjust the ratio between the compressed and uncompressed space. In this case, drag the slider to the right until the host drive shows 0.30MB free space. Notice that as you increase the free space on the host drive, the free space on the compressed drive decreases.

11 Click OK to tell DriveSpace to change the ratio of free space. You have to wait a few minutes while DriveSpace completes the adjustment.

12 When DriveSpace finishes the adjustment, you see a message that tells you the DriveSpace operation is complete. Click OK to return to the DriveSpace dialog box.

13 Select Advanced.

14 Select Change Ratio to display the Compression Ratio for Drive A dialog box. In this case, the dialog box shows that the files currently on the diskette are actually compressed at a 3.0 to 1 ratio.

15 Drag the slider to the far-right side of the scale to make the estimated compression ratio 64.0 to 1. Although it's highly unlikely for you to ever see an actual compression ratio this high, DriveSpace doesn't care if you want to fool yourself into thinking there's more free space available than is reasonable.

16 Click OK to adjust the estimated compression ratio.

17 When DriveSpace completes the adjustment, you see a message similar to the message that tells you the DriveSpace operation is complete. Click OK to return to the DriveSpace dialog box.

You can enter exact values here   or here

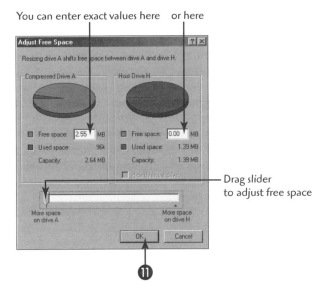

Drag slider
to adjust free space

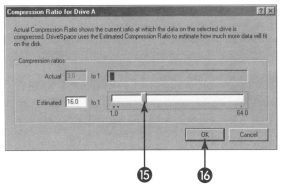

Adjusting compression properties

18 Double-click the drive A icon to display the Compression Properties dialog box. Because you changed the estimated compression ratio to 64.0 to 1, DriveSpace now reports that the diskette has 62.0MB of free space.

19 Click OK to close the Compression Properties dialog box.

20 Click the Close button to close the DriveSpace dialog box.

As you can probably imagine, the DriveSpace report of 62MB of free space on the compressed diskette bears little relationship to reality. If you start copying files to the diskette, you'll run out of disk space long before you come close to adding 62MB of files. It's much safer to assume that DriveSpace was correct in estimating the compression ratio as 3 to 1.

Different types of files can be compressed by differing amounts — that's why the DriveSpace compression ratio is only a rough estimate. You'll find files that are already compressed, such as files with a Zip file extension, can't really be compressed at all. Other files, such as text files or some graphics files, can often be highly compressed.

Windows 98 automatically recognizes when a diskette or a hard disk has been compressed with DriveSpace and loads the appropriate software to read the compressed files. If none of your hard disks are compressed and you have finished removing the compression from a compressed diskette, Windows 98 gives you the option of deleting DriveSpace from memory. It's a good idea to allow Windows 98 to remove DriveSpace when it isn't needed, because this frees up memory so your programs can run faster. Windows 98 reloads DriveSpace if it's needed at a later time.

Adjusting compression properties

When you compress a disk for the first time, the level of compression DriveSpace uses is a compromise between performance and the amount of space saved. DriveSpace can, however, squeeze out more room by compressing files even tighter.

Adjusting compression properties

DriveSpace has three levels of compression. In addition to the standard compression, DriveSpace can perform HiPack compression and UltraPack compression. *HiPack* compression generally reduces files to a smaller size than standard compression, and *UltraPack* compression can make files even smaller.

In this exercise you learn how to adjust the DriveSpace settings to control whether DriveSpace uses standard or HiPack compression during normal operations. In the next exercise you learn how to apply UltraPack compression using the Compression Agent.

1 Click the Start button.

2 Select Programs.

3 Select Accessories.

4 Select System Tools.

5 Select DriveSpace.

6 Select the drive you want to adjust.

7 Click Advanced.

8 Select Settings to display the Disk Compression Settings dialog box.

9 To compress your files to the smallest size, select the HiPack compression radio button. (The remaining compression method options are generally not good choices unless you have a very slow system.)

10 Select the Automatically mount new compressed drives checkbox so that Windows 98 automatically recognizes compressed diskettes.

11 Click OK to close the Disk Compression Settings dialog box.

12 Click the Close button to close the DriveSpace window.

HiPack compression is generally much more efficient than standard compression and may give you as much as 15 to 20 percent more free disk space than if you use standard compression. You can use the DriveSpace Disk Compression Settings dialog box to switch between the two types of compression and determine whether your system experiences any performance degradation when you choose HiPack rather than standard compression.

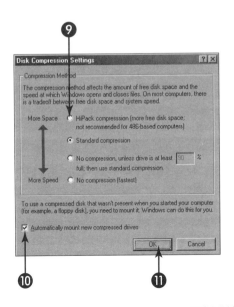

Using the Compression Agent

Using the Compression Agent

The Compression Agent is a special DriveSpace utility that can compress your files even more than DriveSpace alone. The Compression Agent can compress files you don't use often using the UltraPack compression format. Although DriveSpace can't compress files using the UltraPack compression format, it has no problem reading files compressed using the UltraPack compression format.

 Because you can add the Compression Agent as a scheduled task, you can have the best of both worlds in disk compression. You can achieve highest performance by telling DriveSpace not to compress your files when you save them to your hard disk, but still have the largest amount of free disk space by having the Compression Agent compress your files to their smallest possible size.

The Compression Agent only runs if you have a DriveSpace compressed disk. You can use a DriveSpace-compressed diskette or use the Compression Agent to compress the files on a compressed hard disk. In this exercise, the figures show the results of using the Compression Agent on a compressed diskette — you may want to use a compressed diskette until you're comfortable using DriveSpace and the Compression Agent.

❶ Click the Start button.

❷ Select Programs.

❸ Select Accessories.

❹ Select System Tools.

❺ Select Compression Agent. If necessary, choose the compressed disk you want to use for this exercise.

❻ Select Settings to display the Compression Agent Settings dialog box.

Using the Compression Agent

7 For maximum free disk space, select the UltraPack all files radio button.

When you choose this option, the Compression Agent uses the highest level of compression on all files, but because DriveSpace cannot save files using UltraPack compression, any new or modified files are saved using the DriveSpace compression settings.

8 Select UltraPack only files not used within the last x days radio button, if you want to compromise between performance and disk space. This compresses the files you use the least using UltraPack compression format.

9 If you selected UltraPack only files not used within the last x days, make certain the Yes radio button is selected so that any remaining files are compressed using the HiPack compression format.

10 Click the Advanced button to display the Advanced Settings dialog box.

11 To prevent the Compression Agent from reducing the amount of free disk space below an acceptable level, use the up and down arrows to set the amount of free disk space in the spin box.

12 Select the Leave all UltraPacked files in UltraPack format checkbox. Because DriveSpace automatically converts UltraPacked files to another format if the files are modified, you probably don't want the Compression Agent to change any of these files.

13 Click OK to return to the Compression Agent window.

14 Click Start to begin changing the compression formats.

When the Compression Agent finishes, you see a screen that says Compression Agent is completed, similar to the screen shown in the figure on the next page. In this case, changing from standard compression to UltraPack compression increased the free disk space by 98K.

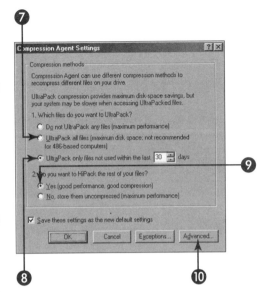

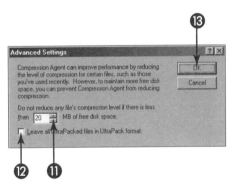

4

Working with Disks

Using FAT32

⑮ Click Exit to close the Compression Agent window.

If you schedule the Compression Agent as a scheduled event after you've selected your desired Compression Agent settings, you probably won't run the Compression Agent manually again. You can run Compression Agent any time you want to adjust the compression settings — by default, any changes you make are stored as the settings that Compression Agent uses until you make further changes. Of course, you wouldn't want to make Compression Agent a scheduled event if the only disk you've compressed is a diskette — you'd have to leave the same diskette in the drive all the time.

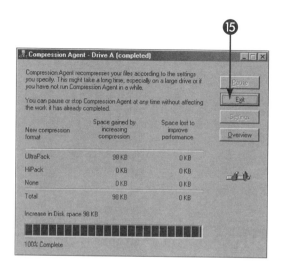

Using FAT32

Since the introduction of the original IBM PC, a *File Allocation Table,* or FAT, has mostly been used to track and control the allocation of space on disk drives. (Windows NT and IBM's unpopular OS/2 both offer additional options, but the majority of PCs use a FAT.) When Microsoft originally created MS–DOS, hard disks were rare, and those that did exist were generally limited to 5 to 10MB. Early versions of MS–DOS included support only for hard disks up to 32MB, while later versions allowed for larger sizes by increasing the minimum amount of space allocated to each file. Unfortunately, these larger allocation units tended to waste a lot of disk space because even the smallest file needed a complete allocation unit. A one byte file could take 32KB of disk space!

Still, until the introduction of FAT32, the maximum size of a drive was limited to 2GB. As PCs become more powerful and users play around with multimedia, combining video and sound, 2GB starts looking smaller every day. FAT32 overcomes this limitation by replacing the old File Allocation Table structure with a new method of allocating disk space. With FAT32, disk space allocation is much more efficient, the 2GB limit on the size of disks is removed, and you can store many more files in the same amount of space because the allocation units are so much smaller. In fact, a one-byte file on a FAT32 disk would take 4KB of space — one-eighth the space needed under the old FAT system.

NOTE *If your PC came with Windows 98 already installed, or if it was built during 1997 and came installed with Windows 95, there's a chance FAT32 may already be installed on your system. To check, open My Computer and right-click the icon for drive C. Select Properties. You'll see an item on the General tab marked "File system." If this says FAT32 rather than FAT, the drive is already formatted in FAT32 format.*

You can convert your hard disks to FAT32 using the Drive Converter tool that comes with Windows 98. However, keep in mind the following limitations:

- The Drive Converter is a one-way tool. You can convert to FAT32, but you cannot reverse the process without destroying all the data on your hard drive.

- You cannot convert a compressed disk to FAT32. DriveSpace and FAT32 are not compatible, so you can choose one but not both.

- If you convert a disk to FAT32, you will not be able to load any other operating system, such as Windows NT.

- FAT32 is intended for drives over 512MB and offers no benefit for smaller drives.

To use the Drive Converter to convert your hard drive to FAT32, follow these steps:

❶ Click the Start button.

❷ Select Programs.

❸ Select Accessories.

❹ Select System Tools.

❺ Select Drive Converter to display the Drive Converter wizard.

❻ Click Next to continue. A warning appears, telling you that after the conversion you will not be able to uninstall Windows 98 or access your hard drive from a previous version of MS-DOS or Windows.

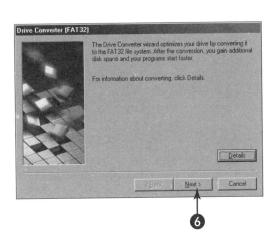

4

Working with Disks

Improving disk performance

7 Click Next to continue. A dialog box appears, notifying you that the Drive Converter must reboot your system. Before you continue, close all other programs and save your work.

8 Click Next to continue.

You won't be able to use your system until the conversion is completed.

 During the conversion, your PC will restart in a special MS-DOS mode, change the file system to FAT32, restart Windows 98, and defragment your hard drive. This may take several hours to complete.

After you've completed the conversion to FAT32, you won't notice much difference in the way your system operates. You may notice additional free space on your hard disk, but all file-related operations should be normal.

IMPROVING DISK PERFORMANCE

You may not realize it, but one of the best ways to speed up your computer is to improve the performance of your disk drives. Your disk drives are mechanical components and are much slower than the electronic components that make up most of your system. Even a small improvement in the performance of your disk drives can make a big difference in the overall performance of your whole PC.

Because disk performance can make such a difference, Windows 98 includes the tools you need to correct any problems that may be slowing down your disk drives. In the following exercises you learn how you can make your computer perform a little better by using these tools.

Defragmenting your disks

The more you use your PC, the more your files become *fragmented* — stored in several noncontiguous pieces on your disks. To understand why this happens, imagine that you and a group of your friends all want to go to your favorite bookstore to look for the latest books from IDG Books Worldwide. There are too many of you to fit in one car, so you drive off together in six different cars. If you go early in the morning and arrive just when the mall opens, you might be able to park your cars together in adjacent parking spots. But if you go later in the afternoon when quite a few people have already gone shopping, you'll probably end up parking at various points around the parking garage because you can't find six spots together.

When you save files on your disks, Windows 98 encounters a similar situation to the parking garage — there's room for the first files you save to be placed in contiguous blocks, but as you delete and save more files, there may not be room to store all the pieces of some files in adjacent blocks. Sure, the small files that only need a single block are okay, but larger files have to be broken up into several pieces — fragmented — in order to find room for them to park on your hard drive.

It takes longer to store and read fragmented files. Rather than reading or writing a complete file in one motion, your disk drive has to jump around to locate all the pieces of a fragmented file. As fragmentation becomes worse, disk operations may seem to take forever. If opening programs or saving documents seems to take longer than it used to, disk fragmentation may be the culprit.

TIP

Anything that writes to your disk drives can cause Windows 98 to start the disk-defragmentation process all over again. Ultimately, you save yourself a lot of time and frustration if you make certain no other programs are running while you defragment your disk drives.

Defragmenting a large hard disk can take quite a bit of time. In this exercise you practice by defragmenting a diskette, which takes less time.

1 Double-click the My Computer icon on your desktop.

2 Insert a diskette into drive A. This diskette should be one you've used so it contains some files. If necessary, copy some files to the diskette — it doesn't matter which files are on the diskette.

3 Right-click the drive A icon.

Defragmenting your disks

4 Select Properties from the pop-up menu to display the Properties dialog box.

5 Click the Tools tab to see the available disk tools, as shown in the figure on the right.

6 Click Defragment Now and wait while Windows 98 checks the fragmentation status of the disk.

While you're defragmenting a diskette, the dialog box shows the progress of the defragmentation process. The progress is usually slow but steady. When you defragment a hard disk, you may notice that Windows 98 starts the process over from the beginning one or more times. This is your clue that some other program you're running is interfering with the defragmentation, and you should exit from the other program unless you really like to waste time.

7 When you see the message shown in the figure on the right telling you the defragmentation is complete, click Yes.

Don't be fooled by the relatively short amount of time it takes to defragment a diskette. It can take quite a bit of time to defragment a large hard disk, especially one that is quite full. Still, if you schedule defragmentation for times when you don't need to use your PC, you improve the performance enough to make up for the time required to defragment your disks.

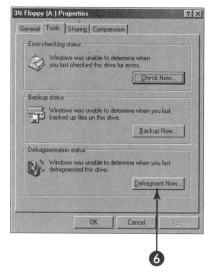

Using ScanDisk to check for damage

I almost hate to tell you this, but your PC and your files may be damaged. I don't want to scare you, but you might have problems right now and not even know about them. Parts of files may be lost, your hard disk may be defective, or there may be pieces of old files eating up space without serving any useful purpose. It doesn't sound too good, does it? Fortunately for you, Windows 98 has just the tool to find and correct most of these types of problems. ScanDisk, the subject of this exercise, comes to your rescue.

Using ScanDisk to check for damage

TIP *ScanDisk serves as a replacement for CHKDSK, a disk-repair tool found in earlier versions of MS-DOS. CHKDSK still exists in Windows 98, but ScanDisk can do a much better job of finding and correcting errors.*

Disk errors fall into two general categories: physical errors and file errors. Physical errors are problems with the surface of the disk that make particular areas on the disk unreliable for storing data. File errors are problems stemming from errors in allocating disk space, making it possible for two files to try to use the same space or part of a file to be lost, or preventing space from being released when a file is deleted.

TIP *Always use the Shut Down option on the Start menu before you turn off your PC. Skipping this step is the surest way to cause file errors.*

For this exercise you can use the same diskette you used in the last exercise. Here, too, the procedure is the same whether you work with a diskette or a hard disk, but the exercise goes much faster if you practice on a diskette.

❶ If you closed the dialog box after the last exercise, double-click the My Computer icon.

❷ Right-click the drive A icon.

❸ Select Properties from the pop-up menu.

❹ Click the Tools tab.

❺ Click Check Now to display the ScanDisk dialog box. Because ScanDisk can take a long time to perform its tests, you can choose more than one drive to test.

❻ Click Advanced to display the ScanDisk Advanced Options dialog box. You may want to make several changes to the default settings.

7 Select the Only if errors found radio button so ScanDisk shows you a report only if there were errors on the disk. This setting enables ScanDisk to continue on to the next selected disk without stopping if there were no errors.

8 Select the Replace log radio button, if it is not selected, to make ScanDisk create a text file (Scandisk.log) in the root folder that you can use to determine which errors were corrected.

9 Select the Make copies radio button, if it is not selected, so ScanDisk makes copies of any files that appear to be sharing the same disk space. If ScanDisk finds *cross-linked* files, you can examine Scandisk.log to see which files were cross-linked. One of each pair of cross-linked files is probably okay, while the other is likely to be unusable.

10 Select the Free radio button to free up the space occupied by *lost file fragments* — left-over pieces of files that are taking up space even though the files were supposed to be deleted.

11 Select the Invalid file names, Invalid dates and times, and Duplicate names checkboxes. You want to make certain ScanDisk finds and corrects all possible errors.

12 Select the Check host drive first checkbox. If you have any disks that are compressed with DriveSpace, ScanDisk checks both the compressed and the host drive for errors.

13 Select the Report MS-DOS mode name length errors checkbox.

14 Click OK to return to the ScanDisk dialog box.

15 Select the Thorough radio button to tell ScanDisk to look for physical errors on the disk surface as well as file system errors. The test takes much longer when ScanDisk examines the disk for physical errors, but the extra time may prevent your PC from writing data to a place on a disk that it can't read later.

16 Click Options to display the Surface Scan Options dialog box.

17 Select the System and data areas radio button so that ScanDisk examines the entire surface of the disk for errors. You don't want to take a chance that either area has a bad spot that isn't detected.

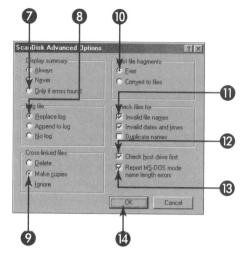

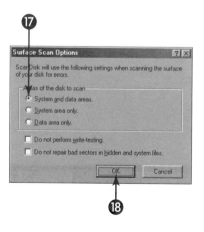

Using ScanDisk to check for damage

NOTE *Do not select the Do not perform write-testing checkbox. If you select this option, ScanDisk only reads the data and does not write to the disk. It's better to find out now whether any spots are failing on your disks than to wait until your system unsuccessfully tries to write data later.*

Do not select the Do not repair bad sectors in hidden and system files checkbox unless you're using old copy-protected software. A long time ago certain software manufacturers used a bizarre method of copy protection that required that certain hidden or system files be located at a specific place on a disk. You're better off allowing ScanDisk to correct any errors than worrying about whether this may cause a problem.

⑱ Click OK to continue.

⑲ Select the Automatically fix errors checkbox in the Scandisk dialog box. If it is not selected, then as the testing proceeds you may see error messages similar to the messages shown in the figure on the right. (You have to respond to each error as it is found.)

⑳ Click Start to begin the disk scan, and then sit back and wait.

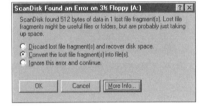

NOTE *When you use ScanDisk to test a large hard disk, be prepared to wait a long time.*

㉑ If any errors were found (or if you selected the Always display summary radio button), ScanDisk may show you a report similar to the one shown in the figure on the right. Click Close when you're done examining the report.

㉒ Click Close to close the ScanDisk dialog box.

If you're lucky, ScanDisk won't find any errors on your disks. If it does find errors, you should consider yourself lucky, too, because ScanDisk probably found the errors before they became a problem for you or your data.

Skills challenge

SKILLS CHALLENGE: MASTERING YOUR DISK DRIVES

Now you can practice some of what you've learned in this chapter to see how much you remember.

1 Format a diskette.

> **1** *What format option can you use to make certain a diskette doesn't contain any bad sectors?*

> **2** *What can you do to prevent a diskette from being formatted and destroying any data it contains?*

2 Copy a file to drive A.

> **3** *How can you copy a file on your desktop to a diskette without using Windows Explorer?*

3 Compress drive A using DriveSpace.

4 Change the estimated compression ratio of the diskette to 3.0 to 1.

5 Change the free space on drive A's host drive to 1MB.

> **4** *How can you specify an exact amount of free space rather than a percentage?*

6 Check to see whether drive A needs to be defragmented.

7 Check for errors on drive A.

> **5** *What setting checks for file-system errors without performing a surface scan?*

> **6** *How can you specify that you want to check all your disk drives for errors in one operation?*

> **7** *What setting is necessary to keep ScanDisk from stopping and showing a summary report if there are no errors?*

8 Check to see which file system is in use on your hard drive.

4

Working with Disks

Troubleshooting

TROUBLESHOOTING

If you encounter problems while working through the exercises, here are some ideas that might help you correct the problems and keep going.

Problem	Solution
When I try to format a diskette, I see an error message telling me the disk is write-protected.	If the diskette is a 3½-inch diskette (the most common size), turn the diskette over and look for a small plastic slider. The slider must be slid towards the center of the diskette to cover the opening. If the diskette is a 5¼-inch diskette, make certain the notch along the side of the diskette isn't covered with a piece of tape.
DriveSpace doesn't appear on the Windows 98 menu.	You need to install DriveSpace using the Add/Remove Programs icon in the Control Panel. Click the Windows Setup tab, choose Disk Tools ➢ Details and make certain DriveSpace is checked. (You don't see the DriveSpace option once DriveSpace is installed.) Click Apply to install DriveSpace.

WRAP UP

You can't work with your PC without using your disk drives. In these exercises you learned a number of important things about using your disks: preparing your diskettes for use, making more room, improving performance, and performing backups of your data. You learned that backing up and restoring your data is a lot easier than most PC users realize.

The next lesson shows you how to make your PC come alive with sound and video. You can have fun playing with some of the advanced capabilities built into today's PCs.

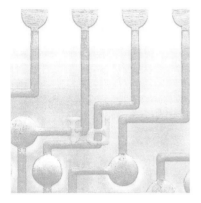

Lights, Action, Multimedia!

50 MINUTES

GOALS

Nothing adds to the fun of using your PC as much as the multimedia capabilities built into virtually all modern systems. Although most PCs have sound and video capabilities built in, making those capabilities work properly can be difficult. This lesson helps you learn how to use the multimedia features in your PC and how to make your PC a more lively companion. In this lesson you learn about:

- Using your PC's sound capabilities

- Viewing video on your PC

- Using the Imaging utility

- Configuring multimedia for performance

Get ready

GET READY

To complete this lesson you need a multimedia PC — one with a sound card, speakers, a CD-ROM drive, and a VGA- or higher-level monitor. You also need your Windows 98 CD-ROM, because some of the exercises use multimedia samples that are included on the CD-ROM. To record sounds with the Sound Recorder, you need a microphone attached to your PC's sound card. If you don't have a microphone, you can still try out most of the features of Sound Recorder. You also need a regular audio CD to complete the "Using the CD Player" exercise. The TV Viewer requires a special video board to display TV programs on your PC screen, but you can download and view the TV listings on any PC as long as you have an Internet connection.

TIP

If you don't have the CD-ROM version of Windows 98, you can find many of the extras from the CD-ROM on on the Internet at `http://www.microsoft. com/msdownload/`.

You may notice a few small differences between some of the dialog boxes pictured in this lesson and what appears on your screen. Audio and video board manufacturers sometimes add their own unique features, or in some cases may even replace the standard Windows 98 dialog boxes with their own variations. Even if this is the case on your system, you should be able to complete the lesson by looking for options similar to those shown in the figures.

Your Windows 98 CD-ROM has over 500 sound files that you can use. You may wish to copy some of those sounds from the CD-ROM to your hard disk to make it more convenient to use the sounds — for example, to attach sounds to events. Some of the exercises use sound files from the Windows 98 CD-ROM.

If you want to copy the sound files to your hard disk before you begin the exercises, follow these steps:

1. Insert your Windows 98 CD-ROM into your CD-ROM drive. If the Windows 98 CD-ROM window appears, click the Close button to close the window.

2. Start Windows Explorer.

❸ Open the \Windows\Media folder.

❹ Select Tools.

❺ Select Find.

❻ Select Files or Folders.

❼ Type this text in the Named text box: ***.wav**.

❽ Click the down arrow at the right side of the Look in list box, and then select the icon for your CD-ROM drive (this is probably D, depending on how many hard disks you have installed).

❾ Click Find Now to begin the search.

❿ When the search is complete, press Ctrl+A to select all the sound files.

⓫ Point to the selected files in the Find dialog box.

⓬ Hold down the left mouse button, and drag the files to the \Windows\Media folder in Windows Explorer.

TIP

Copying all the sound files from the Windows 98 CD-ROM to your hard disk uses a lot of space. If you're short on disk space, you may want to be selective in deciding which files to copy. You'll use mainidle.wav from the \Cdsample\Sounds folder in the exercises.

LET'S MAKE SOME NOISE!

Almost everyone likes to have a computer that makes some noise. Whether it's something simple like playing a sound when you start Windows 98, or a bit more complex like playing audio CDs while you work, Windows 98 can make a lot of noise.

TIP

Although almost everyone likes their computer to make sounds, not everyone appreciates the sounds made by someone else's PC. If you share an office

Playing sounds

with other people, keep the volume down or wear earphones to keep your PC from becoming a nuisance.

Playing sounds

Windows 98 includes a program called Media Player that you can use to play several different types of multimedia files. Windows 98 sound files are one of the types of multimedia files Media Player plays quite well. Windows 98 sound files are also called *wave* files—a reference to their .wav file extension. This type of sound file is simply a digital recording of sounds. Wave files can include everything from sound effects to voice recordings to musical performances. In this exercise you play a sound file using Media Player.

❶ Click the Start button.

❷ Select Programs.

❸ Select Accessories.

❹ Select Entertainment.

❺ Select Media Player. The figure on the right shows the Media Player and identifies the various controls you can use to control the playing of multimedia files.

❻ Select File.

❼ Select Open to display the Open dialog box.

NOTE *Make certain the Media folder is shown in the Look in text box. This is the folder in which Windows 98 normally looks for multimedia files, and it should be the folder in which you store any multimedia files so they're easy to locate.*

❽ Double-click mainidle.wav to open the sound file. This file is one of the sample sound files from the Windows 98 CD-ROM.

❾ Click the Play button to play the file.

Drag slider to change position in a multimedia file

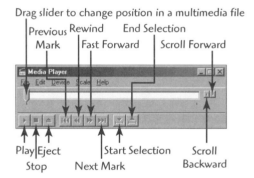

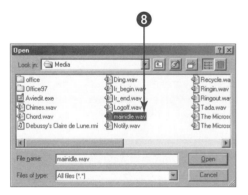

10 Click the Play button again to replay the file. Because you didn't stop the playback before the end, Media Player plays the file from the beginning.

11 Hold down the Rewind button until the slider is about in the middle of the scale.

12 Click the Play button. This time Media Player plays the file from the point at which you left the slider.

13 Drag the slider to the 0:10 mark on the scale.

14 Click the Play button. You can also use the Scroll Forward and Scroll Backward buttons to move to different points in the file.

With so many sound files available, you could spend a lot of time sampling each of them. One method you can use to speed up the process is to have both Media Player and Windows Explorer open at the same time, and drag sound files from the Media folder onto Media Player. As you drop each file onto Media Player, the file automatically plays, saving you quite a few steps as you look for your favorites.

You can find additional sound files in many places. Many of the CD-ROMs of popular office suites contain short sound files. You can probably find additional sound files on many other CD-ROMs, too. Just use the Find ➢ Files or Folders command and look for files with a .wav extension.

Placing an audio clip in a document

Windows 98 documents don't have to be boring. You can easily spice them up with audio clips. You might, for example, want to include an audio "hello" in a note you're sending to someone. In this exercise you learn how to clip out part of an audio file and place the clip in a document. You can select any part of an audio file — you don't have to include the entire file unless you want to.

1 Click the Start button.

2 Select Programs.

3 Select Accessories.

4 Select Entertainment.

5

Lights, Action, Multimedia!

Placing an audio clip in a document

5 Select Media Player.

6 Select File.

7 Select Open to display the Open dialog box.

8 Double-click mainidle.wav to open the sound file in Media Player.

9 Place the slider at the beginning of the file.

10 Click the Start Selection button.

11 Move the slider to the right until the time indicator shows 10:00 (sec) — ten seconds into the sound file.

12 Click the End Selection button to select the first ten seconds of the recording. Media Player highlights your selection.

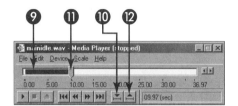

13 Select Edit.

14 Select Copy Object to copy the selected portion of the sound file to the Clipboard.

15 Click the Start button.

16 Select Programs.

17 Select Accessories.

18 Select WordPad to open a new WordPad document.

19 Select Edit.

20 Select Paste to place the audio clip in the WordPad document.

21 Double-click the mainidle.wav icon in the document to play the audio clip. Because you selected the first ten seconds rather than the whole file, only the first part of the file plays.

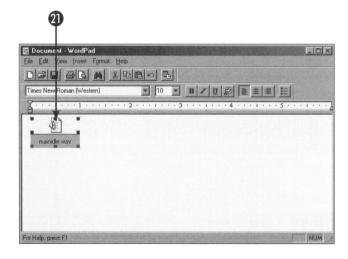

A document file with only a "Main" audio clip probably isn't too useful, so you'd probably want to add additional text if you were really going to send the document to someone. For now, though, you can either save the document and close WordPad, or just leave the document open for later when you add a video clip to the document.

Because you can't easily rename an audio clip you've inserted into a document file, rename the sound file in Windows Explorer before you open it in Media Player. You might, for example, make a copy of main.wav and call it music.wav before you open it in Media Player and clip out the greeting for your document.

Using the volume control

You probably wouldn't put up with a radio or a television that lacked a volume control, so you probably want to be able to control the sound level in Windows 98, too. Windows 98 actually has a quite sophisticated volume control with different settings for different types of sounds. You can choose different levels for audio CDs and wave files, for example. Windows 98 also has a simple volume control that you can use to adjust the overall sound level or to quickly mute all sounds.

In this exercise you access the Windows 98 volume controls and adjust your sound levels.

1. Click the speaker icon on the Taskbar to display the simple volume control. You can move the slider up or down to control the overall volume level. When you use this volume control, all sound sources are adjusted together. You can select the Mute checkbox to mute the speakers.

2. Click a blank space on your desktop to remove the simple volume control from your screen.

3. Double-click the speaker icon to display the full volume control. In the figure on the right, the simple volume control is also shown so you can compare the two.

4. Play a sound file in Media Player while you drag the Volume slider up and down to hear the effect on the volume.

5. Drag the Wave Balance slider left and right as you play a sound file. This slider affects the balance between the right and left speakers.

The full volume control enables you to adjust sound sources individually

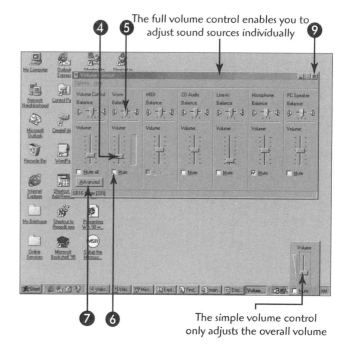

The simple volume control only adjusts the overall volume

Lights, Action, Multimedia!

Using the Sound Recorder

6 Select the Wave Mute checkbox to silence the sound file. Be sure to deselect this checkbox before you close the volume control so you can once again hear wave sounds.

7 Click the Advanced button to display the Advanced Controls dialog box. This dialog box has sliders to adjust the bass and treble response, and it may include additional controls such as a loudness control if your sound card supports additional controls.

8 Click the Close button to close the Advanced Controls dialog box.

9 Click the Close button to close the Volume Control dialog box.

Different sound sources tend to play at different sound levels. By accessing the full volume control you can fine-tune the volume to your liking.

Using the Sound Recorder

Another of the Windows 98 multimedia accessories is the Sound Recorder. This handy little accessory enables you to record and modify sound files. If you have a microphone attached to your PC, Sound Recorder can create wave files of you singing or talking. Even if you don't have a microphone, you can use Sound Recorder to create a wave file from any sounds that pass through your sound card. You can also apply several different types of modifications to existing sounds.

In this exercise you sample some of the capabilities of the Sound Recorder. You start by recording a short sound file using your microphone — if you don't have a microphone attached to your PC, make a copy of main.wav and use the copy to practice modifying sound files.

1 Click the Start button.

2 Select Programs.

3 Select Accessories.

4 Select Entertainment.

5 Select Sound Recorder.

6 Double-click the speaker icon on the Taskbar to display the full volume control.

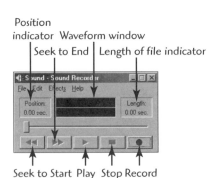

Position indicator Waveform window

Seek to End | Length of file indicator

Seek to Start Play Stop Record

7 Uncheck the Microphone Mute checkbox if it is selected. If you have any other sounds coming from your speakers, select the Mute checkbox for those other sound sources; otherwise, they will be recorded along with your voice.

NOTE

Some sound cards will include all sound sources when you record a sound file, even if the Mute checkbox is selected for those sources. If your sound recordings include unwanted background noise, you may want to reduce all unnecessary sound source volume controls to the minimum before you begin recording.

8 Position your microphone so you can speak into the microphone, and click the Record button.

9 Say **Hello, I'm learning a lot about Windows 98.**

10 Click the Stop button.

TIP

If you make a mistake while recording, select File ➢ New ➢ No to erase the recording so you can start over.

11 Select File.

12 Select Save to display the Save As dialog box.

13 Change the Save in location to the \Windows\Media folder.

14 Type the following text in the File name text box: **Hello 1**.

15 Click Save to save the file and return to Sound Recorder. (If you don't have a microphone, you can select File ➢ Open and open your copy of main.wav.)

16 Click the Play button to play back your recording.

17 Drag the slider to a point about a quarter of the way into the file. You can use the position indicator and the length of file indicator to determine the current position of the slider. Notice, too, how the waveform window shows a thicker line at some points. This thicker line shows where the file contains sounds.

5

Lights, Action, Multimedia!

18 Click the Play button to see where the file starts playing. You should be able to find the point where you finished saying hello and went on to the rest of the message.

19 Select Effects.

20 Select Increase Volume (by 25%).

21 Click the Play button again. Notice that the line in the waveform window increases in thickness as you increase the volume.

22 Select Effects.

23 Select Increase Speed (by 100%).

24 Click the Play button.

25 Select Effects.

26 Select Decrease Speed to return your recorded voice to normal.

27 Select Effects.

28 Select Add Echo.

29 Click Play. Your recording should sound like you were in a large room with a lot of echos.

30 Select Effects.

31 Select Reverse.

32 Click Play. You just learned the secret to putting hidden, backward-playing messages on recordings!

33 Select File.

34 Select Revert.

35 Select Yes to return the file to its original state.

36 Click the Close button to close Sound Recorder.

You can have a lot of fun playing with Sound Recorder. You can even record your own messages to use as sounds to attach to Windows 98 events, which is the subject of the next exercise.

Adding sounds to Windows 98 events ◀

▶ Adding sounds to Windows 98 events

Your PC can make a lot of noise. Almost any *event* — such as starting Windows 98, opening a menu, or closing a program — can be assigned a sound. Assigning sounds to every possible event would probably be overkill in most cases, but you have to determine what's best for you. You may want to consider adding sounds to certain important events, such as error messages or new mail, and leaving most other events silent.

TIP

You can record short descriptions of Windows 98 events using Sound Recorder. Then you can assign the resulting sound files to those events to assist a visually impaired or a young user in using Windows 98.

In this exercise you assign sounds to Windows 98 events.

1 Click the Start button.

2 Select Settings.

3 Select Control Panel.

4 Double-click the Sounds icon to display the Sounds Properties dialog box.

5 To hear the sound already assigned to an event, look for an event that has a speaker icon to the left of the event name, and click the event to choose it.

6 Click the Play button to hear the sound.

7 Choose an event that does not have an assigned sound. In this case choose Open Program to play a sound when you open a program.

8 Click the down arrow at the right side on the Name list box.

9 Select Hello 1.wav to assign the Hello 1.wav sound file you created in the last exercise to the Open Program event (or open your copy of main.wav from the Windows 98 CD-ROM).

10 Click the Play button to hear the sound.

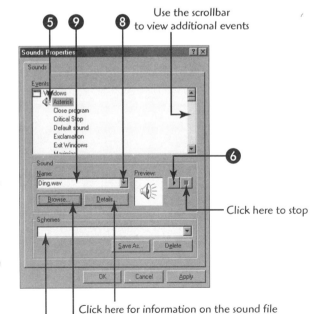

Use the scrollbar to view additional events

Click here to stop

Click here for information on the sound file

Click here to find sound files to assign to events

Select name sound schemes here

⑪ When you have assigned sounds to several events, select Save As to display the Save Scheme As dialog box.

⑫ Type the following text: **My sound scheme**.

⑬ Click OK to save your sound scheme. You can then choose your named scheme or another scheme using the Schemes list box.

⑭ Click OK to close the Sounds Properties dialog box.

Although you can assign any sounds you like to Windows 98 events, it's better to assign relatively short sounds to most events. Otherwise, your PC makes so much noise that the sounds are distracting rather than helpful.

Using CD Player

Most of the time your CD-ROM drive just sits there unused. Oh, sure, you use it when you install programs or when you run programs from a CD-ROM, but that's probably a small fraction of the time you use your PC. There's no reason you can't use the CD-ROM drive at other times to play audio CDs and have some pleasant music while you work. Mozart would certainly have approved of the idea!

Windows 98 includes a CD player to play audio CDs in your CD-ROM drive. There's actually little difference between audio CDs and CD-ROMs. Both use the same type of disc, and a disc can even hold both audio and data tracks.

The Windows 98 CD Player even has some tricks your normal audio CD player probably lacks. You can set up play lists for your favorite audio CDs, and CD Player even remembers audio CDs between sessions.

❶ Place an audio CD in your CD-ROM drive. CD Player should start automatically. If CD Player doesn't start automatically, follow Steps 2 - 6. If it does start automatically, skip ahead to Step 7.

❷ If CD Player doesn't start automatically, click the Start button.

❸ Select Programs.

❹ Select Accessories.

❺ Select Entertainment.

6 Select CD Player.

The figure on the right shows CD Player while it is playing a Mozart CD (after the play list has been manually entered). You may need to select View ➤ Toolbar if the toolbar doesn't appear.

7 You may need to click the Play button to begin playing the CD. Generally CD Player begins playing the first CD automatically, unless you started CD Player before you inserted an audio CD. Subsequent audio CDs don't start playing automatically.

8 Click the Edit Play List button to display the CD Player: Disc Settings dialog box. In this case the information for an audio CD has already been entered, so you can see how a CD Player play list functions.

9 Type the name of the artist in the Artist text box; in this case **Wolfgang Amadeus Mozart**.

10 Type the CD title in the Title text box; in this case **Eine Kleine Nachtmusik**.

11 Type the name of track one in the Track 01 text box; in this case, **Allegro**.

12 Click Set Name.

13 Continue typing in the track names until all of the track names have been entered. CD Player remembers the artist, title, and track names and correctly displays them the next time you play this CD.

14 To prevent a track from playing, choose the track in the Play List box and click Remove.

15 Click Clear All to change the order in which tracks are played.

16 Select a track in the Available Tracks list box.

17 Click Add. (Continue until you've chosen all the tracks you wish to play.)

18 Click OK to return to CD Player.

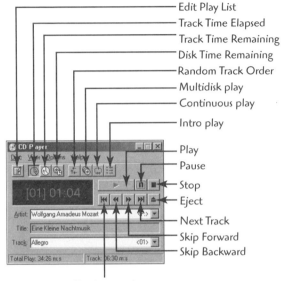

- Edit Play List
- Track Time Elapsed
- Track Time Remaining
- Disk Time Remaining
- Random Track Order
- Multidisk play
- Continuous play
- Intro play
- Play
- Pause
- Stop
- Eject
- Next Track
- Skip Forward
- Skip Backward

Previous track

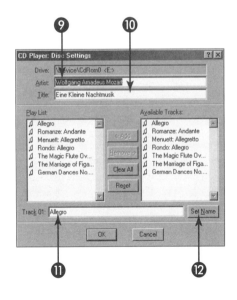

Let's have some action!

⑲ Select the type of time display you prefer by clicking the Track Time Elapsed, Track Time Remaining, or Disk Time Remaining buttons.

⑳ Click the Random Track Order button if you prefer to have the tracks play randomly.

㉑ To play the same CD over again until you click the Stop button, click the Continuous Play button.

㉒ To preview the first ten seconds of each track, click the Intro Play button. (You can change the length of the preview by selecting Options ➤ Preferences ➤ Intro play length.)

㉓ To stop playing and eject a CD, click the Eject button.

The remaining CD Player controls work much like the controls on a standard audio CD player, except that you use your mouse to click the buttons on CD Player. If you enjoy music while you work, you'll find CD Player pretty handy — especially if you take the time to enter play lists for your favorite audio CDs.

LET'S HAVE SOME ACTION!

Windows 98 multimedia isn't only about sound. You can also play video pieces on your screen. Your Windows 98 CD-ROM has some excellent examples that can show you just how impressive multimedia can really be. In the following exercises you see how to use those examples.

Playing video clips takes a lot of computing power. Although you can get by with less, you really should have at least a 120 MHz Pentium system with 16MB of RAM and a quad-speed CD-ROM drive to play most video clips without problems. Slower systems can usually play video clips, but they may display jerky motion in the video or contain gaps in the audio track.

▶ *Playing the fun stuff*

Windows 98 video files use a format where the audio and video
portions are both included — interleaved — in the same file. Your
Windows 98 CD-ROM has several video files. You can play videos
using the Media Player, and in this exercise I show you how.

① Insert your Windows 98 CD-ROM into your CD-ROM drive.

② If the Windows 98 CD-ROM screen appears, select Cool Video
Clips to display the Videos folder, and then go to Step 11.

③ If the Windows 98 CD-ROM screen does not appear, click the
Start button.

④ Select Programs.

⑤ Select Accessories.

⑥ Select Entertainment.

⑦ Select Media Player.

⑧ Select Device.

⑨ Select ActiveMovie to display the Open dialog box.

⑩ Choose your CD-ROM drive (probably drive D) in the Look in
list box, and then choose the \Cdsample\Videos folder.

⑪ Double-click Intro.mpg to open the Intro video file.

⑫ If you manually started Media Player, click the Play button to
view the video.

The figure on the right shows one of the frames of this video
when played using the manually started Media Player.

⑬ You can click the Pause button to stop the video at any point,
and then click Play to resume.

⑭ Drag the slider left or right to move to different frames in the
video.

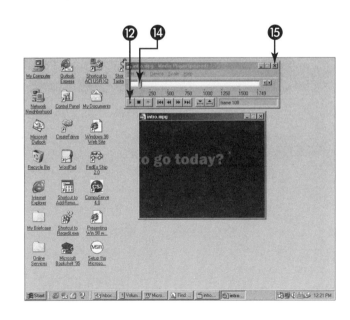

5

Lights, Action, Multimedia!

⑮ Click the Close button to close Media Player. (Depending on how you started the video clip, you may need to click the video window Close button first.)

Although you can easily create your own sound files, creating your own video files is generally beyond the capabilities of most PC users. You need a special video capture board and a video source, such as a video camera, to create digital movies. Unfortunately, this type of equipment is still quite rare and expensive.

Placing a video clip in a document

Video clips tend to be quite large. These large sizes mean that placing a video clip in a document, while possible, isn't always the most practical idea. Still, there may be times when you want to include a video clip in a document—perhaps to add a little excitement to an onscreen presentation. Just remember that a document containing a video clip probably won't be a good candidate for saving on diskettes!

❶ Click the Start button.

❷ Select Programs.

❸ Select Accessories.

❹ Select Entertainment.

❺ Select Media Player.

❻ Select Device.

❼ Select ActiveMovie.

❽ Click the down arrow at the right edge of the Look in list box.

❾ Choose the drive letter for your CD-ROM drive.

❿ Select Videos.

⓫ Double-click Intro.mpg to open the AVI file.

⓬ Select Edit.

⓭ Copy Object to place the AVI file on the Clipboard.

⓮ Click the Start button.

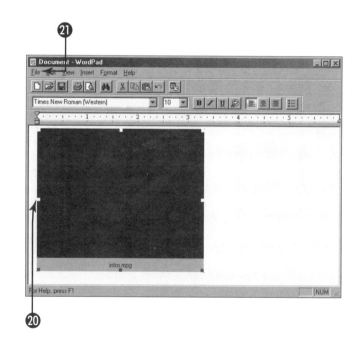

⑮ Select Programs.

⑯ Select Accessories.

⑰ Select WordPad.

⑱ In WordPad, select Edit.

⑲ Select Paste to place the video clip into the document.

⑳ Double-click the video clip in WordPad to play the video clip.

㉑ Select File.

㉒ Select Save.

㉓ Type the following text to name the file: **A video clip**.

㉔ Click Save.

㉕ Click the Close button to close WordPad.

㉖ Click the Media Player Close button.

You don't have to include an entire video file in a document. You can also use the Start Selection and End Selection buttons to clip out a portion of the video file. If you do want to use a portion of a video file, you may also find the Scale ➤ Frames command helpful in locating the exact frames to copy. When you use this command, Media Player shows the frame numbers on the scale rather than the elapsed time.

NOTE

Whenever you include audio or video clips in a document, you must always be aware of the copyright issues. While you probably won't have too much to worry about if you include a small audio or video clip in a personal note to a friend, you need the permission of the copyright owner before you use a clip in a business presentation.

▶ Using TV Viewer

Windows 98 includes a new multimedia component called TV Viewer. If you have a special video adapter compatible with TV Viewer, then you can watch TV programming on your computer. Of course, you

Using TV Viewer

also need a special high-speed Internet connection, a digital cable television connection, or a digital satellite TV connection to see live programming. If you do have all the right pieces, you'll be able to receive high-definition digital TV, get gigabytes of data daily, and see enhanced TV shows that enable you to interact with the show using your computer.

Even if you don't have special video adapters and expensive data connections, you'll find you can still use some TV Viewer features. You can download TV program listings for your local viewing area and even have TV Viewer remind you when your favorite programs will be broadcast.

NOTE *TV Viewer is an optional component that you must install before you can use it. To install TV Viewer, double-click the Add/Remove Programs icon in the Control Panel. Click the Windows Setup tab, choose TV Viewer, and then click Apply.*

To try out TV Viewer, follow these steps:

1 Click the Start button.

2 Select Programs.

3 Select Accessories.

4 Select Entertainment.

5 Select TV Viewer.

6 Click Next.

7 Click Next again.

8 Click StarSight to continue.

9 Enter your postal code as directed by the dialog box that appears.

10 Click the Submit button after you've entered your postal code.

You must select which set of program listings to download. You'll probably have a different set of selections, but you should choose the set that most closely matches your viewing habits.

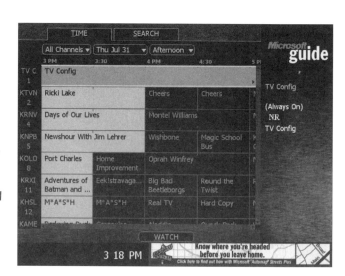

⑪ Select the program listings you wish to download.

⑫ Click Download to begin downloading your local listings.

⑬ Select Guide to view the program guide. As shown in the figure on the right, Programs are listed in a grid that shows the schedule for your local channels as well as a number of special TV Viewer channels.

⑭ Click the Search tab to display a list of categories.

⑮ To view the schedule for your favorite show, choose the show in the listing.

⑯ Click Other Times to find any additional times during the coming week when the show can be seen.

⑰ If you want to be reminded just before a program airs, select the program in the listing.

⑱ Click Remind to display the Remind dialog box.

⑲ Choose the reminder options you prefer.

⑳ Click OK to return to the program guide.

You can continue to look through the program guide for additional programs. As you select programs in the listings, notice that the Remind and Other Times buttons sometimes disappear and the Watch button appears. This indicates a program you may be able to watch on your computer screen.

㉑ Select Guide to return to the programming guide.

㉒ To close TV Viewer, press F10 and then click the Close button.

Because few PCs currently include the necessary hardware to enable viewing programs on screen, TV Viewer is primarily a program guide for now. It's clear, however, that Microsoft would like TV Viewer to be a whole lot more in the near future.

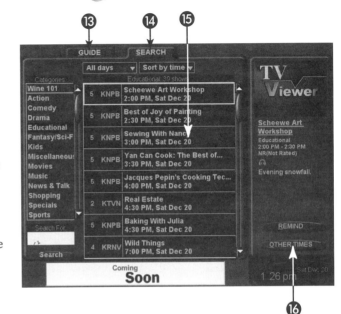

Using Imaging

Using Imaging

If TV Viewer seems to be a little ahead of its time, the Imaging tool will seem much more down-to-earth and useful. This utility enables you to scan images (if you have a Twain-compliant scanner), view faxes, and annotate images. You can, for example, view a fax you've received, add annotations to show your comments about a part of the fax, and then forward the fax to someone else for review.

NOTE *Most modern scanners are Twain-compliant. This is simply a standard that allows different brands of scanners to work with Windows programs so that you can scan directly into many applications. You don't need a scanner to use Imaging, but if you have a scanner, you can easily create and send faxes from almost any printed document.*

To try Imaging, follow these steps:

1 Click the Start button.

2 Select Programs.

3 Select Accessories.

4 Select Imaging.

5 Select File.

6 Select Open.

7 Choose your \Windows folder in the Look in list box.

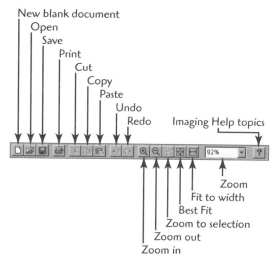

New blank document
Open
Save
Print
Cut
Copy
Paste
Undo
Redo
Imaging Help topics

Zoom
Fit to width
Best Fit
Zoom to selection
Zoom out
Zoom in

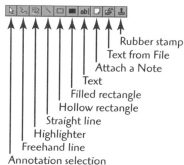

Rubber stamp
Text from File
Attach a Note
Text
Filled rectangle
Hollow rectangle
Straight line
Highlighter
Freehand line
Annotation selection

8 Double-click Setup.bmp to open the Setup image file. If you can't find this image file, choose a different one.

9 Click the Text tool button and drag a text box across the top of the image.

10 Type the following text: **I love learning about Windows 98**.

11 Click the Highlighter tool button.

12 Drag the highlighter over the text you just added to make the text stand out.

13 Select File.

14 Select Save As.

15 Type the following text in the File name text box: **My Setup**.

16 Click Save to save the image.

17 Click the Close button to close Imaging.

If you want, you can use the new image as desktop wallpaper. If the original image had been a fax that someone sent you, you could add your comments to the fax before sending it back or forwarding it to another person. After you save a modified image, any annotations you add become a permanent part of the image. If you need a copy of the original, unmodified image, be sure to use a new name when you save your modified copy.

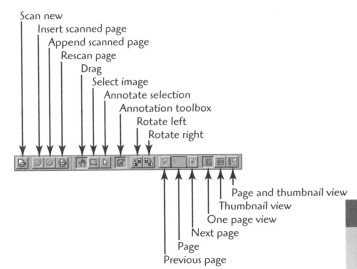

CONFIGURING MULTIMEDIA FOR PERFORMANCE

You can't get around the fact that multimedia uses a lot of your computer's power. To get the best performance from multimedia applications, you have to make certain your multimedia settings are adjusted correctly. Windows 98 gathers all the multimedia settings in one place, the Multimedia Properties dialog box, which you access through the Control Panel.

5

Lights, Action, Multimedia!

Adjusting Multimedia Settings

All of the primary multimedia settings are available on one of the five tabs of the Multimedia Properties dialog box shown in these figures.

Use the Audio tab to change sound settings.

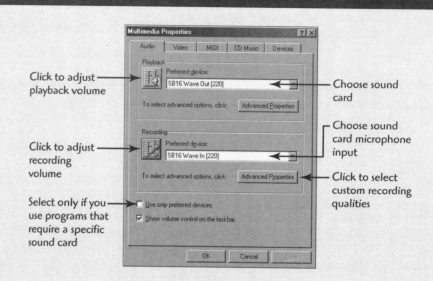

Click to adjust playback volume

Choose sound card

Click to adjust recording volume

Choose sound card microphone input

Click to select custom recording qualities

Select only if you use programs that require a specific sound card

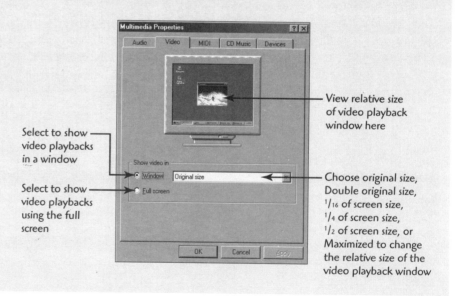

Use the Video tab to change the appearance of video playback.

Select to show video playbacks in a window

Select to show video playbacks using the full screen

View relative size of video playback window here

Choose original size, Double original size, $^1/_{16}$ of screen size, $^1/_4$ of screen size, $^1/_2$ of screen size, or Maximized to change the relative size of the video playback window

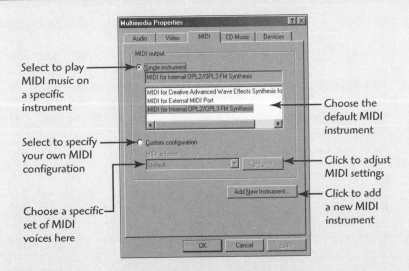

Select to play MIDI music on a specific instrument

Choose the default MIDI instrument

Select to specify your own MIDI configuration

Click to adjust MIDI settings

Choose a specific set of MIDI voices here

Click to add a new MIDI instrument

Use the MIDI tab to change sound synthesizer settings.

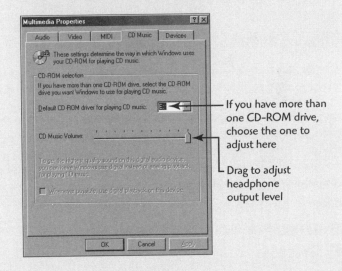

If you have more than one CD-ROM drive, choose the one to adjust here

Drag to adjust headphone output level

Use the CD Music tab to change how audio CDs are played.

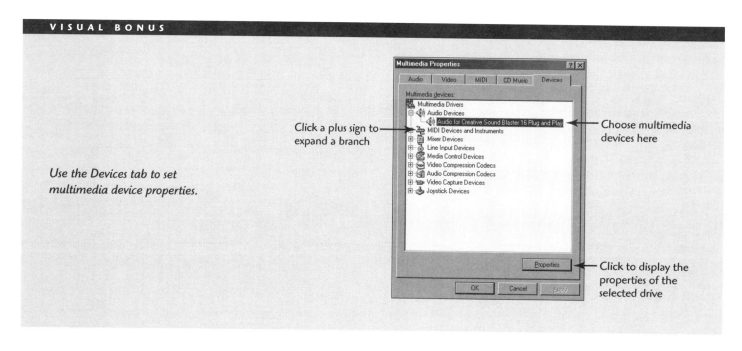

Click a plus sign to expand a branch

Choose multimedia devices here

Use the Devices tab to set multimedia device properties.

Click to display the properties of the selected drive

Adjusting your multimedia settings

You probably use some multimedia settings pretty often, such as the various volume-level settings. On other settings, such as the quality of sound recordings, you are likely either to use the default settings or to adjust them once and use the same settings most of the time. Still others, such as the *MIDI* — Musical Instrument Digital Interface — settings, are of little interest to anyone except those who use their PC to compose music. In this exercise you see how to adjust some of the more common multimedia settings.

1 Click the Start button.

2 Select Settings.

3 Select Control Panel.

4 Double-click the Multimedia icon to display the Multimedia Properties dialog box.

5 Select the Show volume control on the Taskbar checkbox. If the speaker icon ever disappears from the Taskbar, selecting this checkbox brings the icon back.

6 Click the Advanced Properties button to display the Advanced Audio Properties dialog box shown in the figure on the right. (You can use this dialog box to choose the type of recording you need.)

7 Drag the Hardware Acceleration slider to change the way your hardware records sounds. It's generally best to leave the Hardware Acceleration slider set to full unless you experience problems making recordings.

8 Drag the Sample Rate Conversion Quality slider to change the way sounds are sampled. (Higher sampling rates and more data bits usually result in higher-quality recordings, but they use more disk space.)

9 Click OK to return to the Multimedia Properties dialog box.

10 Click the Video tab to display the video playback window settings.

11 Choose a size for the video playback window in the Window list box. For the best performance and highest-quality image, choose Original size. Any other setting (including Full screen) results in a poorer-quality image and may make the video playback jerky.

12 Click the MIDI tab to view the MIDI settings. MIDI files, which share the extension of mid, are a type of music file that plays through your sound card or through an external digital musical instrument. (Unless you're a musician, you probably won't have any reason to change any of the MIDI settings.)

13 Click the CD Music tab to view the audio CD headphone settings. If you use headphones connected directly to your CD player, you can use this tab to adjust the volume.

14 Click the Devices tab to view all of the multimedia devices installed in your system. Depending on what is installed, some devices may have optional settings, but unless you know for certain that you should change a setting, it's best to leave them alone. Incorrect settings could make your multimedia features stop working.

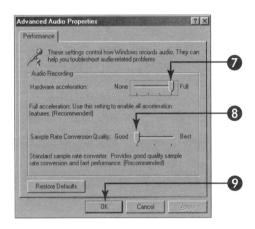

5

Lights, Action, Multimedia!

Skills challenge

15 Click the Close button to close the Multimedia Properties dialog box.

16 Click the Close button to close the Control Panel.

If you make any changes on either the MIDI or Advanced tabs of the Multimedia Properties dialog box, it's always a good idea to note which settings you changed, how they were set before your changes, and the new settings you selected. Include the date and time as well as a brief description of why you changed the settings. This type of record helps you return to the previous settings if you later discover that something is no longer working as you expect.

SKILLS CHALLENGE: MAKING MULTIMEDIA WORK!

Now it's time to try some of the skills you've learned in this lesson.

1 Play the Microsoft Sound wave file.

> **1** *How can you tell the length of a sound file without playing the file?*

> **2** *What artist created the Microsoft Sound?*

2 Add the first three seconds of the Microsoft Sound to a document.

3 Mute the playing of wave sounds.

> **3** *How can you quickly mute all sounds from your PC?*

4 Reenable the playing of wave sounds.

5 Record a message counting from one to ten.

6 Add an echo to your recording.

> **4** *How can you create the effect of having an echo occur before the sound?*

> **5** *How can you remove all changes from a sound recording?*

7 Enter a play list for an audio CD.

⭐**6** *How can you play the songs on an audio CD in reverse order of the way they appear on the CD?*

⭐**7** *How can you make the same set of songs play several times in a row?*

8 Find the current setting for audio recordings.

⭐**8** *How much disk space does the lowest quality PCM format audio recording require for each second of recording?*

9 Download your local TV listings.

10 Open a fax you've received and add a note to the file.

Troubleshooting

TROUBLESHOOTING

If you encounter problems while working through the exercises, here are some ideas that might help you correct the problems and keep going.

Problem	Solution
When I double-click a sound file, I see the Open With dialog box.	You need to install the Media Player from your Windows 98 CD-ROM. Double-click the Add/Remove Programs icon in the Control Panel, click the Windows Setup tab, select Multimedia ➢ Details, and click Media Player. Click OK and then Apply to add Media Player to your hard disk.
My volume control doesn't show the same set of controls shown in the figures.	You can choose which controls are displayed using the Options ➢ Properties command in the volume control menu.
I don't see the speaker icon on my Taskbar.	Select the Multimedia icon in the Control Panel, and make certain the Show volume control on the taskbar checkbox is selected on the Audio tab.

WRAP UP

Multimedia is a lot of fun. In this lesson you learned how to play both audio and video files as well as how to record your own audio files. You also learned how you can use clips from audio or video files in your documents and how you can adjust your multimedia settings to make your PC perform a bit better.

The next lesson gets back down to business and shows you how to install and uninstall programs on your Windows 98 system. It also shows you how to make those old DOS applications work a little better under Windows 98.

Installing and Uninstalling Programs

45 MINUTES

GOALS

Your PC probably came with a number of programs already installed. However, there's no reason for you to use only what's already there and miss out on newer, more capable programs as they become available. Windows 98 makes installing programs a whole lot easier than it used to be, but there are still quite a few considerations in making the process go smoothly. Removing old programs is another task that is easier in Windows 98, but you still need to watch out for a number of potential pitfalls. This lesson guides you along the path and shows you how to keep the problems associated with installing and removing programs to a minimum.

- Installing Windows applications

- Removing Windows applications

- Adding additional Windows components

- Using MS-DOS applications

Get ready

GET READY

To complete this lesson you need the CD-ROM that accompanies this book. You work with the shareware program, ThumbsPlus, and two sample programs, InstallS.exe and Wolf.com, all of which are in the Lesson 6 folder. You also need your Windows 98 CD-ROM so you can install some of the optional components of Windows 98. You may find a printer handy but not absolutely necessary; you can view information onscreen if you can't produce a printout.

INSTALLING WINDOWS APPLICATIONS

In the early days of personal computing, installing a program was fairly easy. If you had enough disk space, you just installed the program and ran it. Of course, each program you installed had to support every piece of your PC or you'd be out of luck. If the program's manufacturer didn't know about your type of printer or monitor, there was a pretty good chance you wouldn't be able to use the program, or at least not to its fullest extent. As bad as that sounds, things got even worse if you wanted to upgrade to a new piece of hardware. Unless the software manufacturer was willing to add support for new hardware, you were probably stuck with your old equipment as long as you wanted to keep using your existing software. You couldn't, for example, upgrade to a new laser printer, a fancy color printer, a higher-resolution monitor, or even a faster modem because your old software didn't support any of those new items.

Although most people look at Windows — Windows 98 or the older Windows versions — and think the graphical user interface is the biggest change between Windows and MS-DOS, there are actually many other changes that are possibly more important under the surface. One of the biggest changes is the difference in the way Windows programs and MS-DOS programs deal with the various components of your system. While MS-DOS programs need to provide direct support for each component, Windows programs only need to know how to communicate with Windows itself. Windows then communicates with the individual components. Your Windows program doesn't have to know anything about your new color holographic-data-sculpting output device, as long as the manufacturer of the device provides drivers so Windows knows how to work with the device.

Adding new Windows 98 programs

What does this all have to do with installing Windows programs? Quite a bit, actually. Because Windows programs don't need to know as much about your PC and its hardware components as MS-DOS programs had to, Windows programs share a lot of software components. This sharing means that some of the pieces a Windows program needs may already be on your system and in use by several other programs. Of course, this also means that removing a program you no longer need may be a bit more complicated; any shared components may still be needed by another program.

But leaving aside for now the issue of removing programs, consider what happens when you install a program that uses shared components. Suppose you want to install program B, which uses a shared component XX.dll. You already have program A installed, and it uses XX.dll, too. If both programs use the same version of XX.dll, there's no problem. But what if there's a newer version of XX.dll, and it happens to be the one installed along with program A? You wouldn't want program B to install the older version and perhaps make program A not function correctly anymore. Well-designed installation programs are supposed to watch for these types of conflicts, but knowing about the potential problems can help you resolve any problems that do pop up.

NOTE *When this lesson refers to programs designed for Windows 98, it's a pretty safe bet that programs designed for Windows 95 will work, too. Although there may be a few Windows 95 programs that won't work correctly in Windows 98, nearly all Windows 95 programs should have no trouble functioning in Windows 98.*

Adding new Windows 98 programs

There are two primary types of Windows programs you may want to install and use on your PC — those designed for Windows 98 and those designed for Windows 3.x. Microsoft created an entire series of guidelines for software manufacturers to follow when creating programs for Windows 98. Some of the most important guidelines relate to how software is installed. Briefly, when you install new programs on your PC, the main items you should be concerned with are whether the program recognizes when newer versions of shared components are already installed, and whether the program includes a method for uninstalling the program.

*The **Windows 98 One Step at a Time** CD-ROM contains a **shareware** program that is used in this exercise. Shareware is a method of software distribution that enables you to try out the software before you buy it. If you decide you like the software and want to continue using it, you must register the shareware with the software author or manufacturer. In some cases, such as the ThumbsPlus software used in this exercise, you receive additional features or functions when you register the software.*

In this exercise you practice installing a program designed for Windows 98 — ThumbsPlus. This is a shareware program that you can use to browse, convert, organize, view, edit, and catalog graphics files. The installation program you use to install ThumbsPlus has some special features. When you install ThumbsPlus, you can choose to place the shared Windows 98 components used by ThumbsPlus in either the ThumbsPlus folder or in the \Windows\System folder. In addition, ThumbsPlus does not automatically assume you always want to use it to view every graphics file. While you may not fully appreciate these features right now, the longer you use your PC, the happier you'll be that some considerate programmers give you the installation options you have with ThumbsPlus.

1. Place the *Windows 98 One Step at a Time* CD-ROM into your CD-ROM drive.

2. Click the Start button.

3. Select Settings.

4. Select Control Panel.

Don't forget to single-click rather than double-click if you have the Active Desktop enabled.

5 Double-click the Add/Remove Programs icon to display the Add/Remove Programs Properties dialog box. The list box in the lower portion of this dialog box shows the Windows 98 programs installed on your system, and you probably won't have the same set of programs shown in the figure.

6 Click the Install button to display the Install Program From Floppy Disk or CD-ROM dialog box.

7 Click Next to continue. Windows 98 then looks for an installation program on a diskette or in the root folder of the CD-ROM. When you install programs that come on their own CD-ROMs, the installation program is usually called something like Setup.exe or Install.exe and is located in the root folder.

8 Because ThumbsPlus is not in the root directory of the CD-ROM, click Browse to display the Browse dialog box.

9 Click the down arrow at the right edge of the Look in list box.

10 Choose the Lesson 6 folder.

11 Choose thmpls32.EXE. (Because you're installing a new program, the Files of type list box displays only program files.)

12 Click Open to continue.

13 Click Finish to begin installing ThumbsPlus.

The figure on the right shows how your screen appears once the installation program begins. Notice that the installation program covers up your desktop. Some installation programs also hide the Taskbar.

14 Click Next to continue. Generally you have the option of choosing a destination folder for the program installation. You can click the Browse button to choose a different folder, or click Next to continue.

15 You can choose to place ThumbsPlus in its own nested menu under the Programs selection on the Start menu, or you can choose to place ThumbsPlus in another menu.

16 Select the Add a ThumbsPlus icon on the desktop, too checkbox if you'd like to have a ThumbsPlus icon on your desktop.

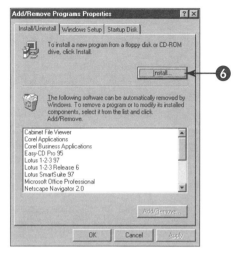

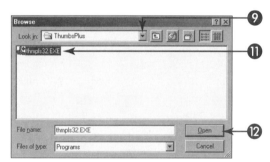

6

Installing and Uninstalling Programs

⑰ Click Next to continue.

⑱ Choose where to install the shared Windows components.

You can choose to install them in the \Windows\System folder or in the ThumbsPlus program folder. If you choose to install these files in the \Windows\System folder, they are shared by other Windows 98 programs. Installing these files in the ThumbsPlus program folder uses a bit more disk space, but it is easier to uninstall the ThumbsPlus program — you won't have to worry whether any other programs are using the files.

⑲ Click Next to continue.

⑳ After you've made all the installation decisions, you're ready to install the program. Click Next to continue, or Back if you want to change any of your selections.

After the installation program finishes installing ThumbsPlus, the Installation Completed message is displayed, as shown in the figure on the right.

㉑ Select the Show me the release notes checkbox so you can see any special information about the program. Not all installation programs include release notes or README files, but when you're given the option to view this type of information, it's always a good idea to view it.

㉒ Click Finish to exit the installation program.

㉓ Click the Close button to close the ThumbsPlus Release Notes screen.

㉔ Check your success by double-clicking the ThumbsPlus icon on your desktop.

㉕ When the credits screen appears, click the thumb icon in the upper-left corner to view the program. (You can learn how to use ThumbsPlus by selecting Help ➢ Contents.)

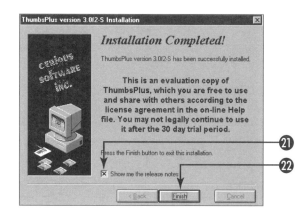

Installing Windows 98 programs using the Add/Remove Programs icon in the Control Panel is fairly straightforward. Not all programs give you as much control over the installation process as ThumbsPlus does. If a program is designed for Windows 98, however, it should at least enable you to choose where to install the program, to choose where the program appears in the menu, and to uninstall the program without too much trouble.

Using old Windows applications in Windows 98

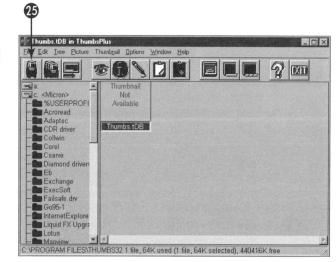

Although programs specifically designed for Windows 95 or Windows 98 generally offer additional features compared to older programs, most programs designed for Windows 3.*x* can still be run in Windows 98. Quite often, however, these older programs lack many of the modern conveniences, such as an uninstall option. If you really need to use an older Windows program — perhaps because a Windows 98 version isn't available — you can probably install the program in Windows 98. You should take a few precautions to protect yourself, however, in case you have problems or later decide you don't want the old program cluttering your hard disk anymore.

In this exercise you learn how to create a log of the changes made to your system when you install a program. This log won't include everything that an installation changes, but it shows you which files were added or changed by the installation. The log is especially helpful if, after you install an older program, you later discover that some of your existing programs no longer work. Generally, this type of problem can be traced to the replacement of one of the shared files with an older version lacking in some of the enhancements that are present in the newer version.

Rather than actually installing an old program, you simulate installing a program by adding a file to your \Windows\System folder — the folder where most installation problems can be found.

1 Click the Start button.

2 Select Programs.

3 Select MS-DOS Prompt to display the MS-DOS Prompt window. You can use this window to enter the commands to create your before and after logs.

4 Type in the following command: **DIR \Windows\System /on > Filesbefore.txt**.

5 Press Enter.

This command creates a text file named Filesbefore.txt that contains a sorted listing of the files in the \Windows\System folder before you install the program. If you're lucky, you won't need to search through this file — it lists hundreds of files!

6 To simulate installing a program that places files in the \Windows\System folder, type the following command: **COPY Filesbefore.txt \Windows\System\Filesbefore.txt**.

7 Press Enter to make a copy of Filesbefore.txt in the \Windows\System folder.

If you were actually installing a program, you would use the Add/Remove Programs dialog box to install the program, as you did in "Adding new Windows 98 programs" earlier in the chapter, and follow through the installation program steps until the program installation was complete. Then you would return here and continue with the next step.

8 Type the following command: **DIR \Windows\System /on > Filesafter.txt**.

9 Press Enter.

This creates a text file named Filesafter.txt that contains a sorted listing of the files in the \Windows\System folder after you install the program.

10 Type the following command: **FC /L /LB99 /N Filesbefore.txt Filesafter.txt > Filechanges.txt**.

11 Press Enter.

This creates a text file named Filechanges.txt, showing you the changes that occurred when you installed the new program.

12 To print a copy of the changes, type the following command: **COPY Filechanges.txt PRN**.

13 Press Enter.

You should write the date, time, and name of the program you just installed on the printout for future reference.

14 To view a copy of the changes onscreen, type the following command: **TYPE Filechanges.txt**.

⑮ Press Enter.

The figure on the right shows how the before and after differences show up in Filechanges.txt. An extra file, filesbefore.txt, appeared in the 115th line, and the directory listing showed 616 files instead of 615 files.

⑯ Type the following command and press Enter to close the MS-DOS prompt window: **EXIT**.

You won't find every change an installation program makes to your system using this method, but you can get a pretty good idea of any major changes that were made. Be sure to continue on to Step 8 immediately after you finish installing the program; otherwise, you won't know for certain that the installation program made the changes you logged. Also, keep in mind that for this method to be useful, you must start the entire procedure from the beginning each time you add new software.

Okay, so you have a printed log of the changes made by an installation program — so what? What good is the printout? If one or more of your programs don't work properly after you install another program, the chances are pretty good that the problem is one of the files that was changed in the \Windows\System folder. Your printout not only shows any new files, but it also shows you any files that have a different size or date. If you call a software technical support line for assistance, knowing what changes were made saves a lot of time in getting to the bottom of the problem. Tell the technical support person that you installed some additional software, and inform the person of the changes you logged. I'm sure he or she will find a solution many times faster with this important information.

TIP

Don't forget the new System File Checker utility if you have a problem after installing a new program. Lesson 2 showed you how to use this important tool to help resolve program installation problems.

6

Installing and Uninstalling Programs

```
MS-DOS Prompt                                      _ □ ×
 Auto

C:\WIN95>TYPE Filechanges.txt
Comparing files Filesbefore.txt and filesafter.txt
****** Filesbefore.txt
  114:  FDECTSP   DLL    116,640  09-02-96  4:52p Fdectsp.dll
  115:  FILESEC   VXD     23,025  07-11-95  9:50a FILESEC.VXD
****** filesafter.txt
  114:  FDECTSP   DLL    116,640  09-02-96  4:52p Fdectsp.dll
  115:  FILESB-1  TXT     35,546  04-29-97  3:29p filesbefore.txt
  116:  FILESEC   VXD     23,025  07-11-95  9:50a FILESEC.VXD
******

****** Filesbefore.txt
  627:  XLCALL32 DLL      5,120  09-27-95 12:00a XLCALL32.DLL
  628:         615 file(s)   50,154,347 bytes
  629:           7 dir(s)   457,539,584 bytes free
****** filesafter.txt
  628:  XLCALL32 DLL      5,120  09-27-95 12:00a XLCALL32.DLL
  629:         616 file(s)   50,189,893 bytes
  630:           7 dir(s)   457,375,744 bytes free
******

C:\WIN95>
```

Removing a Windows 98 program

REMOVING WINDOWS APPLICATIONS

Removing a program should be easy. When you no longer use an old program and want to free up some disk space, you can just delete the program's folder, right? Actually, no. Removing Windows programs is seldom that easy. Because of the way Windows programs share components and the way Windows 98 stores important configuration information, removing old programs can be quite complicated.

Windows 98 uses a special database called the *Registry* to keep track of important information. When you install a program, change your screen saver settings, swap your mouse buttons, or make any other change that's important for Windows 98 to remember, the information is stored in the Registry. When you uninstall a program, you have to use the correct method so Windows 98 can properly update the Registry and adjust the way Windows 98 works when the old program is gone.

Removing a Windows 98 program

In this exercise you see how easy it is to remove a program designed for Windows 98 and installed using the Add/Remove Programs icon. You uninstall ThumbsPlus, which you installed from the CD-ROM earlier. Don't worry—you can always go back and reinstall ThumbsPlus after you've completed this exercise.

1. Click the Start button.

2. Select Settings.

3. Select Control Panel.

4. Double-click the Add/Remove Programs icon.

5. Choose ThumbsPlus from the list of programs that can be removed, as shown in the figure on the right. When you select a program from this list, the Add/Remove button becomes active.

6. Click the Add/Remove button to continue.

   The figure on the next page shows the first uninstall screen for ThumbsPlus. Each program's uninstall screen is different, so if you uninstall other programs, you have to watch the prompts carefully to make certain you know what is happening.

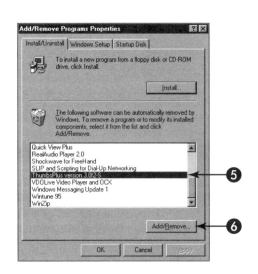

7 Select the Automatic radio button.

8 Select Next to continue.

9 Click Finish to uninstall the program.

Once the program has been removed, you may see a series of screens similar to the figure on the right.

10 Click Yes to delete all the shared files.

In this case the shared files were installed in the ThumbsPlus program folder rather than the \Windows\System folder, so it's highly unlikely any other programs are actually using these copies. You should be safe in deleting all the shared files by clicking Yes for each one. If the shared files were installed in the \Windows\System folder, however, you might want to make note of each one in turn, and decline to delete them. Later you could move them to the Recycle Bin, and if everything still works, delete them from the Recycle Bin after several days.

You probably want to reinstall ThumbsPlus now that you know how easy it is to install and uninstall a program designed for Windows 98. Other programs have different install and uninstall routines than the ones used to install and uninstall ThumbsPlus, of course. Some programs, especially the large, multiapplication office suites, have very complex sets of options that enable you to customize the operation to suit your exact needs. Regardless of the number of options you need to select, always make certain you read and understand the prompts before you continue from one screen to the next.

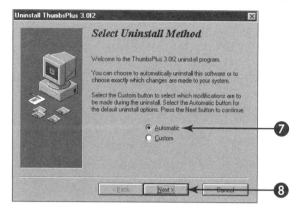

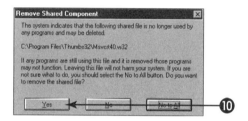

Taking out the garbage

Not all uninstall operations go quite as smoothly as the one you practiced in the last exercise. You may encounter a number of problems that leave behind garbage—files and folders that serve no useful purpose—to clutter up your hard drive. That's when you need to do some cleanup work if you don't want to continue wasting space on the leftovers from programs you no longer use.

The Lesson 6 folder on the *Windows 98 One Step at a Time* CD-ROM contains a sample installation program for this exercise. This sample installation program installs a small program file onto your

Taking out the garbage

hard disk but does not include an uninstall program, which is what you'd probably encounter if you were to install old Windows programs that aren't designed for Windows 98. As a result, you have to uninstall the sample program as part of the exercise. To simulate the problems you may encounter in uninstalling programs that don't include an uninstall program, the installation program places another file on your hard disk, too.

To practice uninstalling programs that lack uninstall programs, follow these steps:

1 Place the CD-ROM that accompanies this book into your CD-ROM drive.

2 Click the Start button.

3 Select Programs.

4 Select MS-DOS Prompt.

5 Type the following command: **DIR \Windows\System /on > Filesbefore.txt**.

6 Press Enter.

7 Click the Start button.

8 Select Programs.

9 Select Windows Explorer.

10 Choose the Lesson 6 folder on the CD-ROM.

11 Double-click InstallS.exe to begin the program installation. The message shown in the figure on the right appears on your screen.

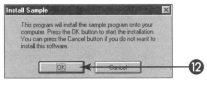

12 Click OK to display the Select Destination Directory dialog box. This dialog box informs you that the sample program will be placed in the C:\Program Files\SampleProgram folder. It doesn't tell you the whole story, however, so you need to do a little detective work to clean up when you uninstall the sample program.

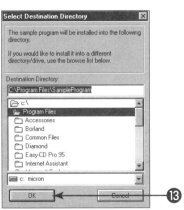

13 Click OK to complete the installation.

14 Go back to the MS-DOS Prompt window.

15 Type the following command: **DIR \Windows\System /on > Filesafter.txt**.

16 Press Enter.

17 Type the following command: **FC /L /LB99 /N Filesbefore.txt Filesafter.txt > PRN**.

18 Press Enter.

In this instance the report shows that no changes were made to the \Windows\System folder, so you don't have to worry about that folder's contents when you uninstall the sample program.

19 Type the following command: **EXIT**.

20 Press Enter to close the MS-DOS prompt window.

21 Open the C:\Program Files\SampleProgram folder to see what was installed.

In this case the program is named Wolfie.com, a program created for this exercise that simply opens and immediately closes an MS-DOS prompt window when double-clicked. In addition to Wolfie.com, the folder also contains a file named Install.log. Like many old Windows programs, however, the installation program created another file that is located in another directory. Before programs were designed for Windows 98, many Windows programs stored their settings in a file with an .ini extension, so our example does as well.

22 Click the Start button.

23 Select Settings.

24 Select Control Panel.

25 Double-click the Add/Remove Programs icon and look for Wolfie in the list of programs Windows 98 can automatically uninstall. (Because our sample program wasn't designed for Windows 98, it's not in the list, and you have to uninstall the program yourself. But first you want to find the .ini file. In most cases the .ini file has the same name as the program file, so the file you want to find is probably called Wolfie.ini.

26 Click the Close button to close the dialog box.

Taking out the garbage

㉗ Click the Start button.

㉘ Select Find.

㉙ Select Files or Folders.

㉚ Type the following text in the Named text box: **Wolfie.***.

㉛ Click Find Now to locate the files.

In this case Windows 98 finds two files, Wolfie.com in the C:\Program Files\SampleProgram folder, and Wolfie.ini in the C:\Windows folder. Now you know where the extra file was installed—your \Windows folder.

㉜ Right-click Wolfie.ini.

㉝ Select Delete from the pop-up menu. (Depending on your Recycle Bin settings, you may also have to click Yes to delete the file.)

㉞ Click the Close button to close the Find dialog box.

㉟ Return to the Windows Explorer window.

㊱ Choose the SampleProgram folder.

㊲ Click the Delete button. (If the Delete Confirmation dialog box appears, click Yes. If you see a message telling you that Wolfie.com is a program and you might not be able to edit some files if it is deleted, click Yes to delete the file.)

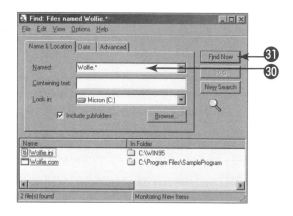

Successfully removing old Windows programs not designed for Windows 98 takes quite a bit more effort than uninstalling Windows 98 programs. Although this exercise showed you some of the pitfalls, there were other issues that simply could not be reliably addressed. If the installation program had made changes to the \Windows\System folder, for example, you would have no way to know for certain that it was safe to remove any files that were added to that folder. You're probably safe in removing any extra files added to the \Windows\System folder when you immediately uninstall programs as you did in this exercise. However, you can't be certain that the files are safe to remove if you have added any additional programs between installing the sample program and uninstalling it.

Installing extra Windows components ◄

TIP

Your computer retailer has programs available that are designed specifically to aid you in uninstalling programs. While these programs are often more capable than the Windows 98 Add/Remove Programs component, you should keep in mind that these uninstaller programs work best if you use them before you install programs you may want to uninstall. That's because the uninstaller program needs to keep track of any changes made to your system.

ADDING ADDITIONAL WINDOWS COMPONENTS

You might be surprised to learn that all of Windows 98 probably isn't installed on your PC. There are a number of optional components you may want to try out, and you'll be pleased to know they're as close as your Windows 98 CD-ROM. In the following exercises you learn how to find and install the additional pieces of Windows 98.

► *Installing extra Windows components*

You install the optional Windows 98 components by selecting them from the various groups on the Windows Setup tab of the Add/Remove Programs Properties dialog box. Table 6-1 lists the optional components you find in each of the component groups. A few of these options, notably the disk compression tools, disappear from the component group after you've installed the option, because these options cannot be removed once installed.

Optional Windows components

TABLE 6-1 OPTIONAL WINDOWS COMPONENTS

Group	Option	Description
Accessibility Options	Accessibility Options	Features to assist disabled users
Accessibility	Enhanced Accessibility	A screen-magnification tool and mouse options
Accessories	Briefcase	Used to synchronize files on two computers
Accessories	Calculator	An onscreen calculator
Accessories	Desktop Wallpaper	Bitmap images you can use on your desktop
Accessories	Document Templates	Assists with creating new documents
Accessories	Games	Windows 98 games to waste your time
Accessories	Imaging	Graphics viewer and Twain scanner support
Accessories	Mouse Pointers	Different mouse pointers you can select
Accessories	Paint	A drawing program
Accessories	Quick View	Enables you to view documents even if you don't have the original program
Accessories	Screen Savers	Enable you to disguise your screen
Accessories	Windows Scripting Host	Task-automation tool
Accessories	Windows 98 Tour	A basic Windows 98 tutorial
Accessories	WordPad	A simple word processor

Group	Option	Description
Broadcast Data Services	Broadcast Data Services	Announcement Listener, Webcast Client, TV Enhancements
Communications	Dial-Up Networking	Enables you to use a modem
Communications	Dial-Up Server	Enables you to access your computer remotely
Communications	Direct Cable Connection	Enables you to connect using a serial or parallel cable
Communications	HyperTerminal	A program for communicating with other computers
Communications	Infrared	Enables you to use wireless infrared devices
Communications	Microsoft Chat 2.0	Enables you to connect to other people via a chat server
Communications	Microsoft NetMeeting	Enables you to communicate over your network or the Internet
Communications	Phone Dialer	Dials your phone through your modem
Communications	Virtual Private Networking	Enables you to connect to your network privately via the Internet
Desktop Themes	Several desktop themes	Provides many different ways to change the appearance of Windows 98
Internet Tools	Microsoft FrontPad	A tool for creating Web sites

continued

6

Installing and Uninstalling Programs

Optional Windows components

TABLE 6-1 (continued)

Group	Option	Description
Internet Tools	Microsoft FrontPage Express	A free version of FrontPage, the Web site editor
Internet Tools	Microsoft VRML 2.0 Viewer	A tool to enable you to see virtual worlds on the Internet
Internet Tools	Microsoft Wallet	Enables you to buy things securely on the Internet
Internet Tools	Personal Web Server	Enables you to host your own Web site
Internet Tools	Web Publishing Wizard	Helps you load your Web pages on a server
Internet Tools	Web-Based Enterprise Management	Enables remote work-station administration
Microsoft Outlook Express	Microsoft Outlook Express	Enables you to use e-mail and read news
Multilanguage Support	Baltic	Estonian, Latvian, and Lithuanian languages
Multilanguage Support	Central European language support	Albanian, Czech, Croatian, Hungarian, Polish, Romanian, Slovak, and Slovenian languages
Multilanguage Support	Cyrillic language support	Bulgarian, Belarusian, Russian, Serbian, and Ukrainian languages
Multilanguage Support	Greek language support	Greek language
Multilanguage Support	Turkish language support	Turkish language

Optional Windows components

Group	Option	Description
Multimedia	Audio Compression	Enables you to record and play compressed audio files
Multimedia	CD Player	Enables you to play audio CDs
Multimedia	DVD Player	Enables you to play DVD movies
Multimedia	Macromedia Shockwave Director	Plays Macromedia Director files
Multimedia	Macromedia Shockwave Flash	Plays Macromedia Flash files
Multimedia	Media Player	Enables you to play audio and video files
Multimedia	Microsoft NetShow Player 2.0	Enables you to play NetShow streaming multimedia broadcasts
Multimedia	Multimedia Sound Schemes	Additional sounds
Multimedia	Sample Sounds	Additional sounds
Multimedia	Sound Recorder	Enables you to record and play sounds
Multimedia	Video Compression	Enables you to record and play compressed video files
Multimedia	Volume Control	Enables you to adjust sound levels
Online Services	AOL	America Online
Online Services	AT&T WorldNet Service	AT&T WorldNet
Online Services	CompuServe	CompuServe
Online Services	Prodigy Internet	Prodigy Internet
Online Services	The Microsoft Network	The Microsoft Network

continued

TABLE 6-1 *(continued)*

Group	Option	Description
System Tools	Backup	Backs up files
System Tools	Character Map	Used to insert characters and symbols into documents
System Tools	Clipboard Viewer	Displays contents of the Clipboard
System Tools	Drive Converter	Converts hard disks to FAT32 file system
System Tools	Group policies	Enables an administrator to establish policies for a workgroup
System Tools	Net Watcher	Enables you to see who is accessing your PC on a network
System Tools	System Monitor	A tool for checking system performance
System Tools	System Resource Meter	A tool for checking system resources
System Tools	WinPopup	Enables you to send messages on a network
TV Viewer	TV Viewer	TV Viewer, Program Guide

Some of these optional components are probably already installed on your PC. For this exercise you install the Multimedia Sound Schemes, a component you probably haven't installed previously.

1 Place your Windows 98 CD-ROM in your CD-ROM drive.

2 Click the Start button.

3 Select Settings.

4 Select Control Panel.

5 Double-click the Add/Remove Programs icon.

6 Click the Windows Setup tab to display the Components list box in the Add/Remove Programs Properties dialog box.

You can tell which items are already installed by looking at the checkboxes. An empty checkbox means the component is not installed. A white checkbox with a check means the component is completely installed. A gray checkbox with a check means the component is partially installed.

7 Select the Multimedia checkbox.

8 Click Details to view the individual multimedia components you can choose.

If the Details button in this dialog box is grayed out, there are no further options for the selected item. If the Details button is not grayed out, you can make further selections by again clicking the Details button.

9 Select the Multimedia Sound Schemes checkbox.

10 Click OK to return to the Add/Remove Programs Properties dialog box. If you wish to add additional components, select them now.

11 Click Apply to copy the added components from the Windows 98 CD-ROM.

12 Click the Close button to close the Add/Remove Programs Properties dialog box.

You can just as easily remove most of the optional Windows 98 components. To remove a component you no longer need, click the Add/Remove Programs Properties dialog box's Windows Setup tab and deselect the component's checkbox. When you click Apply, Windows 98 removes the component from your hard disk. Unfortunately, Windows 98 sometimes simply marks the item as removed without actually erasing it from your hard disk — you just have to take your chances on this one.

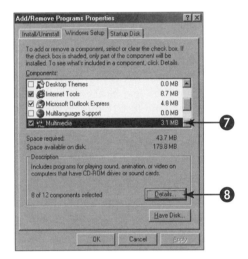

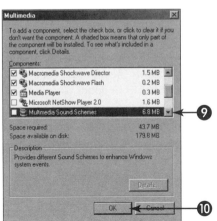

Using the MS-DOS command prompt

USING MS-DOS APPLICATIONS

Even though Windows 98 programs are generally easier to use than MS-DOS programs, there are still some tasks that simply can't be done in the Windows 98 graphical environment. Certain game programs, for example, won't run properly in Windows. Also, you might need to use an old business program that only runs under MS-DOS. Finally, there are some MS-DOS commands that simply have no equivalent in Windows 98 itself.

Using the MS-DOS command prompt

It's important to realize that Windows 98 has two distinct methods you can use to run MS-DOS commands and programs. This exercise deals with the first method, which is to run the *MS-DOS prompt* at the same time as the Windows 98 graphical environment. Using this method, you can switch back and forth between MS-DOS programs and Windows 98 programs, and you can even share data via the Clipboard. Most MS-DOS programs are quite happy to run this way, and it's by far the easiest method to use.

The second exercise shows you how to use *MS-DOS mode*, in which your entire system is dedicated to running the MS-DOS program. Running programs in MS-DOS mode can be a lot more work for you, however, and you cannot run Windows 98 while you're operating in MS-DOS mode.

1 Click the Start button.

2 Select Programs.

3 Select MS-DOS Prompt.

The figure on the right shows the MS-DOS Prompt window. If your MS-DOS prompt hides your entire Windows 98 desktop so only the MS-DOS prompt is visible, press Alt+Enter to switch the MS-DOS prompt to a window.

4 Type the following text: **DIR *.exe > PRN**.

5 Press Enter.

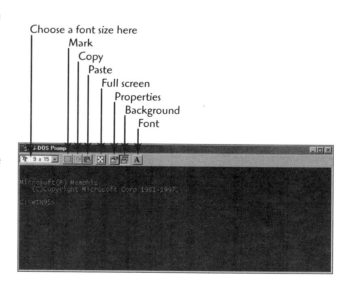

Choose a font size here
Mark
Copy
Paste
Full screen
Properties
Background
Font

Using the MS-DOS command prompt ◀

This MS-DOS command prints a list of all the application programs in the current folder. This is an example of a task that is easy to accomplish using MS-DOS commands but difficult to do within Windows 98 itself. In the Windows 98 graphical environment, there's no simple way to print out a file listing.

6 Click the Start button.

7 Select Programs.

8 Select Accessories.

9 Select WordPad to open a new, blank document.

10 Click the MS-DOS Prompt button on the Taskbar to return to the MS-DOS Prompt window.

11 Type the following text: **DIR /on /b *.bmp**.

12 Press Enter.

13 Click the Mark button.

14 Drag the mouse pointer to highlight the filenames.

If you make a mistake, point to the first letter of the first file, hold down the left mouse button, and drag the mouse pointer down and to the right again until you successfully highlight all the file information.

15 Click the Copy button to copy the selected data to the Clipboard.

16 Click the WordPad button on the Taskbar.

17 Select Edit.

18 Select Paste to paste a copy of the data from the MS-DOS prompt into the WordPad document.

This shows how easy it is to copy information from the MS-DOS prompt to a Windows 98 program. You can also copy information from a Windows 98 program to the MS-DOS prompt, but you may need to copy one line at a time when going in that direction.

19 Click anywhere within the MS-DOS Prompt window to bring the MS-DOS Prompt window to the front.

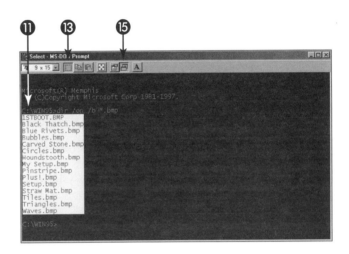

Using the MS-DOS command prompt

20 Click the down arrow at the right edge of the font selection list box.

21 Select 4 × 6 to change the font size in the MS-DOS Prompt window to four pixels wide by six pixels high. Notice that the MS-DOS Prompt window shrinks to a much smaller size and the text becomes very difficult to read.

22 Select 10 × 18 in the font selection list box. Notice the appearance of the type in the MS-DOS Prompt window.

23 Next, select 11 × 18 in the font selection list box.

11 × 18 is one of the *TrueType* fonts — scaleable fonts — so the appearance of the text is better than the 10 × 18 selection. Depending on your display driver, you may have choices other than 11 × 18 — if so, choose a TrueType font in a similar size.

24 Type the following text: **DIR *.bmp**.

25 Press Enter to display a listing of the Windows bitmap files in the current folder.

26 Compare the short filenames in the first column of the listing to the long filenames shown in the last column. When you use most MS-DOS programs (as well as older Windows programs not designed for Windows 98), you must use the short filename. In the MS-DOS Prompt window, you can use either name with MS-DOS commands, but remember to enclose long filenames that include spaces within quotation marks. That is, entering the command **COPY Black Thatch.bmp A:** generates an error message Too many parameters that tells you Windows 98 didn't understand that you wanted to copy the file to a diskette. The correct command would be **COPY "Black Thatch.bmp" A:**.

27 Click the Close button to close the MS-DOS Prompt window.

28 Click the Close button to close WordPad, too. (You can discard the changes in the document.)

If you need to run MS-DOS programs, always try running them in the MS-DOS Prompt window first before you resort to using MS-DOS mode. You may need to press Alt+Enter to run the MS-DOS program full screen, but you can still switch back to your Windows 98

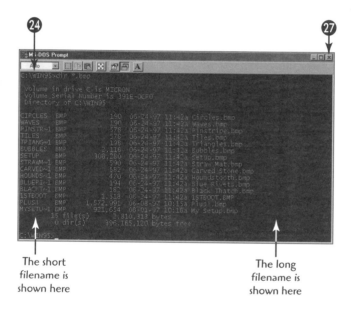

The short filename is shown here

The long filename is shown here

programs by holding down Alt while you press Tab. Each time you press Tab, another of your programs is selected. Release the Tab key when the program you want to use is selected. Press Ctrl+Esc to display the Start menu.

Using MS-DOS mode

When nothing else seems to work, MS-DOS mode may be the key to allowing finicky MS-DOS programs to run on your Windows 98 PC. When you run MS-DOS mode, MS-DOS programs think they're running in plain old MS-DOS. If you have an MS-DOS program that won't run even in MS-DOS mode, it's time to think about dumping the overly picky program and getting something designed for modern PCs.

NOTE *Depending on the specific brand and model of your CD-ROM drive, you may need to load special drivers to access your CD-ROM drive while your PC is operating in MS-DOS mode. Because each CD-ROM drive is different, you have to examine your owner's manual or call the CD-ROM drive technical support line for assistance if you absolutely must access your CD-ROM drive while in MS-DOS mode. Windows 98 includes special drivers that enable most CD-ROM drives to work in MS-DOS mode, but you may still have to edit CONFIG.SYS and AUTOEXEC.BAT to enable those drivers.*

In this exercise, you use the program Wolf.com in the Lesson 6 folder on the CD-ROM accompanying this book to simulate an MS-DOS program that requires MS-DOS mode to run. It's not possible to determine in advance if you are able to access your CD-ROM drive in MS-DOS mode, so you can begin by copying the Wolf.com file to your hard disk. Then you adjust the various settings to enable you to run Wolf.com in MS-DOS mode.

1 Place the CD-ROM into your CD-ROM drive.

2 Click the Start button.

3 Select Programs.

4 Select Windows Explorer.

Using MS-DOS mode

5 Choose your CD-ROM drive.

6 Open the \Lesson 6 folder.

7 Right-click Wolf.com.

8 Select Copy from the pop-up menu.

9 Right-click the \Windows folder on your C drive.

10 Select Paste from the pop-up menu.

11 Right-click Wolf.com.

12 Select Properties from the pop-up menu to display the Properties dialog box General tab. This tab shows very basic information about an MS-DOS program.

13 Click the Program tab. You can make a number of setting changes on this tab, such as specifying parameters for the program in the Cmd line text box. For this exercise you won't need to make any adjustments, however.

14 Click Advanced to display the Advanced Program Settings dialog box. This dialog box contains the important options you use to specify that the program must run in MS-DOS mode.

15 Select MS-DOS mode, and make certain Warn before entering MS-DOS mode is also selected.

Because all other applications must be shut down before you enter MS-DOS mode, it's pretty important to be warned so that you don't lose unsaved data in any programs you may have open. For this example you can select the Use current MS-DOS configuration, because Wolf.com doesn't require any special settings. If you select Specify a new MS-DOS configuration, you can create both a CONFIG.SYS and AUTOEXEC.BAT file just for the particular MS-DOS-mode program.

16 Click OK to continue.

When you select MS-DOS mode, you cannot select any additional settings because Windows 98 won't be controlling programs you run in MS-DOS mode. The figure on the right shows how the Font tab appears for programs that run in MS-DOS mode. The

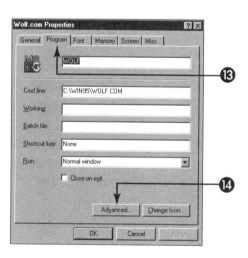

Memory, Screen, and Misc tabs all show the same message shown in this figure, because none of those settings are supported in MS-DOS mode, either.

⑰ Click OK to close the Properties dialog box and save your changes.

⑱ Make certain all other programs are closed and that you have saved any open files, and then double-click the Wolf.com program icon. Windows 98 displays the warning message that appears in the figure on the right.

⑲ Click Yes to run Wolf.com in MS-DOS mode.

When the program runs, your Windows 98 desktop and Windows Explorer both disappear, your screen turns blue, and the following message is displayed: `Windows is now restarting.` If Wolf.com had been a program that actually did anything, you wouldn't see the Windows is now restarting message until you exited from the program. Wolf.com simply turns the MS-DOS screen blue with yellow text and then exits.

Because MS-DOS mode shuts down Windows 98 and allows only a single program to run at a time, you should avoid using MS-DOS mode if possible. If you cannot find a Windows 98-compatible program, at least try to find an MS-DOS program that doesn't require everything else to shut down.

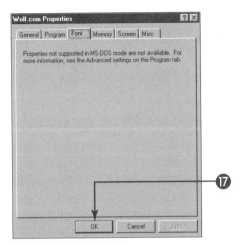

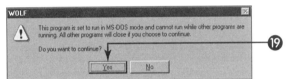

SKILLS CHALLENGE: INSTALLING AND RUNNING PROGRAMS

Now it's time to try out some of the skills you've learned in this lesson.

❶ Install ThumbsPlus.

❷ Install the Multimedia Sound Schemes.

❸ Determine whether the WinPopup accessory is installed.

❹ Install InstallS.exe.

 How can you tell whether a program you installed can be uninstalled using Add/Remove Programs?

Skills challenge

 Which folder generally holds shared program components?

5 Remove the program Install5.exe added to your system and all its related files.

 How can you find the configuration files used by old Windows programs?

6 Add the Help program from the old MS-DOS programs folder on your Windows 98 CD-ROM to the C:\Windows\Command folder.

 How can you find out what additional program is needed to run the MS-DOS Help program?

7 Change the properties for Wolf.com so the program runs at the MS-DOS command prompt rather than in MS-DOS mode.

 How can you run Wolf.com and then run another MS-DOS command in one MS-DOS session?

8 Copy a list of the names of all files in the \Windows folder with a .com extension into a WordPad document.

 How can you print a list of filenames without first copying the list into WordPad?

 What do you need to include in an MS-DOS command if you want to use a long filename that includes spaces?

TROUBLESHOOTING

If you encounter problems while trying to work through the exercises, here are some ideas that might help you correct the problems and keep going.

Problem	Solution
My MS-DOS Prompt window doesn't have buttons to click at the top of the screen.	Right-click the MS-DOS Prompt window title bar and then click Toolbar.
There is no title bar at the top of the MS-DOS Prompt window.	Press Alt+Enter to run the MS-DOS prompt in a window instead of full screen.
When I click the Close button on an MS-DOS window, I see a message telling me Windows 98 cannot close the program.	You need to close the MS-DOS program yourself before you can close the MS-DOS window. Look on the program's menu to find an exit command (or something similar) that closes the program.
When I run Wolf.com, Windows 98 shuts down without any warning.	Make certain the Warn before entering MS-DOS mode checkbox is selected in the Advanced Program Settings dialog box.

WRAP UP

Installing and removing programs is more work than fun, but knowing how to install and remove programs correctly saves you a lot of work and frustration in the long run. In this lesson you learned some tricks that make the whole process less of an ordeal, and you also learned how to make certain you have the information that can help solve problems when things don't work out quite right.

Wrap Up

This lesson also showed you that you're probably missing quite a few interesting pieces of Windows 98, and you learned how to add those missing pieces to your PC. Along the way you discovered how to remove some of those items you never use so it's easier to find what you really want.

In the next lesson you learn how to use WordPad to create something more than the simple files you've seen so far. Because WordPad is essentially a small version of Microsoft Word, you can do quite a bit more with WordPad than you probably realize.

Creating a Letter with WordPad

45 MINUTES

GOALS

You probably have the impression that WordPad isn't much more than a simple text editor. It's funny how far off the mark first impressions can be sometimes. WordPad is a very useful word-processing program. It's true that WordPad lacks some of the more sophisticated features of a full-blown word processor, but you may be surprised by some of the fancy things you can do with WordPad. This lesson gives you pointers on the following:

- Customizing WordPad

- Working with text

- Changing a document's appearance

- Printing a document

Get ready

GET READY

To complete this lesson you need to have WordPad installed and access to a printer. A color monitor is helpful, but if you use a system with a monochrome display, you can simply skip the short section on using color. If your printer can print in color, you can create colorful output, but if your printer is limited to black and white, you can still use color in your onscreen documents.

This lesson uses The Dog and the Shadow.doc (Dog_Shdw.doc), a document found in the Lesson 7 folder on the *Windows 98 One Step at a Time* CD-ROM. When you finish the exercises in this lesson, you will have changed the appearance of this document by adding color, inserting tabs, inserting a date line, and changing the paragraph formatting. You also will have learned how to insert bullets into a list of items by creating the document Bullets.doc.

MAKING WORDPAD WORK YOUR WAY

Do you ever get frustrated because something just doesn't work the way you think it should? It's a lot harder to get much done when you're fighting with a tool that just doesn't work quite right. Even little things can be annoying when you're trying to get some work done and you have to keep working around the problems. Fortunately, you can customize WordPad in a number of useful ways and eliminate some of the frustration of trying to be productive.

Setting WordPad's options

WordPad understands several different types of files and stores separate settings for five types of files. This allows WordPad to work differently when you open a Word document than when you open a simple text document, for example. This also enables you to create your own different settings for each of the five types of files WordPad automatically recognizes.

WordPad has a few settings that apply to all types of files, so you only have to make your selections once and these settings apply to all documents you open or create in WordPad. You probably wouldn't want to use inches as your measurement unit in one type of document and centimeters in another, so it's pretty sensible to make this selection only once.

To view and change WordPad's options, follow these steps:

1 Click the Start button.

2 Select Programs.

3 Select Accessories.

4 Select WordPad.

5 Select View.

6 Select Options to display the Options dialog box.

7 Click the Options tab to display it. The settings on this tab apply to all file types.

8 To choose a different unit of measurement for the ruler, select Inches, Centimeters, Points, or Picas. *Points* and *picas* are *typographic* measurements. There are approximately 72 points in an inch, and 6 points in a pica.

9 Select the Automatic word selection checkbox if you want WordPad to select entire words as you drag the mouse pointer onto a new word.

If you deselect this checkbox, WordPad selects a single letter at a time. At first you may have a hard time understanding how automatic word selection works. Automatic word selection only happens when you already have at least one character selected and you drag the mouse pointer across a space and onto a new word. When you do, WordPad selects the entire original word and the entire new word.

10 Click the Text tab to display the options for text files. Each of the four remaining tabs has the same options, except there is no Status bar option available for embedded files.

11 Select the *Word wrap* option you prefer. Word wrap refers to the action WordPad uses to display lines longer than the width of the WordPad window.

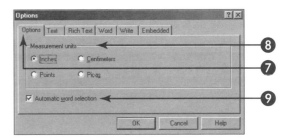

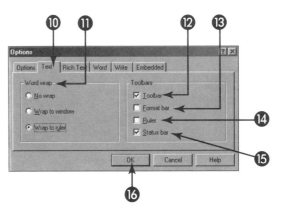

Setting WordPad's options

- *No wrap* allows long lines of text to disappear off the right side of the WordPad window. WordPad displays a horizontal scrollbar when text lines are too wide to fit in the WordPad window.

- *Wrap to window* makes all the text fit within the WordPad window by moving text that would go past the right edge of the window onto a new line. As you resize the WordPad window, WordPad readjusts the line breaks to always display as much text on one line as possible without going past the edge of the window.

- *Wrap to ruler* uses the *ruler* — the measurement line just above the text window — to determine where to break the lines of text. If the WordPad window is too narrow to show the complete lines, WordPad displays a horizontal scrollbar so you can view the remaining text.

⑫ Select Toolbar to include the toolbar just below the WordPad menu line. The toolbar contains a number of useful buttons you can click rather than always using menu commands.

⑬ Select Format bar to display the Format bar below the toolbar. You can use the Format bar to change the appearance of the text, but you cannot save formatting in text files. You must save the file in one of the other file formats if you want to save the formatting.

⑭ Select Ruler to display the ruler. You can use the ruler to set tabs, change the overall width of text lines, and view the final printed appearance of your document before printing.

⑮ Select Status bar to display the document status at the bottom of the WordPad window. The figure on the right shows the WordPad window with all the Toolbars options selected.

⑯ Click OK to close the Options dialog box and return to WordPad.

WordPad saves any changes you made and uses them the next time you open a document of that type. You can have different settings for each of the five file types, so if you prefer not to see the Format bar and ruler for text files, you can still have them visible for any of the other types of files.

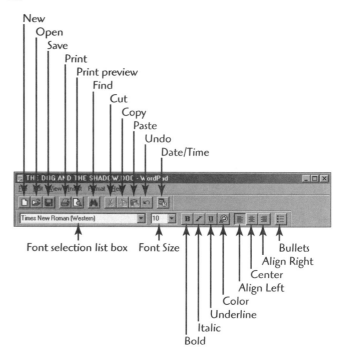

New
Open
Save
Print
Print preview
Find
Cut
Copy
Paste
Undo
Date/Time

Font selection list box   Font Size

Bullets
Align Right
Center
Align Left
Color
Underline
Italic
Bold

Changing the page options

NOTE *WordPad has different options for the different file types because each type of file has different formatting capabilities. Text files, for example, don't contain information on character formatting, so there's no reason to display the Format bar if you're editing a text file.*

Changing the page options

Paper comes in many different sizes, and you probably have occasion to print documents using different layouts. In WordPad you can choose the exact layout you need as long as the settings you choose are compatible with your printer.

TIP *Check your printer manual before adjusting the page options to see what paper sizes and minimum margin settings your printer supports.*

To select the page options for your document, follow these steps:

1 Select File.

2 Select Page Setup to display the Page Setup dialog box.

3 Click the down arrow at the right edge of the Size list box to expand the list of available paper sizes. Of course, you should choose the size of the paper you really intend to use — just because a paper size is shown in the list doesn't mean it's really available.

4 Click the down arrow at the right edge of the Source list box to expand the list of paper sources. This option is only effective if your printer actually has the different paper trays listed. If your printer can only use paper from a single tray, you may not even see the Source list box.

5 Select the Portrait radio button to print with the paper in the normal orientation for letters — tall and narrow.

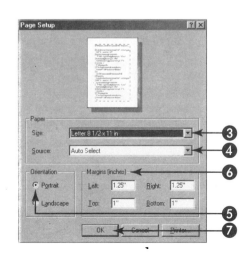

7

Creating a Letter with WordPad

Entering some text

Select the Landscape radio button if you want to swap the print orientation so that the paper is short and wide. You probably won't have to do anything to the paper when you swap the paper orientation, because Windows 98 generally knows how to change the print orientation automatically.

6 Enter the margin settings in the Left, Right, Top, and Bottom text boxes. Margins are the distance printing begins from the edge of the paper. As you change margin settings, the sample page in the top of the dialog box shows a representation of the new settings. Your printer probably has a minimum margin setting. For example, laser printers generally cannot print closer than .25 inches from the edge of the paper.

7 Click OK to close the Page Setup dialog box and return to WordPad.

8 Click the Close button to close WordPad.

Although the standard page settings are a pretty good starting point, you may want to experiment to see the effects different settings have on the appearance of your documents. You aren't locked into the first options you choose because you can always go back and change to a new set at any time.

WORKING WITH TEXT

Working with text is the whole point of using a word processor, so in the following exercises you enter some text, move it around, and replace words. You can do simple typing with a typewriter, but nothing beats a word processor when you want to make changes to existing text. Rather than retyping entire pages, you can create and modify your document onscreen using your keyboard and mouse.

Entering some text

In this exercise you enter a short piece based on Aesop's fable "The Dog and the Shadow" that intentionally contains several errors. These errors provide the opportunity to use WordPad's editing features for correction.

1 Click the Start button.

2 Select Programs.

3 Select Accessories.

4 Select WordPad.

5 Select File.

6 Select New to display the New dialog box.

7 Choose Word 6 Document as the type of document to create.

This document type provides the best formatting options of the three available types and is most useful in the exercises that follow. Rich Text Document format has nearly as many formatting options, while Text Documents retain no text-formatting information. Text Document format is the best choice for creating and editing files such as AUTOEXEC.BAT and CONFIG.SYS — two system files that are sometimes needed to configure PCs.

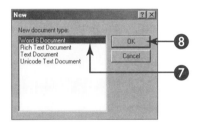

8 Click OK to return to WordPad.

TIP *If you don't want to type the document yourself, you can find Dog_Shdw.doc in the Lesson 7 folder on the Windows 98 One Step at a Time CD-ROM.*

9 Type the following text: **The Dog and the Shadow**.

10 Press Enter twice to end the title line and leave a blank line before the beginning of the body text.

11 Type the following text, making certain you do not correct any errors: **It happened that a Dog had got a piece of meet and was carrying it home in his mouth to eat it in peace. As he crossed, he looked down and saw his own shadow reflected in the water beneath. Now on his way home he had to cross a plank lying across a running brook. Thinking it was another dog with another piece of meat, he made up his mind to have that also. So he made a snap at the shadow in the water, but as he opened his mouth the piece of meet fell out, dropped into the water and was never seen more.**

Moving and copying text

⑫ Press Enter twice to end the paragraph and create another blank line.

⑬ Type the following text: **Beware lest you lose the substance by grasping at the shadow.**

TIP *If you opened Dog_Shdw.doc in the Lesson 7 folder, you'll have to select File ➤ Save As so you can save the file on your hard disk.*

⑭ Select File.

⑮ Select Save.

⑯ Type the following text in the File Name text box: **The Dog and the Shadow**.

⑰ Click Save to save the file and return to WordPad. Your screen should now look like the figure on the right. If necessary, drag the edge of the WordPad window to widen the window so you can see the entire white area of the ruler.

Notice that after you save the file, WordPad displays the filename in the title bar. Always save your work often so you don't accidentally lose work if there's a power failure or a user error (you wouldn't close WordPad without saving your work, would you?).

▶ Moving and copying text

When you typed the fable in the last exercise, you may have thought that some of the text was out of place. If so, you win the gold medal! The second and third sentences were swapped, making the fable somewhat mixed up. In this exercise you correct that error by moving and copying text.

❶ If necessary, open The Dog and the Shadow.doc in WordPad.

❷ Drag the mouse pointer to select the second sentence, "As he crossed, he looked down and saw his own shadow reflected in the water beneath."

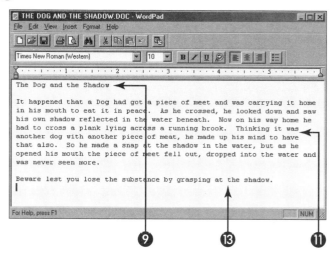

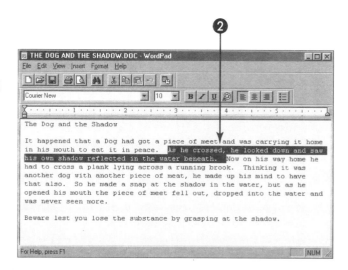

3 Release the mouse button after you've selected the entire sentence.

4 Move the mouse pointer into the selected selection, and hold down the left mouse button.

5 Drag the second sentence to just behind the third sentence.

6 Release the mouse button to drop the sentence into the correct location.

7 Right-click the selection.

8 Select Copy from the pop-up menu to copy the sentence to the Clipboard.

9 Click in the blank space between the third and fourth sentences to move the *insertion pointer* — the blinking cursor that indicates where new text will appear — between those two sentences. The insertion pointer appears as a slowly blinking vertical line.

10 Click the Paste button to insert a copy of the sentence you copied to the Clipboard into the text starting at the insertion point.

11 Click the Undo button to remove the extra copy of the sentence.

If you make a mistake, always make certain you immediately click the Undo button or select Edit ➢ Undo before you do anything else. After you've made another change to the text or selected another command, it's too late to undo any changes you made in error. If you wait too long to use the Undo button, you have to correct the error manually.

12 Click the Save button to save your changes.

You can also use the Edit ➢ Cut and Edit ➢ Paste commands (or the right-click Cut and Paste equivalents) to move text selections, but if you can see both the source and target locations on the screen, drag & drop is probably a little faster and easier to use.

Finding and replacing text

Your copy of The Dog and the Shadow is looking quite a bit better, but there are still some errors to be corrected. In a short document such as this one, you can easily find and replace the errors yourself,

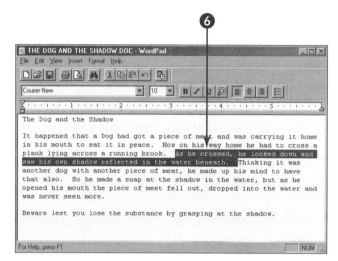

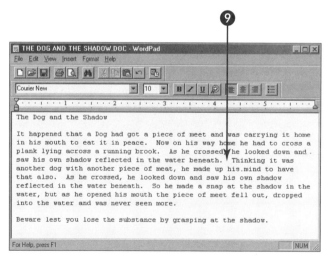

Creating a Letter with WordPad

7

Finding and replacing text

but in a longer document it's pretty handy to have WordPad locate the errors for you. The errors left in the document are two instances where you entered the word **meet** instead of **meat**. In this exercise you learn how to tell WordPad to find and replace words and phrases.

1 If necessary, open The Dog and the Shadow.doc in WordPad.

2 Select Edit.

3 Select Replace to display the Replace dialog box.

Edit ➢ Find works almost like Edit ➢ Replace, except that you don't have the option of specifying a replacement word or phrase.

4 Type the following text in the Find what text box: **meet**.

5 Type the following text in the Replace with text box: **meat**.

Your dialog box should now look like the figure on the right.

6 Click Find Next to locate the first instance of the word "meet" in the document. Find Next selects the word but doesn't replace it.

7 Click Replace to replace the incorrect word with the correct one and locate the next instance, as shown in the figure on the right.

8 Click Replace to replace this instance of the incorrect word and continue to search for additional instances. Because WordPad cannot find any more instances of "meet" in the document, the message shown in the figure on the right is displayed.

9 Click OK to confirm the message and return to the Replace dialog box, because you don't have any more words to replace.

10 Click Close to return to WordPad.

11 Click the Save button to save your work.

You may be wondering why you didn't just click the Replace All button to replace all copies of "meet" with "meat" at once. Because "meet" is actually a correctly spelled word, there's a possibility that it might be used correctly somewhere in your document. You wouldn't want to write a memo telling your boss that you were going to "meat a client" would you? It's much safer to use Replace All only when the word or phrase you're replacing clearly is not an actual word that might legitimately appear in your document.

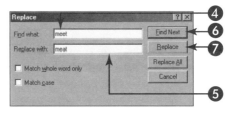

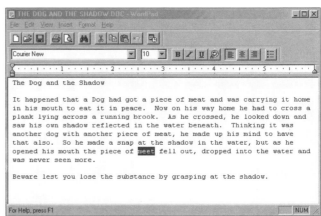

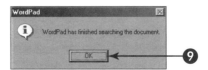

Using different characters

> **TIP**
>
> *You can use Edit ➤ Replace to make WordPad automatically type long or difficult phrases. Whenever you need to include your special phrase, just enter a sequence of characters that would never appear in normal text, such as x#@, and then use Replace All to change that sequence throughout your document.*

CHANGING THE DOCUMENT'S APPEARANCE

Okay, now you have a corrected copy of the Dog and the Shadow fable, but it just doesn't look too fancy, does it? With just a few steps you can turn the plain-looking text in your document into something that really reaches out and grabs the reader. In the following exercises you see how you can make your copy of the fable look quite special.

Using different characters

No, you're not going to replace the dog in the fable with your favorite politician, you're going to see how to use some different fonts, font sizes, and a few other font characteristics to make the fable look a bit fancier. Windows 98 uses *TrueType* fonts, which are fonts that can be *scaled* — displayed in a number of different sizes — and that appear the same onscreen and in the printed document. (You learn a lot more about fonts in Lesson 9.)

> **NOTE**
>
> *If you can't find the exact fonts used in this exercise, choose a different font. Windows 98 comes with a number of standard fonts, but not all fonts are available on every PC.*

1 If necessary, open The Dog and the Shadow.doc in WordPad.

2 Press Ctrl+A to select the entire document.

3 Click the down arrow at the right edge of the Font Selection list box.

4 Choose Times New Roman.

If you have more than one font labeled Times New Roman, select the one with two T's to the left, indicating a TrueType font. If there's more than one of those, select the one that says Western. This changes the entire document to the Times New Roman TrueType font.

5 Select the title line by dragging the mouse pointer across the first line of the document.

6 Choose 16 in the Font Size list box to increase the title line to 16-point type.

7 Select the last line of the document.

8 Click the Bold button to change the font to bold.

9 Click the Italic button to add the italic attribute to the font.

10 Click the Underline button to apply that attribute as well.

11 Press the End key to move the insertion point to the end of the line.

12 Click the Save button to save your changes.

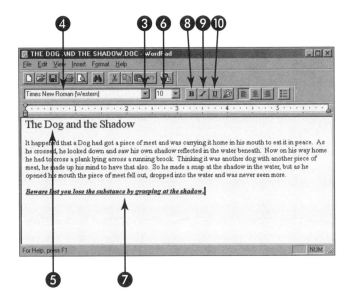

Your document looks a lot more lively after just a few simple changes. You may not have noticed one of the more subtle differences that resulted from the change from Courier New to Times New Roman — your document looks a bit softer and a little less mechanical. Careful font selection can result in a number of small improvements like this one.

Adding some color

Color is something most people don't usually consider when they think about what they can do to change the appearance of their documents. Until color inkjet printing started to become more common in the past few years, nearly all PC printers gave you any color you wanted — as long as you wanted black. Many people now have the option of adding a bright splash of color or maybe just a

Adding some color

subtle tint to their documents. Even if you lack a color printer, however, you probably have a color monitor and can use color to spice up your onscreen views.

To add color to your document, follow these steps:

1. If necessary, open The Dog and the Shadow.doc in WordPad.
2. Select the title line of the document.
3. Click the Color button.
4. Click Lime to change the title to a bright lime-green color.
5. Press the End key to remove the highlight from the title line. (You won't be able to see the effects of your color selection until you remove the highlight from the selection.)
6. Click the Save button to save your changes.

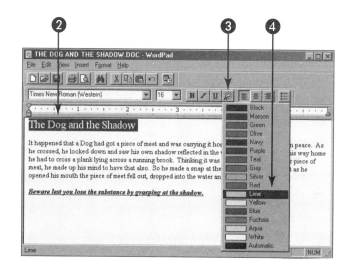

Although the color selection list shows 17 choices, in WordPad the Black and Automatic choices produce identical results. White is generally a poor choice because white text on a white background is invisible.

Don't fall into the trap of using too many colors simply because you can use them. Too many colors make your document garish and detract from its readability.

Keeping tabs

Tabs are a handy little tool in your word-processing bag of tricks. Tabs are fixed points you use to specify precise text positioning. If you've ever tried to line up text by pressing the spacebar, you know that there has to be an easier way to make your text line up the way you want. Tabs are that answer. If you want to line up a list of words indented exactly one inch from the rest of your text, you can use a tab to do the job. If you want to create two or more columns in your list, tabs are the answer here, too, because you can set multiple tabs on your ruler.

To practice setting tabs, follow these steps:

1. If necessary, open The Dog and the Shadow.doc in WordPad.
2. Select the main paragraph of the document.
3. Click the 1" mark on the ruler to place a tab at that point.

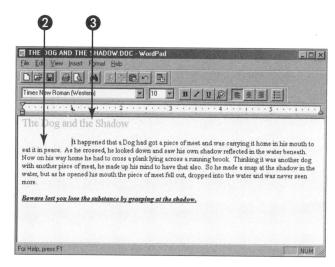

Keeping tabs

4 Press the Home key to move the insertion point to the beginning of the paragraph. (If you don't remove the selection by moving the insertion point, your text will be replaced when you press another key to insert a tab or a character. If this happens, be sure to click Undo immediately.)

5 Press the Tab key to indent the first line of the paragraph to the first tab position.

6 Select Format.

7 Select Tabs to display the Tabs dialog box.

8 Click the tab listed as 1". Because only one tab was set, you can clear the tab by clicking Clear All. If you had set additional tabs, you would need to select the tab you want to clear.

9 Click Clear to remove the tab you set. You can also drag tabs off the ruler to clear them.

10 Click OK to return to WordPad.

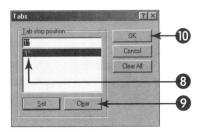

Were you surprised that the indent of the first line of the paragraph changed from 1 inch to ½ inch? If you don't set tabs manually, WordPad automatically places tabs every ½ inch. These automatic tabs aren't visible on the ruler, but they exist even if you can't see them.

11 Click the Save button to save your work.

Tabs work with any font. You've probably noticed that different fonts use different amounts of space for the same characters. That's one reason why using the spacebar to align lines of text doesn't work too well. If you use tabs, you can be sure the alignment works out correctly.

Making a date

Dates and times are often an important part of a document. You probably show the current date when you write a letter, and adding the current date and time to a memo can help ensure that you can keep track of a sequence of events. Rather than checking the correct date and time, why not just let WordPad enter the information automatically?

To add the date or time to a document, follow these steps:

1 If necessary, open The Dog and the Shadow.doc in WordPad.

2 Press Ctrl+End to move the insertion point to the end of the document.

3 Press Enter twice to insert a blank line and move to the beginning of a new line.

4 Click the Date/Time button to display the Date and Time dialog box. Your dialog box should show the current data and time when you're doing the exercise. Times are shown at the bottom of the Available formats list box.

5 Select the full day name, month name, day number, and year choice in the Available formats list box.

6 Click OK to add the date to your document.

Notice that the date is formatted in bold, italic, underlined characters. When you moved the insertion point to the end of the document, WordPad assumed you wanted to continue with the current formatting, which at that point was bold, italic, underlined characters.

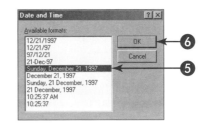

7 Drag the mouse pointer across the date entry to select the entire line.

8 Click the Bold button to remove the bold attribute from the date entry.

9 Click the Italic button to remove the italic attribute from the date entry.

10 Click the Underline button to remove the underline attribute from the date entry.

11 Click Save to save your changes.

The date or time you add to your WordPad document is a static entry — it won't change as the actual date and time change. To update the date or time shown in your document, select the date or time and click the Date/Time button again. Select your choice of formats and click OK to update the entry.

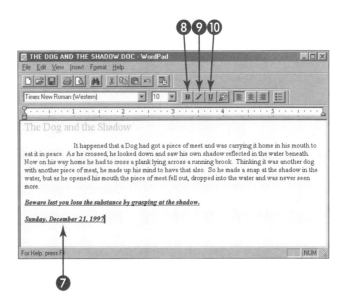

Changing paragraph formatting

▶ Changing paragraph formatting

In WordPad, paragraph formatting refers to *alignment* — whether the text is flush with the left or right margins or centered between them — and *indents* — extra distance between the document margins and the paragraph margins. In this exercise you see examples of each of these options.

1 If necessary, open The Dog and the Shadow.doc in WordPad.

2 Move the insertion point to the beginning of the main paragraph and press Home.

3 Press Delete to remove the tab and begin the first line flush with the left margin. This enables you to better see how indents work.

4 Select Format.

5 Select Paragraph to display the Paragraph dialog box.

6 Type the following text in the Left text box: **1.5″**.

This indents the left edge of the paragraph 1 ½ inches from the left document margin.

7 Type the following text in the Right text box: **1″**.

This indents the right edge of the paragraph 1 inch from the right document margin.

8 Type the following text in the First line text box: **.5″**.

This indents the first line of the paragraph ½ inch from the left edge of the rest of the document. Your dialog box should look similar to the figure on the right.

9 Click OK to return to WordPad.

10 Move the insertion point into the title line. It's not necessary to select the line.

11 Click the Center button to change the title line alignment to centered between the margins.

12 Move the insertion point into the last line of the fable (the line that ends with the word "shadow").

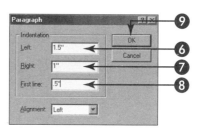

⓭ Click the Right button on the toolbar to align the line flush with the right margin. (You may need to drag the WordPad window borders a little to view the entire document.)

⓮ Click Save to save your work.

No one can say your document looks dull now! Of course, few people would say the combination of formatting, indents, alignment selections, and so on looks all that good combined as they now appear. You probably shouldn't look on the current document settings as a shining example of exceptional document design. Probably the best thing you can say is that you've learned about the range of options you can use in WordPad documents.

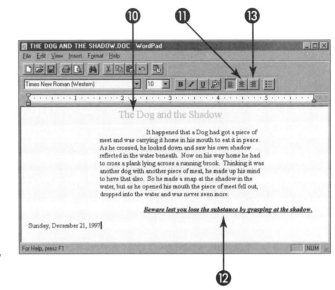

Duck, we're using real bullets

Bullets are those markers you often see at the left of a list of summary points. You use bullets to make each point stand apart from the remaining points. In this exercise you learn how to create a bulleted list in a WordPad document.

❶ If necessary, open WordPad.

❷ Select File.

❸ Select New.

❹ Select Word 6 Document.

❺ Select OK.

❻ Type the following text: **In WordPad, you can use the following options to modify the document appearance:**

❼ Press Enter twice.

❽ Click the Bullets button. WordPad inserts a bullet and moves the insertion point to the first tab position.

❾ Type the following text and press Enter: **Different characters**.

When you press Enter, WordPad moves the insertion point to the first tab position on the next line and inserts a bullet at the beginning of the line.

⑩ Type the following text and press Enter: **Colors**.

⑪ Type the following text and press Enter: **Alignment**.

⑫ Type the following text and press Enter: **Indents**.

⑬ Click the Bullets button to stop the bulleted list.

⑭ Click the Save button and save your documents as Bullets.doc.

You don't have to create a bulleted list from scratch. You can change a list of items into a bulleted list by selecting the list and clicking the Bullet button. When you click the Bullet button, WordPad adds a bullet at the beginning of each paragraph. You begin a new paragraph by pressing Enter. Items in a bulleted list can span more than one line, but only the first line of each individual item has a bullet. When bulleted items span more than one line, each line is lined up at the first tab position.

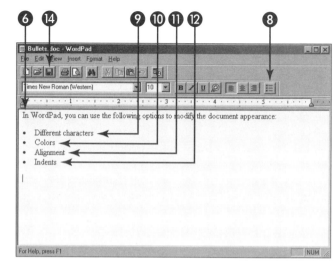

PRINTING A DOCUMENT

It's pretty hard to share your documents without printing them. The paperless office that many people thought would result from everyone using computers is still far from reality. It's likely that you need to print copies of most of your documents, so the following brief exercises show you some of the basics of printing in Windows 98.

Selecting your printer

If your PC is connected to a network, you may have several printers to choose from when you want to print a document. If you're not connected to a network, you may be surprised to learn that you may have more than one choice, too. It's likely that you have a fax/modem board installed in your PC, and it probably shows up as a fax option in the printer selections. You can even have the option to print documents to printers not connected to your PC.

TIP

To create a print file for a printer not connected to your PC, use the Add Hardware icon in the Control Panel to add the printer. When you're asked to specify where the printer is connected, click File. Windows 98 then asks for a filename for the print file whenever you print to this printer. You can copy the print file to the PC connected to the printer, and print the file on that system.

You need to use a little imagination to complete this exercise. You probably won't have the same printer options shown in the exercise, so you need to choose from what's available on your system. The point of the exercise isn't to select the exact same printer or printer options shown in the figures, but rather to learn how you can select your printer and its options.

1 Open The Dog and the Shadow.doc in WordPad.

2 Select File.

3 Select Page Setup.

4 Select Printer to display the Page Setup dialog box with the printer selection options.

5 To see which printers are installed on your system, click the down arrow at the right edge of the Name list box. You also choose the printer you want to use from this list box.

6 To set the options for the currently selected printer, click Properties. The figure on the right shows a typical printer's Properties dialog box. In this case the printer is an HP LaserJet 4 Plus. Each type of printer has different options. The best way to learn what each option does is to click the question mark icon in the dialog box title bar, and then click the option to see a short description of the option.

7 Click OK to close the Printer Properties dialog box.

8 Click OK twice more to return to WordPad. Any changes you made are saved and used the next time you print a document.

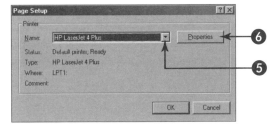

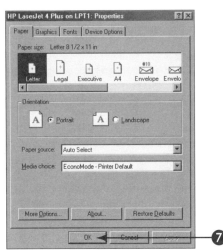

7

Creating a Letter with WordPad

Previewing and printing documents

If you have more than one printer, check to see which printer is selected before you begin printing so you aren't surprised when your document prints on a printer other than the one you expect. This may be especially important if you're printing a copy of your resume — you wouldn't want that to print on the network printer down the hall!

Some Windows 98 applications change the Windows 98 default printer when you select a different printer in the Page Setup dialog box, while others change only the printer setting for the one application. You should make a habit of always checking which printer is selected before you begin a print job.

Previewing and printing your document

A funny thing often happens when people see a printed copy of their document — they often find something that isn't quite right and should really be fixed before the final copy is printed. If this sounds like the way you do things, this exercise shows you how to cut down on wasted paper by viewing a copy of the printout onscreen before you print. There's no reason to end up with piles of waste paper simply because of an error you can easily catch using the onscreen print preview.

1 If necessary, open The Dog and the Shadow.doc in WordPad.

2 Click the Print Preview button to display the print preview window.

3 Click the Zoom In button to magnify the view so you can see the text a little better. You can zoom in one more level, or zoom out to see more of your document.

Examine your document to see if it appears to be ready to print. The dotted lines in the print preview represent the current margin settings. Don't worry if some of the text seems to be missing at the ends of the lines — Windows 98 may not be able to correctly show the entire text and still be able to show how formatting will appear in the printed document.

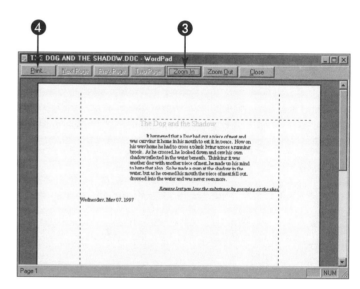

④ If you're satisfied that the formatting appears to be correct, click Print; otherwise, click Close to return to WordPad and make your corrections.

⑤ If you clicked Print, select the All radio button to print the entire document. (To print specific pages, select the Pages radio button and then specify the from and to page numbers.)

⑥ Click the up or down arrow at the right edge of the Number of copies box to print more than one copy. If you intend to print more than one copy of your document, it's much faster to specify the number of copies one time rather than printing one copy many times.

⑦ Click OK to print your document.

It's always a good idea to print one test copy before doing a long print run with many copies. You can cut down on the number of trial printouts by using print preview, but nothing quite matches an actual printout.

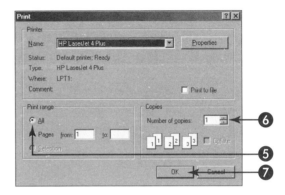

SKILLS CHALLENGE: USING WORDPAD

Now it's time to practice your skills with WordPad. You should be able to complete these steps without any additional help.

❶ Open WordPad.

❷ Set the word wrap options for text files to no wrapping.

 How can you make the text adjust to the width of the WordPad window?

❸ Remove all the toolbars except the toolbar from the text file displays.

 Which toolbars contain options you can't save in text files?

Skills challenge

4 Check the current automatic word-selection setting.

 3 *What do you need to cross before automatic word selection occurs?*

5 Change the unit of measurement to points.

6 Set the paper orientation to landscape.

 4 *What effect does changing the paper orientation have on the margin settings?*

7 Determine the current top margin setting.

8 Open The Fox and the Grapes.txt from the Lesson 7 folder on the CD-ROM.

9 Save the file as a Word 6 document.

10 Move the first sentence of the main paragraph after the third sentence using drag & drop.

 5 *How can you copy text using drag & drop?*

 6 *Which buttons can you use in place of using drag & drop?*

11 Undo the move.

12 Use the Find button to determine how many times the word "again" appears in the document.

⓭ Make the title font twice the size of the rest of the text.

⓮ Right-align the main paragraph.

 7 *How can you move a paragraph closer to the right margin while keeping the paragraph left-aligned?*

⓯ Make the characters in the moral of the fable red.

8 *How can you keep text in a document but prevent it from printing?*

⓰ Place a tab at 2 inches in the moral sentence, and move the beginning of the moral to the tab.

⓱ Determine which printer you want used.

⓲ Preview and then print the document.

Troubleshooting

TROUBLESHOOTING

If you encounter problems while trying to work through the exercises, here are some ideas that might help you correct the problems and keep going.

Problem	Solution
When I try to print a document, Windows 98 tells me there's something wrong with my printer.	Make certain your printer is turned on, that the On Line light is lit (if your printer has this light), and that there's paper in the printer.
When I try to open a document in WordPad, Windows 98 opens it in Word instead.	If you have both Word and WordPad installed on your system, you'll have to open WordPad and use File ➢ Open to open your document.

WRAP UP

In this lesson you learned how to use WordPad to create something interesting. You probably found that you can do quite a bit more with WordPad than you thought possible. While you probably wouldn't want to write a book using WordPad, the program is certainly powerful enough to use for many small documents. Even if WordPad isn't your word processor of choice, you probably learned a lot about Windows 98 and documents in this lesson.

The next lesson is another fun lesson. You learn how to use the Paint program to create and modify drawings. If you've ever wanted to try your hand at being an artist or at creating useful signs, you should enjoy playing around with Paint.

Creating a Masterpiece with Windows Paint

50 MINUTES

GOALS

Have you ever wondered what masterpieces of art you might be able to create if only you had the right tools? Don't worry — no one expects you to be a great artist just because you complete this lesson. If you're already an artist, that's fine, but this lesson isn't really an art lesson — it's an introduction to using Paint, a Windows 98 accessory that you can use to create or modify Windows 98 bitmap image files. You probably remember Windows 98 bitmap image files — they're the same files you can use as desktop wallpaper. When you finish this lesson, you will have your own customized wallpaper file. This lesson shows you a number of things you can do with Paint:

- Starting and setting up Windows Paint

- Using the Paint toolbox

- Editing a painting

- Creating special effects

Get ready

GET READY

For this lesson you need to have Paint installed. A color printer would be nice, but most black-and-white printers should be fine. You want to set your display for at least 256 colors (more would be better) and 800 × 600 or higher screen resolution.

The Lesson 8 folder on the *Windows 98 One Step at a Time* CD-ROM contains a bitmap image file, 3Horses.bmp, that you use in this lesson. When you finish the exercises in this lesson, you will have created three paint files using the Paint toolbox, corrected mistakes in one image, and created special effects in another.

STARTING AND SETTING UP WINDOWS PAINT

Proper preparation is the key to ensuring the outcome you want in almost any task you take on. In just a few minutes of set up you can make certain that Paint is ready to work for you instead of making the whole project harder than necessary. In the following short exercises you learn how to set up Paint so you can have fun, not frustration!

 Windows 98 actually includes two tools you can use to work with image files. In Lesson 5 you learned about Imaging — a program designed to help you work with scanned images and faxes. In this lesson you learn about Paint — a program better suited to creating your own image files from scratch.

Starting Paint and setting up the page

Before you begin to set up Paint, you need to consider how you intend to use any images you create. If you intend to create wallpaper for your Windows 98 desktop, you have different considerations than if you want to create an image for the cover of a report. One primary difference between these two applications is the page layout. Your monitor likely uses landscape orientation; the display is wider than it is high. Printed reports, however, generally use a portrait orientation, which orients the paper so it is higher than it is wide.

Starting Paint and setting up the page

To start Paint and adjust the page settings, follow these steps:

1 Click the Start button.

2 Select Programs.

3 Select Accessories.

4 Select Paint.

5 Select File.

6 Select Page Setup to display the Page Setup dialog box. If this dialog box seems familiar, it probably is — Paint uses the same Page Setup dialog box as WordPad.

7 Select the orientation setting appropriate to the way you want to use the printed output. Choose Portrait or Landscape as needed for your purposes.

8 Enter the margin settings in the Left, Right, Top, and Bottom text boxes.

9 Click OK to close the dialog box.

Most images print at about 96 pixels per inch, so a 672×912 pixel drawing is the largest size you can fit on a page without adjusting the margins. This means you can fit a full-size 640×480 pixel VGA screen on a page printed in portrait orientation, but you need to select landscape to keep a Super VGA 800×600 screen on one page. Of course, if you're not concerned with desktop wallpaper images or don't care about printing the image on a single sheet, you don't need to worry about the paper orientation or margin settings.

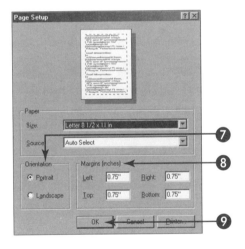

Setting up the tools

Paint has a useful set of tools you use as you create your drawings. In this exercise you see how to choose the tools and the options for those tools.

1 If necessary, open Paint.

2 Click the Select button.

You use the Select button to select a rectangular area, or the Free-Form Select button to choose any area you like. When you

Setting up the tools

click the Free-Form Select, Select, or Text button, the Tool Option box includes the Draw Transparent and Draw Opaque options, as shown in the figure on the right. The Cursor Position box shows the cursor position until you begin dragging a tool and the *anchor* position — the beginning of the object or selection — while you drag the mouse pointer. The Object Size box shows the height and width of an object or selection.

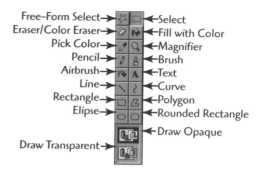

3 Click the Eraser/Color Eraser button.

The Tool Option box changes to offer you choices for the eraser size. When you hold down the left mouse button, the eraser changes to the right-click color anything you drag across. You can also use the eraser to change one specific color to another by dragging the eraser while holding down the right mouse button. When you hold down the right mouse button, areas you drag across having the left-click color are changed to the right-click color. If this seems confusing, remember that the left mouse button changes all colors, while the right mouse button changes only one color.

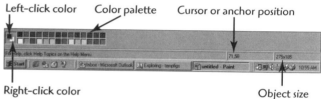

4 Click the Fill With Color button.

When you use this tool, Paint fills an area with color by finding a contiguous block that has the color under the paint spout. The Fill With Color tool has no optional settings, so the Tool Option box is blank when you select this tool.

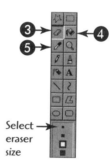

5 Click the Pick Color button.

6 Right- or left-click a specific color in your drawing to place that color in the right-click or left-click color box. You can use this tool when you want to exactly match a color that is already in your drawing. The Pick Color tool has no optional settings, so the Tool Option box is blank when you select this tool.

7 Click the Magnify button to zoom in to view your drawing in closer detail.

The Tool Option box changes to offer you choices for the zoom level. You can use the other tools while the view is zoomed for finer control over the changes you make to your drawing.

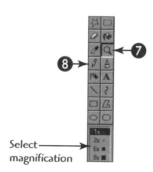

8 Click the Pencil button to use the Pencil tool.

This tool draws a thin line using the current color selections. If you hold down the left button, the line is drawn using the left-click color. The line is drawn using the right-click color if you hold down the right button. The pencil has no optional settings, so the Tool Option box is blank when you select this tool.

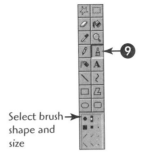

Select brush shape and size

9 Click the Brush button.

10 Choose the brush shape and size in the Tool Option box. This tool also draws in either the left-click or right-click color, depending on which button you hold down.

11 Click the Airbrush button.

12 Choose the airbrush pattern in the Tool Option box. Choose the color by holding the right or left mouse button.

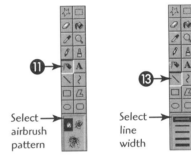

Select airbrush pattern

Select line width

13 Click the Line button.

14 Choose the line width in the Tool Option box. The Curve tool also offers the same line width options.

15 Click the Rectangle button.

The Rectangle, Ellipse, Polygon, and Rounded Rectangle buttons all display the Tool Option box. Choose to draw a border only, a filled object with a border, or a filled object without a border. If you hold down the left mouse button, the border uses the left-click color, and the fill uses the right-click color. The right mouse button reverses the colors.

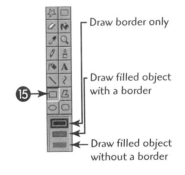

Draw border only

Draw filled object with a border

Draw filled object without a border

16 Click a color square in the color palette with the right or left mouse button to select the color as the right-click or left-click color.

NOTE

You may find that the color selections don't always work quite as you expect. Some bitmap images use a special internal color table to re-map your color selections to match the colors already in the image.
This enables you to use the same colors as you see in the image, but can be a little confusing when the colors you select aren't the ones used to draw new objects. You're more likely to encounter this unexpected behavior in scanned photographs than in drawings created with Paint.

8

Creating a Masterpiece with Windows Paint

Adjusting the image attributes

To make the tools work the way you want, remember to check the Tool Option box whenever you select a new tool. If you don't, you might find yourself using the Edit ➢ Undo command much more than you'd like.

Adjusting the image attributes

The final step in getting ready to use Paint is to make certain you've selected the correct image attributes. You can choose both the size of the image and whether to create a color or black-and-white image. While it's possible to change the size later, it's usually best to select the correct image size first. Changing the size of an image can distort the appearance of the image.

To set the image attributes, follow these steps:

1 If necessary, open Paint.

2 Select Image.

3 Select Attributes to display the Attributes dialog box.

4 Select the unit of measurement.

The default selection is pixels — the unit used to measure your screen resolution.

5 Specify the Width and Height for the image.

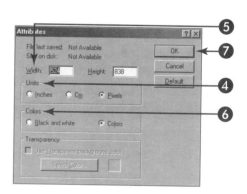

If you're creating an image to use as desktop wallpaper, you probably want to limit the image size to no more than your screen resolution. The three most common screen resolution settings are 640 × 480, 800 × 600, and 1024 × 768.

6 Select either a color or black-and-white image. (If you select Black and white, Paint uses patterns rather than colors to fill objects.)

7 Click OK to close the dialog box. (If you selected to change the image to Black and white, you have to confirm your decision before you can return to Paint.)

Now that you've set the image attributes and you know how to select the options for the tools, it's time to have some fun and create a drawing.

Drawing lines and curves

USING THE PAINT TOOLBOX

Let's face it — not everyone is an artist! Drawing a straight line, a circle, or even a respectable-looking rectangle can be hard work. Fortunately, you can cheat a little and use the tools in the Paint toolbox to create these and many other objects, and no one will know you had help.

Drawing lines and curves

Are you one of those people who just can't draw a straight line? In this exercise you learn how to draw lines in all directions, including ones that are straight and level. In addition, you see how you can even draw smooth curves.

TIP *You may find it easier to move the pointer to exact locations if you zoom in on your drawing.*

1 If necessary, open Paint.

2 Click the Line tool button.

3 Move the pointer down and to the right until the Cursor Position indicator shows 50, 50. This means the cursor is 50 pixels from the top edge of the drawing space and 50 pixels to the right of the left edge.

4 When you have the pointer at the correct position, hold down the left mouse button and drag the point until the Object Size indicator shows 100 X 100. This means that the *bounding box* — an imaginary rectangular box as wide and as high as the object you're drawing — is 100 pixels square. Because both the height and width are the same, when you release the mouse button, your line extends down and to the right at a 45-degree angle.

5 Move the mouse pointer to the end of the line. The Cursor Position indicator should show 150, 150.

6 Hold down the left mouse button and drag the pointer to the right until the Object Size indicator shows 100 X 1. This means

Drawing lines and curves

the line is 100 pixels long and 1 pixel high — a straight and level line. Release the mouse button to draw this line segment.

7 Move the pointer to 50, 200.

8 Hold down the Shift key as you drag the mouse pointer down and to the right until the Object Size indicator reads 100 × 100.

9 Release the mouse button. (Because you held down the Shift key, Paint drew the line at exactly 45 degrees, and you probably found it a whole lot easier to draw the line correctly.)

10 Move the pointer to 150, 300.

11 Hold down the Shift key as you drag the mouse pointer to the right until the object size is 100×1.

12 Release the mouse button. This time Paint kept the line perfectly level.

13 Click the Curve button.

14 Move the pointer to 250, 300.

15 Drag the pointer to 250, 150.

16 Release the mouse button. The straight line Paint drew between the ends of the two lines doesn't look like a curve yet, but it will soon.

17 Move the pointer to 250, 225.

18 Drag the line left until the Object Size is -100 × -75, and then release the button.

19 Move the pointer to 250, 225 and click the left mouse button. Your drawing should now look something like the figure on the right.

20 Select File.

21 Select Save.

22 Type the following text in the File name text box: **Drawing 1**.

23 Click Save to save the file and return to Paint.

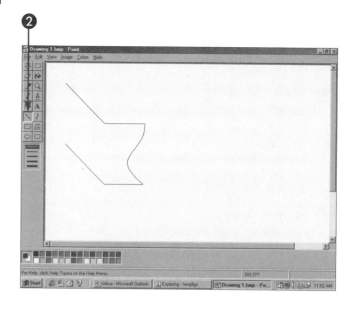

Drawing solid objects

You don't have to draw just straight lines and S curves, of course. You can draw a line at any angle, but Paint helps out and makes your line perfectly horizontal, vertical, or at a 45-degree angle if you hold down Shift while you're drawing the line. If you want to draw a simple curve rather than an S curve, double-click when you release the curve. You can also choose different line widths in the Tool Option box before you begin drawing a line.

Drawing solid objects

Lines and curves make a good start, but you probably want to use some solid objects in your drawing, too. Solid objects are simply things like rectangles, circles, or *polygons* — multisided objects. You can draw just the border, a filled object with a border, or a filled object with no border.

TIP

To control the width of the border on solid objects, click the Line tool button and choose a line width before you choose a solid object tool.

To practice drawing solid objects, follow these steps:

1 If necessary, open Paint.

2 Click the Rectangle tool button.

3 Select the type of solid object you want to draw by choosing one of the options in the Tool Option box.

4 Click a color with the left mouse button to choose the border color.

5 Choose a fill color with the right mouse button.

6 Move the pointer to one corner where you'd like to begin drawing a rectangle, and drag the pointer to draw the rectangle. To draw a square, hold down Shift as you drag out the shape. The Rounded Rectangle tool works just like the Rectangle tool, but Paint adds a curve to each corner.

7 Click the Ellipse tool button.

8

Creating a Masterpiece with Windows Paint

Adding some paint

8 Drag out an ellipse. (To draw a perfect circle, hold down Shift as you drag out the shape.)

9 Click the Polygon tool button.

10 Click the starting point for the multisided shape.

Continue clicking at each corner point until you've completed drawing the polygon. If you double-click the final point, Paint adds the final line from that point to the starting point. If you click the starting point after you've created additional points, Paint closes the object, too. If you've chosen a filled object in the tool option box, Paint fills any enclosed spaces in your polygon. You can draw horizontal, vertical, or 45-degree lines by holding down shift as you draw.

11 Select File.

12 Select Save to save your changes.

You don't have to add solid objects randomly as you did in this exercise. There's no reason you can't use the Cursor Position and Object Size indicators to precisely align and size your objects. If you were going to draw a toy car, for example, you'd probably want to be precise in making certain the wheels were the same size and that they were on a level plane.

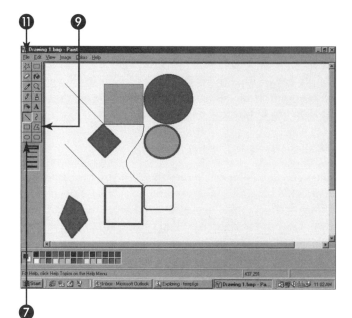

Adding some paint

The real fun of using Paint comes when you start playing with the painting tools — Pencil, Brush, Airbrush, and Fill With Color. When you use these tools, you feel more like a real artist as you add freehand effects to your drawings. The painting tools work somewhat differently than the tools you've used so far. Rather than creating straight lines and precisely defined objects, you use the painting tools to let your imagination have more control over the drawing.

To try out the painting tools, follow these steps:

1 If necessary, open Paint.

2 If you still have Drawing 1 open, select File.

3 Select New to create a new drawing. (If you haven't saved your work, Paint asks if you want to save the file first.)

4 Click the Pencil button.

5 Draw a line near the top of the drawing area. Be sure to loop the line across itself a time or two.

6 Click the Brush button.

7 Select the long diagonal line brush style in the left column of the third row of the Tool Option box.

8 Use the Brush tool to draw another line similar to the Pencil line, again making certain to loop the line a few times.

9 Click the Airbrush button.

10 Select the mid-sized airbrush pattern.

11 Draw a third line similar to the first two, and notice how the coverage increases as you draw more slowly. If you move the mouse quickly, little color is sprayed onto the drawing, but if you go slowly, a lot more color is sprayed.

12 Point to the color palette and click a contrasting color with the left mouse button.

13 Click the Fill With Color button.

14 Move the pointer so the end of the paint pouring out of the can is within one of the loops of the pencil line.

15 Click the left mouse button to fill the loop with the contrasting color you selected.

16 Click inside one of the loops of the brush line to fill that loop, too.

17 Try filling one of the loops in the airbrushed line. Unless you drew the line slowly or went over the line to fill it in completely, the contrasting color probably escaped from the loop and filled the drawing area. The Fill With Color tool fills as much space as possible without crossing another color. Because the airbrushed line probably wasn't solid, the fill color was able to find its way out through the gaps in the line.

18 Select File.

19 Select Save.

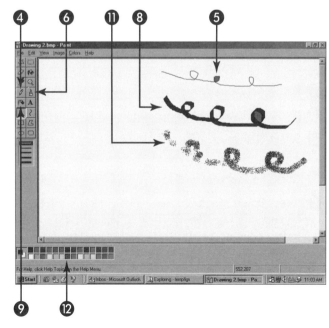

8

Creating a Masterpiece with Windows Paint

Adding some text

⑳ Type the following text in the File name text box: **Drawing 2**.

㉑ Click Save to save the file and return to Paint.

You can combine the painting tools and the object tools in creating a single drawing — there's no rule that says you must keep them apart. But if you do use both, try to keep their differences in mind. The object tools are best suited to creating well-defined items, while the painting tools are more suited to free form additions.

Adding some text

Everyone has heard the old saying "A picture is worth a thousand words," but I wonder how many people realize that sometimes a few well-chosen words are worth as much as any picture? If you wish to convey a message with a sign, you probably want to add a few words so no one has to ponder your meaning. In this exercise you see how easy it is to add some text to your drawings.

TIP
If possible, enter text into a Paint image using a contrasting color that doesn't already appear in your drawing. That way, you can use the color eraser to remove the text if necessary — once text is entered, it can't be edited.

❶ If necessary, open Paint.

❷ If you still have Drawing 2 open, select File.

❸ Select New to create a new drawing. (You can add text to an existing drawing, but for this exercise, create a new file.)

❹ Click the Text tool button.

❺ Select Draw Opaque to have the right-click color appear behind your text. (Select Draw Transparent if you want the text to be drawn on a transparent background so any existing objects show through the background.)

❻ Left-click the color you want to use for the text.

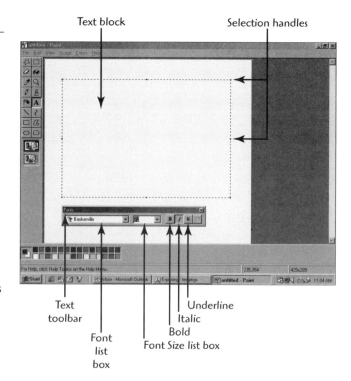

Text block   Selection handles

Text toolbar
Font list box
Font Size list box
Bold
Italic
Underline

7 If you selected Draw Opaque, right-click the color you want for the background.

8 Use the mouse pointer to drag out a box for your text. If you make a mistake, drag out a new box of the correct size.

9 Select View.

10 Select Text Toolbar to display the toolbar.

You can only display the text toolbar when a text block is selected, and the text toolbar provides the only method of choosing a font, size, and attributes for text. In addition, after you've closed a text block, you cannot reopen the text block. This means you cannot edit the text or change any text attributes after you close the text block.

11 Type the following text: **Windows 98**.

12 Click the down arrow at the right edge of the Font list box.

13 Choose Baskerville. (If you don't have this font installed, select another font so you can see the effect of changing the font.)

14 Click the down arrow at the right edge of the Font Size list box.

15 Choose 72 to change the type to 72 points — approximately one inch high when you print the image.

16 Depending on how large a text block you dragged out, changing the font size to 72 points may cause part of the text to disappear. If so, move the mouse pointer over one of the selection handles, and when the pointer changes to a double-headed arrow, drag the text block out until all of the text reappears. (You may need to make the block higher as well as wider.)

17 Click the Italic button. (Make certain that neither the Bold nor the Underline button is selected.)

18 Select File.

19 Select Save.

20 Name your file **Drawing 3**.

21 Click Save.

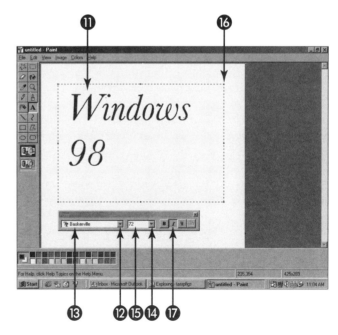

Creating a Masterpiece with Windows Paint

8

Editing a painting

Any font settings you select affect the entire text block. You can't, for example, make part of a text block italic and part regular text. What you can do is create separate text blocks that appear to be contiguous, and apply different attributes to each block as you create each one. You may have some difficulty trying to perfectly line up separate text blocks, but you can use a couple of tricks to make your task easier. First, you can use the Cursor Position indicator to help align your text blocks. You may want to write down the cursor positions as you add each text block. Another trick that may help is to add a horizontal or vertical line as appropriate and use it as an alignment guide. Be sure to use a contrasting color so you can use the Color Eraser tool to remove the extra lines when they're no longer needed.

EDITING A PAINTING

If you're one of those people who never makes mistakes, you can skip this section while the rest of us have a look at editing an image. Editing a Paint image really means erasing a mistake, moving part of an image from one place to another, or covering up one object with another.

There are two primary types of image-creating programs for your PC. These are generally defined as *draw* programs and *paint* programs. Draw programs create objects that can be stretched or moved independently of any other objects in the image. Paint programs create objects that are part of a *bitmap* image, which does not keep objects separate from each other, but rather adds them to the whole picture. One way to think of the difference between the two types of programs is to think of drawing programs as keeping each object on separate glass sheets stacked one on top of the next. Paint programs, by contrast, have a single layer, so when you add something new, whatever it covers up no longer exists.

This difference is important when you want to edit an image. Because Paint creates a bitmap image, you can't select an object and move it around without destroying whatever you pass over. On the other hand, you can easily change individual points in a bitmap image, which is difficult or impossible to do in a draw program.

▶ *Oops, correcting mistakes*

There are several techniques you can use to correct mistakes in Paint, but the proper technique depends on what you'd like to accomplish. In this exercise you see how to use some of these techniques and see how they differ.

This exercise uses a photo, called 3Horses.bmp, that was taken by the author and scanned for use in this exercise. The colors were modified to use standard Windows colors to make this exercise a little less confusing. In addition, I added four blocks of color in the lower-left corner of the image to help you select the correct colors for this exercise. You can find a normal color version of this image in the Images folder on the *Windows 98 One Step at a Time* CD-ROM.

① Insert the *Windows 98 One Step at a Time* CD-ROM into your CD-ROM drive.

② If necessary, open Paint.

③ Select File.

④ Select Open.

⑤ Click the down arrow at the right edge of the Look in list box.

⑥ Choose the Lesson 8 folder on your CD-ROM drive.

⑦ Choose 3Horses.bmp.

⑧ Click Open.

The figure on the right shows how 3Horses.bmp appears before you begin making modifications.

⑨ Click the Pick Color button.

⑩ Right-click the top color in the sample block. This makes the top color the background or right-click color.

⑪ Click the Pick Color button again.

⑫ Left-click the second color in the sample block to make the selected color the foreground or left-click color.

⑬ Click the Eraser/Color Eraser tool button.

Oops, correcting mistakes

⑭ Choose the largest size for the eraser.

⑮ Hold down the left mouse button while you move the eraser back and forth over the lower-right corner of the image. As the figure on the right shows, the eraser changes everything it crosses to the right-click color.

⑯ Select Edit.

⑰ Select Undo to return the original colors to the block you just erased. (If you didn't erase the entire block in one step, select Edit ➤ Undo again. Paint restores only the last three sections you erased. If necessary, reload 3Horses.bmp from the CD-ROM, and then reselect the right-click and left-click colors.)

⑱ Hold down the right mouse button while you drag the eraser back and forth over the same general area in the lower-right corner of the image. When you hold down the right mouse button, the eraser becomes the color eraser and changes only the left-click color areas to the right-click color. All other colors remain untouched.

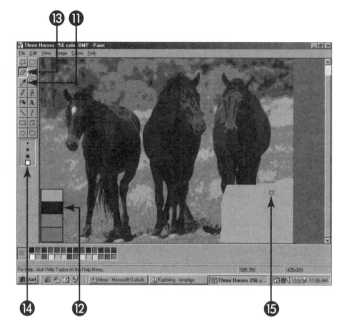

⑲ Select Edit.

⑳ Select Undo to restore the colors.

㉑ Click the Select button. (You can use the Free-Form Select tool in the same way as the Select tool if you want to choose a nonrectangular area.)

㉒ Select Draw Transparent.

When you use the Draw Transparent option, Paint acts as if the right-click color in the selection is transparent, and does not cover up existing colors when you move a block. If you select Draw Opaque, Paint moves the right-click color along with the block. You may need to experiment a little to fully understand the difference between these two options.

㉓ Move the pointer to 550, 100.

㉔ Drag the mouse to select a block 100 × 100.

㉕ Release the mouse button after you've selected the block.

㉖ Move the mouse pointer into the selected block.

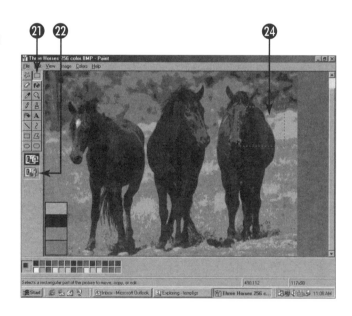

27 Hold down the left mouse button and drag the block to 550, 300.

28 Select Edit.

29 Select Undo to restore the block to its original location.

You've seen how the Eraser tool and the Select tool can remove mistakes from an image. While these tools are useful, you've probably noticed that the changes they make aren't exactly subtle. It's true that the Color Eraser tool can selectively remove a specific color from an image, but there's another method you can use to create softer-looking changes that won't stand out quite as much. The next exercise shows you how to use this method.

TIP

If you want to create colored objects that have a patterned fill instead of a solid fill, start by creating the image in black and white. Draw the objects you wish to fill with a pattern, and then change the image to color. Finally, use the Color Eraser tool to change the black pattern to the color you want.

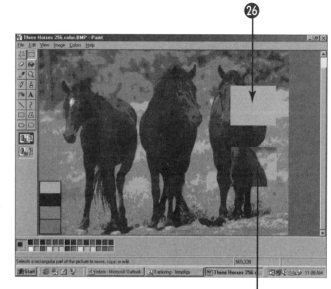

Airbrushing away mistakes

An airbrush is an interesting type of tool because the changes it makes to an image can be much more subtle than the changes made by most of Paint's tools. In this exercise you see how you can use the airbrush tool to remove mistakes from an image.

1 If necessary, open Paint.

2 Open 3Horses.bmp from the *Windows 98 One Step at a Time* CD-ROM.

3 Click the Pick Color button.

4 Right-click the bottom color in the sample block.

5 Click the Pick Color button again.

6 Left-click the second color from the bottom of the sample block.

7 Click the Airbrush button.

Flipping and rotating selections

8 Choose the largest airbrush pattern in the Tool Option box.

9 Use the left and right mouse buttons to alternately spray the left-click and right-click colors over the middle horse. For a more realistic effect, you may want to use the Pick Color tool to select additional colors to spray. The figure on the right shows how your screen might look after a few minutes of work.

10 Select File.

11 Select Save As.

12 Type the following text in the File name text box: **2Horses.bmp**.

13 Click Save to save your modifications.

As this exercise showed, the airbrush is a powerful touch-up tool. With just a little effort you can remove unwanted objects from an image. Just think, now you can boot your old flame right out of your vacation pictures!

CREATING SPECIAL EFFECTS

Playing with Paint is a lot of fun, isn't it? In this section you have even more fun applying some special effects to images. You may be surprised at what you can do to change the appearance of images through special effects.

Flipping and rotating selections

The first special effect you try is flipping and rotating selections. Do you want to make someone stand on their head or face in a different direction? In this exercise you learn just how easy it is to make these types of changes.

1 If necessary, open Paint.

2 Open 3Horses.bmp from the *Windows 98 One Step at a Time* CD-ROM.

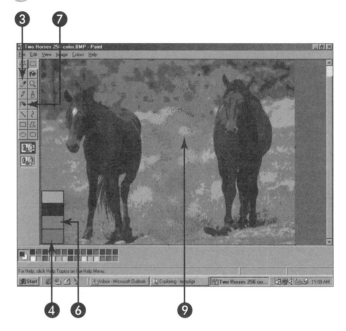

Flipping and rotating selections

3 Click the Select tool button. You need to select an area before you can flip or rotate the area.

4 Move the pointer to 255, 50.

5 Hold down the left mouse button.

6 Drag the selection box out to 170 × 425. (This selection includes the entire middle horse—yes, you're going to pick on him again!) Release the mouse button once the area is selected.

7 Select Image.

8 Select Flip/Rotate to display the Flip and Rotate dialog box.

9 To make the horse face to his right rather than to his left, select the Flip horizontal radio button.

You can make the horse appear to stand on his head by selecting Flip vertical. Use the Rotate by angle options when you want to turn the selection 90, 180, or 270 degrees clockwise.

10 Click OK to flip or rotate the selected area.

The figure on the right shows the selection flipped horizontally. With a little airbrush touch up, no one will know you flipped the horse to face a different direction.

11 Select File.

12 Select Save As.

13 Type the following text in the File name text box: **3Horse_F.bmp**.

14 Click Save to save your modifications.

Flipping a rectangular selection horizontally or vertically places the flipped selection in the exact position necessary to cover the original selection. Rotating a selection either 90 or 270 degrees isn't quite so neat. You want to make sure the selection box is exactly square before you rotate a selection 90 or 270 degrees so that the rotated selection covers the same space. Otherwise, you'll probably have extra cleanup work to do to make the effect just what you want.

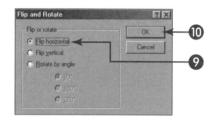

8

Creating a Masterpiece with Windows Paint

Stretching and skewing selections

Stretching and skewing selections

Before you start this exercise, I'm giving you fair warning — stretching or skewing images of your in-laws may be hazardous to your health! That poor middle horse, though, is fair game.

Stretching a selection makes the selection grow or shrink by a percentage you specify. You can only stretch a selection in one direction — horizontally or vertically — at a time. To stretch a selection in both height and width, first you need to stretch the selection in one direction and then in the other. Whenever possible, Paint keeps the upper-left corner — the anchor point — of the selection at the same position.

Skewing a selection leans the selection at an angle. Depending on the skewing option you select, either the horizontal or the vertical edges of the selection retain their original orientations when the selection is skewed.

1 If necessary, open Paint.

2 Open 3Horses.bmp

3 Click the Select button.

4 Move the pointer to 255, 50.

5 Drag the selection box out to 170 × 425.

6 Select Image.

7 Select Stretch/Skew to display the Stretch and Skew dialog box.

8 Type the following text in the Horizontal text box (make certain you choose the text box in the Stretch section): **125**.

Your screen should now look like the figure on the right. If the text box is grayed out, select the Horizontal radio button.

9 Click OK to stretch the selection. The middle horse now appears to be a bit wider than before.

10 Select Edit.

11 Select Undo to return the selection to its original size.

12 Select Image.

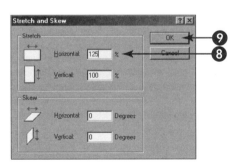

⑬ Select Stretch/Skew.

⑭ Type the following text in the Horizontal text box (make certain you choose the text box in the Skew section): **30**.

⑮ Click OK to skew the horse as shown in the figure on the right.

⑯ Select Edit.

⑰ Select Undo to return the selection to its original orientation.

You can both stretch and skew an image in a single step by specifying both a stretch percentage and a skew angle before you click OK. If you don't select an area of an image before you select Image ➢ Stretch/Skew, Paint applies the changes to the entire image. You can use this technique to adjust images to be a better fit as desktop wallpaper.

Inverting colors

One of the most interesting and bizarre special effects you can create in Paint is to *invert* the colors. When you invert colors, each color is replaced by its complement. The effect can be quite shocking!

❶ If necessary, open Paint.

❷ Open 3Horses.bmp from the *Windows 98 One Step at a Time* CD-ROM.

❸ Click the Select button.

❹ Move the pointer to 320, 0. (If you have trouble selecting an area so close to the edge of the image, try 320, 1 or 320, 2.)

❺ Hold down the left mouse button and drag the selection box down until the selection size is 320 × 480 (if you started a little below the top edge, the maximum height will be a little less than 480). You may have to drag the selection box down into the gray band below the image to make the full selection.

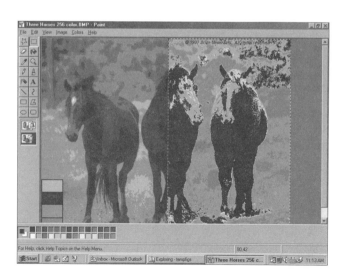

❻ Click Image.

❼ Select Invert Colors to invert the colors in the selection. Your screen should now look similar to the figure on the right.

❽ Select Edit.

Creating your own colors

9 Select Undo to return the selection to its original colors.

If you don't select an area of the image before you invert the colors, Paint inverts the colors in the entire image. If you invert the colors in a black-and-white image, you create a negative image.

Creating your own colors

No matter how many colors your system supports, Paint only gives you a choice of a limited number of colors. If you're trying to create an exact match to a color, it can be pretty hard to find just what you need in such a limited palette. Fortunately, there's an easy way around this limitation — create your own colors.

Creating a new color to match an existing object is not unlike going to a paint store to buy touch-up paint. At the paint store you find a rack containing an assortment of color samples. When you make your selection, the paint store uses a formula that tells how many drops of red tint, green tint, blue tint, black tint, and so on to add to the base color to get just the color you want. After all the tints are mixed with the base, your paint is ready to use. In Paint you use a similar process to create colors, but luckily you don't have to know the formula for your custom colors — Paint figures out the formula based on your selections. Considering that Paint can create over 231,000,000,000,000 color shades, it's a good thing you don't have to know the formulas!

NOTE *If your display is set to 256 or fewer colors, many of the custom color selections appear as patterns rather than solid colors. To correct this, you can either select custom colors that show as solid colors or set your display for a higher number of colors.*

To create custom colors for your Paint images, follow these steps:

1 If necessary, open Paint.

2 Select Colors.

3 Select Edit Colors to display the Edit colors dialog box.

④ Click Define Custom Colors to expand the dialog box so the color selection area is shown.

⑤ Click one of the empty boxes in the Custom colors area to define a new color.

⑥ Drag the color balance slider to the general color you wish to create.

⑦ Drag the brightness slider down until the Color|Solid box shows a color similar to the color you want to create.

⑧ Continue dragging the color balance slider and the brightness slider until you have just the color you want.

⑨ Click Add to Custom Colors. (You can specify exact values in the Hue, Sat, Lum, Red, Green, and Blue text boxes, but Paint automatically enters values in these boxes as you drag the sliders.)

⑩ To create additional custom colors, click a different empty box in the Custom colors area, and then repeat Steps 6-8.

⑪ Select the custom color you wish to use.

⑫ Click OK. Paint places the selected color in the upper-left corner of the color palette and automatically makes the color the left-click color.

⑬ Select Options.

⑭ Select Save Colors to display the Save Colors dialog box.

⑮ Type the following text in the File name text box: **My colors**.

⑯ Click Save to save the custom colors.

If you need to use more than 16 custom colors in an image, save each set of 16 custom colors under a separate name. Then use Options ➢ Get Colors to load the custom color palettes as you need them.

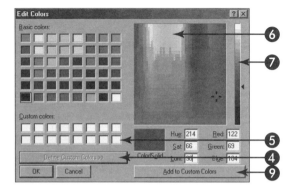

| TIP |

To create a custom color to match a color already in an image, use the Pick Color tool to make the color the left-click color. Then select Options ➢ Edit Colors ➢ Define Custom Colors ➢ Add to Custom Colors. Be sure to save the colors.

8

Creating a Masterpiece with Windows Paint

Skills challenge

SKILLS CHALLENGE: USING PAINT

Here's your chance to have some fun and practice what you've learned about Paint.

1 Change the page orientation to landscape.

2 Set all the margins to ½ inch.

3 Create a text block with a transparent background using a 24-point bold Arial font.

4 Enter your first and last name in the text block.

 How can you adjust the text block so your first name appears on one line and your last name on the next line?

 How can you make your last name appear in a larger-size font?

5 Create a rounded rectangle.

 How can you create a rounded rectangle around the text block without covering up your name?

6 Fill the rounded rectangle with a contrasting color.

7 Draw a straight line that extends down and to the right at a 45-degree angle.

4 *How can you create an octagon with all sides exactly horizontal, vertical, or at 45-degree angles?*

8 Create an ellipse that is 200 pixels wide and 100 pixels high.

5 *How can you create a perfect circle?*

9 Open 3Horses.bmp.

10 Make the color of the center of the spot on the left horse's head the left-click color.

11 Add a similar spot to the forehead of the horse on the right.

12 Remove the horse on the left from the image.

13 Move the middle horse left about 100 pixels.

6 *How can you change the image size to 800 by 600?*

14 Invert the colors in the image.

7 *How can you change the dark brown areas of the horses to the bright pink color you see when you invert the colors, while keeping all the other colors in the image as their normal colors?*

15 Create a custom color that has the following settings: Hue **214**, Sat **67**, Lum **90**, Red **122**, Green **69**, and Blue **104**.

8

Creating a Masterpiece with Windows Paint

Troubleshooting

TROUBLESHOOTING

If you encounter problems while trying to work through the exercises, here are some ideas that might help you correct the problems and keep going.

Problem	Solution
Paint doesn't appear on my menu.	Double-click the Add/Remove Programs icon in the Control Panel. Paint is in the Accessories group on the Windows Setup tab.
Some colors appear to have patterns in them.	Your display is set to show too few colors. Right-click your desktop, select Properties from the pop-up menu, click the Settings tab, and select a higher number of colors in the Color Palette list box.

WRAP UP

If you didn't have fun learning about Paint in this lesson, you weren't trying. In this lesson you learned how to make a lot of unusual modifications to images, and, along the way, you picked up a number of useful techniques you can use as you create your own masterpiece. You also got to play with some interesting images you can use as desktop wallpaper and learned how to create fat, pink horses. Now there's a skill you don't learn every day!

In the next lesson you learn how to use and organize fonts. You may be surprised to see what's available on your system. Not only can you find interesting typefaces, but you can also find a whole lot of fancy symbols to dress up your documents. You may also find you can save some space and get better performance by cutting down the number of redundant fonts that are installed.

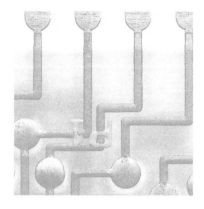

Working with Fonts

30 MINUTES

GOALS

If you're an average Windows 98 user, you probably don't even know how many fonts are installed on your PC. You probably use the same fonts most of the time, and you've probably never used quite a few fonts. In fact, you likely have a hard time choosing a font simply because no one has ever helped you figure out what's what in your font folder. Would you be surprised to discover that you have a lot of virtually identical fonts installed on your PC? Would you be happy to learn that all those extra fonts not only take up space on your hard disk and make selecting a font more cumbersome, but that having too many fonts installed can actually slow down your computer? Would you be interested in knowing about some special fonts that let you place arrows and other interesting symbols in your documents? This lesson covers all of that and more.

- Figuring out what fonts you have

- Installing and deleting fonts

- Inserting Wingdings and Dingbats in your text

Get ready

GET READY

In this lesson you primarily use Windows Explorer and WordPad to work with and view your fonts. You may find it handy to have a printer available, although this isn't an absolute requirement.

You use the FontList.doc and WingDing.doc files, which are located in the Lesson 9 folder on the *Windows 98 One Step at a Time* CD-ROM, to complete this lesson. When you finish this lesson, you will have figured out what fonts you have, learned how to install and delete fonts from your system, and how to insert Wingdings and Dingbats in your documents.

 NOTE *A lesson on Windows 98 fonts runs head on into a major problem — there's no way I can determine which fonts you might have installed on your system. Windows 98 has a set of standard fonts that are automatically installed, but depending on what other software has been added to your PC, you may have hundreds of additional fonts available. You may not have the same set of fonts you see in the figures, but you probably have others that aren't shown. You need to keep these possibilities in mind as you go through the exercises in this lesson; don't get confused if your screen looks a little different than some of the figures.*

 NOTE *If you wanted to be completely accurate, you'd probably use the term* **typeface** *instead of* **font** *to describe the different styles of type available on your PC. In the old days of printing presses, each different type size in a particular typeface was a font. Thus you might have a 10-point font and a 12-point font in the Courier typeface. Today, however, computers can scale type to different sizes, so most people tend to use* **font** *to describe the type style. In this book we follow the convention of using* **font** *to describe a typeface, and* **size** *to describe the point size.*

WHAT FONTS DO I HAVE?

Okay, how about a totally unfair pop quiz? How many fonts are installed on your PC? No fair peeking, just make a guess.

Give up? Don't feel bad. It's pretty unlikely that even the most experienced PC users can give a good answer to that question. One reason for this is simple—you probably don't know which fonts came with Windows 98 and which came with other applications.

Let's try an easier question. Would you rather your computer was easier to use and ran faster, or that it was confusing and slow? There's probably no reason to wait around for the answer to that one, is there?

Believe it or not, these two questions are closely related. You can install hundreds of fonts on your Windows 98 system, but there are some very good reasons why you shouldn't. If you have too many fonts installed, everything you run in Windows 98 moves a little bit slower. Each font you add won't make much of a difference, but you've probably heard about the straw that broke the camel's back—one straw by itself, like one extra font, seems to be almost nothing. But when you keep adding straws or fonts, eventually the system (or the camel) just can't keep up.

There's another reason you want to do a better job of managing the fonts installed on your PC. Long before you get so many fonts that your PC runs noticeably slower, you may find that just choosing a font is too confusing. If you have 15 fonts that all appear to be the same, how do you choose one to use? Wouldn't it be better to select the best of the 15 and take the others off your system?

NOTE *Windows 98 can use several different types of fonts. The most common are the system fonts and TrueType fonts. PostScript fonts are another type of font you may encounter; they are also called Type 1, or Adobe fonts. To use PostScript fonts you need a special driver program that is not part of Windows 98. PostScript fonts are not covered in this book, but many of the same considerations apply to PostScript fonts as well as the standard Windows 98 font types.*

Previewing your fonts

▶ *Previewing your fonts*

If you don't know the difference between Arial, Courier, and Times New Roman, this exercise was designed just for you. Here you learn how to preview your fonts and print out samples. With this information you are better able to choose the fonts you want to use.

① Turn on your printer.

② Click the Start button.

③ Select Programs.

④ Select Windows Explorer.

⑤ Open the Windows\Fonts folder.

The figure on the right shows a fairly typical Fonts folder. You probably won't have the same set of fonts installed on your system, and you probably have others that don't appear in the figure, too. Notice that the toolbar looks a little different when you're viewing the Fonts folder. Because fonts need to be installed to be usable, many of the normal Windows Explorer toolbar buttons simply won't work correctly in the Fonts folder.

⑥ Click the Large Icons button if Windows Explorer isn't displaying the fonts in the large icon view.

⑦ Double-click the Arial icon to preview the appearance of the Arial font.

Arial is one of the TrueType fonts that is installed when you install Windows 98. The font name and the type of font are shown in the top line of the font preview dialog box, but don't be fooled into thinking the top line is a sample of the font. The font samples are shown below the font information.

⑧ Click Print.

⑨ Click OK to print a sample page.

The printed sample shows the font in seven different sizes and gives you a pretty good idea how documents using this font will appear.

Go to different folder

Up one level
Large icons
List
Similarity
Details

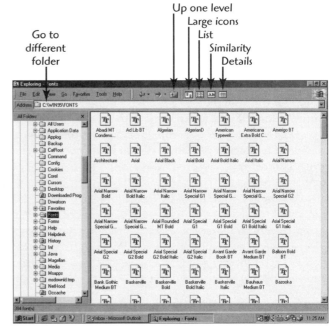

Font name

⑩ Font type **⑧**

Samples of this font

⑩ Click Done to close the font preview dialog box.

You may want to print a few samples of some of the fonts installed on your system to compare how each looks. For example, you might want to see how Arial and Arial Bold differ. If you're short of disk space, you can uninstall the variations of a font such as Bold, Bold Italic, and Italic. Windows 98 can simulate these variations with the basic font, but the quality of the simulated font won't be quite as high as the separate font files provide.

Creating a list of your fonts

If you have a large number of fonts installed on your system, you may soon decide that individual pages of print samples for each font are just too cumbersome. This exercise shows you how you can create a single reference list showing all the fonts you have installed. You get a little help from the FontList.doc document, which is found on the *Windows 98 One Step at a Time* CD-ROM and previews many of the more common fonts you may have installed.

① Make certain your printer is turned on.

② Insert the CD-ROM from this book into your CD-ROM drive.

③ Click the Start button.

④ Select Programs.

⑤ Select MS-DOS Prompt.

⑥ Type the following command: **cd fonts**.

⑦ Press Enter.

⑧ Type the following command: **dir /on > prn**.

⑨ Press Enter.

If you use a laser printer, you may need to press the On Line button, the Form Feed button, and then the On Line button on your printer to print the final page.

⑩ Type the following command: **exit**.

⑪ Press Enter.

Creating a list of your fonts

⑫ Click the Start button.

⑬ Select Programs.

⑭ Select Accessories.

⑮ Select WordPad.

⑯ Select File.

⑰ Select Open.

⑱ In the Look in list box, choose the Lesson 9 folder on the CD-ROM.

⑲ Double-click FontList.doc.

The figure on the right shows how your screen should appear if you have all the fonts included in FontList.doc installed on your system. If some of the fonts in the document are missing from your system, Windows 98 substitutes a different font in the Sample column.

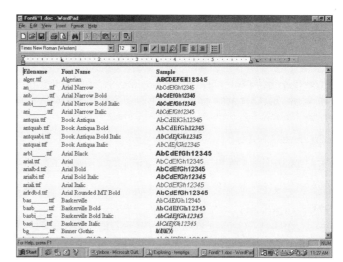

Compare the file listing you printed at the MS-DOS prompt to the list of filenames in the first column of FontList.doc. If your printout shows the same filename shown in the document, go to the next line. If FontList.doc shows a filename that isn't in your printout, delete the entire line from FontList.doc. Finally, add any filenames that are on your printout but missing from FontList.doc.

If you add any filenames to FontList.doc, you need to check the Fonts folder to determine the correct name of the font.

- Click the Start button.

- Select Programs ➤ Windows Explorer.

- Open the Windows\Fonts folder.

- Click the Details button. You can find the filenames in the second column. Type the corresponding font names in the second column of FontList.doc—press Tab to move to the second and then the third column.

⑳ Type the following text in the third column of any lines you add to FontList.doc: **AbCdEfGh12345**.

㉑ Select the text you just added.

㉒ Click the down arrow at the right of the Font list box.

㉓ Select the same font name as shown in the second column. For bold and italic, click the appropriate toolbar buttons.

㉔ When you have finished making your changes, select File.

㉕ Select Save As.

㉖ Select the Windows folder on drive C to save the file.

㉗ Click Save.

㉘ Select File.

㉙ Select Print to display the Print dialog box.

㉚ Depending on the number fonts used in column 3 of FontList.doc and the type of printer installed on your system, you may be able to print the document by clicking OK. Otherwise, you have to print one page at a time by entering a single page number in the from text box, clicking OK, and then printing the next page.

You can use the printed samples to compare the different fonts installed on your computer. You may notice that your system is very slow when you're working in FontList.doc. When a document contains a large number of fonts as this document does, Windows 98 tends to run a little short of breath. If your PC doesn't speed up once you close FontList.doc, close all open programs and restart Windows 98. Although you may not notice it, just having a large number of fonts installed slows down your PC a little.

▶ *Seeing how fonts compare*

You've probably noticed something funny about your printed font samples—a lot of the fonts look almost alike! Wouldn't it be handy to know which fonts were quite similar to each other so you could decide which fonts to keep and which to discard? In this exercise you see how to compare different fonts.

9

Working with Fonts

Seeing how fonts compare

NOTE *Windows 98 uses information contained in the font files to determine how fonts compare. Not all font files contain the necessary information, so Windows 98 may not be able to determine how similar certain fonts are to your other fonts. When font files lack the information to allow comparisons with other fonts, Windows 98 displays those font files at the bottom of the comparison list along with the message* No PANOSE information available.

① Click the Start button.

② Select Programs.

③ Select Windows Explorer.

④ Open the Windows\Fonts folder.

⑤ Click the Similarity button. When you select this view, Windows Explorer organizes the fonts by similarity.

⑥ Click the down arrow at the right edge of the List fonts by similarity to list box.

⑦ Choose Courier New as the comparison font.

⑧ Double-click Courier New in the list of fonts to view the font preview dialog box for the Courier New font.

⑨ Double-click one of the other fonts that is listed as being similar to Courier New.

In the figure on the right, MS LineDraw is being compared to Courier New. The two dialog boxes were dragged to the side so the two could appear next to each other.

⑩ Click Done in the MS LineDraw font preview dialog box.

⑪ Click Done in the Courier New font preview dialog box.

You may want to compare a number of fonts to see which fonts are similar. To do this, you can use your printed font sample from the "Creating a list of your fonts" exercise to mark the fonts you prefer and the fonts you probably won't use. If one of a set of similar fonts is

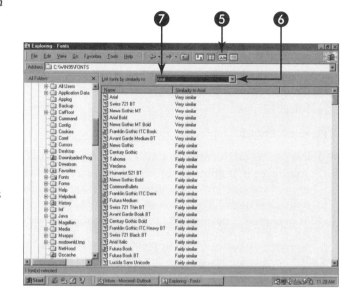

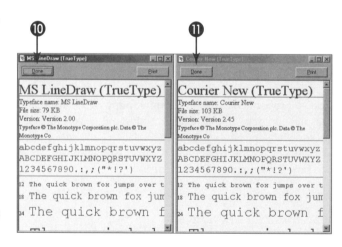

listed as an MS core font version (as Courier New is), you probably want to keep the MS core font because it's one of the Windows 98 standard fonts. There's probably little reason to keep several fonts that are virtually identical to each other.

INSTALLING AND DELETING FONTS

If a lot of fonts are similar, why would you want to add more fonts to your system? One reason is that there are many nice fonts that aren't simply a visual clone of another font. Another reason might be to make certain that documents that result from the collaboration of several authors have a unified appearance.

You've already seen some of the reasons for removing some of the fonts from your system. If two fonts are essentially identical, why have the extra clutter on your hard disk, and why have all those extra redundant choices when you want to select a font?

In the following exercises you see how to install and remove fonts. For practice, you first remove and then reinstall the WingDings font, one of the standard Windows 98 fonts. You cannot install the same font twice without first removing the first copy, so you have to start by deleting WingDings.

▶ Deleting extra fonts

You probably already have a list of fonts you don't use and can delete, but in this exercise you remove the WingDings font. This font contains symbols in place of the letters and numbers contained in normal fonts. A little later in this lesson you learn more about WingDings and other related types of fonts. WingDings is a good font to use for this exercise because it's on your Windows 98 CD-ROM and you can easily add it back in the next exercise.

❶ Click the Start button.

❷ Select Programs.

❸ Select Windows Explorer.

❹ Open the Windows\Fonts folder.

Installing new fonts

⑤ Place a diskette in drive A. (You can copy the WingDings font file to the diskette before deleting it so that you can reinstall it later.)

⑥ Point to the WingDings icon and hold down the left mouse button.

⑦ Drag the file to drive A to copy the file to the diskette.

⑧ Right-click WingDings.

⑨ Select Delete from the pop-up menu. (The right-click menu for fonts reflects that fewer options are available when you're dealing with installed fonts.)

⑩ Click Yes to delete any fonts currently selected. You can confirm the number of fonts you've chosen to delete by looking at the status line in the lower-left corner of the Windows Explorer window.

⑪ Click the Close button to close Windows Explorer.

Before you delete fonts, you should always copy them to a diskette. Then you can reinstall the font from the diskette if necessary. You may want to list all the fonts on the diskette label when you've copied them to the diskette so you can more easily locate the correct diskette later.

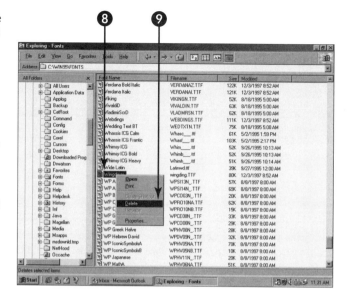

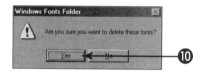

Installing new fonts

You have to install fonts before you can use them. Installing fonts is easy, but you must use the proper command to install fonts.

❶ Place the diskette containing Wingding.ttf in drive A. (If you're installing fonts from a different source, such as a CD-ROM, substitute the correct drive letter when you tell Windows 98 where to find the font file.)

❷ Right-click the Start button.

❸ Select Explore from the pop-up menu.

❹ Open the Windows\Fonts folder.

❺ Select File.

6 Select Install New Font to display the Add Fonts dialog box.

7 Click the down arrow at the right edge of the Drives list box.

8 Choose drive A.

9 Choose WingDings from the List of fonts list box.

10 Select the Copy fonts to Fonts folders checkbox. If this checkbox is not selected, Windows 98 still installs the font but always tries to access it from the location it was in when you installed it. In this case, you would have to always leave the diskette in drive A in order to use the WingDings font.

11 Click OK to install the font. (If you see a message like the one shown in the figure on the right, click OK, because the font is already installed.)

12 Click the Close button to close the Add Fonts dialog box.

If you buy a software package, such as one of the office suites, that includes extra fonts as a bonus, you may find that you need to use a different method to install the fonts that come with the package. These types of programs often have their own special installation programs rather than using the Windows 98 method of installing fonts. If so, be sure to follow the directions that came with the software package to correctly install the bonus fonts.

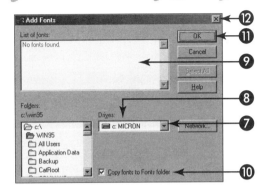

Using only TrueType fonts

Fonts come in a number of different types, but it's usually best to use TrueType fonts in Windows 98. TrueType fonts offer several advantages over other types of fonts. TrueType fonts are scalable, so no matter what size characters you use, the font has a high-quality appearance in the printed document. TrueType fonts also have the same appearance both onscreen and in the printed report. Finally, because TrueType is built into Windows 98, you don't need any extra font-management software to use TrueType fonts.

You can choose to have only TrueType fonts appear as the font selections in your applications. This prevents you from accidentally selecting a different type of font and perhaps reducing the quality of your printouts.

9

Working with Fonts

Wingdings and Dingbats

To specify that only TrueType fonts are offered as options, follow these steps:

1 Right-click the Start button.

2 Select Explore from the pop-up menu.

3 Open the Windows\Fonts folder.

4 Select View.

5 Select Options to display the Folder Options dialog box.

6 Click the TrueType tab. This tab only appears in the Options dialog box when the Fonts folder is open.

7 Select the Show only TrueType fonts in the programs on my computer checkbox.

8 Click OK to close the dialog box.

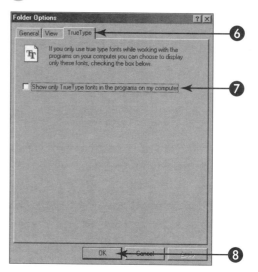

Because most of the fonts installed on your PC are probably TrueType fonts, telling your system to show only TrueType fonts doesn't cut down on the number of font selections very much. But it does ensure that you don't accidentally select a poorer quality font in place of a TrueType font.

LOOK OUT, IT'S WINGDINGS AND DINGBATS

No, this section isn't about Archie Bunker or his wife, Edith. It's about fonts made up of symbols such as arrows, flowers, smiling faces, and other strange things in place of the characters you normally expect to see. Why would you want strange symbols in place of letters and numbers? You can use these symbols in documents just as if they were normal text, that's why. If you want to add happy faces as bullet points, or maybe arrows to make a point stand out, symbols are just the ticket.

Why are they called WingDings, Dingbats, or other such strange names? Mostly so you know that these fonts aren't your everyday, ordinary text fonts.

▶ ## Using those strange symbols

The best way to get a feel for the appearance of symbol fonts is to create a small document and then change the character formatting to use a symbol font. In this exercise you see the strange results this produces.

1 Click the Start button.

2 Select Programs.

3 Select Accessories.

4 Select WordPad.

5 Type the following text: **This will show me how a symbol font changes the appearance of text I type in Windows 98**.

Or open WingDing.doc in the Lesson 9 folder on the *Windows 98 One Step at a Time* CD-ROM if you do not want to type the text yourself.

6 Press Enter twice to create a blank line and start a new line.

7 Point to the beginning of the text you just typed and hold down the left mouse button.

8 Drag the mouse pointer to select the entire sentence.

9 Release the mouse button.

10 Point to the highlighted text, hold down Ctrl, and hold down the left mouse button.

11 Drag the mouse pointer to the last line of the document to make a copy of the text.

12 Click the down arrow at the right edge of the Font list box.

13 Select WingDings to change the copy of the sentence to the WingDings font. (If you have the choice of more than one WingDings font, choose the one with the double T symbol, which indicates it is a TrueType font.) Believe it or not, only the font has changed—the second copy of the sentence *still* has the same text as it did before you changed the font!

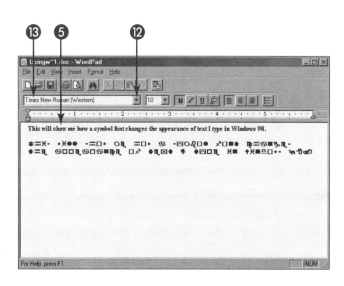

9

Working with Fonts

⑭ Drag the mouse pointer across the last two words in the second copy of the sentence. In the WingDings text, you can tell where words start and end by looking for the spaces between the words.

⑮ Choose Arial from the Font list box to change the font for these two words back into a human-readable font.

⑯ Select File.

⑰ Select Save.

⑱ Save your document as: **WingDing.doc**.

Symbol fonts can add a lot of character to your documents. They can also make documents impossible to read. Unless you're trying to create your own secret code, you may want a better way to use symbols than the method you used in this exercise. The next exercise shows you a better way to use symbols in your documents.

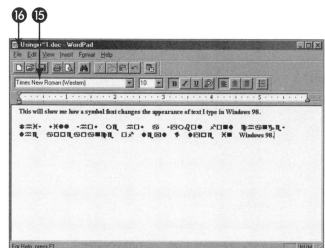

Inserting symbols with the Character Map

Symbol fonts may be interesting, but if all they do is make your documents unreadable, they're not too useful. Symbol fonts weren't really designed to format most document text, though. Their real purpose is to add an accent here and there—when you want something a little fancier than a standard round bullet to make a point stand out, for example. As the previous exercise demonstrated, though, finding just the right symbol can be pretty difficult—unless you know the trick. Windows 98 includes a handy tool, Character Map, that is designed to make using special symbols much easier.

TIP

Many programs, such as Microsoft Word, include an Insert ➢ Symbol command on their menus to make using Character Map a bit easier.

To practice using Character Map, follow these steps:

① If necessary, open a new WordPad document.

② Click the Start button.

③ Select Programs.

4 Select Accessories.

5 Select System Tools.

6 Select Character Map.

7 Click the down arrow at the right edge of the Font list box.

8 Choose WingDings.

9 Point to the first clock face symbol and hold down the left mouse button to magnify the view of the symbol. The magnified view shows that this clock symbol represents a clock showing one o'clock.

10 Double-click the one o'clock symbol to place it in the Characters to copy box.

11 Double-click the two o'clock, three o'clock, and four o'clock symbols to add them to the Characters to copy box, too. These clock symbols seem like good choices for a series of bullet points.

12 Click Copy to copy the selected symbols to the Clipboard.

13 Click the Close button to close Character Map.

14 Click the WordPad window to return to WordPad.

15 Click the Paste button to add the four clock symbols to your document.

16 Move the insertion point between the first and second symbols.

17 Press Enter.

18 Press Enter between the remaining symbols to place each symbol on a new line.

19 Press Ctrl+A to select all four symbols.

20 Choose 22 in the Font Size list box to increase the size of the symbols.

21 Move the insertion point to the first line just to the right of the one o'clock symbol.

22 Press Tab to move the insertion point to the first tab position.

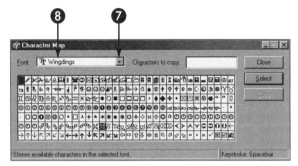

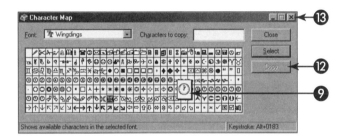

9

Working with Fonts

㉓ Choose Arial in the Font list box and 12 in the Font Size list box.

㉔ Type the following text: **My first point**.

㉕ Move the insertion point to the end of the second line, press Tab, choose the Arial font, and choose 12 as the font size.

㉖ Type the following text: **My second point**.

㉗ Move the insertion point to the end of the third line.

㉘ Press Tab.

㉙ Choose the Arial font.

㉚ Choose 12 as the font size.

㉛ Type the following text: **My third point**.

㉜ Move the insertion point to the end of the fourth line.

㉝ Press Tab.

㉞ Choose the Arial font.

㉟ Choose 12 as the font size.

㊱ Type the following text: **My fourth point**.

㊲ Select File.

㊳ Select Save and save your work as **Symbols for Bullets.doc**.

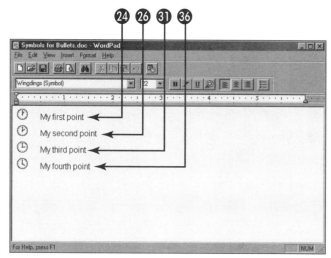

You can also insert symbols from the Character Map into an existing document. You might even find it easier to create your list of bullet points first, and then add the symbols once all the text has been entered and formatted. One advantage of this method is that you don't have to keep reselecting the text font as you add each point on the list.

TIP *You can also use Character Map to insert foreign and accented characters into a document by selecting the same font in Character Map as you're using for the document text.*

If a symbol you insert seems to change to a different character than it was in Character Map, select the character and change the font back to WingDings. You can also experiment with different font selections in Character Map. WingDings is only one of the many symbol fonts available.

SKILLS CHALLENGE: USING FONTS

Now it's time for you to play with fonts a bit on your own. The following steps should be pretty easy to follow.

1 Determine how many fonts are installed on your PC.

2 Print samples of several different fonts.

3 Create a WordPad document with at least four different fonts.

 How can you format text using the Arial Bold, Arial Italic, and Arial Bold Italic fonts?

4 Determine which fonts are most similar to Courier New.

 How can you tell which fonts are Windows 98 standard fonts?

 What symbol tells you that a font is a TrueType font?

5 Copy several fonts to a diskette.

6 Delete the fonts you just copied from Windows 98.

 How do you know for certain how many fonts will be deleted?

7 Reinstall the deleted fonts.

 What do you need to do before you can install a new version of a font?

Skills challenge

 6 *How can you make certain that your documents use only TrueType fonts?*

8 Reformat your WordPad document using the WingDings font.

9 Change the font back to Arial.

 7 *How can you add accents to characters in a document?*

TROUBLESHOOTING

If you encounter problems while trying to work through the exercises, here are some ideas that might help you correct the problems and keep going.

Problem	Solution
Character Map doesn't appear on my menu.	Double-click the Add/Remove Programs icon in the Control Panel. Character Map is in the System Tools group on the Windows Setup tab.
I don't have the same font choices shown in the figures.	Windows 98 includes a number of standard fonts, but application programs often add additional fonts. You may want to check the CD-ROMs for any large programs such as an office suite to see if there are additional fonts you can install.
When I try to print the font list, my printer stops printing and reports that it is out of memory.	Try printing the list one page at a time. You may also want to upgrade the amount of memory in your printer if you encounter this problem when printing other documents.

WRAP UP

In this lesson you learned how to use and organize fonts. You found out how to compare your fonts so you can choose the ones you prefer, and you learned how to clean up your system to remove fonts you don't really need. You also had some fun with symbol fonts and learned how you can spice up a document by adding fancy symbols.

The next lesson shows you how to share information between applications. You learn how you can use the best tools for each part of a job and then combine their efforts into a single document. You'll see that Windows 98 makes sharing a lot easier than you probably realize, so you don't have to struggle quite so hard to create the document you really want.

Don't Be Stingy; Share Your Data

45 MINUTES

GOALS

There are a number of avenues to data sharing in Windows 98, and this lesson shows you how to use the ones that are most useful to you. This lesson also teaches you some of the basics of using more than one application to create a single document so you can pick and choose the best tools for the job. In this lesson you learn about the following topics:

- Cutting, copying, and pasting data

- Figuring out what's on the Clipboard

- Dragging and dropping text

- Building compound documents with OLE

- Creating shortcuts on your desktop

Get ready

GET READY

You use several of the Windows 98 accessories in this lesson, so you may need your Windows 98 CD-ROM to install any that are missing. You also use three practice files from the CD-ROM that accompanies this book: Rose_Ama.doc, Des_Rose.bmp, and Hare_Frg.doc. These files can be found in the Lesson 10 folder on the CD-ROM.

A few of the examples in this lesson are a bit more interesting and fun if you have some Windows 98 programs, such as one of the major office suites, installed on your PC. It's not too important which office suite you have, because each of them provides objects you can use. If you don't have one of the office suites installed, you can still complete the lesson; however, you won't have quite as many toys to play with in some of the later exercises.

WHAT'S THIS CUT, COPY, AND PASTE ALL ABOUT?

In earlier lessons you copied and pasted objects a number of times, but you haven't really learned all that much about how cut, copy, and paste work. It's time to change that, and I'll show you how to make the most of the Windows 98 Clipboard.

Think of all you can do with the *Clipboard*; it is a pretty powerful tool, isn't it? You can use the Clipboard to copy a word or a phrase from a text document, but you can also use the Clipboard to copy a huge file from one disk to another. You can use the Clipboard to place an image into a document or to move a whole series of files from one place to another.

Cutting, copying, and pasting data

This exercise is mostly a review of some things you've done before, but that doesn't mean it's just a waste of your time. You probably haven't given too much thought to how you use the Clipboard, so it's time to make certain you understand how the Clipboard really works. Then you can see how to get the most benefit from the Clipboard.

It's important to understand one principal characteristic of the Clipboard — only one thing can be on the Clipboard at a time. When

Cutting, copying, and pasting data

you copy something new to the Clipboard, anything that's already there is erased. If you cut an object to place it on the Clipboard and then place something else on the Clipboard, the first object is gone forever. The most important point to keep in mind is that the Clipboard can only hold a single item at a time.

To practice cutting, copying, and pasting, follow these steps:

1. Click the Start button.

2. Select Programs.

3. Select Accessories.

4. Select WordPad.

5. Type the following text: **A Rose and an Amaranth blossomed side by side in a garden, and the Amaranth said to her neighbor, "How I envy you your beauty and your sweet scent! No wonder you are such a universal favorite." But the Rose replied with a shade of sadness in her voice, "Ah, my dear friend, I bloom but for a time: my petals soon wither and fall, and then I die. But your flowers never fade, even if they are cut; for they are everlasting."**

   If you don't want to type the text, open Rose_Ama.doc in the Lesson 10 folder on the book's CD-ROM.

6. Press Enter twice.

7. Type the following text: **"Greatness carries its own penalties."**

8. Select File.

9. Select Save As.

10. Type the following text in the File name text box: **The Rose and the Amaranth**.

    This is another of Aesop's fables. If you opened the file from the CD-ROM, you need to specify a folder on your hard disk to save the file.

10

Don't Be Stingy; Share Your Data

Cutting, copying, and pasting data

TIP

Files you copy from a CD-ROM always have their Read-only property set. To change this setting after you've copied a file from a CD-ROM, right-click the file, select Properties, and remove the check from the Read-only checkbox.

⑪ Click Save to save the file.

⑫ Double-click the first occurrence of Amaranth to select the word.

⑬ Select Edit.

⑭ Select Cut to remove the selected word and place it on the Clipboard.

The figure on the right shows the document after Amaranth has been cut.

⑮ Click the Paste button to paste the word Amaranth back into the document.

⑯ Double-click the first occurrence of Rose.

⑰ Click the Copy button to place a copy of the word Rose on the Clipboard.

⑱ Select Edit.

⑲ Select Undo. Were you surprised to see Amaranth disappear again?

⑳ Click the Paste button to paste the word currently on the Clipboard back into the document.

The figure on the right shows the result, which may not have been what you expected. Because the last word you copied to the Clipboard was Rose, that's the word that was pasted back where Amaranth used to be.

㉑ Double-click the word Amaranth, which appears later in the first sentence.

㉒ Select Edit.

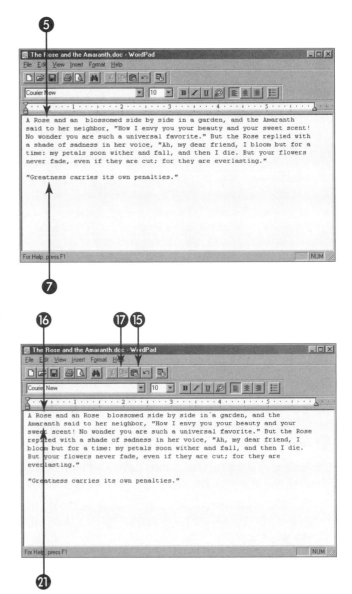

㉓ Select Copy to place another copy of `Amaranth` on the Clipboard.

㉔ Select Edit.

㉕ Select Undo.

Even though the last command you used was Edit ➤ Copy, the command that is undone is the pasting of the word Rose. The Edit ➤ Undo command reverses the last change made within the WordPad document, not commands that place objects on the Clipboard.

㉖ Select Edit.

㉗ Select Paste.

You probably guessed that the word `Amaranth` would come back, as shown in the figure on the right.

㉘ Click the Save button.

This exercise demonstrated an important point that would be a little difficult to grasp without such a graphic example. The Clipboard is an independent part of Windows 98 and isn't affected by the Edit ➤ Undo command. When you place something on the Clipboard, whatever was already there disappears without a trace or a warning. If you need to recover something you placed on the Clipboard, use Edit ➤ Paste immediately before you accidentally lose it forever!

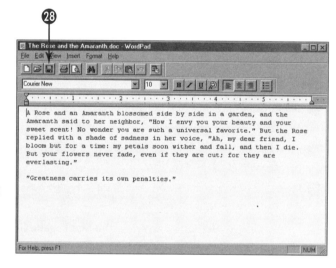

Using keyboard shortcuts

Sometimes it's more convenient to use the keyboard than to grab for the mouse and choose commands from a menu or click buttons. Many Windows 98 commands have keyboard shortcuts that allow you to keep your hands right on the keyboard and not break your concentration while you cut, copy, or paste.

You need to press two keys at the same time to use most keyboard shortcuts. In most instances, you first press and hold the Ctrl key and then press the second key to tell Windows 98 which shortcut you want to use. In this short exercise you try out a few common keyboard shortcuts.

10

Don't Be Stingy; Share Your Data

Using keyboard shortcuts

TIP

If you're unable to press two keys at the same time, install the Accessibility options on the Windows Setup tab of the Add/Remove Programs dialog box.

1 Insert the *Windows 98 One Step at a Time* CD-ROM into your CD-ROM drive.

2 Open The Rose and the Amaranth.doc in WordPad.

3 Use the arrow keys to move the insertion point to the beginning of the first occurrence of the word `Amaranth`.

4 Hold down Shift.

5 Select the entire word by using the right arrow key. (Shift acts as an anchor so you can extend the selection.)

6 Press Ctrl+X to cut the selected word to the Clipboard. (Ctrl+X is a shortcut for Edit ➢ Cut.)

7 Press Ctrl+V to paste the word back into the document. (Ctrl+V is a shortcut for Edit ➢ Paste.)

8 Press Shift+Ctrl+left arrow to select the word again. In this case, Ctrl+left arrow is a shortcut for moving the insertion point one word to the left, and Shift anchors the selection.

9 Press Ctrl+C to copy the selected word to the Clipboard. (Ctrl+C is a shortcut for Edit ➢ Copy.)

10 Press the left arrow to move the insertion point and deselect the selected word.

11 Press Ctrl+V to paste a second copy of Amaranth into the document.

12 Press Ctrl+Z to undo the insertion. (Ctrl+Z is a shortcut for Edit ➢ Undo.)

Some commands have more than one keyboard shortcut, but the second shortcut isn't considered to be an "official" Windows 98 shortcut. Still, you may find some of the unofficial shortcuts handy. The following table shows several of the more common keyboard shortcuts and a few unofficial shortcuts that may come in handy—especially if you find them easier to remember than the official shortcut.

TABLE 10-1 SOME COMMON KEYBOARD SHORTCUTS

Command	Official Shortcut	Unofficial Shortcut
Edit ➢ Copy	Ctrl+C	Ctrl+Insert
Edit ➢ Cut	Ctrl+X	Shift+Del
Edit ➢ Find	Ctrl+F	
Edit ➢ Paste	Ctrl+V	Shift+Insert
Edit ➢ Undo	Ctrl+Z	
Edit ➢ Select All	Ctrl+A	
File ➢ Save	Ctrl+S	
File ➢ New	Ctrl+N	
File ➢ Open	Ctrl+O	
File ➢ Print	Ctrl+P	
File ➢ Exit		Alt+F4

TIP

Windows Explorer has another handy shortcut. Press F2 to rename a selected file.

▶ Copying information to a dialog box

Windows 98 programs often use dialog boxes to request information from you. In this exercise you learn how to use the Clipboard to make it a little easier to enter some of the information required in dialog boxes. This technique is especially helpful when you need to enter a long or unusually difficult filename, but the same technique may well be useful when you enter other information in a dialog box, too.

1 Insert the *Windows 98 One Step at a Time* CD-ROM into your CD-ROM drive.

2 Open The Rose and the Amaranth.doc in WordPad.

3 Drag the mouse pointer across the words `Greatness carries its own penalties` to select the moral of the fable.

4 Click the Copy button to copy the selection to the Clipboard.

5 Select File.

6 Select Save As to display the Save As dialog box.

7 Right-click the File name text box.

8 Select Paste.

The dialog box should now appear as shown in the figure on the right.

9 Click Save to save the file using the new name.

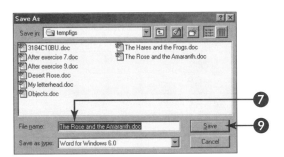

> *You can also use the Ctrl+V or Shift+Insert keyboard shortcuts to paste information into a dialog box text box.*

When you copy information into a dialog box, watch out for a trailing space after the final word of a multiple word selection. WordPad, as well as most other word processing programs, automatically selects the space following a word if the word isn't followed by a period or other punctuation. If you include the extra trailing space, that space becomes part of the filename. This can be confusing because the extra space may not be readily apparent.

Capturing screens with the Clipboard

There are times when nothing but a picture tells the full story. Sometimes the picture you need is a copy of your computer screen, or at least a portion of your screen. This can be especially true if you've made a number of settings in a dialog box, and you need a printed record so you can redo the settings in the event of a problem.

> *Make a copy of the registration information screen when you install new software so you have the*

information immediately available if you have to call the program's technical support line.

You can use the Clipboard to capture copies of your screen and then paste those images into a program. Using the Clipboard for capturing screens isn't as convenient as using software designed for screen capturing, but if you only need an occasional screen, the Clipboard suffices. If you need something more sophisticated, you may want to try one of the shareware screen capture programs included on the *Windows 98 One Step at a Time* CD-ROM.

① Open WordPad.

② Press Alt+Print Scrn to capture the active window on your screen (your keyboard may show Prt Scr, Print Screen, or some similar variation).

③ Click the Paste button to paste a copy of the Clipboard contents into the document.

The figure on the right shows the image of the WordPad window inserted into the document.

You can capture the entire screen by pressing Print Scrn alone. In most cases, however, it's probably more useful to capture the active window by pressing Alt+Print Scrn. Make certain the window you want to capture is the active window by clicking the window's title bar before you capture the active window; otherwise, you may not capture the window you expect to capture.

WHAT'S ON THE CLIPBOARD?

It's Lesson 10, do you know what's on your Clipboard? The last thing you copied to the Clipboard, of course, but are you sure you remember the last time you copied something to the Clipboard? To view your Clipboard, you can just use Edit ➢ Paste and paste a copy of whatever is on the Clipboard into your document, but there's an easier way — use the Clipboard Viewer. You can even use the Clipboard Viewer to save Clipboard contents for future use, so if you want to place new objects on the Clipboard, you don't have to lose what's already there.

③ This is an image of the WordPad window inserted into a WordPad document

10

Don't Be Stingy; Share Your Data

Using the Clipboard Viewer

Using the Clipboard Viewer

The Clipboard Viewer extends the Clipboard so you can view and save the Clipboard contents. The Clipboard Viewer also provides a handy little option that enables you to clear the contents of the Clipboard. If you share your PC with someone else, you can use this feature to make certain no one else sees sensitive information you've been using. You can also use this feature to clear the Clipboard after you've used it to copy a large object. Your system may slow down quite a bit if too much data remains on the Clipboard after it is no longer needed.

TIP

To quickly replace the Clipboard contents, copy a single letter or a single word to the Clipboard.

❶ Insert the *Windows 98 One Step at a Time* CD-ROM into your CD-ROM drive.

❷ Open The Rose and the Amaranth.doc in WordPad.

❸ Press Alt+Print Scrn to copy an image of the WordPad window to the Clipboard.

❹ Click the Start button.

❺ Select Programs.

❻ Select Accessories.

❼ Select Clipboard Viewer (if you've installed ClipBook Viewer, you can either select ClipBook Viewer or reinstall Clipboard Viewer to complete this exercise). The figure on the right shows the Clipboard Viewer as it should appear.

❽ Select File.

❾ Select Save As to display the Save As dialog box.

❿ Type the following text in the File name text box: **Rose**.

⓫ Click OK to save the Clipboard contents for future use.

⓬ Click the WordPad title bar.

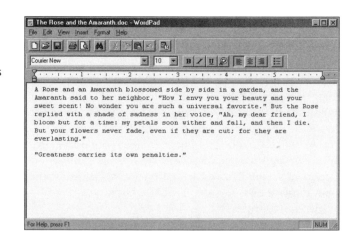

⑬ Drag the mouse pointer to highlight the final sentence, `Greatness carries its own penalties.`

⑭ Click the Copy button to replace the current Clipboard contents.

⑮ Click the Clipboard Viewer title bar to verify that the selected text has replaced the screen you captured earlier on the Clipboard, as the figure on the right shows.

⑯ Select File.

⑰ Select Open to display the Open dialog box.

⑱ Double-click Rose.clp to indicate you wish to open the Clipboard contents you saved earlier. Windows 98 displays the message shown in the figure on the right, asking you to verify that you wish to replace the current Clipboard contents.

⑲ Select Yes to place the saved image back on the Clipboard.

⑳ Select Edit.

㉑ Select Delete to remove the image from the Clipboard.

㉒ Click Yes again to confirm your action and clear the Clipboard.

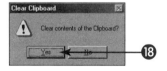

NOTE *You run into a bit of strange behavior if you try to save the Clipboard contents using a name longer than eight characters or one that includes spaces: Clipboard not only won't save the contents, but it also neglects to tell you there's a problem. If you need to be certain that you've successfully saved the Clipboard contents, use the File ➢ Open command to verify that the file was saved before you place anything else on the Clipboard.*

DRAG IT AND DROP IT

Windows 98 is a highly visual environment, so naturally you think you can perform many of the common tasks visually, too. This turns out to be the case, and the visual method is often the easiest method, too. Copying and moving data using drag & drop is one of those examples where the visual method is so easy, it becomes almost second nature after you've tried it a few times.

10

Don't Be Stingy; Share Your Data

Moving data from one place to another

▶ Moving data from one place to another

How would you move a box or a book from one place to another? Most likely you'd simply pick it up, carry it where you want it, and drop it. That's the idea behind drag & drop — you use your mouse to pick up the data at its source, drag it to the destination, and drop it. (Don't you wish you could use your mouse next time the sofa needs moving?) There's no need to worry about finding the right menu commands when you can simply move the data right on the screen without ever opening a menu.

TIP

Hold down Ctrl while you're dragging and dropping to copy rather than move the selected item.

Drag & drop doesn't use the Windows 98 Clipboard, so if you already have data on the Clipboard, you won't affect that data by using drag & drop. This makes drag & drop an excellent companion to the commands that do use the Clipboard. You can use drag & drop to copy or move data when that's the most convenient method, and use the Clipboard when that's easier.

❶ Insert the *Windows 98 One Step at a Time* CD-ROM into your CD-ROM drive.

❷ Open The Rose and the Amaranth.doc in WordPad.

❸ Point to the quotation mark at the beginning of the moral and hold down the left mouse button.

❹ Drag the pointer to the end of the line so that "Greatness carries its own penalties." is completely highlighted.

❺ Release the mouse button.

❻ Move the mouse pointer over the selected section of text and hold down the left mouse button.

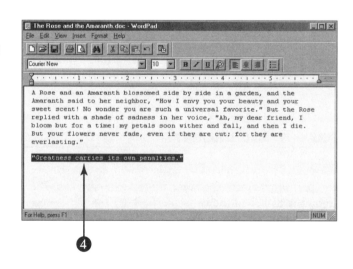

7 Drag the selection to the beginning of the document.

8 Hold down Ctrl.

9 Drag the selected section of text back to its original position at the end of the document. The Ctrl key enables drag & drop to copy rather than just move text.

10 Drag across the extra copy of the moral at the beginning of the document.

11 Click the Cut button to remove the extra copy from the document.

You may want to practice using drag & drop to move and to copy data until you're completely comfortable with the process. People sometimes have trouble learning to use drag & drop because they forget to release the left mouse button after they've selected the data they want to move or copy, or they forget to hold down the left mouse button once they move the mouse pointer back into the selection. If you make a selection and don't release the left mouse button before you use drag and drop, the selection simply continues to grow as long as you continue to hold down the mouse button. If you make a selection and then click the left mouse button rather than hold down the button, you remove the highlight and the data is no longer selected. You may want to try both of these errors yourself so you can see what happens. The WordPad document, The Rose and the Amaranth.doc, is a good place to practice using drag & drop because you can always reload the copy from the *Windows 98 One Step at a Time* CD-ROM if the document becomes too messed up.

Dragging data between programs

Many Windows 98 programs enable you to drag and drop data from one program to another. This makes sharing data very easy because you can simply select the data you want to use, and then drag and drop it onto the target document.

7

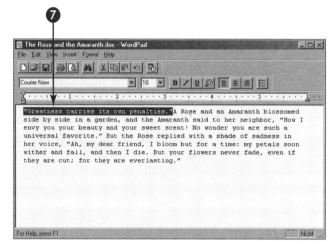

10

Don't Be Stingy; Share Your Data

Dragging data between programs

*While many Windows 98 programs support drag and drop between programs, not all programs support this feature. Without getting too technical, to send data, programs must be **OLE servers**; to receive drag and drop information, programs must be **OLE clients**. Because it takes a bit more programming effort to support these features, you're considerably more likely to find that more modern, full-featured programs support drag and drop between programs, while simple programs don't include this support. The best way to determine if your programs support drag and drop between programs is simply to give it a try.*

In this exercise you learn how you can use drag & drop to place a copy of an image into a WordPad document. WordPad can both accept and send data via drag & drop.

1 Insert the *Windows 98 One Step at a Time* CD-ROM into your CD-ROM drive.

2 Open The Rose and the Amaranth.doc in WordPad.

3 Click the Start button.

4 Select Programs.

5 Select Windows Explorer.

6 Choose the Lesson 10 folder on the *Windows 98 One Step at a Time* CD-ROM.

7 Click Des_Rose.bmp to select the file.

8 Drag the icon onto the Taskbar icon for The Rose and the Amaranth.doc in WordPad. The Taskbar icon only shows `The Rose and the` followed by three periods because there isn't room for the entire title in the icon.

9 Drop the Des_Rose.bmp icon on the Taskbar icon. When you do, Windows 98 displays the message shown in the figure on the next page. This message appears because you can't drop data on a Taskbar icon; you must wait for the destination document to open and then drop the data into the document.

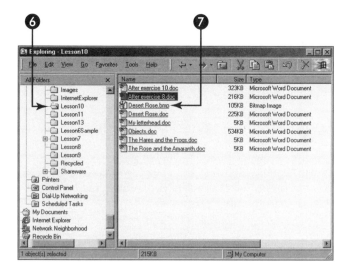

⑩ Click OK.

⑪ Go back to Windows Explorer and click the Des_Rose.bmp icon.

⑫ Drag the icon onto the Taskbar icon for The Rose and the Amaranth.doc, and continue to hold down the left mouse button while you wait for the WordPad window to appear on top of all other windows.

⑬ While still holding the left mouse button down, move the pointer into the WordPad window.

⑭ Drop the image at the end of the document. You may want to move the insertion point to the end of the moral and press Enter to move the image down a line. You may also want to drag the WordPad window borders a bit so you can see the entire document, as shown in the figure on the right.

⑮ Click the Save button to save your document.

Dragging and dropping data between applications is a pretty easy way to do some neat things with your documents, isn't it? In the next section you learn how you can do quite a bit more by sharing data between applications — even when the applications don't fully support the drag-and-drop method of sharing data.

BUILDING COMPOUND DOCUMENTS WITH OLE

Windows 98 uses something called *OLE* — Object Linking and Embedding — to share data between programs. OLE is actually a pretty sophisticated way to share data because it allows you to create *compound documents*, which are nothing more than documents containing data from a number of sources. The document you saved when you completed the last exercise was a compound document because it contained text from WordPad and an image from Paint.

Compound documents allow you the freedom to use the tools best suited to each task while still producing a single, unified document. The WordPad document containing the desert rose image is a good example of this on a small scale. WordPad has no way to create the image file itself, and Paint isn't too good when it comes to formatting text. Between the two applications, however, you were

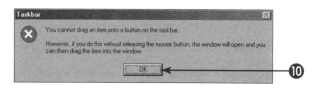

10

Don't Be Stingy; Share Your Data

Embedding information

able to create a document containing nicely formatted text and a pretty image of a flower. If you use one of the major Windows 98 office suites, you find that each of the several programs in the suite is best suited to one type of task — such as word processing, spreadsheets, and graphics. When you combine their talents into a single compound document, you can create a pretty fancy document that none of the programs could produce independently.

OLE actually has two parts — *linking* and *embedding*. These refer to how the object is placed in the document. For the most part you can ignore the difference between the two, but there are some differences worth pointing out:

- Embedded objects take more room than linked objects, because the document contains an actual copy of embedded objects rather than a simple pointer to the original file.

- Editing is slightly different for the two types of objects. You can edit either embedded or linked objects by double-clicking them, but editing linked objects starts the source application rather than editing the object right in the compound document.

- Linked objects are updated if information is changed in the source file.

- Embedded objects remain as they were when you added them to the compound document, even if the source file is updated.

- Linked objects need access to their source files, which makes linking a poor choice if you need to send the compound document to someone else so they can work on the document on their computer.

Embedding information in your documents

In most cases, embedding information into a document rather than linking to the source is probably the best choice. While it's true that documents containing embedded data tend to be larger than those containing linked information, this difference in size is usually offset by the convenience of having everything in one file. With all the data in one file, you don't have to worry that part of a compound document might become unavailable if you accidentally move or delete a source file because you forgot that it was linked to another document.

In this exercise you use your old friends WordPad and Paint to create a compound document. You could use many other programs to create compound documents, but these two work okay, and they offer the advantage of being available on every Windows 98 PC.

1 Click the Start button.

2 Select Programs.

3 Select Accessories.

4 Select WordPad.

5 Type the following text: **This is the desert rose, the cactus flower.**

6 Press Enter twice.

7 Click the Start button.

8 Select Programs.

9 Select Accessories.

10 Select Paint.

11 Select File.

12 Select Open.

13 Click the down arrow at the right side of the Look in list box.

14 Choose the Lesson 10 folder on the CD-ROM that accompanies this book.

15 Double-click Des_Rose.bmp to open the image file.

16 Select Edit.

17 Select Select All to select the image.

18 Select Edit.

19 Select Copy to place a copy of the image on the Clipboard.

⑳ Click the WordPad icon on the Taskbar to return to WordPad.

㉑ Select Edit.

㉒ Select Paste Special to display the Paste Special dialog box.

You can choose from the available formats in the As list box — these are the image formats Paint makes available. Other applications provide different formats. Because Paint does not directly support linking, only the Paste (embedding) options are available.

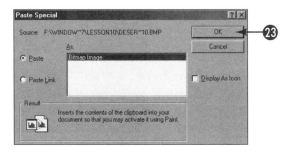

㉓ Click OK to paste the Bitmap Image format into your document.

㉔ Select File.

㉕ Select Save.

㉖ Type the following text in the File name text box: **Desert Rose**.

㉗ Click Save to save the compound document.

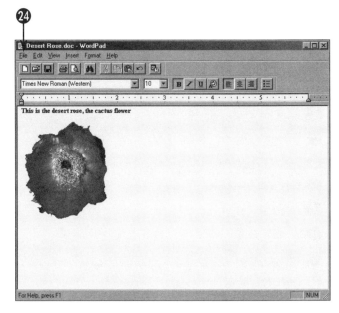

Embedding information in a compound document using the Clipboard is quite similar to the drag and drop method you used earlier, but there are important differences. When you drag and drop information into a document, the information is always embedded — you don't have the choice of linking the information rather than embedding it. Also, an object you drag and drop always is embedded in the default format. While this may be what you want most of the time, it won't be true all the time. For example, when you embed information from a database program or from a spreadsheet program, you have the option to embed the information as a database (or spreadsheet) object, as a bitmap image, or as one or more types of text. You can choose the data format that works the best in your document.

If the source application directly supports linking, selecting the Paste Link radio button displays different format options in the Paste Special dialog box. For example, if the source application is a spreadsheet program, you are likely to have an option to link to a worksheet file.

Inserting an object into your document

Inserting an object into your document

In the previous exercises you learned a couple ways to add existing objects to form a compound document. Sometimes, though, you want to build the various pieces of the document as you go. One way to do this is to insert objects into the document. In this exercise you learn how to insert objects into a document by creating a new object when you need one.

1 Click the Start button.

2 Select Programs.

3 Select Accessories.

4 Select WordPad.

5 Select Insert.

6 Select Object to display the Insert Object dialog box.

The object types shown in your Object Type list box depend on the programs installed on your system, and they probably won't match what is shown in the figure.

7 Choose Bitmap Image as the type of object to insert.

8 Click OK to insert the object.

WordPad's appearance changes to reflect the type of object you're creating. In this case, WordPad looks like Paint, because you're editing a bitmap image, which is done in Paint. This appearance change is temporary and is often referred to as *in-place editing* because the toolbars of the source application are displayed so you can edit the object without leaving the document.

9 Select the Airbrush tool.

10 Spray paint the word **OBJECT** in the box as shown in the figure on the right. You can create any sort of fancy image you like using the Paint tools, but for the purpose of this exercise, just about anything is okay.

11 Click anywhere in the document window outside the object box to restore the WordPad toolbars.

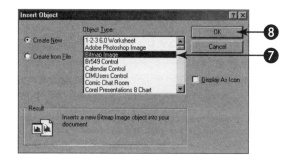

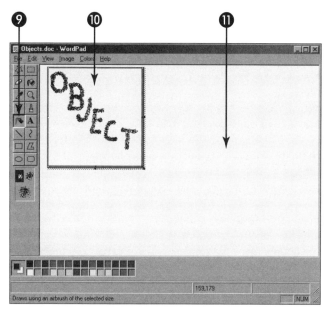

Inserting a file into a document

12 Select File.

13 Select Save.

14 Type the following text in the File name text box: **Objects**.

15 Click Save to save the document.

Using the Insert ➢ Object command allows you to create the pieces of your compound document as you need them. But the Insert ➢ Object command has other advantages, too:

- **Disk space.** Compound documents containing embedded objects take up more disk space because the embedded objects are actually contained in the compound document. If you use Insert ➢ Object and create the embedded objects as you need them, those embedded objects only exist within the compound document file. You won't be wasting disk space for a second copy of the object as you would if you created the object first and then assembled the compound document from a set of existing objects.

- **Document updating.** Embedded objects created using the Insert ➢ Object command can only be accessed through the compound document itself. Thus, there is no risk of updating one of the objects in the original application and then forgetting to update the compound document itself.

Inserting a file into a document

You can also use the Insert ➢ Object command to insert an existing file into a compound document. In some cases this is the only way you can create a linked rather than an embedded object. For example, even though Paint doesn't directly support linking, you can still use Insert ➢ Object to create a link to a Paint image file. To see the advantage of this, suppose that you want to link several compound documents to a master image file, but there is a possibility that the master image might need to be edited or updated later. Because the compound documents are linked to the master image file, any subsequent changes you make to the master image file are included in each of the compound documents.

Inserting a file into a document

TIP

You can only link to an object after you've saved the object to a file.

To insert a file into a document, follow these steps:

1 Insert the *Windows 98 One Step at a Time* CD-ROM into your CD-ROM drive.

2 Open Objects.doc in WordPad.

3 Select Insert.

4 Select Object.

5 Select the Create from File radio button.

When you select this radio button, the Insert Object dialog box changes appearance as shown in the figure on the right.

6 Select the Link checkbox to create a link to the file rather than embedding the object in the compound document.

7 Click the Browse button to display the Browse dialog box.

8 Click the down arrow at the right edge of the Look in list box.

9 Choose the Lesson 10 folder on the CD-ROM accompanying this book.

10 Double-click Des_Rose.bmp.

11 Click OK to insert the file link into your compound document. Your screen should now appear similar to the figure on the right. The first bitmap image, which contains the spray painted word "OBJECT," is embedded, while the second bitmap image is linked.

12 Double-click the Des_Rose.bmp image to edit the image.

Editing a linked object opens the source application — Paint in this case — rather than simply changing the toolbars. There's a good reason for this difference. Changes you make in a linked object must be saved in the original file so that any other compound documents linked to that object are also updated.

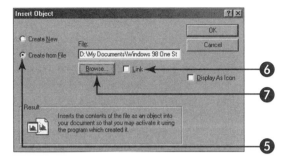

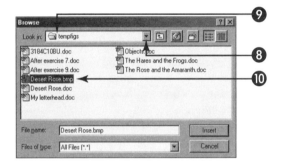

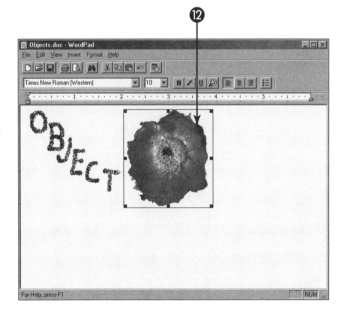

10

Don't Be Stingy; Share Your Data

Creating document shortcuts

NOTE

If you make any changes to Des_Rose.bmp, select File > Save As and save the file (you won't be able to save any changes to the CD-ROM).

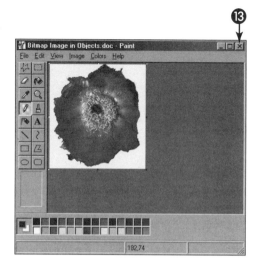

13 Click the Close button to close Paint and return to WordPad.

14 Click the Save button to save your changes.

When you create a compound document that contains links to other files, the source files must always be available before you open the compound document. Because of this, it's much more difficult to share such compound documents with others. You not only need to provide the compound document file, but also all of the source files. Even if you do, it's likely some of the links will be broken and need to be fixed, which may not be easy to do. If you intend to share compound documents, it's best to plan ahead and use embedded rather than linked objects.

MAKE SOME SHORTCUTS ON YOUR DESKTOP

Sharing your data isn't only about creating compound documents or using the Clipboard to copy and paste information. Sometimes, sharing your data may be something a whole lot simpler, like making it easier to access information quickly. In this section you learn about a couple of techniques you can use to make information available right on your desktop.

Creating document shortcuts

You probably create a lot of documents that have a number of identical elements. If you own a small business, for example, you probably send business letters that start out by printing your letterhead at the top of the first page. Why not create a document that has the letterhead already entered, and then save a shortcut to that master document on your desktop so you can quickly start a new letter just by double-clicking an icon on your desktop?

Creating document shortcuts

1 Click the Start button.

2 Select Programs.

3 Select Accessories.

4 Select WordPad.

5 Type the following text and press Enter: **My Wonderful Company**.

6 Type the following text and press Enter: **PO Box 123**.

7 Type the following text and press Enter: **My Town, NV 89898**.

8 Drag the mouse pointer across the first line of text.

9 Choose 20 in the Font Size list box.

10 Drag the mouse pointer across all three lines.

11 Click the Center button.

12 Click the Save button.

13 Type the following text in the File name text box: **My letterhead**.

14 Click Save to save the file.

Your document should look similar to Myletter.doc in the Lesson 10 folder on the CD-ROM that accompanies this book.

15 If WordPad is taking up the entire screen, click the Restore button so you can see part of your Windows 98 desktop.

16 Click the Open button to display the Open dialog box.

17 Right-click Myletter.doc.

18 Select Properties to display the Properties for Myletter.doc dialog box as shown in the figure on the right (your dialog box may look a little different).

19 Select the Read-only checkbox. Because you're going to use the document as a master document, you want to make certain you don't accidentally overwrite Myletter.doc when you save a letter that you started from the master document. Making the file read-only prevents you from saving a modified copy of the document unless you specify a new name for the file.

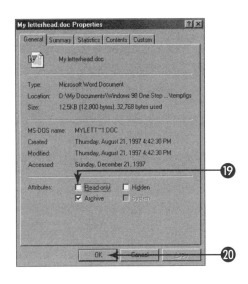

Creating document shortcuts

⑳ Click OK to return to the Open dialog box.

㉑ Point to Myletter.doc and hold down the right mouse button.

㉒ Drag the pointer onto your desktop. When you release the mouse button, Windows 98 displays a shortcut menu.

㉓ Select Create Shortcut(s) Here to add a shortcut to the document to your desktop.

㉔ Click Cancel to close the Open dialog box and return to WordPad.

㉕ Click the Close button to close WordPad.

㉖ Double-click the Shortcut to Myletter.doc icon on your desktop to open the document — if you have Microsoft Word installed, the document will probably open in Word rather than in WordPad.

㉗ Select File.

㉘ Select Save As and give the document a new name.

If you attempt to save the document as Myletter.doc, WordPad displays a message similar to the one in the figure on the right because the file is read-only and must be saved under a new name.

㉙ Click OK and save the file with a different name.

㉚ Click the Close button to close WordPad.

Although you used this technique to save a shortcut to a document created by WordPad, you can use this same technique to save any type of document shortcut on your desktop. Once you've saved document shortcuts on your desktop, you can use those shortcuts to create new documents as you did in this exercise, or you can drag the shortcuts into a master document to quickly create a compound document.

▶ *Creating document scraps*

One of the important things you've learned about the Clipboard is that when you copy something new to the Clipboard, any existing data on the Clipboard is replaced by the new data. There are times, though, when it would be a lot handier if you could save items for future use without having them destroyed by the next thing copied to the Clipboard. It turns out that Windows 98 provides a method for you to do just this. You can save *scraps* — pieces of documents — on your desktop. These scraps can then be added back to the original document or even used in a different document whenever you need them. In this exercise you learn how to create and use scraps.

1 Click the Start button.

2 Select Programs.

3 Select Accessories.

4 Select WordPad.

5 Type the following text: **The Hares and the Frogs**.

6 Press Enter twice.

7 Type the following text (or open Hare_Frg.doc in the Lesson 10 folder on the *Windows 98 One Step at a Time* CD-ROM): **The Hares were so persecuted by the other beasts, they did not know where to go. As soon as they saw a single animal approach them, off they used to run. One day they saw a troop of wild Horses stampeding about, and in quite a panic all the Hares scuttled off to a lake hard by, determined to drown themselves rather than live in such a continual state of fear. But just as they got near the bank of the lake, a troop of Frogs, frightened in their turn by the approach of the Hares scuttled off, and jumped into the water. "Truly," said one of the Hares, "things are not so bad as they seem:**

8 Press Enter twice.

9 Type the following text: **"There is always someone worse off than yourself."**

10 Click the Save button.

11 Type the following text in the File name text box: **The Hares and the Frogs**.

12 Click Save to save the file.

13 Drag the mouse point across `As soon as they saw a single animal approach them, off they used to run.` to select the sentence.

14 Release the left mouse button.

15 Point to the selected sentence and hold down the left mouse button.

16 Drag the pointer onto your desktop to create the first scrap on the desktop.

17 Drag the mouse pointer across `One day they saw a troop of wild Horses stampeding about, and in quite a panic all the Hares scuttled off to a lake hard by, determined to drown themselves rather than live in such a continual state of fear` to select the sentence.

18 Release the left mouse button.

19 Point to the selected sentence and hold down the left mouse button.

20 Drag the pointer onto your desktop to create the second scrap.

Your screen should now appear similar to the figure on the right.

21 Drag the mouse pointer across the second and third sentences starting with `As soon as` and ending with `state of fear` so that both sentences are selected.

22 Select Edit.

23 Select Clear to remove the selection.

24 Double-click the first occurrence of the word `Hares`.

25 Click the Copy button to replace anything that is on the Clipboard.

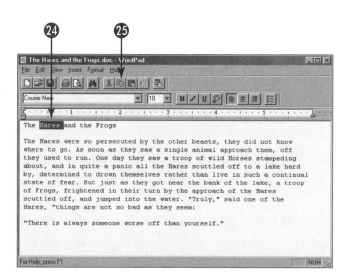

㉖ Point to the WordPad document scrap 'As soon as they . . .' icon on your desktop, and hold down the left mouse button.

㉗ Drag the scrap back into the correct position following the first sentence of the main paragraph.

㉘ Drag the second scrap back into its correct position. Your document should now once again be complete.

Scraps are useful for purposes other than simply short-term storage of text as you rearrange a document. Just as you created a letterhead shortcut on your desktop, you might use scraps to hold other text you frequently need to insert into documents. For example, if you regularly include a limited warranty clause in documents, you could save the text of the warranty in a scrap. If you often need to insert a set of directions in your documents, the directions might be a good scrap candidate, too. The only real limit to how you can use scraps is the amount of free desktop space you have available.

SKILLS CHALLENGE: SHARING DATA

You'll want to practice the important data sharing skills you learned in this lesson. The following steps suggest tasks for you to try.

❶ Open The Rose and the Amaranth.doc.

❷ Cut the second sentence to the Clipboard.

❸ Drag the first sentence to the end of the document.

 How does dragging and dropping affect the Clipboard contents?

❹ Undo the move.

❺ Paste the missing sentence back into the document.

Skills challenge

6 Capture a copy of the screen to the Clipboard.

> **2** *How can you copy just the active window instead of the entire screen?*

7 View the Clipboard contents.

8 Save the captured screen for future use.

> **3** *Which Windows 98 accessory can you use to change the size of a captured screen image?*

> **4** *How can you add a captured screen image to a WordPad document?*

9 Clear the Clipboard.

10 Drag the Des_Rose.bmp file into the WordPad document.

11 Edit the Des_Rose.bmp image.

> **5** *How can you tell whether an object inserted into a compound document is embedded or linked?*

> **6** *How can you create a link to an object when the source application doesn't directly support linking?*

12 Create a scrap of Des_Rose.bmp on your desktop.

> **7** *What happens to the current Clipboard contents when you create a scrap?*

TROUBLESHOOTING

If you encounter problems while trying to work through the exercises, here are some ideas that might help you correct the problems and keep going.

Problem	Solution
Clipboard Viewer doesn't appear on my menu.	Double-click the Add/Remove Programs icon in the Control Panel. Clipboard Viewer is in the Accessories group on the Windows Setup tab.

WRAP UP

In this lesson you learned how to share information between applications. You learned how you can use the best tool for each part of a job and then combine their efforts into a single document. You also learned some tricks for sharing information between different documents by creating scraps.

The next lesson covers some very important information on working with Windows 98 applications. You learn quite a few tricks to make your life a lot easier. You also learn more about many of the basic, but often confusing, aspects of using Windows 98 applications.

Working with Windows 98 Applications

GOALS

You can learn many little tricks and techniques to help you get more done with less work and in less time in Windows 98. This lesson brings these tricks and techniques together to help you really understand the best ways to work with Windows 98 applications. Most of the exercises in this lesson are fairly short and, at first, may seem like a review of things you already know. On the other hand, you may be surprised at how much you still can learn about better ways to work with Windows 98. In this chapter you learn about the following topics:

- Choosing menus and commands

- Opening several programs at once

- Selecting options from dialog boxes

- Controlling the size and position of windows

- Working with programs and documents

Get ready

GET READY

As with many of the earlier lessons, you use some of the optional Windows 98 accessories in this lesson. If you've followed through the earlier lessons, you should have all the programs you need installed already. If not, you probably need your Windows 98 CD-ROM. You may also want to have the CD-ROM that accompanies this book available so you can access the practice files, Fox_Grps.txt, Myreport.doc, and Aesop_Fb.doc, in the Lesson 11 folder.

CHOOSING MENUS AND COMMANDS

You use menus and select commands whenever you use your PC, so understanding a bit more about them helps remove some of the confusion you may feel from time to time. In the following exercises you review some of the conventions typical to Windows 98 applications so you aren't surprised when dialog boxes appear or when extra menus pop up.

Let the mouse do it!

There's just no getting around the fact that Windows 98 works better when you use a mouse. With a mouse you can open a menu, move the mouse pointer down to view the available selections, and click the button to make your choice. But did you ever wonder why the menus work the way they do? In this short exercise you learn the answers.

TIP *If you enable the Web style view of the Active Desktop, your mouse will activate desktop items with a single click, just as it does when you make menu selections.*

To practice using the mouse to make menu selections, follow these steps:

1 Click the Start button.

2 Select Programs.

3 Select Accessories.

Let the mouse do it!

④ Select Paint.

⑤ Select Edit to drop down the Edit menu.

*Commands such as Copy To and Paste From that are followed by three periods (an **ellipsis**) display a dialog box when you select them. Most other commands, such as Undo, are complete by themselves, so no* further input is necessary to execute the command — when you click one of these choices, the command is carried out immediately.

⑥ Select Undo to confirm that this command does not display any additional choices.

⑦ Select Edit.

⑧ Select Paste From to confirm that this command displays a dialog box, as shown in the figure on the right.

⑨ Select the View menu.

⑩ Move the mouse pointer down to Zoom.

The View menu is interesting because some items display a check, while Zoom has an arrow to indicate that it will display an additional *cascading* menu when selected. Choices such as Tool Box use a check to indicate whether the tool box is displayed (checked) or not displayed (unchecked). This action is called a *toggle*.

All Windows 98 applications use these same conventions to indicate how menu selections react when you choose them. An item followed by an ellipsis always displays a dialog box. An item followed by an arrow always displays a cascading menu. Items that lack the ellipsis and the arrow are immediate action selections. Items that are toggles show a check when the option is turned on and no check when the option is turned off.

Discover the purpose of the Alt key

Your keyboard has several keys that may seem like they have no purpose. In reality, though, there are uses even for the key cryptically

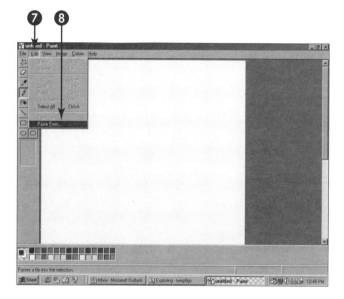

11

Working with Windows 98 Applications

Discover the purpose of the Alt key

marked Alt. You've probably noticed that pressing the Alt key doesn't seem to do anything, but in this exercise you find out the true purpose of this lonely key.

TIP *The Alt key works a little differently than the Shift and Ctrl keys. If you prefer, you can press the Alt key first, and then press the hotkey. For example, you can press Alt, and then press V, and finally press Z to display the Zoom cascade menu.*

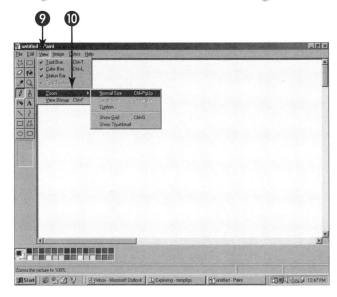

❶ Open Paint.

❷ Press Alt+V to open the View menu.

❸ Press Alt+Z to open the Zoom cascade menu.

❹ Press Alt+U to select Custom and display the Custom Zoom dialog box.

Are you starting to see the pattern of how the Alt key works? The underlined letter in a menu name or a menu selection is the letter you press while you hold down Alt to open the menu or make the selection.

❺ Press Alt+1 to select 100%, and then click OK to return to Paint.

Quite a few menu items show keyboard shortcuts, but these keyboard shortcuts use the Ctrl key rather than the Alt key, which can be rather confusing until you understand the difference between the two. Keyboard shortcuts that use the Ctrl key are true shortcuts — you don't have to open a menu and make selections to use a Ctrl key shortcut. The Alt key, on the other hand, simply provides a means to open menus and choose commands without using your mouse. To compare the differences between the two, you might want to use the keyboard to alternately remove and redisplay the tool box. Using the Alt Key, you need to press Alt+V and then Alt+T to toggle the tool box display. Using the Ctrl key, you just press Ctrl+T without ever opening a menu. But because many menu commands lack a Ctrl key shortcut, sometimes using the Alt key is the only option for someone who doesn't want to use a mouse.

Switching gears with the Taskbar ◀

LET'S OPEN SEVERAL PROGRAMS AT ONCE

You've seen how handy it can be to have more than one program open at the same time. Not only can you jump back and forth between programs as you need to, but you can easily share data in many cases, too. In the following quick exercises you practice several different methods of moving between different programs, and you learn some tricks that enable you to switch between programs even when it seems impossible.

▶ Switching gears with the Taskbar

The Windows 98 Taskbar is a pretty handy tool that you've used quite a few times in the earlier lessons in this book. You already know quite a bit about the Taskbar. It usually appears at the bottom of your Windows 98 screen, it contains a button for each program you have running, and it holds the Start button that leads you to the Start menu. You can move the Taskbar to any side of your screen, or you can hide the Taskbar altogether.

What you may not know is that the Taskbar is always available, even when certain programs go to extraordinary lengths to keep you from accessing it. Software installation programs, for example, often hide the Taskbar and simply refuse to let you do anything else while you're installing a new program. This is usually okay, but there are times when you just have to be able to do something else. If an installation program asks for the location of your existing data files, you may need to open Windows Explorer and search your hard disk. If the installation program determines that you're a little short on disk space, you probably want to delete some old files. These are just two instances when you need to do something else before the installation program continues, but what happens when the Taskbar is totally hidden and won't appear? In most cases you'd probably click Cancel, do your cleanup work, and start over. Why not learn how to make things work your way instead?

To practice accessing the Taskbar to switch between programs, follow these steps:

1 Click the Start button.

2 Select Programs.

Switching gears with the Taskbar

3 Select Accessories.

4 Select WordPad.

5 Click the Start button again.

6 Select Programs.

7 Select Accessories.

8 Select Paint.

9 Click the WordPad button on the Taskbar to switch to WordPad.

10 Right-click the Taskbar and select Properties.

11 Deselect the Always on top checkbox by removing the check from this item.

12 Click OK to confirm the dialog box.

13 If necessary, click the Maximize button so WordPad expands to cover the whole screen as shown in the figure on the right. (You may need to click the button twice to make the Taskbar disappear.)

14 Move the mouse pointer to the bottom of the screen to try to make the Taskbar appear.

No matter where you move the mouse, the Taskbar won't reappear. If you recall hiding the Taskbar in Lesson 2, this was probably not what you expected — but it is exactly what you may encounter when you're installing programs that hide the Taskbar during the installation.

15 Press Ctrl+Esc to display the Start menu. (Because the Start menu is connected to the Taskbar, the Taskbar also reappears when you press Ctrl+Esc.)

16 Click a blank space on the Taskbar.

17 Right-click the Taskbar.

18 Select Properties.

19 Click the Always on top checkbox to reselect this item.

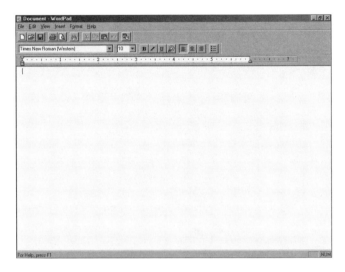

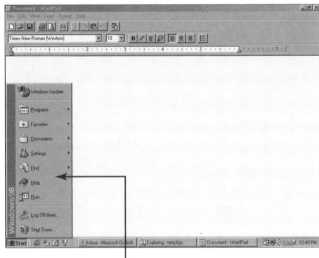

Press Ctrl + Esc to display the
Start menu and the Taskbar

Changing programs with the keyboard

The Taskbar is always available, even when some programs try to prevent you from using the Taskbar. In this exercise you learned a technique for displaying a hidden Taskbar. This is a trick that few Windows 98 users know about, but one that can save you a lot of time and frustration. After you've displayed the Taskbar and Start menu, you can run whatever programs you need and return to the program that hid the Taskbar when it's convenient for you.

Changing programs with the keyboard

The Taskbar isn't the only way to switch between programs. If the program windows are visible, you can simply click within a program's window to make that window the active window. You can also use the keyboard to switch between open programs even if the programs are running full screen and therefore preventing you from seeing the other programs.

To practice switching between running programs using the keyboard, follow these steps:

1 Click the Start button.

2 Select Programs.

3 Select Accessories.

4 Select WordPad.

5 Click the Start button again.

6 Select Programs.

7 Select Accessories.

8 Select Paint.

9 Hold down Alt while you press Tab several times.

Each time you press Tab, the selection box moves to the next open program as shown in the figure on the right.

10 Release the Alt key when the program you want to use is in the selection box. The program and document name in the bottom of the dialog box will help you determine when you've selected the correct program.

Hold down Alt and press Tab several times to select the program

Using the mouse in dialog boxes

TIP *You can reverse the direction of the selector by holding down the Shift key along with the Alt key.*

To quickly switch back to the last program you used, press Alt+Tab once. When you use this trick, you don't have to wait for the dialog box to appear, because you automatically go back to the last program you used, even if you have a number of programs running. This means that you can continue switching back and forth between two programs with a quick press of Alt+Tab; many users find that this is even quicker than using the Taskbar buttons.

SELECTING OPTIONS FROM DIALOG BOXES

It would be impossible to use Windows 98 and not encounter dialog boxes several times in each session. Dialog boxes may sometimes seem complex and intimidating, but they serve an important purpose — they help organize related information and often make it much easier to enter data by enabling you to provide several pieces of information in one place. In the following exercises you learn some advanced techniques for working with dialog boxes.

Using the mouse in dialog boxes

The mouse and the dialog box were really made for each other. In this exercise you review some of the common elements you encounter in dialog boxes, and you see how to use the mouse to interact with those elements.

1 Click the Start button.

2 Select Programs.

3 Select Accessories.

4 Select Paint.

5 Click File.

6 Select Print to display the Print dialog box.

Using the keyboard in dialog boxes

It's much faster to print multiple copies of a document by selecting the number of copies in the Print dialog box rather than printing the copies one at a time.

7 Click the up arrow at the right edge of the Number of copies spin box to increase the number of copies. (If you hold down the left mouse button, the number continues to change as long as you hold down the button.)

8 Select the Print to file checkbox. Checkboxes are always square boxes, and they are generally independent of each other. You can usually select as many checkboxes as necessary.

9 Select the Pages radio button. Radio buttons are always round and grouped together. When you select one radio button, all other radio buttons are deselected.

10 Click the down arrow at the right edge of the Name list box. List boxes usually provide a set group of options and do not allow you to enter new information. Some list boxes include a text box that does allow you to enter new information — these combinations of a list box and a text box are called *combo boxes*.

11 Click the Pages from text box to move the insertion point into the text box. (The insertion point must be in a text box before you can enter information in the text box.)

12 Click the Cancel button to close the dialog box. (Clicking a command button executes the command associated with the button.)

Dialog boxes are usually designed so you can specify a number of related options in one dialog box. You can save time by making certain you select all of your choices at the same time if possible.

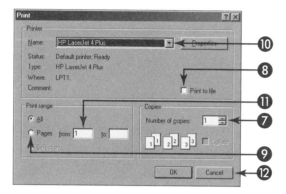

Using the keyboard in dialog boxes

It's not always possible to totally ignore the keyboard when you're working in dialog boxes. It's a little difficult to enter text into text boxes, for example, without using the keyboard. In some cases you can copy information from another source before you access the

Working with Windows 98 Applications

dialog box, and then paste the information into the text box using the right-click mouse menu, but that only works when you need to enter information into a single text box. In the following exercise you learn how to use the keyboard for those times when the mouse just isn't quite up to the task.

1 Click the Start button.

2 Select Programs.

3 Select Accessories.

4 Select Paint.

5 Select File.

6 Select Print.

7 Press Tab to move the *focus* — the dotted outline showing which dialog box element is currently active — to the Properties button. (The dialog box element that currently has the focus is the element that reacts to any keyboard input.)

8 Press Enter to display the Properties dialog box for your printer. (This dialog box is specific to your printer.)

9 Press Esc to close the Properties dialog box. Pressing Esc in a dialog box is generally the equivalent of selecting Cancel.

10 Press Shift+Tab to move the focus back to the Name list box. When you move the focus to a list box or a text box, the current value in the box is highlighted to further emphasize which element has the focus.

11 Press Alt+down arrow to view the choices in the Name list box.

12 Select a printer from the Name list box.

While the list box is expanded, you can choose from it using the up arrow or down arrow (you can also use left arrow and right arrow as substitutes for up arrow and down arrow).

13 Press Enter when your choice is highlighted.

14 Press Alt+G to select the Pages radio button and move the focus to the text box. (When you select the Pages radio button, the All radio button is deselected.)

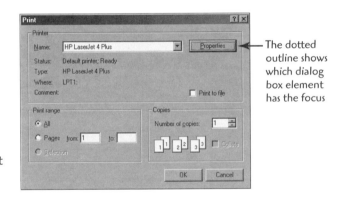

The dotted outline shows which dialog box element has the focus

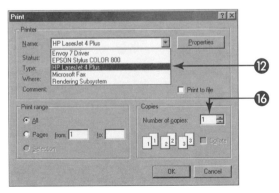

⑮ Press Alt+C to select the Number of copies spin box.

⑯ Type the following text: **20**.

⑰ Hold down the down arrow until the value in the Number of copies spin box returns to 1. You can enter values in spin boxes by typing the entry or by using the arrow keys. Spin boxes only accept whole numbers and generally have a specified range of acceptable values. For example, you cannot print a negative number of copies, nor can you print zero copies. You can enter **0** in the Number of copies spin box, but you get an error message when you try to print.

⑱ Press Alt+L to place a check in the Print to file checkbox. Press Alt+L again to remove the check. Checkboxes function as toggles, so each time you press a checkbox's *hotkey*—Alt + the underlined character—the checkbox changes its current state.

⑲ Press Tab to move the focus to the OK button. (If you press Enter while the focus is not on another command button, the effect is the same as pressing the OK button, but it's safer to make certain you know which command button is activated before you press Enter.)

⑳ Press Esc to close the dialog box.

Using the keyboard to navigate and make selections in dialog boxes is a little trickier than using the mouse to navigate and make selections. Still, the fastest way to print a Paint image never requires you to touch the mouse. Just press Ctrl+P and then Enter. No matter how fast you can click mouse buttons, you can't beat that!

Editing text in text boxes

Sometimes the fastest way to retype something isn't to retype it at all. You can save a lot of time by editing rather than retyping, and you'll probably make fewer mistakes, too. You may not realize it, but you can apply this knowledge to the text boxes within dialog boxes to edit the existing information rather than retype an entire entry. One situation where you may find this trick quite useful is when you're creating a number of files with similar names, such as the chapters in a book. In this exercise you see how you can make use of editing in text boxes.

Editing text in text boxes

1 Click the Start button.

2 Select Programs.

3 Select Accessories.

4 Select WordPad.

5 Type the following text: **This is report # 1**.

6 Select File.

7 Select Save As.

8 Type the following text in the File name text box: **My sample report on what I have learned about Windows 98 #1**.

9 Click Save to save the file.

10 Select File.

11 Select New.

12 Click OK.

13 Type the following text: **This is report # 2**.

14 Select File.

15 Select Save As.

16 Click `My sample report on what I have learned about Windows 98 #1.doc` **once to place** the filename in the File name text box. (Make certain you don't double-click the filename.)

17 Click once in the File name text box.

18 Press End to move the insertion point to the end of the name. (If the filename were short enough so you could see the entire name in the File name text box, you wouldn't need to press End.)

19 Drag the mouse pointer across the number 1 in the filename, and type **2** to change the filename to `My sample report on what I have learned about Windows 98 #2.doc`.

20 Click Save to save the file under the new filename.

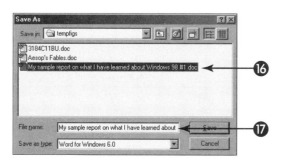

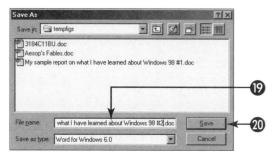

Changing the size of a window

Although you edited only a single character of the filename, there's nothing to prevent you from selecting any part of the text in a text box and editing it rather than retyping the entire entry. This exercise showed you a useful trick that is very handy whenever you want to create a series of files with similar names. There's no real reason to risk making a typing mistake when you can simply "borrow" an existing filename and make a quick edit.

CONTROLLING THE SIZE AND POSITION OF WINDOWS

Each Windows 98 program runs in a separate window. Depending on the size of your monitor and the types of programs you run, you may run those programs in full-screen windows, or you may choose to shrink each window so you can see more than one program at a time. In the following exercises you learn how you can control the size and positioning of the windows on your screen.

NOTE *Some display adapters have the ability to create a* ***virtual desktop***, *which is an area larger than your actual display. If your display adapter has these capabilities, you may need to scroll the desktop to see all the windows that are open. You have to refer to the documentation from the display adapter manufacturer to determine how to zoom and scroll your desktop display.*

Changing the size of a window

There are several ways to adjust the size of program windows, but before you change the size of windows, you should consider what size is optimal. If you wanted to see a large number of program windows at the same time, you'd probably be tempted to make each window as small as possible. Unfortunately, if you did this, you'd probably find that the windows were too small to use effectively. For example, you probably expect to have to scroll up and down in a word-processing document, but if you make the window so narrow that you have to scroll side to side, you probably discover that writing and editing the

Changing the size of a window

document is a real pain. Likewise, if you make program windows too narrow, you probably won't be able to use all of the toolbar buttons. On the other hand, there's really little reason to expand program windows to the point where most of the space they encompass is simply blank, wasted space. Experiment to see what is the best size window for each of your favorite applications.

In this exercise you practice changing the size of the WordPad window. WordPad is a little different than most of the programs you use on your PC because you can set WordPad's options so that the text adjusts to fit the width of the WordPad window. Most programs don't have such an option, so if you make the window narrower than the document, you have to use the horizontal scrollbar to view the entire width of the document.

1 Insert the *Windows 98 One Step at a Time* CD-ROM into your CD-ROM drive.

2 Click the Start button.

3 Select Programs.

4 Select Accessories.

5 Select WordPad.

6 Select File.

7 Select Open.

8 In the Look in list box, choose the Lesson 11 folder on the CD-ROM accompanying this book.

9 If you don't see Fox_Grps.txt, choose All Documents (*.*) in the Files of type list box.

10 Double-click Fox_Grps.txt to open the file shown in the figure on the right.

11 Press Alt+Spacebar to display the Control menu. (This menu enables you to control the window size using the keyboard. You can also click the Control menu button to display the Control menu.)

12 Select Size to resize the WordPad window.

Control menu button

Maximize or Restore button

Minimize button

Changing the size of a window

When you select Size, a four-headed pointer appears in the WordPad window.

13 Press the right arrow to indicate that you wish to adjust the size of the window by moving the right edge of the window. (The first arrow key you press after selecting Size determines which border moves.)

14 Press the left arrow several times to move the gray border as shown in the figure on the right.

15 Press Enter to complete the resizing.

16 Move the mouse pointer over the right edge of the WordPad window.

17 When the pointer changes to a double-headed arrow, hold down the left mouse button, and drag the right side of the window back to approximately the original width.

18 Click the Maximize button to expand the WordPad window to full screen. (When the window is maximized, the Maximize button is replaced by the Restore button.)

19 Click the Restore button. (This button always returns the window to its previous size.)

20 Click the Minimize button to shrink the WordPad window to an icon on the Taskbar.

21 Click the WordPad icon on the Taskbar to restore the window to its previous size.

If you resize the WordPad window, the size you select is automatically saved so that the WordPad window defaults to your selected size the next time you open WordPad. Most Windows 98 applications remember the last size of their windows and restore the windows to the same size the next time you use the program. Some programs, however, have a default size to which they always return the next time you open the program, so don't get frustrated if this happens to you.

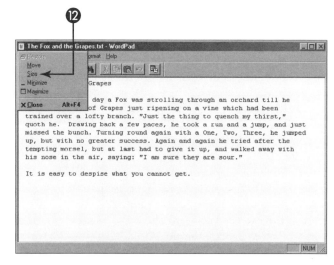

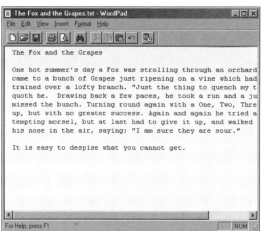

11

Working with Windows 98 Applications

Using the Taskbar to arrange windows

Using the Taskbar to arrange windows

If you start working with a lot of open program windows, eventually you realize that a little organization would probably make your life a lot easier. Rather than having windows randomly scattered all over the desktop, you can have them neatly arranged so it's easier to see what's in each window. If you're using drag & drop to share data, arranging the windows properly enables you to see both the source and destination windows — a major plus for this type of operation! Even if you're simply switching between several programs and not sharing data between them, proper organization makes it easier for you to keep track of your applications.

In this exercise you learn about the window arrangement options you can access through the Taskbar. The Taskbar window arrangement options offer you one feature that is pretty hard to duplicate manually — each window is at least partially visible. If you have only a few windows open, this isn't much of a feat, but when you open several windows at the same time, it can be difficult to see each one. To practice using the Taskbar window arrangement options, follow these steps:

1. Click the Start button.

2. Select Programs.

3. Select Accessories.

4. Select WordPad.

5. Click the Start button.

6. Select Programs.

7. Select Accessories.

8. Select Imaging.

9. Click the Start button.

10. Select Programs.

11. Select Accessories.

12. Select System Tools.

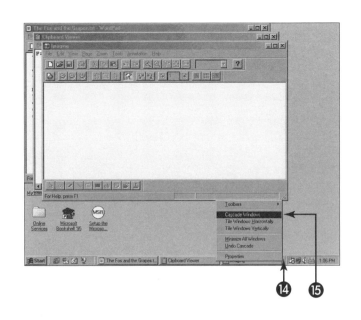

Using the Taskbar to arrange windows

⑬ Select Clipboard Viewer.

⑭ Right-click a blank spot on the Taskbar.

⑮ Select Cascade to arrange the open windows as shown in the figure on the right.

When you choose the cascaded arrangement, Windows 98 arranges the open windows so the title bar of each window is shown. To use any of the windows, just click that window's title bar.

TIP

Some programs, such as Paint, don't tile well because their windows have a minimum size setting, which may be larger than necessary if you want all open windows to be visible.

⑯ Right-click a blank spot on the Taskbar.

⑰ Select Tile Horizontally to arrange the open windows as shown in the figure on the right.

Each of the open windows is stacked between the top and bottom of the screen. You may find it useful to hide the Taskbar or move the Taskbar to one side of the screen if you use the horizontally tiled arrangement to maximize the available vertical screen space.

⑱ Right-click a blank spot on the Taskbar.

⑲ Select Tile Vertically to arrange the open windows as shown in the figure on the right.

This option stacks the open windows next to each other between the right and left edges of the screen.

⑳ Right-click a blank spot on the Taskbar.

㉑ Select Minimize All Windows to drop all open windows down to a Taskbar button. You can also use the Show Desktop button on the Quick Launch toolbar (next to the Start button) to minimize all open windows.

You can then access your desktop, and use any shortcuts you may have placed on the desktop. Click any of the buttons to restore the associated window to its former size.

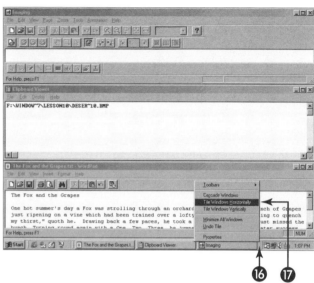

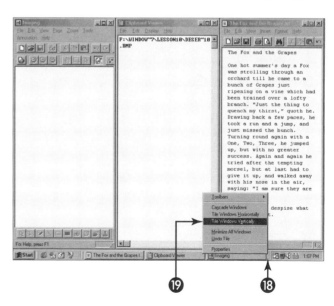

Working with Windows 98 Applications

11

Opening, saving, and closing

> **TIP**
> *If you find you don't like the window arrangement after selecting one of the tiling options, right-click the Taskbar and select Undo Tile.*

The horizontal and vertical tiling arrangements work best if you have only a few program windows open. If you have several program windows open, the tiled arrangements create windows that really are too small to be very useful. Unfortunately, you can't tell Windows 98 to tile some windows while leaving others shrunk to Taskbar buttons. If you want to do so, you have to resize the windows manually. You can start by selecting the tiling arrangement you prefer, minimizing the unneeded windows, and then manually resizing the others.

WORKING WITH PROGRAMS AND DOCUMENTS

If your PC is going to be of any use to you, you spend a lot of time working with programs and documents. It makes sense to learn any special little tricks that can help you get more done in less time and with less frustration. In the following exercises you see how you can spend more of your time being productive, and less of your time wondering how to get things done.

Opening, saving, and closing

This exercise reviews opening, saving, and closing programs and documents. You have, of course, done quite a bit of each of these activities in the past, so this exercise simply brings together some of the shortcuts and tricks you may have missed earlier. It also provides a few reminders of potential problems to avoid.

1. Click the Start button.

2. Select Programs.

3. Select Accessories.

4. Select WordPad.

5. Select File to display the drop-down File menu.

Opening, saving, and closing

Like WordPad, most Windows 98 programs include a list of the most recently used documents near the bottom of the File menu. If you've saved files in several different locations, selecting a file from the list of most recently used documents is much faster than browsing in the Open dialog box.

6 Choose the file you wish to open. In this case choose Fox_Grps.txt by pressing 1. As long as the file can still be found in the same location where it was last saved, WordPad quickly opens the file.

7 Click the Save button frequently to save any changes you've made. If the file has already been named, a quick click is all it takes to make certain you won't lose your work in the event of a power failure or a system crash.

8 Select File.

9 Select Save As to save the file under a new name.

If you're creating a new document that you're basing on an existing document, use File ➢ Save As and rename the file before you make any changes to the original. That way, you won't accidentally click the Save button and overwrite the original document with the changes.

10 To quickly close the document and the program, click the Save button.

11 Click the Close button. (If you forget to click the Save button first, you'll have to go through several steps confirming whether you want to save or lose your changes.)

Many Windows 98 programs, such as Microsoft Word, allow you to have more than one document open at a time. If you're working in a program with several documents open, you can generally close your open document by pressing Ctrl+F4. You can close programs by pressing Alt+F4. In both cases, save your changes by clicking the Save button first to avoid being asked if you want to save your changes.

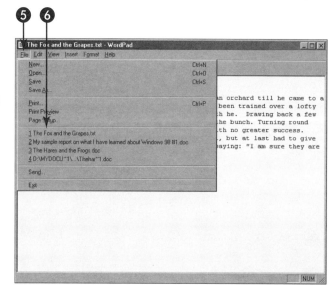

Scrolling in a document

TIP

In applications that allow you to open more than one document at the same time, you can move between document windows by pressing Ctrl+F6.

Scrolling in a document

Unless you always create extremely small documents, you probably find that only a small portion of most documents is visible at one time. To see the rest of a document, you need to scroll through the document. In this short exercise you learn some tricks that help you scroll through documents more quickly and efficiently.

1 Insert the *Windows 98 One Step at a Time* CD-ROM into your CD-ROM drive.

2 Click the Start button.

3 Select Programs.

4 Select Accessories.

5 Select WordPad.

6 Click the Open button to quickly display the Open dialog box.

7 In the Look in list box, choose the Lesson 11 folder on the CD-ROM.

8 Double-click Aesop_Fb.doc.

9 Drag the WordPad window borders so the window is sized as shown in the figure on the right.

10 Click the down arrow at the bottom of the vertical scrollbar.

The arrows at the ends of the scrollbars scroll the document one line vertically or one character horizontally each time they're clicked. Hold down one of the arrows to scroll continuously.

11 Click the blank space below the box in the vertical scrollbar.

Clicking in a blank space on a scrollbar scrolls the document one screen in the direction toward the point you clicked. If you click

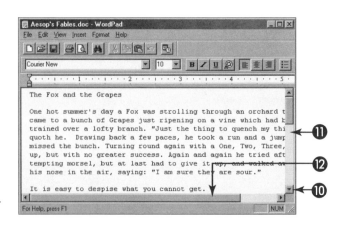

below the box, the document scrolls down. Pressing PageDown or PageUp also scrolls the document one screen. If you know the approximate location you want to find, point to that spot on the scroll bar and hold down the left mouse button to quickly scroll to that point.

12 Point to the box in the horizontal scrollbar and drag the box to the right. (The document scrolls continuously as you drag the box.)

13 Press Ctrl+End to scroll to the end of the document in one step. (Pressing End by itself moves the insertion point to the end of the current line.)

14 Press Ctrl+Home to scroll to the beginning of the document in one step. (Pressing Home by itself moves the insertion point to the beginning of the current line.)

15 Press Ctrl+right arrow to move the insertion point to the beginning of the next word.

16 Press Ctrl+left arrow to move the insertion point to the beginning of the current word, and press the combination again to move to the beginning of the previous word.

Scrolling through long documents isn't difficult, but people often waste a lot of time because they don't know how to move quickly through their documents. In particular, clicking the blank space on a scrollbar or dragging the box on the scrollbar is much faster than clicking the arrows at the ends of the scrollbars.

Using simple editing techniques

There are a number of simple editing techniques that are common to most Windows 98 programs. In this exercise you review a number of those techniques, such as making a selection, anchoring a selection, and extending a selection, and you see how to save even more time working with your documents. Here, too, you find some new tricks that might surprise you a little. You certainly learn some ways to save time and effort.

1 Open Aesop_Fb.doc (from the *Windows 98 One Step at a Time* CD-ROM) in WordPad.

Using simple editing techniques

2 Drag the WordPad window borders to increase the window size so you can see the entire ruler and more of the text, as shown in the figure on the right. Ideally, you should be able to see a complete paragraph as well as a few separate lines.

3 Double-click the word `hot` in the first sentence of The Fox and the Grapes. (Double-clicking a word selects the entire word so you can edit or format the word.)

4 Hold down Shift and click just after the period that ends the first sentence. (Holding down Shift anchors the current selection, and when you click, you extend the selection to the point you clicked.)

5 Quickly click three times anywhere within the first paragraph.

TIP *Triple-clicking selects the entire paragraph and is probably the fastest method of selecting an entire paragraph. You may need to practice triple-clicking to get a feel for just how quickly you must click the mouse button.*

6 Click at the beginning of the paragraph to move the insertion point just before the first word.

7 Hold down Shift and Ctrl.

8 Press the right arrow several times. (Each time you press the right arrow, the selection extends by an additional word.)

9 Press Home to move the insertion point back to the beginning of the line.

10 Hold down Shift.

11 Press End to extend the selection to include the entire line.

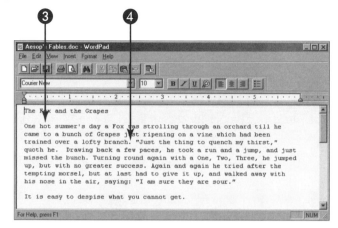

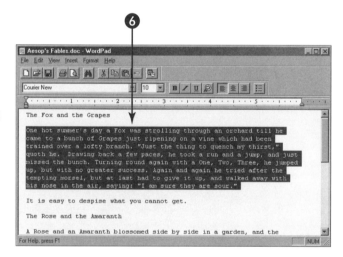

⑫ Continue to hold down Shift and press the down arrow key. (Each time you press the down arrow key, the selection extends down to include a complete additional line.)

⑬ Hold down Shift and Ctrl.

⑭ Press End. This time you extend the selection to the end of the document.

⑮ Hold down Shift and Ctrl.

⑯ Press Home. This extends the selection to the beginning of the document, but you may be surprised by the size of the selection as shown in the figure on the right.

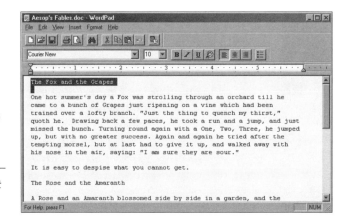

NOTE

Remember that Shift anchors the selection starting at the insertion point, so only the text between the beginning of the document and the start of the first paragraph is selected.

⑰ Press Ctrl+A to select all of the document text.

Another way to select the entire text is to press Ctrl+Home to move to the beginning of the document, hold down Shift, and press Ctrl+End. This method usually works even in programs that don't allow you to select the whole document by pressing Ctrl+A. You can also use Edit ➢ Select All to select everything in a document.

After you've selected a part of a document, you can copy, move, delete, or format the selection as necessary. Because selections tend to remain selected until you move the insertion point or make another selection, you can usually perform several tasks, such as changing the font and making the text bold, without reselecting that section of text.

11

Working with Windows 98 Applications

Skills challenge

SKILLS CHALLENGE: WORKING WITH PROGRAMS AND DOCUMENTS

It's time for a little practice so you can make certain you remember the important tricks and techniques you learned in this lesson.

1 Open Paint and find one of the menu items that displays a dialog box.

 How can you open the Open dialog box without going through the File menu?

 How can you tell (without actually using the Text tool) whether the text toolbar will be displayed when you add text to a Paint document?

2 Determine which Paint menu selections display a cascading menu.

3 Change the Windows 98 settings so the only thing shown on the screen is the Paint window.

 How can you access the Taskbar when the Always on top check box is deselected?

4 Open WordPad and then use the keyboard to switch between WordPad and Paint.

5 Open the Print dialog box and use the keyboard to determine what printer selections are available.

 How can you open the Print dialog box without going through the File menu?

 How can you select Print to file using the keyboard?

6 Open My sample report on what I have learned about Windows 98 #1.doc in WordPad.

7 Save the open document as My sample report on what I have learned about Windows 98 #3.doc without typing any more of the filename than absolutely necessary.

8 Tile the WordPad and Paint windows horizontally.

 How can you tile just two windows when you have three programs running?

9 Open Aesop_Fb.doc in WordPad.

10 Select the first line of the first paragraph using the keyboard.

11 Select the first fable's title line by pressing two keys.

 How can you select an entire paragraph with the mouse without dragging the mouse pointer?

Troubleshooting

TROUBLESHOOTING

If you encounter problems while trying to work through the exercises, here are some ideas that might help you correct the problems and keep going.

Problem	Solution
Some of my program windows disappear off the edge of my screen.	Click the Minimize button and then click the program button on the Taskbar. If you can't see the Minimize button, click the Control menu in the upper-left corner of the window and select Minimize, and then click the program button on the Taskbar.
I can't resize some windows.	Some programs have windows that cannot be resized. This is usually to prevent the controls in the window from being hidden by making the window too small.
Some of the shortcuts I learned in this lesson don't always work.	Not all Windows 98 programs include every standard shortcut. You may be able to find other shortcuts by looking on the program's menu.

WRAP UP

In this lesson you learned quite a few tricks that make your life a lot easier when you're working with Windows 98 applications. The techniques for selecting text, using the Alt key shortcuts, and navigating in documents that were covered in this lesson help you get more done with less work. They also help you avoid a lot of needless frustration as you create and edit your documents.

The next lesson shows you how to venture out onto the Internet. You've probably heard more people talk about the Internet than anything else in the whole world of computers. If you haven't tried out the Internet yourself, you're probably ready to jump in. The next lesson is just what you need to get your feet wet in beginning to surf the Internet.

Let's Get Connected to the Internet

50 MINUTES

GOALS

Getting connected to the Internet can be a frustrating experience. Without some first-class help it's pretty easy to find yourself yelling "Why won't this work?" When you're connected, it's easy to forget about all the problems, and maybe that's why it can be so difficult to find someone who knows how to lead you through the process and help you make the connection. This lesson helps you overcome these potential problems and then shows you how to start using the Internet. You learn about the following topics:

- Getting ready to explore the Internet

- Using Internet Explorer

- Surfing the Internet

- Creating a simple Web site

- Communicating over the Internet

Get ready

GET READY

The Internet probably generates more excitement and interest than any other topic in the world of computing today. It's become almost impossible to read anything about computers without seeing some reference to the Internet. If you're not already connected, you probably feel as though you're being left out—it's almost like knowing there's a big, fun party going on and you weren't invited. That's about to change as you learn how to get connected and start surfing the Internet yourself.

This lesson requires access to the Internet. For most people, this means you must open an account with an *Internet service provider*, or ISP; you must have a modem; and you must have access to a telephone line. There are hundreds of ISPs, from small, local operations to large companies serving millions of users. An ISP is a company that provides connections to the Internet, mail servers so you can send and receive electronic mail, and news servers so you can browse news groups on the Internet. If you don't already have an account with an ISP, you need to set up an account so you can complete this lesson. (Refer to the first four exercises in this lesson for help in setting up an account with an ISP.)

Make sure Dial-Up Networking is already installed on your system, or else you also need your Windows 98 CD-ROM to complete this lesson.

GETTING READY TO EXPLORE THE INTERNET

There are a number of important steps you need to complete before you're ready to begin exploring the Internet. The first step is one you have to take on your own—opening an account with an ISP. The following "mini" exercise makes certain you have the information you need to continue.

Obtaining information from your ISP

The ISP should provide you with a list of technical information you need in order to connect. At the very least, this list includes the following information:

Obtaining information from your ISP

- The **dial-in phone number.** The phone number your computer must call.

- Your **user name.** May or may not be case-sensitive.

- Your **password.** May or may not be case-sensitive, too.

- The **IP address.** Either a series of four numbers separated by periods, as in 255.12.27.67, or the instruction to obtain an IP address automatically from the server.

- The **default gateway.** Similar to the IP address.

- The **DNS addresses.** Similar to the IP address. There are usually two of these.

- The **mail server.** May be two names, one being the *SMTP outgoing host*, and the other being the *POP (or POP3) server host*.

- The **Usenet News Server.** Another name.

If possible, obtain all the above information in writing before you continue. If you aren't sure you understand part of the information, check now before you go on. It's a lot easier to enter the correct information in the first place than to try to figure out what is causing problems later. If you enter any one of the pieces of information incorrectly, you probably won't be able to connect to the Internet, and you'll encounter nothing but frustration trying to correct the situation!

Dial-in phone number: _____

User name: _____

Password: _____

IP address: _____

Default gateway: _____

DNS addresses: _____

Mail server(s): _____

Usenet News Server: _____

Installing Dial-Up Networking

Installing Dial-Up Networking

Dial-Up Networking is the Windows 98 component that enables you to use your modem to connect to a network. Because the Internet is just a huge collection of computers connected to networks, you need to have Dial-Up Networking installed on your PC before you can connect to the Internet through your modem. To install Dial-Up Networking, follow these steps:

1 Click the Start button.

2 Select Settings.

3 Select Control Panel.

4 Double-click the Add/Remove Programs icon.

5 Click the Windows Setup tab.

6 Select Communications.

7 Select Details to display the Communications dialog box.

8 Make certain Dial-Up Networking is checked.

The remaining four items aren't too important right now, but, because they don't require much disk space, you can select them if you want.

9 Click OK to return to the Add/Remove Programs Properties dialog box.

10 If you chose to add any new components, click Apply. (You may need to insert your Windows 98 CD-ROM to continue.)

11 Click OK to close the dialog box. If Dial-Up Networking was not already installed, you probably need to restart your PC.

When your system has restarted, you can continue on with the rest of the setup.

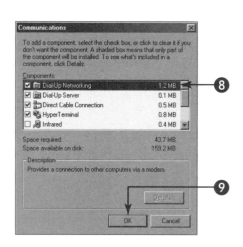

Connecting to your ISP

To complete the setup, you use the information you obtained from your ISP. Sorry, you can't delay any longer—if you haven't taken the time to get all the required information, you won't be able to go any farther.

Okay, now that you're ready, you can continue. The next steps use the Internet Connection Wizard to help you enter all the necessary information for a successful connection. Because different ISPs require different settings, you need to be careful to enter the correct information for your connection.

1 Double-click The Internet icon on your desktop to display the Internet Connection Wizard. (If you don't see the Internet Connection Wizard, someone has already set up an Internet connection on your PC—click the Start button, select Programs ➢ Internet Explorer ➢ Connection Wizard.)

2 Click Next to continue.

3 Select the Setup Options.

4 Select the radio button named I want to set up a new connection on this computer to my existing Internet account using my phone line or local area network.

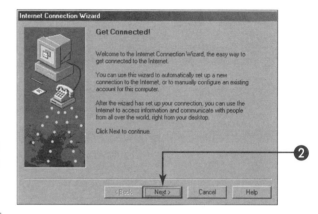

 NOTE

If you don't already have an ISP, you can use the I want to choose an Internet service provider and set up a new Internet account option. This enables you to establish an account with one of the national Internet service providers. You likely won't be able to select a local Internet service provider if you choose this option.

5 Click Next to continue and display the Internet Connection Wizard.

6 Select the Connect using my phone line radio button.

Even if your PC is connected to a network, it's unlikely that your network is connected directly to the Internet. If your network is connected directly to the Internet, you want to select the Connect using my Local Area Network radio button.

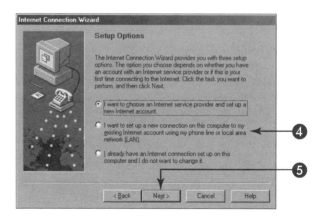

12

Let's Get Connected to the Internet

7 If you see the message shown in the figure on the right, select the Create a new dial-up connection radio button, unless you want to use one of the existing connections.

8 Click Next to continue.

9 Type the correct information to connect to your ISP in the Area code and Telephone number text boxes. The information you want to use is the dial-in phone number your ISP provided. You must include the area code even if the dial-in number is a local call.

10 If necessary, choose the correct country from the Country name and code list box. This code represents the dialing prefix used to initiate a long-distance call.

11 Click Next to continue and display the user name and password entries. Enter your correct user name and password.

12 Click Next to continue and display the Advanced Settings options. For now, choose No to indicate you do not want to change these settings. If you have problems connecting, you can adjust these settings later.

13 Enter a name for the connection. (Type the name of your ISP in the Connection name text box.)

14 Click Next to continue.

15 Select the Yes radio button. This allows you to send electronic mail more easily, because you won't have to set up a separate program.

16 Click Next to continue.

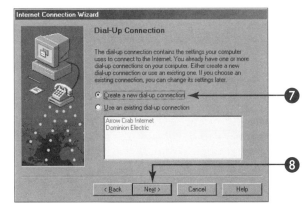

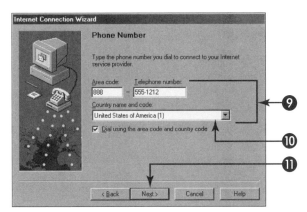

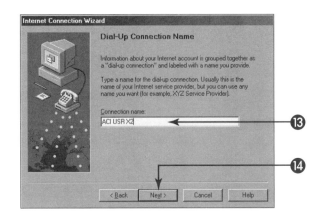

Connecting to your ISP

⑰ If you already have an Internet mail account, you can use the existing account as shown in the figure on the right. Otherwise, you'll have to set up a new account to use Internet mail. Click Next to continue.

⑱ If you chose to use an existing account, confirm your account. (If the settings are correct, make certain the Accept settings radio button is selected.)

⑲ Click Next to continue.

⑳ Choose whether to set up an Internet news account.

㉑ If you selected Yes, click Next and make certain your name is shown correctly in the Display name text.

㉒ Click Next to continue.

㉓ Enter your email address.

㉔ Click Next to continue.

㉕ Enter the name of the news server.

㉖ Click Next to continue.

㉗ Enter a friendly name for the news server or leave the name as is.

㉘ Click Next to continue.

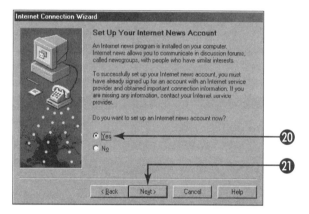

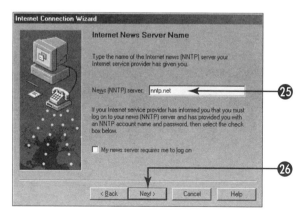

Using Internet Explorer

㉙ Decide whether to use a directory service. (Unless you've already signed up for an LDAP account, choose No.)

㉚ You're almost done setting up your connection. Click Next to continue.

After your Internet connection has been completely configured, you are ready to give the Internet a try. Fortunately, you probably won't have to go through the setup process again. Make certain, though, that you keep all of the information about your connection in case you need to redo any of the settings in the future. You may want to see if your ISP will provide you with a printed copy of all your account information.

USING INTERNET EXPLORER

Internet Explorer is a *Web browser*—a program that enables you to view the contents of pages on the *World Wide Web*, the graphical portion of the Internet often simply called the *Web*. Internet Explorer isn't the only Web browser you can choose, but because it's included free with Windows 98, it's pretty hard to go wrong using Internet Explorer as your Windows 98 Web browser.

In Windows 98, Internet Explorer is more than just a Web browser. Internet Explorer is also the tool you use to view the files and folders on your PC. In fact, in Windows 98 there's little difference between looking at a Web page and viewing a file on your local hard drive. Because you already know how to explore your PC, the following exercises concentrate on how to use Internet Explorer to explore the Internet.

Web browsers do more than simply display graphical information on your screen. They also play sounds, show animations, play movies, allow you to choose the sites you want to visit on the World Wide Web, keep track of where you've been, enable you to buy items online, and much more. In short, Internet Explorer is your window to the Internet. In the following exercises you get a feel for Internet Explorer and see how to make Internet Explorer work best for you.

Unless your computer is attached to a network directly connected to the Internet, most of the time you're using Internet Explorer, your computer has to be connected to the Internet through your modem. If you have a single telephone line that you use for both voice and modem calls, you won't be able to make or receive voice calls while you're using Internet Explorer. Also, if someone picks up an extension phone while you're using Internet Explorer, it's quite likely that your connection to the Internet will be disrupted. Make certain you keep these factors in mind, and free up the telephone line when you're not actively using Internet Explorer.

Starting Internet Explorer

Although you use Internet Explorer for some offline tasks, such as viewing Web pages you've stored previously or looking at the files and folders on your PC, start Internet Explorer by clicking the desktop icon labeled `The Internet`. Before you begin this exercise, make certain you're ready to connect to the Internet with Windows 98 on your screen, your modem turned on (if your modem is an external modem), and your telephone line available.

TIP

You may want to set your screen to a higher resolution setting, such as 800 × 600 or 1024 × 768 before you start Internet Explorer so you can see more of each Web page without so much scrolling.

12

Let's Get Connected to the Internet

Starting Internet Explorer

To start Internet Explorer, follow these steps:

1 Double-click the icon labeled `The Internet` on your desktop (or the Internet icon on the Quick Launch toolbar next to the Start button).

This begins the loading of Internet Explorer and displays the connection dialog box, as shown in the figure on the right. The dialog box that appears on your screen shows the information you entered for your connection.

When your account has been verified, Internet Explorer loads and displays a start page similar to the figure on the right. Keep in mind, however, that the information shown on Web pages is constantly being updated, so your start page will certainly include a different set of articles.

2 Move your mouse around the screen and notice when the pointer changes to a hand. The hand indicates that you're pointing to a *link* — a connection to another Web page. If you click one of the links, Internet Explorer displays a different page.

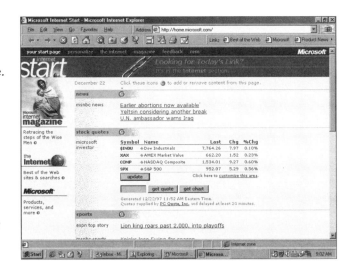

3 Click the Close button to exit from Internet Explorer. Windows 98 asks if you wish to disconnect from your ISP.

4 Click Yes to close the connection and free up the phone line.

You should always make certain you disconnect from the Internet when you're finished browsing. If you don't, your ISP will likely automatically disconnect you after several minutes to half an hour of inactivity.

Your first session with Internet Explorer was a short one, but you at least saw a glimpse of the Internet. Later, you learn more about surfing the Internet.

Internet Explorer

There's a lot on the Internet Explorer screen. This Visual Bonus helps you identify the important elements that help you use Internet Explorer. Note that in the accompanying figure the Address list box was dragged to the top toolbar row so that the toolbar buttons would be visible.

Return to previous page
Go forward to a page you've already visited
Stop loading the current page
Reload the current page
Return to the home page
Search for Web sites
Add, organize, or visit your favorite Web pages
See a list of the pages you've visited
View the available channels
Click to adjust the font size of the pages
Send e-mail
Print the current page
Open Front Page Express
Drag here to change the size of the address and links section
Enter or view the Web page address here

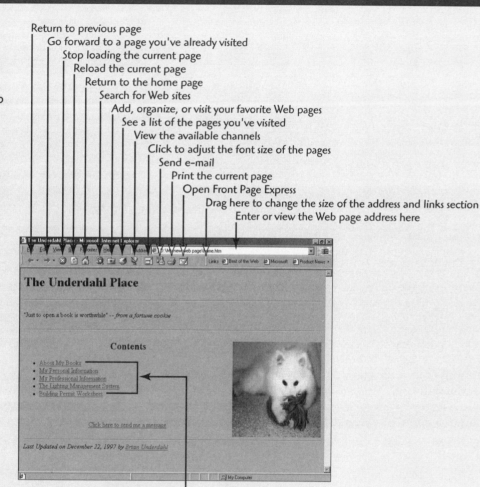

The Internet Explorer screen gives you a lot of tools for browsing the Internet.

Click to visit the associated Web site

12

Let's Get Connected to the Internet

Controlling your Internet Explorer view

Controlling your Internet Explorer view

There are many changes you can make to the way Internet Explorer displays the Web sites you visit. Some of these changes are simply cosmetic, some affect the speed with which pages load, and others are just for fun. In the following exercise you see examples of a number of settings you can use to change the Internet Explorer view. You won't be changing all the possible settings in this exercise—you can play with the remaining settings another time.

1 Double-click the The Internet icon on your desktop.

2 If necessary, click Connect.

3 Select View.

4 Select Internet Options.

5 Click the Advanced tab of the Options dialog box.

6 Select the Multimedia options you prefer (you may need to scroll down to see the multimedia options).

In most cases you want to leave the Show pictures, Play Animations, Play videos, Play sounds, and Smart image dithering checkboxes selected, but removing the checks enables you to view Web pages more quickly. Of the five, the Show pictures checkbox is the one that is likely to have the most effect because so many Web pages include graphics. If you remove the check from the Show pictures, Play Animations, or Play videos checkboxes, you can view the pictures or videos after the page has loaded by right-clicking and selecting Show picture.

7 To change the colors used for text or for the background, click the General tab.

8 Click Colors to display the Colors dialog box.

9 Remove the check from the Use Windows colors checkbox.

10 Click the rectangle to the right of Text or Background to display the color selection palette.

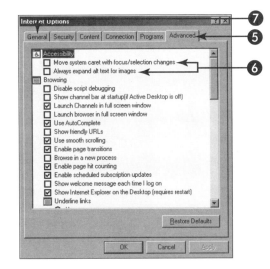

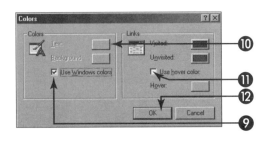

Changing the connection settings

NOTE

Links are generally shown underlined and in a contrasting color. You can use the Visited color palette to change the color of links you've already visited and the Unvisited color palette to change the color of links you haven't visited.

⓫ Select the Use hover color checkbox to make links change color as your mouse pointer is over a link.

⓬ Click OK to close the Colors dialog box.

⓭ Click the Font Settings button if you prefer to use different fonts to display Web pages. (You can choose a fixed and proportional font, but the default settings are generally good choices.)

⓮ Click Apply.

⓯ Click OK to apply any changes and close the dialog box.

If you changed the Multimedia settings, you may need to click the Refresh button to see the effects of those changes on the current Web page. You see the difference immediately if you load a new Web page.

Changing the connection settings

Because most of your use of Internet Explorer is on the Internet, it's important to make certain that Internet Explorer is using the best connection settings. In this exercise you learn how to view and adjust the connection settings.

❶ Start Internet Explorer.

❷ Select View.

❸ Select Internet Options.

❹ Click the Connection tab.

❺ Click the Settings button to display the Dial-Up Settings dialog box.

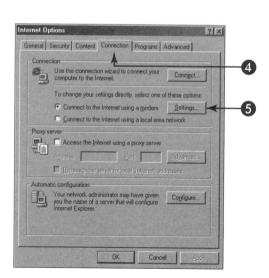

6 Select the checkbox labeled Connect automatically to update subscriptions. This ensures that your Web site subscriptions will be automatically updated. You can deselect this checkbox if you're on a network directly connected to the Internet.

7 If you have more than one Dial-Up Networking connection defined, you can select the correct one to use for connecting to the Internet by clicking the down arrow at the right edge of the Use the following Dial-Up Networking connection list box.

8 Click the Add button to create a new Dial-Up Networking connection. (You would use this option if you changed to a new ISP.)

9 Click the Properties button to make a change in your current Dial-Up Networking connection, such as to change to a new phone number or to modify the IP address settings.

10 Use the up and down arrows at the right side of the Disconnect if idle for *x* minutes spin box to change the length of time Internet Explorer waits before disconnecting you when you haven't done anything for some time.

Most ISPs automatically disconnect idle users, too, but you can use this setting to ensure you are disconnected if you forget to close Internet Explorer after a session online. You may find this setting even more beneficial if you have to access the Internet through long distance or if you use an ISP that charges for connect time.

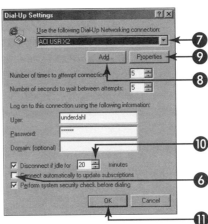

TIP

Leave the Perform system security check before dialing checkbox selected to make certain there are no problems with your password.

11 Click OK to confirm your changes and return to the Internet Options dialog box.

NOTE *Most users won't have a need to use the Access the Internet through a proxy server option. This option only applies if you access the Internet through a network and special software that controls that access. Your network administrator can advise you if you need to use these options.*

⑫ Click Apply and then OK to apply any changes and close the dialog box.

You probably won't need to change the connection settings very often. If you experience difficulty establishing the connection to the Internet, you may need to adjust some of the settings for your Dial-Up Networking connection, but when these settings are correct, you shouldn't need to adjust them further.

▶ Changing the navigation settings

The navigation settings control which Web page is used as your start page as well as which pages are connected to the toolbar links. These settings also control how long Internet Explorer maintains a historical record of Web pages you've visited. As a bonus, you can also quickly clear the Web page history list so other people can't find out where you've been on the Web. To view and change the navigation settings, follow these steps:

❶ Start Internet Explorer.

❷ Select View.

❸ Select Internet Options to view the General tab.

Changing your program settings

4 Enter the address for the page you want to use as your home page in the Address text box.

You can click Use Current to make the currently displayed page your home page, Use Default to return to the original page, or Use Blank to use an empty home page. For example, you could visit `http://www.idgbooks.com` and assign the address to your home page.

5 Use the up and down arrows at the right edge of the Number of days to keep pages in history spin box to specify how often Web pages should be obsolete and no longer kept on your hard disk. (It's a good idea to keep this number quite low to save disk space and to make certain you always are viewing the most current information. If you use the Internet quite a bit, you may want to reduce this number to seven days or less.)

6 Click Clear History to remove all the stored pages. (You may want to do this if you've accidentally visited Web sites that might not be approved by your employer, for example.)

7 Click Apply to apply any changes.

8 Click OK to close the dialog box.

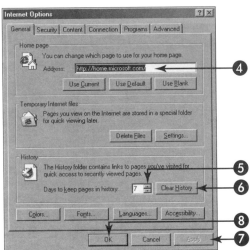

You can also modify the pages assigned to the Links toolbar by right-clicking a link and selecting Properties. You can do this to store addresses of Web pages you've visited. As you learn later, it's generally easier to save those page addresses in your Favorites list. You may, however, want to change your start page, especially if you create you own Web site.

Changing your program settings

The settings on the Programs tab of the Options dialog box control which programs are used for things like mail and news and which programs are used to keep your calendar and address listings. You probably won't be too concerned with these settings, but you may want to change the mail setting so that you can better organize all of your mail. To view and change the program settings, follow these steps:

1 Start Internet Explorer.

② Select View.

③ Select Internet Options.

④ Click the Programs tab.

⑤ Click the down arrow at the right side of the Mail list box to see which options are available on your system. Because Outlook Express works with your other Windows 98 programs as well as with Internet Explorer, you are able to keep all of your mail in one place if you choose Outlook Express.

TIP

If you have Microsoft Office 97 installed, you'll want to use Outlook rather than Outlook Express.

⑥ Click the down arrow at the right side of the News list box to see which options are available on your system.

⑦ Choose the option you prefer in the News list box. (Here, too, you'll probably want to choose Outlook Express so you can keep everything in one place.)

⑧ If you wish, choose an option in the Calendar list box.

⑨ You'll probably want to select Windows Address Book as the Contact list option because the Windows Address Book also works well with Outlook Express.

⑩ Select the Internet Explorer should check to see whether it is still the default browser checkbox. This causes Internet Explorer to verify that you haven't switched to another Web browser whenever Internet Explorer is started.

⑪ If you want to make long distance calls on the Internet, choose an option in the Internet call list box. You'll probably want to use NetMeeting since it comes with Windows 98.

⑫ Click Apply to apply any changes.

⑬ Click OK to close the dialog box.

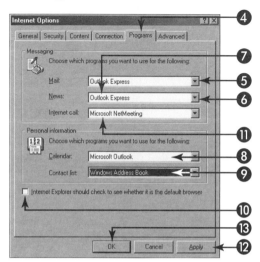

12

Let's Get Connected to the Internet

Changing your security settings

After you've selected your desired program settings, you probably won't need to adjust them again. Internet Explorer is able to use any newly registered file types automatically as you add new programs to your PC, without any special adjustments.

Changing your security settings

The Internet can be a really nasty, dangerous place to visit. There are not only criminals who would love to steal your credit card numbers, but also Web sites with raw adult material, and even places where your computer can easily be damaged by viruses and other dangerous programs. You can use the Internet Explorer security settings to protect yourself from most of these perils. To adjust your security settings, follow these steps:

1 Start Internet Explorer.

2 Select View.

3 Select Internet Options.

4 Click the Content tab.

5 Click Enable to display the Supervisor Password Required dialog box. (If you haven't set up Internet Explorer security before, you may see the Create Supervisor Password dialog box in place of the Supervisor Password Required dialog box.)

6 Type the password in the Password text box. (If you see the Create Password dialog box, type the same password in the Password and Confirm Password text boxes. Make certain you remember the password you type; otherwise, you won't be able to change any of the settings in the future.)

7 Click OK twice to return to the Options dialog box.

8 Click Settings.

9 Enter your password.

10 Click OK to continue to the Content Advisor dialog box.

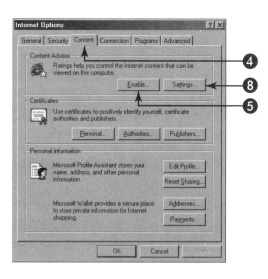

⑪ Click one of the Category keys to display the current rating.

⑫ Drag the Rating slider to the right or left until you are satisfied with the setting. Continue on to set each of the categories to your preference.

⑬ Click the General tab.

⑭ For the most complete protection against material you feel may be objectionable, deselect both checkboxes. Be aware, however, that many Web sites have no rating even though they do not contain anything objectionable. If you clear both checkboxes, you won't be able to visit unrated Web sites.

⑮ Click the Advanced tab.

If you wish to use a third-party rating system, you can specify the system you wish to use here. Some rating systems are continually updated by a special Web site that lists changes to Web page ratings. If you use one of these rating systems, you can specify the rating update page in the Rating Bureau text box.

⑯ Click Apply.

⑰ Click OK to apply any changes and close the dialog box.

⑱ You can view the current certificate settings by clicking the Personal, Sites, or Publishers button.

Certificates are electronically encrypted messages that authenticate the identity of Internet users and Web sites, giving you more confidence in the integrity of businesses you encounter on the Internet.

⑲ Click the Security tab to view the security level settings.

⑳ Select the High radio button to provide the maximum protection to your system. (When you choose this setting, Internet Explorer tries to prevent programs running on Web sites you visit from damaging your system.)

㉑ Click Apply.

㉒ Click OK to apply any changes and close the dialog box.

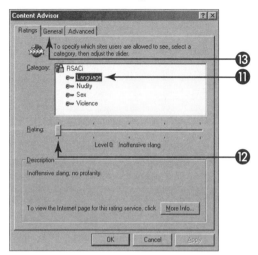

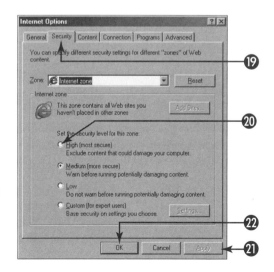

Changing your Advanced Settings

Remember that even the best security measures can be compromised if you're not careful. When in doubt, don't provide information or accept questionable content. This goes a long way toward keeping you and your computer safe.

Changing your Advanced Settings

Several remaining Internet Explorer settings are lumped together under the title Advanced Settings. You probably want to use the default options for most of these settings, but you find a few quite useful items here, too. To adjust the Advanced Settings, follow these steps:

1 Start Internet Explorer.

2 Select View.

3 Select Internet Options.

4 Click the Advanced tab.

5 Scroll down to the security settings.

6 Select each of the checkboxes starting with "Warn."

By default, the Always accept cookies radio button is selected. This option allows Web sites to store information on your system without your knowledge.

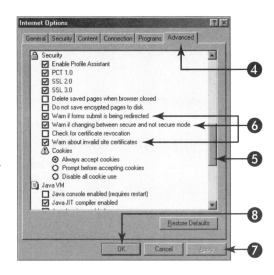

Cookies are text files that contain information about you and your visits to Web sites. Cookies are supposed to be available only to the Web site that stored the information on your PC, but there's no reason you shouldn't be informed before the cookie files are created. Choose Prompt before accepting cookies to select this option.

7 Click Apply.

8 Click OK to apply any changes and close the dialog box. (You can leave the rest of the advanced settings set to their defaults.)

Internet Explorer has many optional settings, but you've had a chance to learn about the changes you can make to improve both your speed and your security when you're browsing the Web. You can return to the Options dialog box at any time if you feel the need to further fine-tune the way Internet Explorer works.

SURFING THE INTERNET

Now that you've adjusted the Internet Explorer settings, you're ready to try a little surfing. The Internet is a pretty big place, but it may not be exactly what you'd expect. You probably find many Web sites that are top quality and offer real value, but you also find a lot of sites that aren't even worth a visit. It's pretty hard to determine in advance what you'll find, but it's pretty easy to predict that you'll find yourself heading off in directions you never imagined.

The Internet doesn't belong to anyone. Some years ago the U.S. government created an interconnection between the computer networks at government sites around the country. Eventually this interconnected group of networks expanded to include universities and other nongovernment sites, such as large companies. Standards were developed to allow all these computers to talk to each other and to make certain messages were sent to the correct destinations. In the past few years, millions of people have jumped in and made the Internet one of the hottest topics of conversation both in and out of computer circles.

How do I find what I want?

At first you're bound to find the Internet a bit confusing. There aren't any road maps, and, because the Web is in a constant state of change, you may be reminded of what it's like trying to get directions to someone's house in an unfamiliar town. There are a lot of dead ends, but there may well be several paths that all lead to your destination. In this exercise you learn how you can start finding your way around the Web.

How do I find what I want?

NOTE *Web site addresses change faster than the weather. It's impossible to predict whether a particular Web site will be available tomorrow, much less between the time this book was written and when you're reading it. Rather than rely on specific Web site addresses you may see in the examples, treat the examples as a general guide.*

1 Start Internet Explorer.

2 Click the Search button on the toolbar to load the search page.

This page provides links to several *search engines*—services that index Web pages. These search engines provide the means for you to find Web pages based on keywords that you feel identify pages you'd like to find. You may want to try out several of the available search engines because they don't all produce the same results.

3 Type the following text in the text box: **"IDG Books"**.

When you enclose the keywords in quotation marks, most search engines treat the keywords as a single phrase rather than separate words to find. If you omitted the quotation marks, the search would look for sites that had either IDG or books, which would probably match many more sites not of interest to you.

4 Click the Search button next to the text box—not the Search button on the toolbar—to begin looking for Web pages that include the keywords. It turns out there are thousands of Web pages that include the keyword phrase "idg books" (notice that the search ignores differences in the case of the letters).

5 You can visit one of the Web pages by clicking one of the underlined links. In this case, however, it's pretty easy to guess that many of the pages are part of the same Web site, and you want to see the home page of that Web site. Because each of the links shows a *URL*—the address—for the page, you can see that several of the pages start out the same: `http://www.idgbooks.com`. To go directly to that page, type the following text in the Address text box: **http://www.idgbooks.com**.

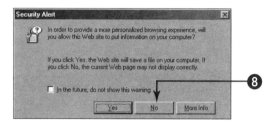

NOTE

*In many cases you don't have to type the entire address. You can, for example, just type **idgbooks** rather than **http://www.idgbooks.com**, but typing the complete address generally loads the page quicker.*

6 Click the Close button on the Search bar to close the bar.

7 Press Enter to go to the `http://www.idgbooks.com` Web page as shown in the figure on the right. It turns out this indeed is the home page for the IDG Books Worldwide Web site.

8 If you selected the Warn before accepting cookies check box, you probably see messages similar to the message shown in the figure on the right as you move to certain pages. Click Yes or No to continue. (In most cases you can click No without encountering problems.)

9 If you're not sure just what you want to find, click Best of the Web in the Links section of the toolbar. If you can't see any of the links, drag the separator between the Address and Links sections to expand the links section.

The different search engines index Web pages quite differently. As you search for Web sites, you may discover that some search engines find very few pages that match your keywords, while others may find so many that it's hard to know which to visit. You may want to try out several different search engines to see which of them produces the best results in finding the Web sites you seek.

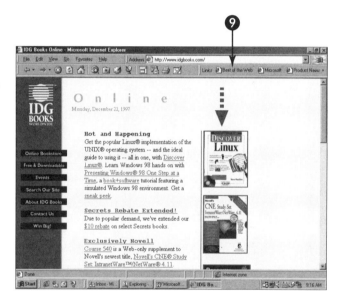

TIP

Web pages quite often include links to related sites. If you click those links, you probably find other quite interesting pages that may not show up when you use one of the search engines.

Keeping track of your favorite sites

Keeping track of your favorite sites

You will no doubt discover Web pages that are interesting and worth a repeat visit. You can try to remember how you got to your favorite pages, but there's a much easier way to keep track of the sites you like. You can tell Internet Explorer to remember the addresses for your favorite pages so that when you're ready for a return visit, you can simply pick out the page from your list of favorites. To keep track of your favorite Web pages, follow these steps:

1 Start Internet Explorer.

2 Type the following text in the Address text box:
http://www.idgbooks.com.

3 Press Enter to go to the IDG Books Worldwide home page.

4 Click Favorites.

5 Select Add To Favorites to display the Add to Favorites dialog box.

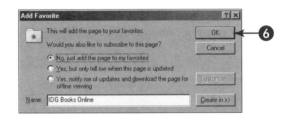

6 Click OK to add the page to your list of favorite Web sites.

7 Click the Favorites button on the toolbar to display the list of your favorite Web sites.

8 Select Favorites.

9 Select Organize Favorites to display the Organize Favorites dialog box.

You can create folders for your favorites, remove items from the list, or move items to different folders. You probably want to use folders to organize your favorites, perhaps by creating separate folders for different types of Web sites.

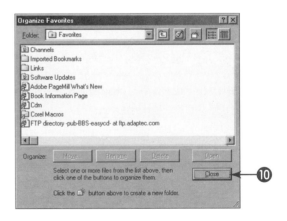

10 Click Close to close the dialog box.

The Organize Favorites dialog box includes everything in your Windows\Favorites folder, not just your favorite Web sites. When you're organizing your favorites, you can simply ignore any items in the Organize Favorites dialog box that aren't related to your favorite Web sites.

CREATING A WEB SITE

What's the fun of only looking at someone else's Web pages? Windows 98 has everything you need to create and publish your own simple Web pages. In the following exercises you learn how you can become famous by designing your own Web page in Windows 98.

 NOTE

You can't learn everything about creating fancy Web sites in just a few pages, of course. But this quick overview can give you a taste of what it takes to design Web pages. If you decide you'd like to get a bit fancier, you may want to check out the many fine books by IDG Books Worldwide at your local bookstore or at `http://www.idgbooks.com`*.*

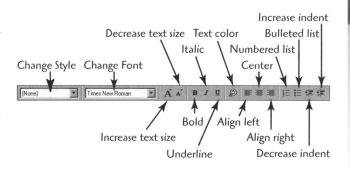

Using FrontPage Express

FrontPage Express is a Web page design tool you get free with Windows 98. FrontPage Express is a slightly smaller version of FrontPage, a full-featured Web page design tool you can buy from Microsoft. FrontPage Express is missing a few FrontPage features, but you can always upgrade to FrontPage later if you prefer.

In this exercise you learn how to quickly create a Web page using one of the FrontPage Express Web page creation wizards. Once you've created a Web page, you can use FrontPage Express to modify the page to suit your needs, of course.

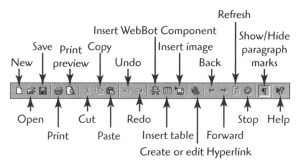

1 Click the Start button.

2 Select Programs.

3 Select Internet Explorer.

4 Select FrontPage Express to open FrontPage Express.

5 Select File.

6 Select New to display the New Page dialog box.

7 Select Personal Home Page Wizard as the type of page to create. You can experiment with the other types later after you've learned the basics of creating a Web page.

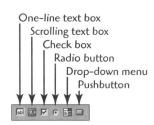

Using FrontPage Express

8 Click OK to display the Personal Home Page Wizard dialog box. (You choose the basic elements of your home page in this dialog box.)

9 Remove the check from Employee Information to deselect it.

10 Add a check to Personal Interests to select it.

11 Click Next to continue.

As the figure on the right shows, you can now enter a filename (Page URL) and Page Title for your home page. For this exercise you can use the default names, but you may want to enter more descriptive names when you create Web pages in the future.

12 Click Next to continue. (Because you are including a list of your favorite Web sites, you must now choose the style for the list. The default, Bullet list, will do just fine.)

13 Click Next to continue.

14 Type the following text in the Personal Interests text box: **Windows 98**.

15 Click Next to continue.

16 Type your e-mail address and any additional personal information you'd like to include on your Web page. (It's probably not a good idea to include your home telephone number unless you really like to receive calls from strange people at any hour of the day.)

17 Click Next to continue.

18 If you want comments and suggestions about your Web page sent to you, select the Use link radio button and enter your email address.

19 Click Next to continue and display the list of home page sections. (If you'd like to rearrange the sections, select a section and click Up or Down to move the section. The sections will appear on your home page in the order shown in this list.)

20 Click Next and then Finish to create the sample home page, as shown in the figure on the right.

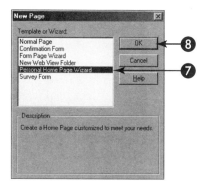

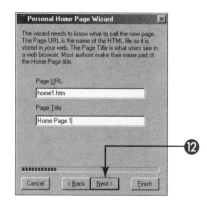

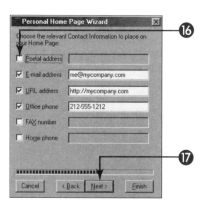

㉑ Select File.

㉒ Select Save As.

㉓ Click the As File button.

㉔ Click Save to save the page.

You can change the text in your Web page by simply selecting the old text and typing your new text. You can edit items by right-clicking them and selecting the appropriate options. If you wish to add images, sound, or other items, choose options from the Insert menu.

It's often better to create relatively small Web pages—at least as the top page of a Web site—and link to your more complex pages. That way people who visit your Web site won't have to endure long delays while your entire Web site loads.

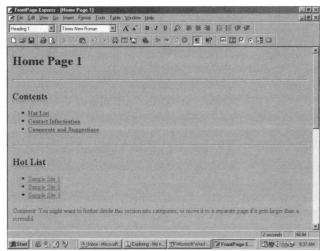

Using the Web Publishing Wizard

After you've created your Web pages, you're ready to publish them on the Internet. Windows 98 includes the Web Publishing Wizard to help make this an easy project.

You need some information from your ISP before you can use the Web Publishing Wizard to publish your Web pages. You need to know where to send your files as well as any passwords necessary for access to the Web server. If you don't already have all the necessary information, ask your ISP to supply you all the necessary information to place your Web pages on the Web server. Follow these steps to publish your Web pages using the Web Publishing Wizard:

❶ Click the Start button.

❷ Select Programs.

❸ Select Internet Explorer.

❹ Select Web Publishing Wizard to open the Web Publishing Wizard.

❺ Click Next to continue.

❻ Enter the name of the file or folder for your Web page.

If your Web site will include multiple pages, make certain you select the folder containing the entire set of pages. If your site is contained in several folders, make certain the Include subfolders checkbox is selected. Be sure to include any graphics files or other items you've included on your Web pages, too.

7 Click Next to continue.

8 Type a descriptive name for the Web server.

9 Click Next to continue.

10 Unless your ISP has specified otherwise, select Automatically Select Service Provider.

11 Click Next to continue.

12 Type the URL (address) for your Web site. (Your ISP must provide this information.)

13 Click Next to continue.

14 Click Next to continue again.

15 The Web Publishing Wizard will then dial your ISP and transmit your Web pages.

Depending on your ISP, you may have to enter a password or some additional information to complete the process, as shown in the figure on the right.

After you've published your Web pages, you can update them using FrontPage Express. It's a good idea to make certain your site is up-to-date; otherwise, no one will want to visit your site.

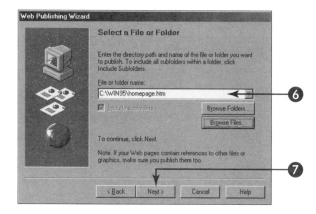

COMMUNICATING ON THE INTERNET

You can do a lot more on the Internet than visit Web sites. The following two exercises will give you a feel for a couple of the exciting new features of Windows 98 that enable you to communicate using both voice and video if you have the right equipment. You'll also be able to share applications and use the Internet as a secure extension of your private network.

Using NetMeeting

NetMeeting takes communicating via the Internet to the limits. With the right hardware you can use the Internet as a free telephone line, as a carrier for video conferencing, as an electronic whiteboard, or even to share Clipboard objects. To use the full capabilities of NetMeeting, you'd need a high-speed Internet connection, a video camera connected to your PC, and a few additional pieces of hardware. For this exercise, however, you don't need to go out and spend a lot of money. Instead, you'll see what's possible with the equipment you probably already have.

1 Click the Start button.

2 Select Programs.

3 Select Internet Explorer.

4 Select Microsoft NetMeeting. (The first time you start NetMeeting, you'll see a series of screens that will help you set up NetMeeting for use.)

5 Click Next to continue.

You must choose a directory server if you want people to be able to see your name and place a call to you. You should choose the same directory server selected by the people you normally call.

6 Click Next to continue.

7 Enter your first name, last name, and e-mail address. (The remaining information is optional.)

8 Click Next to continue.

9 Choose the category for your information.

10 Click Next to display the Audio Tuning Wizard.

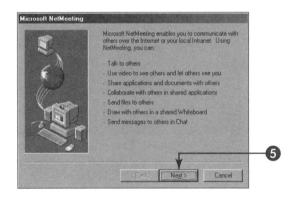

Using NetMeeting

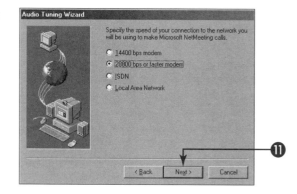

⑪ Click Next to select the type of connection you will use. (Make certain you select the correct type of connection since the connection directly affects the audio and video quality NetMeeting can provide.)

⑫ Click Next to continue.

⑬ Click the Start Recording button to begin testing your settings. (Once you click the Start Recording button, speak into your microphone until the timer indicates the test has completed.)

⑭ Click Next to continue. You're now ready to begin using NetMeeting.

⑮ Click Finish to display the NetMeeting window. (Depending on the type of connection you selected, the Connection Wizard may establish a connection to the Internet.)

⑯ Click the Call button to display the New Call dialog box.

⑰ Type the necessary information to reach your party in the Address text box. You can use an e-mail address, computer name, network address, or modem telephone number as appropriate.

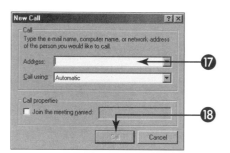

⑱ Click the Call button to dial the call.

⑲ When you've completed your call, click the Hang Up button to disconnect.

⑳ Click the Close button to close NetMeeting.

If you're using NetMeeting to make a call to someone over the Internet, you may want to coordinate your call in advance by sending an e-mail telling them when you intend to call. If you connect to the Internet using a modem, this advance scheduling will be particularly important because both parties must be connected and running NetMeeting for the call to be connected.

If you're connected to a LAN (Local Area Network), you'll probably find NetMeeting even more useful than if you use NetMeeting via modems. Networks typically offer much higher data transmission rates than do modems, so you'll be able to have much higher quality audio and video on a LAN than you will over modems.

Using Virtual Private Networking

Using Virtual Private Networking

Virtual Private Networking is the name Microsoft uses for a special networking protocol that enables you to access your network securely via the Internet. This special protocol is also called *Point-to-Point Tunneling Protocol* (PPTP). When you use Virtual Private Networking, you are able to access your network remotely, but unauthorized users are prevented from accessing your files.

Virtual Private Networking acts as if it were a new type of modem adapter. When you use Virtual Private Networking, your connection to the Internet and ultimately your remote network is routed first through the Virtual Private Networking Adapter and then through your modem. This extra layer provides the security to prevent unauthorized access to your network.

In this exercise you learn how to set up Virtual Private Networking so that you can access your network remotely. Your network administrator will have to add and configure the PPTP services on the network server.

① Double-click the My Computer icon on your desktop.

② Double-click the Dial-Up Networking icon to open Dial-Up Networking.

③ Double-click the Make New Connection icon.

④ Select Microsoft VPN Adapter (if this adapter is not shown, you'll need to go to the Windows Setup tab of the Add/Remove Programs dialog box and choose Virtual Private Networking from the Communications options). You can also enter a more descriptive name for the connection, but this is optional.

⑤ Click Next to continue.

⑥ Enter the name or IP address for your network server. (You may need to ask your network administrator for this information.)

⑦ Click Next.

⑧ Click Finish to complete the setup.

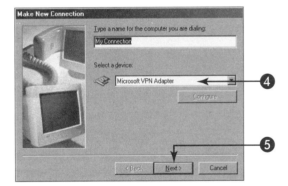

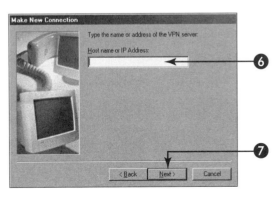

Skills challenge

9 To use your Virtual Private Networking connection, first open your dial-up connection to the Internet. After you're logged on to the Internet, open your Virtual Private Networking connection to establish the secure connection to your network.

Virtual Private Networking also enables you to access your server through a high speed Internet connection. This means you can connect two or more offices via the Internet and not have to worry about people stealing or damaging your files.

SKILLS CHALLENGE: USING THE INTERNET

Now it's time for a little practice. If you have trouble remembering any of the steps, go back and have another look at the exercises.

1 Open My Computer.

2 Open Dial-Up Networking.

3 Right-click the icon for your Internet connection and select Properties.

4 Check to see what phone number this connection uses.

5 Click Server Type.

6 Check your TCP/IP settings.

7 Close the Dial-Up Networking dialog boxes.

8 Connect to your ISP without first loading Internet Explorer.

 Where can you find out the speed of your Internet connection?

9 Disconnect from the Internet.

10 Open Internet Explorer.

 How can you tell the URL for the current page?

⑪ Go to `http://www.idgbooks.com`.

⑫ Go back to your start page.

 How can you return to the previous page with a single click?

 How can you go back to `http://www.idgbooks.com` with a single click?

⑬ Click one of the links to go to one of the featured pages.

 How can you tell which part of the text on a page is a link?

 How can you tell which links you've already followed?

⑭ Check to see which program Internet Explorer uses for e-mail.

⑮ Search for Web pages that refer to "Area 51".

⑯ View your list of favorite Web sites.

⑰ Disconnect from the Internet.

⑱ Open the sample Web page you created.

⑲ Make a call using NetMeeting.

Troubleshooting

TROUBLESHOOTING

If you encounter problems while trying to work through the exercises, here are some ideas that might help you correct the problems and keep going.

Problem	Solution
I can't connect to the Internet.	Check to make certain you've correctly entered your user name and password, including using the proper combination of upper- and lowercase characters. Make certain your modem is dialing the correct number. Check the IP address settings—if you aren't completely accurate you won't be able to connect.
I can connect, but I get messages telling me none of the names I enter are valid.	Check your DNS Server settings. The DNS Server is used to convert the names you enter into valid addresses. Also make certain you're using a forward slash (/) in addresses rather than the backward slash (\) generally used on the PC.
Internet Explorer won't allow me to visit most of the Web sites I'd like to see.	You probably enabled the Content Advisor ratings on the Security tab of the Options dialog box and didn't adjust any of the rating levels. You need to either adjust the rating levels or disable the ratings—you need the password you entered to do so.

WRAP UP

This lesson showed you how to connect to and begin using the Internet. You learned what you need to do to set up your PC for a successful connection, and you learned how to customize Internet Explorer to suit your needs. You also learned some of the basics of finding information and interesting places on the Web. With these

Wrap up

basics you have a good foundation for continuing your explorations of the countless places you can go on the Internet.

The next lesson shows you how to use e-mail. Now that you're connected to the Internet, you can send messages virtually instantly anywhere in the world. In the next lesson you see how you can use Windows 98 applications to create and send those messages.

Just the Mail, Please

30 MINUTES

GOALS

In today's world everyone needs to communicate, and it seems like no one has the time to wait for old-fashioned mail delivery. When you need to send a message, there's no better time for the message to arrive than immediately. That's why electronic mail — e-mail — has become such a part of modern life. In Windows 98 you can send and receive e-mail right from many of your favorite programs. The primary goal of this lesson is to introduce you to using the e-mail capabilities in Windows 98 and to show you how to integrate these capabilities into your everyday computing environment. You learn about the following topics:

- Sending e-mail

- Reading your e-mail

- Creating your own address book

Get ready

GET READY

This lesson requires that you have a modem connected to your PC. You also need access to the Internet, but if you completed Lesson 12, that shouldn't be a problem, either. You use one practice file from the *Windows 98 One Step at a Time* CD-ROM, Myfileat.doc, which is in the Lesson 13 folder. When you complete the exercises in this lesson, you will not only have learned how to send and receive e-mail, but you will also have learned how to attach a file to an e-mail message.

Outlook Express is used as the basis for this lesson. It will probably show up on your desktop as Inbox. If you don't have Inbox on your desktop, use the Windows Setup tab in the Add/Remove Programs dialog box to install Outlook Express before starting this lesson.

You need to know your e-mail address. You're going to send yourself some messages, and you may want to try out sending messages to other people, too.

OUTLOOK EXPRESS: SEND SOME MAIL

In the following exercises you learn how to create and send e-mail messages.

E-mail differs from ordinary mail in a number of ways. Some of the most important differences are its speed and immediacy, its capability to send more than just text in a message, and its extremely low cost. These same benefits of e-mail can work against you, however. It's pretty easy to send an angry note without considering the consequences. Once you've cooled down, it's also pretty easy to wish you hadn't hit that Send button. Just because e-mail is easy to use doesn't mean you should throw good manners out the window!

Creating an e-mail message

There are many ways you can create e-mail messages. Outlook Express includes a simple text editor that you can use for a quick message. You can also use WordPad or many other Windows 98 programs to create e-mail messages. In this exercise you use the most straightforward method — the Outlook Express text editor.

Creating an e-mail message

The e-mail messages you create using the Outlook Express text editor consist of long lines of text that Outlook Express automatically wraps to a new line to suit the width of the text editor window. Many other e-mail programs commonly used on the Internet don't wrap long lines of text to a new line. This can make it difficult for some people to read your e-mail messages because they have to use the horizontal scrollbar to view the complete line. In extreme cases, people not using Outlook Express may not be able to read your complete message if the lines are too long. If someone complains about not being able to read your complete messages, consider pressing Enter at the end of each line to place the following text on a new line.

To create an e-mail message, follow these steps:

1 Double-click the Inbox icon to open Outlook Express. The following figure shows the Inbox folder of Outlook Express.

2 Click the Compose Message button to display the Outlook Express text editor as shown in the following figure.

3 Type your e-mail address in the To text box. Normally you'd type someone else's address to send them a message, but for this exercise, you can send yourself a message.

4 Type the following text in the Subject text box: **My test message**.

5 Type the following text in the body of the message: **This is a test message I'm sending to myself to try out sending e-mail.**

6 Click the Send button to place the outgoing message in the Outbox folder as shown in the figure on the next page. Your message, of course, will contain your own e-mail address in the To column.

7 Select Tools.

8 Select Send and Receive to send the message.

Until it leaves your Outbox folder, you can reopen the message by double-clicking it in the Outbox folder. You might need to do this if you create a message and then discover that you forgot part of the message. You also can cancel messages that are still in the Outbox

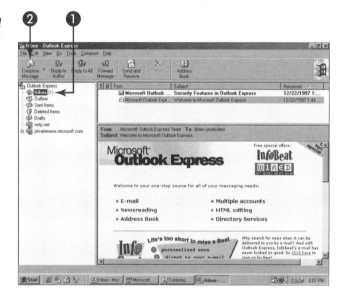

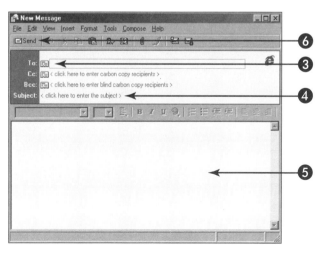

Sending files

folder by selecting the message and clicking the Delete button. After a message has left the Outbox folder, however, there's no way to stop it from being delivered.

TIP

> *You don't have to use Tools > Send and Receive to send each message. Select Tools > Options, and select the Send messages immediately checkbox on the Send tab to send messages as soon as you click the Send button.*

Sending files

Although simple text messages probably take care of your needs most of the time, sometimes you just have to send a file, too. In Windows 98 you generally have two options for sending files. The first, which is always available, is to create a message using the Outlook Express text editor and *attach* a file to the message. The second method is to send a file from within an application. Each method produces the same result, although there are some minor differences between the two. For example, sending a file from within an application isn't always possible — the application must be designed for Windows 98, and it must include a File > Send command.

TIP

> *Don't forget to check whether someone can actually receive file attachments before you spend the time to e-mail large files to them.*

In this exercise you send yourself another message. This time, however, you send the message as a file attachment.

To send a file along with a message, follow these steps:

1 If necessary, double-click the Inbox icon to start the Outlook Express.

2 Click the Compose Message button.

3 Type your e-mail address in the To text box. For this exercise you send the message to yourself as you did with the earlier message.

4 Type the following text in the Subject text box: **My text file attachment**.

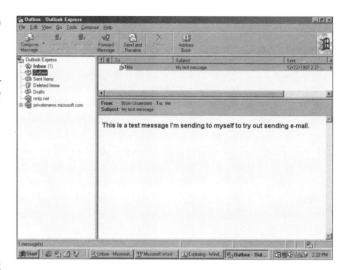

Reading your e-mail messages

⑤ Type the following text: **This is an example of sending a file attached to a message.**

⑥ Click the Insert file button.

⑦ Select Myfileat.doc in the Lesson 13 folder on this book's CD-ROM.

⑧ Click the Send button to send the message.

Because you're sending a message to yourself, there was no need to add additional text to the body of the message. It's a good idea, however, to include some explanation of the file attachment when you send a file to someone else. After all, would you want to open a mystery package?

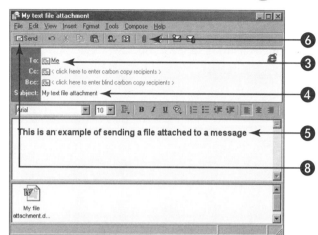

READING YOUR MAIL

Reading your mail — unless it's all bills — is even more fun than sending mail. In the following exercises you learn how to read and reply to e-mail messages. You also learn how to handle files attached to messages you receive.

Reading your e-mail messages

Because the Outlook Express collects all your messages in one place — the Inbox — you only have to look in the Inbox to find your messages. In this exercise you learn how to read one of the messages you sent yourself earlier.

TIP

You may want to use Sound Recorder to create a voice message to attach to the New Mail Notification event to tell you when you have new messages. Double-click Sounds in Control Panel to add your voice message to an event.

❶ If necessary, double-click the Inbox icon on your desktop to open the Outlook Express.

❷ Select Tools.

Replying to and forwarding messages

③ Select Send and Receive to check for new messages. The messages you sent earlier may already be in your Inbox, but there's no harm in checking to see if you have any additional messages.

④ If necessary, click the Inbox folder icon so you can see any messages. As the figure on the right shows, new messages that you haven't read are shown in bold type, while messages you have read are shown in normal type.

⑤ Double-click the new message to open it. (If you prefer, you can also read messages in the preview pane located below the list of messages, but this will be a bit more cumbersome for longer messages.)

⑥ Click the Print button to print a copy of the message. Notice that your printed copy of the message includes a header with information about the message to help you keep track of your messages.

⑦ Click the Close button to close the message.

It really doesn't matter whether a message was one you sent to yourself or one sent by someone halfway around the world. When you use Outlook Express, it's just as easy to read any message, regardless of its origin.

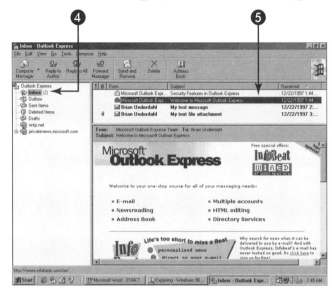

Replying to and forwarding messages

One thing that sets e-mail apart from old-fashioned, hand-delivered mail is the ease with which you can reply to an e-mail message or forward a copy of the message to someone else. In this exercise you learn how to reply to an e-mail message and see how you can forward a copy when necessary.

① Double-click the message entitled "My test message" to open the message again.

② Click the Reply To Author button to open the reply window.

In the figure on the next page, notice that the To text box and the Subject text box are already filled in, and a copy of the original message is included in the body of the message. The copy of the original message is indented to show that it is the copy.

❸ Type the following text in the message body: **This is my reply**.

❹ Click the Send button to place your reply in the Outbox.

❺ Select Tools.

❻ Select Send and Receive to connect to your ISP and send your reply.

Forwarding a message is almost as simple as replying to a message. Rather than clicking the Reply To Author button, you click the Forward button. When you forward a message, you must choose the recipient. Also, the message subject line begins with FWD rather than RE to indicate that the message is a forwarded message, not a reply to a message.

Saving file attachments

E-mail messages that contain file attachments require slightly different handling than simple text messages. In most cases you probably want to save the attached file for future use. In the following exercise you learn how to view and save file attachments in your e-mail messages.

❶ Double-click the message entitled "My text file attachment" to open the message.

❷ Right-click the icon for Myfileat.doc in the message body.

❸ Select Open in the menu that appears to open the attached document. Notice that all the character formatting you added to the original document remains in the document.

❹ Click the Close button to close WordPad (or Word, if you have Word installed on your PC).

❺ Right-click the icon for Myfileat.doc.

❻ Select Save As to display the Save As dialog box.

❼ Click the down arrow at the right edge of the Save in list box.

❽ Select the folder in which you'd like to save the file. Be sure you know where the file is saved — it's easy to forget where you saved a file attachment.

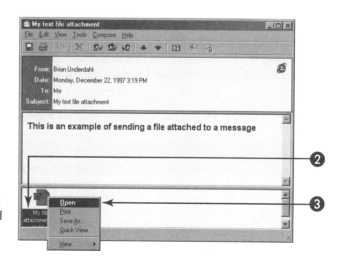

13

Just the Mail, Please

9 Click Save to save the file.

10 Click the Close button to close the message.

It's a good idea to be a little cautious about saving file attachments if you don't know the person who sent the message or if you're not certain of the origin of the file. File attachments can contain computer viruses, and once they're saved on your hard disk, they're free to damage your system.

CREATE YOUR OWN ADDRESS BOOK

It can be a little inconvenient to always have to type in the e-mail address whenever you want to send a message. It's much easier to save the addresses and phone numbers in the Outlook Express Address Book, and then just select the recipient from the list when you want to send a message.

Adding names to your Address Book

You probably use a telephone that stores some of the phone numbers you frequently call. When you want to call one of these stored phone numbers, you just push a button or two and your telephone dials the number for you. The Outlook Express Address Book provides a similar capability for your e-mail messages. In this exercise you learn how to add people to your Address Book.

1 If necessary, double-click the Inbox icon to start the Outlook Express.

2 Click the Address Book button to display the Address Book as shown in the figure on the right. (Your Address Book probably won't have any entries yet.)

3 Click the New Contact button to display the Properties dialog box.

4 Type the name of the person in the Display text box. The name you type doesn't have to be the person's real name — you can use an easy-to-remember nickname if you like.

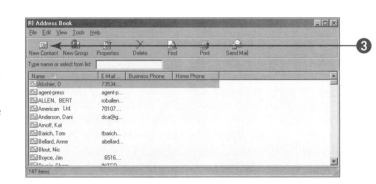

5 Type the person's e-mail address in the E-mail Address text box. This is something like `someone@somecompany.com`.

6 Click OK to add the new entry to your Address Book. If you like, you can add more information on the other tabs of the Properties dialog box before you close the dialog box, but the two entries you've added are all that is required.

7 Click the Close button to close your Address Book.

TIP

Right-click the sender's name when you receive e-mail and select Add to Address Book to quickly add new entries to your Address Book.

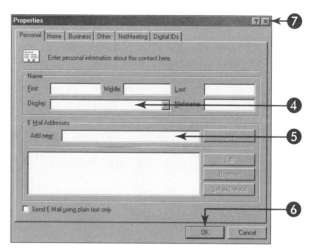

Using your Address Book names

After you've added names to your Address Book, it's a lot easier to send messages. Rather than typing out the complete e-mail address, you can simply type the person's name or choose an entry from your Address Book.

1 If necessary, double-click the Inbox icon to start Outlook Express.

2 Click the Compose Message button to begin creating a new message.

3 Type the name of the recipient in the To text box. You should type the same name you added to the Display Name text box when you created the Address Book Entry.

4 If you're not certain you entered the name correctly, click the Check Names button.

5 To add additional names to either the To or the Cc text boxes, type the additional names separated by a semicolon (;). If you're not certain of the correct names, click the To or the Cc buttons and choose names from the Address Book.

6 Complete your message and click the Send button.

13

Just the Mail, Please

Using your Address Book names

TIP

*To send a **blind carbon copy** — a copy that the other recipients don't know about — add the additional recipient in the Bcc text box.*

SKILLS CHALLENGE: USING MAIL

Now it's time to try out the skills you've learned in this lesson.

1 Start Outlook Express.

> **1** *How can you tell whether the same mail server provides both incoming and outgoing mail delivery to your PC?*

2 Determine how often the Outlook Express checks for new Internet mail.

> **2** *How can you tell Outlook Express not to check for Internet mail automatically?*

3 Check to see if you have any new mail in your Inbox.

> **3** *How can you tell if a message includes an attachment?*

4 Send yourself a message with a file attachment.

5 Create a new message in WordPad.

6 Send the WordPad message to yourself.

7 Add your e-mail address to your Address Book.

> **4** *How can you quickly add someone who sent you a message to your Address Book without actually opening your Address Book?*

8 Send yourself a message using your name rather than your e-mail address.

Troubleshooting

TROUBLESHOOTING

If you encounter problems while working through the exercises, here are some ideas that might help you correct the problems and keep going.

Problem	Solution
I can receive but not send e-mail over the Internet.	Check to make certain your ISP uses the same mail server for incoming and outgoing mail. You may need to use the Advanced settings in Internet Mail to specify a different outgoing mail server.

WRAP UP

This lesson showed you how to use e-mail. Now you can send messages virtually instantly anywhere in the world. You learned you can use Windows 98 applications to create and send those messages. You learned how you can manage all your e-mail addresses in your Address Book.

In the next lesson you learn how to use another Windows 98 accessory that enables you to connect directly to another PC — HyperTerminal. If you want to share files with a friend, HyperTerminal can be an easy solution, and you don't even need to connect to the Internet.

Hyper HyperTerminal

45 MINUTES

GOALS

Even if you're connected to the Internet, you may need to connect directly to other computers from time to time. Whether you want to swap some files with your friends or download an updated file from a manufacturer, you need a way to make your computer communicate with other computers. HyperTerminal, one of the Windows 98 accessories, may be just what you need. HyperTerminal is a *terminal* program — no, that's not a dying program, it's a program that turns your PC into a communications terminal so that you can upload and download files. In this lesson you learn about the following topics:

- Connecting to another computer

- Exchanging files with a remote computer

- Capturing and saving text from the HyperTerminal screen

Get ready

GET READY

To complete this lesson, you need a modem or a direct-cable connection to another PC. You also need someone you can call. This can be a friend with a PC or an online service — it's really up to you. You should also have HyperTerminal installed. You will need your Windows 98 CD-ROM if HyperTerminal doesn't appear in your Accessories menu.

If you intend to use a direct-cable connection between two PCs, you need a *null modem cable* — a special cable that enables two PCs to talk directly to each other without a modem. Before you buy a null modem cable, be sure you know the type of connector needed at each end of the cable. The standard null modem cable for PCs is connected as shown in Table 14-1.

TABLE 14-1 NULL MODEM PIN CONNECTIONS

Connector 1	Connector 2
Pin 2	Pin 3
Pin 3	Pin 2
Pin 4	Pin 6
Pin 5	Pin 5
Pin 6	Pin 4
Pin 7	Pin 8
Pin 8	Pin 7

It doesn't matter whether you want to connect to another computer through your modem or through a cable connected directly between the two computers. HyperTerminal works pretty much the same either way. Direct connections are usually faster than modem connections, but you probably won't notice too many other differences.

Connecting to another computer

Windows 98 provides another means of connecting two computers — Dial-Up Networking. While both HyperTerminal and Dial-Up Networking enable two computers to communicate, HyperTerminal offers you the opportunity to connect to computers that aren't running Windows 98.

MAKING THE CONNECTION

Computers really aren't a whole lot different than people — they must speak the same language in order to communicate. When you use a program such as HyperTerminal to connect two computers, you need to make certain both computers have the same communications settings and that they use the same *file transfer protocol* to exchange files. In the following exercises you learn how to make certain your PC can communicate with another computer.

Connecting to another computer

In this exercise you use HyperTerminal to connect to another computer. If you have access to an online service such as CompuServe or a local computer bulletin board, either would be a good choice for this exercise. You need to know the correct phone number to dial as well as any log-in information you must type to access the service. If you don't have access to an online service, you may want to try connecting to another computer.

1. Click the Start button.

2. Select Programs.

3. Select Accessories.

4. Select HyperTerminal to open the HyperTerminal folder. (Your HyperTerminal folder probably has a different set of icons than are shown in the figure on the right.)

5. Double-click the Hypertrm.exe icon to start HyperTerminal.

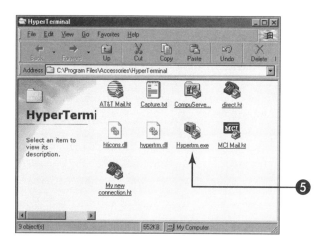

Connecting to another computer

6 If you see a dialog box asking if you'd like to use HyperTerminal as your Telnet application, click Yes to continue.

7 Type the following text in the Name text box: **My new connection**.

8 If you like, choose a different icon for the connection.

9 Click OK to display the Phone Number dialog box.

10 Verify that the correct country is chosen in the Country code list box.

11 Check the Area code entry to make certain it is correct.

12 Type the access phone number in the Phone number text box.

13 Make certain the correct modem or port is chosen in the Connect using list box.

14 Click OK to display the Connect dialog box. The dialog box should show the correct phone number for your connection.

15 Click Dial to begin making the connection.

16 After the connection has been made, you are probably greeted with a log-in screen where you must type your user name and password to access the online service, as shown in the figure on the next page. (If all you see is a blank screen, try pressing Enter a couple of times so the remote computer realizes you've connected. If all you see on your screen is gibberish, you need to change your terminal settings, which you learn to do in the next exercise.)

After you enter the information necessary to log on to the online service, you are usually greeted with a menu of options. The figure on the next page shows a typical menu you might see on CompuServe.

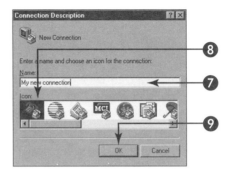

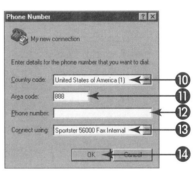

Configuring the terminal settings ◀

17 Type the command necessary to log off the online service. (This is often **bye** or **off** followed by Enter.)

18 Click the Disconnect button.

19 To view something that has scrolled off the top of the terminal window, use the vertical scrollbar to scroll back.

20 Click the Close button to close HyperTerminal.

21 Click Yes to save the session. (This places an icon for the connection in your HyperTerminal folder so you can later make the same connection without redoing all the connection-setting entries.)

You can create a number of different HyperTerminal connection icons, and each can have different settings. You might create one for a commercial online service such as CompuServe and a different one for your connection to a friend's PC.

Configuring the terminal settings

HyperTerminal is usually able to determine the correct settings for connecting to other computers, but there are some settings you must make yourself if you have problems connecting or if your screen doesn't display information correctly. In this exercise you learn how to correct these types of problems by adjusting HyperTerminal's terminal settings.

1 If necessary, open the HyperTerminal folder.

2 Double-click My new connection.ht.

3 Click Cancel to prevent HyperTerminal from dialing.

4 Click the Properties button to display the Properties dialog box.

5 Click the Settings tab.

New
Open
Connect
Disconnect
Send
Receive
Properties
Status bar

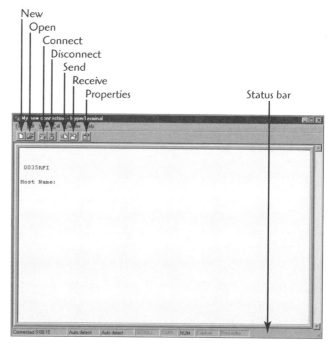

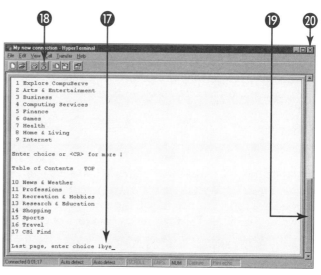

14

Hyper HyperTerminal

HYPER HYPERTERMINAL **381**

Answering a call

6 Click the ASCII Setup button to display the ASCII Setup dialog box.

7 Select the Send line ends with line feeds checkbox if everything you type appears on the same line on the remote computer. (If everything you type appears double-spaced on the remote computer, make certain this checkbox is not selected.)

8 Select the Echo typed characters locally checkbox if you can't see anything you type. (If everything you type appears doubled, such as `eevveerryytthhiinngg iiss ddoouubblleedd`, make certain this check box is not selected.)

9 Click the Append line feeds to incoming line ends checkbox if everything coming from the remote computer appears on one line thus overwriting the existing text. (If everything coming from the remote computer appears double-spaced on your screen, make certain this checkbox is not selected.)

10 Select the Force incoming data to 7-bit ASCII checkbox if everything coming from the remote computer appears garbled.

11 Select the Wrap lines that exceed terminal width checkbox.

12 Click OK twice to return to HyperTerminal.

Most online services should work using HyperTerminal's default terminal settings, but if you attempt to connect to a friend's PC, experimentation determines which settings work the best. If necessary, you can adjust your terminal settings while you're connected to another computer and then try out those settings during the current session.

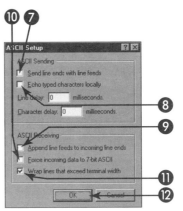

Answering a call

If you want to connect to another PC via modem, one PC must dial and the other PC must answer. HyperTerminal provides an easy way to dial the call, but you won't find any HyperTerminal commands for answering a call. Fortunately, you can easily get around this limitation by typing a command to tell your modem to answer an incoming call.

1 Open the HyperTerminal folder.

2 Double-click My new connection.ht.

③ Click Cancel to prevent HyperTerminal from dialing.

④ To tell your modem to answer the next incoming call on the second ring, type the following text: **ATS0=2**.

⑤ Press Enter.

You should see OK in the HyperTerminal window. If you don't, make certain you type the command in uppercase letters and that the character following the S is the number zero, not the letter O.

⑥ If a call is already coming in, type the following text: **ATA**.

⑦ Press Enter to immediately begin answering.

⑧ To hang up, type **ATH** or click the Disconnect button.

If your modem does not respond to your commands, type **+++** and wait for OK to appear on your screen. This command won't have any effect if your modem is responding to your other commands.

EXCHANGING FILES WITH A REMOTE COMPUTER

You've probably heard people talk about *uploading* — sending — and *downloading* — receiving — files. You can use HyperTerminal to exchange files in both directions with other computers. If you have a really neat scanned image you'd like to share with a friend, or if you need to download a software update from a manufacturer's computer service, HyperTerminal can do the job.

▶ ## Selecting a file transfer protocol

Computers use *error-correcting file transfer protocols* to ensure files are transferred properly. These protocols are simply methods of breaking up files into relatively small pieces and verifying that each of those pieces is received properly. If any piece contains an error, only the piece with the error needs to be retransmitted — not the entire file. The exact methods of breaking up the files, checking for errors, and reassembling the received files aren't too important to you. All that's really important is that the files you receive are identical to the files that were sent by the other computer.

14

Hyper HyperTerminal

Selecting a file transfer protocol

File transfer protocols do matter to you in one important way. Both the sending and receiving computer must use the same protocol. HyperTerminal can use several of the popular protocols, so you should be able to find one that works. To select the file transfer protocol in HyperTerminal, follow these steps:

1 Open the HyperTerminal connection you wish to use.

2 To select a file transfer protocol for sending a file, select Transfer.

3 Select Send File to display the Send File dialog box.

4 Click the down arrow at the right edge of the Protocol list box to display the protocol options.

5 Choose the protocol you wish to use.

In some cases you have to choose a specific protocol because you can only find one that is available both in HyperTerminal and on the remote computer. If you have a choice of several common protocols, Zmodem is a very good choice because the Zmodem protocol is usually the easiest to use.

6 Click Close to return to HyperTerminal.

7 To select a file transfer protocol for receiving a file, select Transfer.

8 Select Receive File to display the Receive File dialog box.

9 Click the down arrow at the right edge of the Use receiving protocol list box to display the protocol options.

10 Choose the protocol you wish to use. You probably want to choose the same protocol for both sending and receiving files.

11 Click Close to return to HyperTerminal.

If you encounter problems transferring files even if it appears that the same protocol has been selected on both the sending and receiving computers, it's possible that the two computers aren't using completely compatible versions of the protocol. Unless both computers are running the same program, such as HyperTerminal, you can't be sure that there won't be slight differences in how a protocol is implemented. If this happens, the two computers may try to send the files and be unable to successfully complete the transfer. Often the problem can be solved simply by choosing a different protocol.

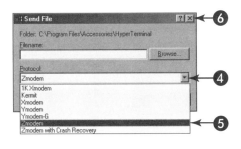

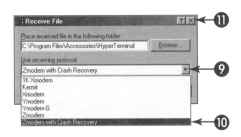

Uploading and downloading files ◀

▶ Uploading and downloading files

When you've determined which file transfer protocol to use, you can upload and download the files. The exact procedure you use depends on whether you're transferring files from an online service or between two PCs. Transferring files between two PCs can be a bit more complicated because you won't have a menu of options on your screen like you see when you connect to an online service. In this exercise the figures show you how to download a file from a typical online service such as CompuServe. If you're transferring files between your PC and a friend's PC, you can use the same HyperTerminal commands, but you will have to work without the prompts on your screen. To download a file from an online service using HyperTerminal, follow these steps:

❶ Start the HyperTerminal connection to the other computer and log on to the system if that is required. (If you're transferring files from another PC, skip to Step 4.)

If you're using an online service, use the onscreen menus to locate the file you want to download and tell the online service you want to download the file. You need to follow the prompts for the particular online service you use to locate the file areas.

❷ Choose a file transfer protocol. (You need to pick a protocol available in HyperTerminal.)

❸ If prompted as shown in the figure on the right, type a filename for the file. (You probably want to use the same name the file has on the online service.)

❹ Select Transfer.

❺ Select Receive File.

❻ Click Receive to begin the transfer.

If you're transferring files between PCs, the PC sending the file should issue the command to begin sending the file, too.

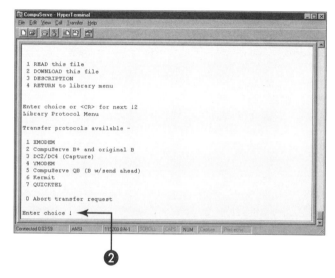

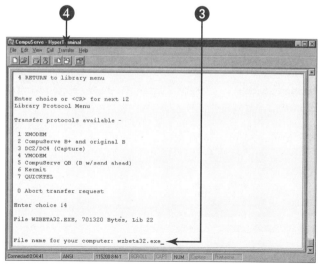

Working with text files

While the file is being transmitted, you see a dialog box similar to the one shown in the figure on the right. The dialog box looks a little different if you're using a file transfer protocol other than Ymodem as shown in the figure.

7 When you complete the file transfer, press Enter to signal the online service that the transfer is complete.

8 When you're finished transferring files, log off and click the Disconnect button to hang up the phone.

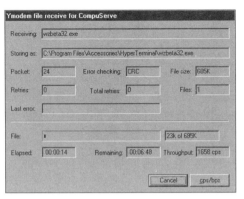

If you're transferring files between two PCs that are using HyperTerminal, or if the other computer supports Zmodem, choose Zmodem as the file transfer protocol. When you choose Zmodem, the file transfer starts automatically on the receiving computer as soon as the sending computer is ready to begin sending the file.

You can upload files using HyperTerminal by selecting Transfer ➢ Send File rather than Transfer ➢ Receive File. If you're transferring files to or from a friend's PC, you may want to decide in advance on a signal to use so each person knows when to begin sending or receiving files. For example, the person sending files could type the name of the next file they were going to send and press Enter before issuing the Transfer ➢ Send File command.

WORKING WITH TEXT FILES

Working with text in HyperTerminal is pretty easy. You can collect, or *capture*, all the text that appears on your HyperTerminal screen in a file or print a copy of the text. You can also send the contents of a file rather than type everything during a session. In the following exercises you learn how to work with text in HyperTerminal.

Capturing text to a file or to the printer

Capturing text to a file or to the printer

It's pretty useful to be able to save text that appears on your HyperTerminal screen into a file or to your printer. Imagine how much easier it is to have a printed copy of directions to someone's party than to try to remember what you read on the screen. In this exercise you learn how to capture the text on your HyperTerminal screen by saving the text in a file or by printing a copy.

① Open a HyperTerminal connection.

② When you want to begin printing any text that follows, select Transfer.

③ Select Capture to Printer. (When this option is selected, the Print echo indicator at the right edge of the HyperTerminal status line changes to black rather than gray.)

④ To stop printing text, select Transfer.

⑤ Select Capture to Printer again.

⑥ To begin capturing text in a file, select Transfer.

⑦ Select Capture Text to display the Capture Text dialog box.

⑧ If you want to use a file other than Capture.txt, type the name in the File text box.

⑨ Click Start to begin capturing text.

⑩ To temporarily stop capturing text into the file, select Transfer.

⑪ Select Capture Text.

⑫ Select Pause.

⑬ To resume capturing text into the file, select Transfer.

⑭ Select Capture Text.

⑮ Select Resume.

⑯ To completely stop capturing text into the file, select Transfer.

Sending a text file

17 Select Capture Text.

18 Select Stop.

TIP *If you think you want to capture text during a session, select Transfer ➢ Capture Text and click the Start button. Then select Transfer ➢ Capture Text ➢ Pause to halt the capture until you're ready to begin capturing text. That way you're ready to immediately begin capturing text by selecting Transfer ➢ Capture Text ➢ Resume.*

When you capture text to a file or to the printer, text that already appears on your screen is ignored. If you need to capture something that has already appeared on your screen, use your mouse to highlight the text, right-click the selection, and select Copy to place a copy on the Clipboard.

Sending a text file

HyperTerminal isn't exactly the world's greatest word processor. If you make a mistake typing into the HyperTerminal window, the person sitting at the remote computer immediately sees your mistake. There are a couple of things you can do to prevent this from happening. If you have a lot of text to send, you can send an entire text file that you've prepared in advance. For smaller amounts of text, you can use the Windows 98 Clipboard to paste text. To send text from a file or the Clipboard, follow these steps:

1 Open a HyperTerminal connection.

2 To send a complete text file, select Transfer.

3 Select Send Text File to display the Send Text File dialog box.

4 Select the file containing the text. (For example, if a technical support person asked you to send your Config.sys file, you'd select C:\Config.sys.)

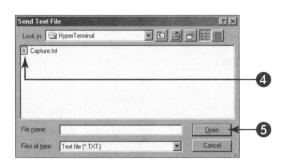

5 Click Open to send the text contained in the file. (Unless you have selected the Echo typed characters locally checkbox in the ASCII Setup dialog box or are connected to an online service that echoes what you type, you may not see the text.)

6 To send a small amount of text, first copy the text to the Clipboard. (For example, if you noticed a file you'd like to download, select the filename in the HyperTerminal window, right–click the selection, and choose Copy.)

7 When you're ready to send the text from the Clipboard, right-click in the HyperTerminal window.

8 Select Paste to Host. (The same rules apply as with sending a text file on whether you see the text on your screen.)

TIP *If you know in advance much of the text you need to type during an online session, you might want to type that text into a WordPad document. Place each piece of text you need to send in a separate paragraph and keep WordPad open while you're working in HyperTerminal. When you need to send text, copy it from the WordPad document and paste it into HyperTerminal. Anyone on the other end of the connection thinks you're the world's fastest typist!*

You can also combine typing with sending text from the Clipboard. If you have a phrase you need to include quite often, copy it to the Clipboard before you begin the HyperTerminal session. When you're typing information into the HyperTerminal window, press Ctrl+V to paste the saved phrase into the text.

Skills challenge

SKILLS CHALLENGE: USING HYPERTERMINAL

Now you can practice using HyperTerminal on your own. You should find these exercises quite easy.

1 Open a new connection in HyperTerminal.

2 Choose a different icon for the new connection.

3 Connect to another computer.

 What setting do you need to adjust if you can't see anything you type?

 What do you need to do if everything sent by the remote computer overwrites the previous line of text?

 What can you do if you can't read anything sent by the remote computer because all of the text appears in strange characters?

4 Determine what file transfer protocol HyperTerminal uses for sending files.

 Which file transfer protocol automatically begins sending the file as soon as the sending computer tries to start sending the file?

5 Start printing all new text.

6 Begin capturing the text in a file.

7 Send the contents of a text file to the remote computer.

 How can you send Clipboard text to the remote computer?

TROUBLESHOOTING

If you encounter problems while trying to work through the exercises, here are some ideas that might help you correct the problems and keep going.

Problem	Solution
HyperTerminal doesn't appear on my Accessories menu.	Install HyperTerminal from the Communications group on the Windows Setup tab of the Add/Remove Programs dialog box.
I can't transfer files to or from a friend's PC even though we are both using the same file transfer protocol.	Try selecting a different protocol. Some protocols may be implemented slightly differently in different programs even though they have the same names.

WRAP UP

This lesson showed you how to use HyperTerminal to connect directly to another PC or to an online service. HyperTerminal enables you to share files even if you aren't connected to the Internet. HyperTerminal also enables you to connect two PCs directly without using modems, so you can share files in a small office without the expense of a network.

Installing Windows 98

If you buy a new PC after Windows 98 is released, it's likely your PC will come with Windows 98 already installed. If you upgrade to Windows 98, you'll find it's pretty easy to install it yourself. In this appendix you learn what you need to do to prepare for installing Windows 98, and then actually proceed with the installation.

Preparing to install Windows 98

PREPARING TO INSTALL WINDOWS 98

Here are a few steps you need to follow before you install
Windows 98:

1 Make sure your computer is compatible with Windows 98.
Basically, it must have an 80386, 80486, Pentium, Pentium Pro,
Pentium II, or compatible processor; 8MB of memory; and
about 50MB or more of free disk space. You'll be a lot happier if
you don't try to run Windows 98 on a 386, and even most 486
systems will be pretty slow. You're also a lot better off with at
least 16MB of memory and 100MB or more of free disk space.

2 Make sure you don't have any unresolved hardware problems or
conflicts. If something isn't working right before you install
Windows 98, it won't be working right afterwards, either.

3 Back up any of your critical files. Installing Windows 98 shouldn't
cause any data to be lost, but why take the chance?

4 Make sure you have a blank, high-density diskette available.

5 If you're connected to a network, make certain you have a list
of your user names and passwords.

INSTALLING WINDOWS 98

You need about an hour to install Windows 98—maybe longer if you
encounter any problems or have a slow system. When you're ready,
follow these steps:

1 Place the Windows 98 CD-ROM in your CD-ROM drive (or the
first Windows 98 diskette in drive A).

2 If you're running Windows 3.x, select File ➢ Run.

3 Type the following text (if your CD-ROM drive is not drive D or
if you are installing from diskettes, use the correct drive letter):
d:\setup.

4 Follow the prompts and click the Next button when necessary.

⑤ If the setup program prompts you to choose a directory, choose the option to install Windows 98 in the same directory as your existing version of Windows; otherwise, you'll have to reinstall all of your programs.

⑥ At one point the setup program will direct you to make a startup disk. This creates a diskette you can use to start your PC in case there's a problem with your hard disk.

⑦ Continue to follow the prompts and finish the installation. Be sure to remove any diskettes before allowing the system to restart.

If Windows 98 has any problems restarting, wait a few minutes before you do anything. Remember that it may take an hour or so to complete the installation.

A

Installing Windows 98

Answers to Skills Challenge Questions

Answers to skills challenge questions

 How would you create a shortcut that opens Windows Explorer with the C:\Windows\Start Menu\Programs\Accessories folder visible in the contents pane?

Open the Windows Explorer, point to the C:\Windows\Start Menu\Programs\Accessories folder icon in the left pane, hold down the right mouse button, and drag the pointer onto your desktop. (If the Windows Explorer window is covering the entire desktop, click the Restore button to reduce the size of the Windows Explorer window so you can see your desktop.) Click Create Shortcut(s) Here.

 How would you create a shortcut that opens Windows Explorer with the contents of your CD-ROM drive visible?

Open the Windows Explorer, point to the icon for your CD-ROM drive, hold down the right mouse button, and drag the pointer onto your desktop. (If the Windows Explorer window is covering the entire desktop, click the Restore button to reduce the size of the Windows Explorer window so you can see your desktop). Click Create Shortcut(s) Here.

 How can you add WordPad as an option to the Send To command?

Create a shortcut to WordPad in the \Windows\SendTo folder.

 What could you do to make it easy to copy files to a specified folder using the right-click menu?

Create a shortcut to the specified folder in the \Windows\SendTo folder.

 What would you do to make Windows Explorer run automatically whenever you start Windows 98?

Create a shortcut to Windows Explorer in the \Windows\Start Menu\Programs\StartUp folder.

 How would you find files created during June, 1997?

Specify 6/1/97 in the "between" and 6/30/97 in the "and" text boxes on the Date Modified tab of the Find dialog box and select the Find all files created or modified radio button before you click Find now.

 How can you find out which files were created or modified by a program you installed today?

Select the During the previous *x* days radio button, select 1 in the spin box, and select the Find all files created or modified radio button on the Date Modified tab of the Find dialog box before you click Find now.

 How can you find a document file someone created on your computer yesterday if you don't know the name or location of the file?

Although you could simply select 2 in the During the previous *x* days spin box and perform the search, you might want to set both the "between" and "and" text boxes to yesterday's date and use that option to limit the search.

 How would you find and open the help file called Backup.hlp?

Click the New Search button, type **Backup.hlp** in the Named text box, click Find Now, and then double-click Backup.hlp in the results panes.

LESSON 2

 How would you change to the High Contrast White (Extra Large) color scheme?

Answers to skills challenge questions

Right-click a blank space on the desktop, select Properties, click the Appearance tab, and choose High Contrast White (Extra Large) in the Scheme list box.

 2 *How would you increase the size of the onscreen text to five times normal so a vision-impaired user could read the Windows 98 screen?*

Right-click a blank space on your desktop, select Properties, click the Settings tab, click Custom, and specify 500% in the Scale fonts to be *x* of normal size text box.

 3 *How do you make a picture into wallpaper that covers your entire desktop?*

Choose the picture in the Wallpaper list box on the Background tab of the Display Properties dialog box, and then select the Tile radio button.

 4 *What can you do to protect your privacy when you step away from your desk?*

Select a screen saver and a password on the Screen Saver tab of the Display Properties dialog box, and set the screen saver Wait time to a very short time.

 5 *How can you hide the title bar text?*

Select Active Title Bar in the Item list box of the Appearance tab of the Display Properties dialog box, and set the font color to the same color as the title bar.

 6 *How would you find out where someone hid the Taskbar?*

Move your mouse off each edge of the screen. If the Taskbar is hidden at that edge, it will appear after a short delay.

 7 *How would you make it easier for someone with limited physical abilities to double-click the mouse?*

Answers to skills challenge questions

Double-click the Mouse icon in the Control Panel, and set the Double-click speed to the slowest setting.

 8 *What would you do to make the mouse pointer easier to find for someone who's never used a mouse before?*

Select the Show pointer trails checkbox on the Motion tab of the Mouse Properties dialog box.

 9 *What two settings can you use to make the keyboard easier to use for someone who's just learning to type?*

Set the Repeat delay and Repeat rate settings in the Keyboard Properties dialog box.

LESSON 3

 1 *What is the one step you must always remember to do before saving a find files search if you want Windows 98 to remember any date specification you entered?*

You must make certain Options ➢ Save Results is selected, and that you've selected Find Now before you select File ➢ Save Search.

 2 *What is the fastest way to find the first item that starts with W in the Windows Explorer contents pane?*

Press W to jump to the first item beginning with W.

 3 *How can you remove one item from a selection?*

Hold down Ctrl while you click the item you wish to remove.

How can you add an option to open the Text
Document file type with WordPad in addition to
keeping the default action?

Open Windows Explorer, select View ➢ Options, click the File
Types tab, select text, click Edit, select New, and type **Open** in the
Action text box and **WordPad** in the Application used to perform
action text box.

LESSON 4

 What format option can you use to make certain
a diskette doesn't contain any bad sectors?

Make certain the Full format type radio button is selected.

 What can you do to prevent a diskette from being
formatted and destroying any data it contains?

Slide the write-protect tab open.

 How can you copy a file on your desktop to a
diskette without using Windows Explorer?

Right-click the file icon, select Send To, and choose the diskette
as the destination.

 How can you specify an exact amount of free
space rather than a percentage?

Click the Start button, select Programs ➢ Accessories ➢
System Tools ➢ DriveSpace, select the icon for the drive, click Drive
➢ Adjust Free Space, and enter an exact value in either the
compressed drive or the host drive free space text box.

 What setting checks for file system errors without
doing a surface scan?

Select the ScanDisk Standard type of test rather than the Through type of test.

 6 *How can you specify that you want to check all of your disk drives for errors in one operation?*

Select all of the drives in the Select the drive(s) you want to check for errors list box before you click Start.

 7 *What setting is necessary to keep ScanDisk from stopping and showing a summary report if there are no errors?*

Click the Advanced button and select Only if errors found.

LESSON 5

 1 *How can you tell the length of a sound file without playing the file?*

Right-click the sound file, choose Properties, and look on the Details tab.

 2 *What artist created the Microsoft Sound?*

Right-click the sound file, choose Properties, and look on the Details tab to see that the artist was Brian Eno.

 3 *How can you quickly mute all sounds from your PC?*

Click the speaker icon on the Taskbar, and choose Mute.

 4 *How can you create the effect of having an echo occur before the sound?*

Use the Sound Recorder Effects ➤ Reverse command to reverse the sound. Then use Effects ➤ Add Echo. Finally use Effects ➤ Reverse again.

Answers to skills challenge questions

 How can you remove all changes from a sound recording?

Select File ➢ Revert.

 How can you play the songs on an audio CD in reverse order of the way they appear on the CD?

Edit the play list and add the songs starting from the end of the titles.

 How can you make the same set of songs play several times in a row?

Either click the Continuous Play button, or add the songs to the play list several times.

 How much disk space does the lowest-quality PCM format audio recording require for each second of recording?

8 Hz, 8-bit mono requires 8K per second.

LESSON 6

 How can you tell whether a program you installed can be uninstalled using Add/Remove Programs?

If a program can be uninstalled, it will appear on the Install/Uninstall tab of the Add/Remove Programs dialog box.

 Which folder generally holds shared program components?

C:\Windows\System

 How can you find the configuration files used by old Windows programs?

Look for files with an INI extension.

4 *How can you find out what additional program is needed to run the MS–DOS Help program?*

If you try to run the help program, you'll see the message Can not find file QBASIC.EXE, which tells you that Help.COM needs QBASIC.EXE.

5 *How can you run Wolf.com and then run another MS–DOS command in one MS–DOS session?*

Click the Start button and select Programs ➢ MS–DOS Prompt. Then run the programs from the command line.

6 *How can you print a list of filenames without first copying the list into WordPad?*

When you're at the MS–DOS prompt command line, redirect the output of the DIR command to the printer by adding **> PRN** to the end of the command line.

7 *What do you need to include in an MS–DOS command if you want to use a long filename that includes spaces?*

Enclose the long filename in quotes.

LESSON 7

1 *How can you make the text adjust to the width of the WordPad window?*

Select View ➢ Options ➢ Wrap to window.

2 *Which toolbars contain options you can't save in text files?*

The Format bar and the ruler.

Answers to skills challenge questions

 3 *What do you need to cross before automatic word selection occurs?*

A space between two words.

 4 *What effect does changing the paper orientation have on the margin settings?*

The top and left margins and the bottom and right margins are swapped.

 5 *How can you copy text using drag & drop?*

Select the text, and then hold down Ctrl while you drag the mouse pointer.

 6 *Which buttons can you use in place of using drag & drop?*

Cut, Copy, and Paste.

 7 *How can you move a paragraph closer to the right margin while keeping the paragraph left aligned?*

Select Format ➢ Paragraph ➢ Left to set the left indent.

 8 *How can you keep text in a document but prevent it from printing?*

Select Format ➢ Font ➢ Color and select White.

LESSON 8

 1 *How can you adjust the text block so your first name appears on one line, and your last name on the next line?*

While the text block is still selected, drag one of the vertical borders so your last name wraps to a second line.

Answers to skills challenge questions

 2 *How can you make your last name appear in a larger size font?*

You must create a second text block to apply different attributes to some of the text.

 3 *How can you create a rounded rectangle around the text block without covering up your name?*

Make certain you select the Draw border only option in the tool option box.

 4 *How can you create an octagon with all sides exactly horizontal, vertical, or at 45-degree angles?*

Hold down Shift to force lines to be exactly horizontal, vertical, or at 45-degree angles.

 5 *How can you create a perfect circle?*

Hold down Shift as you drag out the circle.

 6 *How can you change the image size to 800 by 600?*

Select Image ➢ Attributes, and then specify **800** in the Width text box and **600** in the Height text box.

 7 *How can you change the dark brown areas of the horses to the bright pink color you see when you invert the colors, while keeping all the other colors in the image as their normal colors?*

Invert the colors, pick the bright pink color and add it to the custom colors, invert the colors again, and use the Color Eraser tool to change the colors. You might also try the Fill tool to quickly fill an area.

B

Answers to Skills Challenge Questions

Answers to skills challenge questions

LESSON 9

 1 *How can you format text using the Arial Bold, Arial Italic, and Arial Bold Italic fonts?*

You need to apply the bold and italic attributes using the toolbars or the Format ➤ Font options. Windows 98 will automatically use the correct font file when you apply these attributes.

 2 *How can you tell which fonts are Windows 98 standard fonts?*

When you view fonts using the Font Viewer, the version information will include the text `MS core font` in the description.

 3 *What symbol tells you that a font is a TrueType font?*

The TT icon.

 4 *How do you know for certain how many fonts will be deleted?*

Watch the status line at the lower-left corner of the Windows Explorer window.

 5 *What do you need to do before you can install a new version of a font?*

You must first delete the existing version.

 6 *How can you make certain that your documents will use only TrueType fonts?*

Select View ➤ Options and click the TrueType tab. Make certain the Show only TrueType fonts in the programs on my computer checkbox is selected.

Answers to skills challenge questions

 7 *How can you add accents to characters in a document?*

Use the Character Map application to copy the accented characters to the Clipboard and paste them into your document.

LESSON 10

 1 *How does dragging and dropping affect the Clipboard contents?*

Dragging and dropping does not affect the Clipboard contents.

 2 *How can you copy just the active window instead of the entire screen?*

Press Alt+Print Scrn.

 3 *Which Windows 98 accessory can you use to change the size of a captured screen image?*

You can change the image size in Paint.

 4 *How can you add a captured screen image to a WordPad document?*

Select Edit ➢ Paste.

 5 *How can you tell whether an object inserted into a compound document is embedded or linked?*

One way is to double-click the object to edit the object— editing linked objects starts the source application rather than editing the object right in the compound document.

 6 *How can you create a link to an object when the source application doesn't directly support linking?*

Use the Insert ➢ Object command to insert an existing file into a compound document.

B

Answers to Skills Challenge Questions

ANSWERS TO SKILLS CHALLENGE QUESTIONS **409**

7 *What happens to the current Clipboard contents when you create a scrap?*

Nothing, because creating a scrap doesn't use the Clipboard.

LESSON 11

 1 *How can you open the Open dialog box without going through the File menu?*

Press Ctrl+O.

 2 *How can you tell (without actually using the Text tool) whether the text toolbar will be displayed when you add text to a Paint document?*

Look on the View menu for a check next to Text Toolbar.

 3 *How can you access the Taskbar when the Always on top checkbox is deselected?*

Press Ctrl+Esc.

 4 *How can you open the Print dialog box without going through the File menu?*

Press Ctrl+P.

 5 *How can you select Print to file using the keyboard?*

Press Ctrl+P to open the Print dialog box, and then press Alt+L.

 6 *How can you tile just two windows when you have three programs running?*

One way would be to right-click the Taskbar, select Tile Horizontally (or Tile Vertically), click the Minimize button on the window you don't want to see, and drag the other two windows to their desired sizes.

How can you select an entire paragraph with the mouse without dragging the mouse pointer?

Triple-click the paragraph.

LESSON 12

 Where can you find out the speed of your Internet connection?

Double-click the modem icon on the Taskbar.

 How can you tell the URL for the current page?

Look in the Address text box.

 How can you return to the previous page with a single click?

Click the Back button.

 How can you go back to `http://www.idgbooks.com` *with a single click?*

Display the history list using the down arrow at the right edge of the Address text box, and click `http://www.idgbooks.com`.

 How can you tell which part of the text on a page is a link?

It will be underlined and a different color.

 How can you tell which links you've already followed?

They will be in a different color than the other links.

Answers to skills challenge questions

LESSON 13

 How can you tell whether the same mail server provides both incoming and outgoing mail delivery to your PC?

Look in the Advanced Options dialog box. If your ISP specifies both a POP3 and an SMTP mail server, the POP3 server is incoming, and the SMTP server is outgoing.

 How can you tell Outlook Express not to check for Internet mail automatically?

Select the Work off-line and use Remote Mail checkbox.

 How can you tell if a message includes an attachment?

Look for the paper clip icon.

 How can you quickly add someone who sent you a message to your Address Book without actually opening your Address Book?

Right-click their name and select Add to Address Book.

LESSON 14

 What setting do you need to adjust if you can't see anything you type?

Click the Echo typed characters locally checkbox.

 What do you need to do if everything sent by the remote computer overwrites the previous line of text?

Click the Append line feeds to incoming line ends checkbox.

 What can you do if you can't read anything sent by the remote computer because all of the text appears in strange characters?

Select the Force incoming data to 7-bit ASCII checkbox.

 Which file transfer protocol will automatically begin sending the file as soon as the sending computer tries to start sending the file?

Zmodem.

 How can you send Clipboard text to the remote computer?

Right-click in the HyperTerminal window and select Paste to Host.

What's on the CD-ROM

The CD-ROM in the back of the book includes the exclusive *One Step at a Time On-Demand* software. This interactive software coaches you through the exercises in the book's lessons while you work on a computer at your own pace.

USING THE ONE STEP AT A TIME ON-DEMAND INTERACTIVE SOFTWARE

One Step at a Time On-Demand interactive software includes the exercises in the book so that you can search for information about how to perform a function or complete a task. You can run the software alone or in combination with the book. The software consists of three modes: Concept, Demo, and Teacher.

- **Concept** mode displays an introduction to each exercise.

Installing the software

- **Demo** mode provides a movie-style demonstration of the same steps that are presented in the book's exercises, and works with the sample exercise files included on the CD-ROM in the Exercise Files folder.

- **Teacher** mode simulates the software environment and permits you to interactively follow the exercises in the book's lessons.

■ Installing the software

The *One Step at a Time On-Demand* software can be installed on Windows 95, Windows 98, and Windows NT 4.0. To install the interactive software on your computer, follow these steps:

1 Place the *Windows 98 One Step at a Time* CD-ROM in your CD-ROM drive.

2 Launch Windows (if you haven't already).

3 Click the Start menu.

4 Select Run. The Run dialog box appears.

5 Type **D:\Setup.exe** (where D is your CD-ROM drive) in the Run dialog box.

6 Click OK to run the setup procedure. The On-Demand Installation dialog box appears.

7 Click Continue. The On-Demand Installation Options dialog box appears.

NOTE

Full/Network installation requires 150MB of hard disk space. If you don't have enough hard disk space, click the Standard radio button to choose Standard installation. If you choose Standard installation, you should always insert the CD-ROM when you start the software to hear sound.

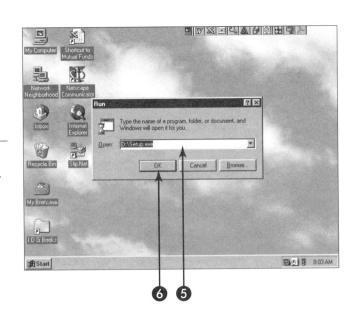

Running the software

8 Click the Full/Network radio button (if this option is not already selected).

9 Click Next. The Determine Installation Drive and Directory dialog box appears.

10 Choose the default drive and directory that appears, or click Change to choose a different drive and directory.

11 Click Next. The Product Selection dialog box appears, which enables you to verify the software you want to install.

12 Click Finish to complete the installation. The On-Demand Installation dialog box displays the progress of the installation. After the installation, the Multiuser Pack Registration dialog box appears.

13 Enter information in the Multiuser Pack Registration dialog box.

14 Click OK. The On-Demand Installation dialog box appears.

15 Click OK to confirm the installation has successfully completed.

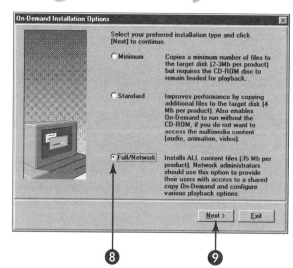

■ Running the software

After you've installed the software, you can view the text of the book and follow interactively the steps in each exercise. To run Concept, Demo, or Teacher mode, follow these steps:

1 Launch Windows 98 (or Windows 95 or NT).

2 From the Windows desktop, click the Start menu.

3 Select Programs ➤ IDG Books ➤ Windows 98 One Step. A small On-Demand toolbar appears in the upper-right corner of your screen.

4 The On-Demand Reminder dialog box appears, telling you that the On-Demand software is active. If you don't want to display the dialog box, deselect the Show Reminder check box. Then Click OK.

5 Click the icon of the professor. The Interactive Training—Lesson Selection dialog box appears.

6 Select the Contents tab, if it isn't selected already. A list of the lessons appears, divided into X parts.

7 Click the plus icon next to the part you want to explore, or click the Lessons radio button. A list of the lessons appears.

8 Click the plus icon next to the lesson you want to explore. Topics appear.

9 Double-click a topic of your choice. A menu appears.

10 Select Concept, Demo, or Teacher.

11 Follow the onscreen prompts to use the interactive software and work through the steps.

NOTE *In Demo mode, you only need to perform actions that appear in red. Otherwise, the software automatically demonstrates the actions for you. All you need to do is read the information that appears onscreen. (Holding down the Shift key pauses the program; releasing the Shift key activates the program.) In Teacher mode, you need to follow the directions and perform the actions that appear on screen.*

■ Getting the most from the One Step at a Time software

It is strongly recommended that you read the topics in the book as you are using the software. In those instances where the onscreen instructions don't match the book's instructions exactly, or the software appears to stop before completing a task, the book provides the instructions necessary for you to continue.

■ Stopping the program

To stop running the program at any time, press Esc to return to the Interactive Training — Lesson Selection dialog box. (To restart the software, double-click a topic of your choice and select a mode.)

■ Exiting the program

To exit the program, press Esc when the Interactive Training — Lesson Selection dialog box appears. The On-Demand toolbar appears in the upper-right corner of your screen. Click the icon that displays the lightning bolt image. A menu appears. Choose Exit. The On-Demand — Exit dialog box appears. Click Yes to exit On-Demand.

■ Copying exercise files to your hard drive

Generally, your computer works more efficiently with files located on the hard drive rather than on a floppy disk or CD-ROM. To make your work in this book easier, copy the exercise files into a folder on your hard drive. You can then open and work with the files from that location when instructed to do so.

1 Double-click the My Computer icon on your desktop.

2 Double-click the hard drive (C).

3 Select File ➤ New, and then choose Folder from the submenu that appears.

   A new folder appears, with the name New Folder.

4 Type **One Step** to name the folder.

5 Press Enter.

6 Close the My Computer window.

7 Place the *Windows 98 One Step at a Time* CD-ROM into the CD-ROM drive.

8 Double-click the My Computer icon again and, in the My Computer window, double-click the CD-ROM icon to open the drive where you inserted the CD-ROM.

9 Click the folder named Exercise Files.

10 Copy the selected folder by pressing Ctrl+C.

11 Close the CD-ROM window.

12 Double-click the My Computer icon on your desktop.

13 In the My Computer window, double-click the hard drive (C).

⑭ Double-click the One Step folder.

⑮ Paste the Exercise Files folder into the One Step folder by pressing Ctrl+V. All of the exercise files are now located within this folder on your hard drive.

■ Using the Exercise Files

You need to make sure you have removed the Read-only attribute from any files you copy to the hard drive before you start using them. Otherwise, you will not be able to save changes to the files. To remove the Read-only attribute, open the One Step folder on your hard drive and press Ctrl+A to select all the files in the folder. From the File menu, select Properties. The Properties dialog box appears. Click the Read-only attribute to remove the check from the checkbox.

FINDING OUT MORE ABOUT ON-DEMAND INTERACTIVE LEARNING

You may install additional modules of On-Demand Interactive Learning and find out more about PTS Learning Systems, the company behind the software, by using a file on the CD-ROM included with this book. Follow these steps:

❶ Start your browser.

❷ Select File from the menu.

❸ Select Open.

❹ Type **D:\info\welcom.htm**, where D is your CD-ROM drive.

❺ Click OK to view the contents.

The *Windows 98 One Step at a Time* CD-ROM also contains a number of bonus items that I hope you find quite useful and fun. In addition to the *One Step at a Time On Demand* interactive tutorial, you find two quite interesting folders, the Images folder and the Shareware folder.

■ **The Images folder**

The Images folder contains a number of scanned images you can use as desktop wallpaper to make your PC look a bit different from anyone else's PC. These images are photos provided by the author for your private use. You may use these images in noncommercial ways only — that is, you can use them on your desktop, but you are not permitted to use them in a commercial presentation.

■ **The Shareware folder**

The Shareware folder contains 25 shareware and trial versions of software. You may well be wondering just what shareware is. Shareware is a method of making it easy for you to try programs for a limited period of time before you decide whether the program really fills your needs. After you've tried a shareware program and decide that it's just what you need, you register the program and you can keep on using it. If you decide the program isn't worthwhile, all you need to do is to stop using the program.

It's very important to understand that shareware isn't free. The software authors who create shareware really do depend on your honesty — otherwise, why would they bother creating more shareware, updating their current products, or providing any support for their programs? If you decide to keep on using a shareware program once you've seen what it can do for you, do your part and register the program. It doesn't cost very much, and you can sleep a lot better knowing you didn't try to cheat the program's author.

The following short descriptions will give you an idea of what you find in the shareware folders. You'll find more information in each folder on the CD-ROM — look for the Readme.txt file at the top of each folder as a starting point.

Shareware

AMAZING AVI SCREEN SAVER

The Amazing AVI Screen Saver from Esm Software is perfect for livening up your screen with your favorite animations. You can cycle through a list of animations and have the animations sit at the center of your screen, appear at random positions, or float about your screen. Options include image-size adjustment, sound/mute control, and password protection.

AMAZING IMAGES SCREEN SAVER

Watch your favorite JPEG, GIF, BMP or PNG images float gracefully about your screen with the Amazing Images screen saver for Windows 95, 98, and NT 4.0 from Esm Software. The easy-to-use, tabbed dialog interface makes customizing your screen saver a snap. Options include choosing different image movements, setting the float speed, cycling through an unlimited number of images, setting password protection, and much more.

BATTLEGRID

BattleGrid, from Bob Dolan Software, is a version of the classic board game. Play against the computer or another person. Watch the computer play itself using different strategies.

CARDS+MORE

Cards+More, from Informatik, Inc., is a label and cards maker. It includes 10 graphics formats, many text attributes, rotation, Code39 bar codes, POSTNET, import, merge, drag & drop, snap to grid, auto-numbering, high-quality printing, and so on.

ECOPAD32

Ecopad32, from Azure D'or Software, is a text editor replacement for Windows Notepad that can print up to eight pages of text on one sheet of paper (on both sides!). Ecopad is compatible with all TrueType fonts/point sizes and supports any printer that can be used with Windows 95 or 98.

FIRST AID 97

Cybermedia's First Aid 97 corrects many systems problems on your PC and can warn you of serious hard drive problems.

GREEN SCREEN SAVERS

"Jumping Frog Green Saver," "Jumping Cricket Green Saver," "Jumping Katydid Green Saver," and "Kangaroo Rat Green Saver" are Windows 95, 98, and NT applications included with Digital Control Systems' Green Screen Savers. These screen savers display an animated picture (with optional sound) on your screen for a user-selected period of time.

HYPERSNAP

HyperSnap-DX from Hyperionics brings professional-quality, conveniently executed Windows 95, 98, and NT screen captures to your fingertips. It was designed for ease of use, with powerful and useful features to aid the professional as well as support the needs of the occasional user.

JOKER

The Joker, from Bob Dolan Software, is a Windows application that gives you a laugh whenever you need it. Just as your day is getting completely boring, a window will appear with a joke to break the ice. If one joke doesn't do it for you, then press the ANOTHER button for more.

MEDIACHANGER

Media Changer Deluxe from Swoosie Software is a suite of applications designed to make your Windows desktop more fun. It provides the ability to automatically change your system sounds, wallpaper bitmap, screen saver, and desktop theme.

OIL CHANGE

Cybermedia's Oil Change will search the Internet for software updates, notify you of available updates, and install the updates for you.

Shareware

PAINT SHOP PRO

Paint Shop Pro, from JASC, Inc., is a powerful and easy-to-use image-viewing, editing, and conversion program.

ROLODIAL

RoloDial/MemoPad, from Wells Software, is three programs in one. It includes an address/phone book (with envelope printing), phone dialer (with rate calculator and automatic phone log), and memo/post/sticky pad.

SCAT

SCAT, from Bob Dolan Software, is a card game involving four players that can be as simple or challenging as you want. Features include defining strategy levels, setting the game speed, and leaving the cards face up or face down as you play. This game even includes conversational chitchat between the players!

SIDEKICK 97 TRIAL

Sidekick 97, from Starfish Software, Inc., is the best-selling organizer with full-featured calendars that let you schedule unlimited calls, appointments, and to-do items. View your calendar by day, week, month, or year; set customizable alarms; and reschedule with drag-and-drop ease. Flexible contact files keep track of vital information and include powerful search features. Internet Scheduling lets you schedule anything with anyone, anywhere, anytime — as easily as sending an e-mail! Caller ID, mail merge, and more let you manage all your communications effortlessly. And Sidekick 97 lets you print to all of the popular paper formats, so you can take your schedule with you!

SMARTDRAW

SmartDraw, from SmartDraw Software, Inc., is the Windows program that lets anyone draw great-looking flowcharts, diagrams, and business graphics. Providing an easier-to-use interface and better value than Visio, SmartDraw provides drag-and-drop drawing and lines that stay connected between shapes. SmartDraw works with the Microsoft Office and other programs as an OLE server, and much more!

STARFISH INTERNET UTILITIES 97 TRIAL

Internet Utilities 97 from Starfish Software, Inc. is the number one Internet utilities survival kit; it includes a power-packed collection of utilities designed specifically to help you solve today's Internet problems. Whether you're new to the Internet or a professional Webmaster, this high-powered collection of utilities, including QuickMarks, InternetMeter, QuickZip, InternetClock, and InternetTools, helps you get more out of every Internet session. From organizing and tracking your favorite Web sites, to downloading or uploading files via QuickFTP, to pinpointing Internet connection problems with QuickRoute, Internet Utilities 97 is the best way to safely store all your bookmarks and favorites, and it helps you solve many of today's Internet problems.

THUMBSPLUS

ThumbsPlus, from Cerious Software, Inc., helps with browsing, converting, organizing, viewing, editing, and cataloging graphic files. It supports over 40 file formats internally, with many more formats that can be configured or accessed via OLE.

TURBOBROWSER

Turbo Browser is designed to provide you with convenient file-management and file-viewing capabilities. The Files and Folders window is similar to that of Windows 95/98/NT 4.0 Explorer. When you choose a file in the Files and Folders window, the file contents are automatically displayed in the Preview window. By moving up and down the file list, you can easily view additional files.

TURBOZIP

TurboZIP from Pacific Gold Coast Software is a powerful ZIP archive and e-mail manager for the most commonly used Internet compressed file formats (zip, exe, gz, z, tar, taz, tgz), as well as Microsoft Windows compressed file formats and e-mail file formats — UU Encode (uue), MIME (mme, b64), and Binhex (hqx). TurboZIP provides seamless zipping/unzipping, disk spanning, creation of self-extracting (SFX) files, and encoding/decoding features.

C

What's on the CD-ROM

Shareware

From Bob Dolan Software, WinGO! is the latest version of the original BINGO game for Windows. Many new features have been added to make this game the most fun for all BINGO players.

WRACKO

WRackO, from Bob Dolan Software, is a challenging, card-type strategy game that you can play against the computer or another person. It is easy to learn and simple to master. Quick thinking and risk taking are essential to being a winner in WrackO.

■ The Text folder

The Text folder contains a PDF (portable document format) version of *Windows 98 One Step at a Time*, and the Adobe Acrobat Reader, which enables you to view, navigate, and print PDF files.

A

alignment Positioning of text relative to the left or right margin.

anchor position The beginning of the object or selection.

animated cursor A mouse pointer that includes movement.

Argument A piece of additional information controlling how a program runs. Also known as a *parameter*.

Attach To include a file with a message.

Audio Visual Interleave (AVI) Windows 98 video files in which the audio and video portions are both included — interleaved — in the same file.

B

bitmap An image file in which all objects are part of a single object.

Blind carbon copy (Bcc) A copy that the other recipients don't know about.

boot disk A disk you can use to start Windows 98.

Boss key The key that quickly hides 3D Pinball - the Esc key.

bounding box An imaginary rectangular box as wide and as high as the object being drawn.

bullets Markers often seen at the left of a list of summary points.

C

cascading menu A menu that appears and offers additional choices when a menu item that has an arrow is selected.

Clipboard A Windows 98 tool you can use to cut, copy, and paste objects.

combo box A list box that includes a list box and a text box.

command-line interface The MS-DOS window where you type commands. Also known as the *prompt*.

compound documents Documents containing data from a number of sources.

Compressed Volume File (CVF) A special file used by DriveSpace to create additional space on a disk by storing everything in a single, compressed file.

cookie A text file that contains information about a Web surfer's visits to Web sites.

cover page An extra sheet sent at the beginning of a fax.

cross-linked Multiple files that seem to be using the same disk space. At least one of each pair of cross-linked files will probably be unusable.

D

desktop theme A special collection of color schemes, wallpaper, animated cursors, and sounds in Plus!

destination disk

destination disk The target disk.

Distribution Media Format (DMF) Diskettes specially formatted to prevent them from being copied.

downloading Receiving files.

dragging Holding down the left mouse button while moving a selected object.

draw program A program that creates objects that can be stretched or moved independently of any other objects in the image.

dropping Releasing an object by letting up on the mouse button.

E

ellipsis Three periods that follow a menu command, indicating that a dialog box will appear when the command is selected.

embedding Placing an OLE object in a document.

error-correcting file transfer protocol A method of breaking up files into relatively small pieces and verifying that each of those pieces is received properly to ensure that files are transferred properly.

event Something that can be assigned a sound, such as starting Windows 98, opening a menu, or closing a program.

F

file transfer protocol A method ensuring that files are transferred properly.

focus The dotted outline showing which dialog box element is currently active.

formatting The process of creating the electronic marks that allow your disk drives to write in the right places on a disk.

fragmented Stored in several noncontiguous pieces on a disk.

G

Graphical User Interface or **GUI** ("gooey") The Windows 98 visual-style interface. In contrast, MS-DOS uses a *command line interface* or *prompt*.

H

host drive The drive letter used to access the physical drive rather than the compressed drive.

hotkey Alt + the underlined character, which activates a menu command.

I

icon A small picture that represents a program or document.

indent Extra distance between the document margin and the paragraph margin.

in-place editing A temporary appearance change that allows use of a source application's toolbars so an object can edited without leaving the document.

insertion pointer The slowly blinking vertical line where new text will appear.

Internet service provider (ISP) A company that provides access to the Internet.

invert A special effect in which each color is replaced by its complement.

L

link A connection to another Web page.

linking Placing a reference to an OLE object in a document.

lost file fragments Leftover pieces of files that are taking up space even though the file was deleted.

M

margin The distance printing begins from the edge of the paper.

MS-DOS mode The operating mode in which your entire system is dedicated to running an MS-DOS program.

MS-DOS prompt The MS-DOS command line you use to issue DOS commands.

Musical Instrument Digital Interface (MIDI) A method of generating music using a synthesizer.

N

Null modem cable A special cable that enables two PCs to talk directly to each other.

O

Object Linking and Embedding (OLE) A way to share data that allows you to create *compound documents*.

OLE client A program that can receive drag and drop information.

OLE server A program that can send drag and drop data.

P

paint program A graphics program that creates *bitmap* images.

parameter A piece of additional information that controls how a program runs. Also known as an *argument*.

password A secret word that allows access to a resource such as a folder.

pica A typographic measurement approximately $1/12$ of an inch.

pixel A unit of measure of screen resolution. Short for picture element.

point A typographic measurement. There are approximately 72 points in an inch.

polygon A multisided object.

R

Registry A special database Windows 98 uses to keep track of a lot of important information about your system. If the Registry is damaged, you may not be able to use your computer.

Restore The process of making backed-up files available for use.

root directory The ultimate parent of all the folders on a disk.

ruler The measurement line just above the text window in a word processor.

S

sampling rate The number of times per second sound is recorded.

scrap A piece of a document saved on the desktop.

search engine A service that indexes Web pages.

shortcut A copy of an icon used to access a program or document.

skewing Leaning a selection at an angle.

source disk The original disk used in a copy operation.

stretching Making a selection grow or shrink by a percentage.

T

tabs Fixed points used to specify precise text positioning.

terminal program A program that makes your PC into a communications terminal so you can upload and download files.

toggle A command that changes states from selected to deselected, or deselected to selected, each time the command is selected.

Tooltips Hints that appear when the mouse pointer is held over Toolbar buttons.

TrueType fonts Scalable fonts.

U

uploading Sending files.

Uniform Resource Locator (URL) The address for a Web page.

V

virtual desktop An area larger than the actual monitor display provided by some display adapters.

W

wave files Windows 98 sound files that are simply a digital recording of sounds.

Web browser A program that enables a Web surfer to view the contents of pages on the *World Wide Web*, the graphical portion of the Internet.

word wrap The action used to display lines longer than the width of the window.

World Wide Web The graphical portion of the Internet. Often simply called the *Web*.

write-protect slider A small plastic rectangle on the diskette that prevents your PC from writing anything on this diskette until you move the slider back to cover the hole.

Glossary

A–C

D

D–F

Index

FAT32 incompatibility, 125-126
HiPack compression, 131
operating systems and, 125
troubleshooting, 144
UltraPack compression, 131

E

e-mail. *See* Outlook Express
Echo typed characters locally
checkbox, HyperTerminal, 382
Edit Colors dialog box, Paint utility,
248-249
Edit Play List button, CD Player, 157
editing
file types, 112
in-place, 291
Paint utility, 240-244
shortcut names, 34
text in text boxes, 313-315
Windows 98 applications, 323-325
Effects tab, Display Properties dialog
box, 60-61, 69
ellipses, Windows 98 applications and,
305
embedding
dragging and dropping comparison, 290
OLE (Object Linking and Embedding),
288-290
energy-saving feature, screen savers,
65-66
Eraser/Color Eraser button, Paint
utility, 230, 243
events, adding sounds to, 155-156
exercise files, *One Step at a Time
On-Demand* interactive
software, 420
Explorer. *See* Internet Explorer;
Windows Explorer

F

FAT32 file system, 134-136
Drive Converter utility, 135-136
DriveSpace incompatibility, 125-126
favorite sites, browsing with Internet
Explorer, 352
Favorites option, Start menu, 5
faxes, Imaging tool, 164-165
File Allocation Table. *See* FAT32 file
system
file listings, MS-DOS command prompt,
195
file previews (Quick View), right
mouse button, 14
file transfer protocols, HyperTerminal,
383-384
file types, 110-112
displaying or hiding, 108-109
editing, 112
registering, 110-111
WordPad and, 207
filenames
finding files with, 23-25
long. *See* long filenames
files, 87-116
copying, 96-98
copying to diskettes, 122-123
creating folders for, 95-96
deleting, 27-28, 98-101
finding, 23-27, 87-92
inserting into documents, 292-294
long filenames, 23-25, 101-105
moving and copying, 96-98
naming, 96-97, 103-104
recovering from Recycle Bin, 28-29
selecting, 92-94
Send To command, 41-42

sending via Outlook Express (e-mail),
368-369
Skills Challenge, 115
sorting, 105-107
System File Checker, 79-80
Task Scheduler, 112-114
types of. *See* file types
viewing, 105-109
Fill with Color button, Paint utility,
230, 237
Find option, Start menu, 6
finding files, 23-27, 87-92
advanced techniques, 26-27
by dates, 25-26
by filenames, 23-25
Containing text box, 27
Date tab, 91
quotation marks (") and, 25, 104
Save Results command, 90, 91
Save Search command, 90, 91
selecting files and folders, 92-94
finding and replacing text, WordPad,
211-213
flipping and rotating selections, Paint
utility, 244-245
floppy disks. *See* diskettes
focus, defined, 312
Folder Options dialog box, mouse
single-click option, 75-76
folders
copying, 96-98
creating, 95-96
deleting, 98-101
moving and copying, 96-98
naming, 23, 96-97, 103-104
selecting, 92-94
shortcuts for, 33
sorting, 105-107
Windows Explorer, 20

INDEX **435**

Index

K–M

K

keyboard
    adjusting settings, 76–77
    dialog boxes and, 311–313
    switching between programs with,
        309–310
keyboard shortcuts, 277–279
    Accessibility options, 278

L

**Label text box, formatting diskettes,
    121**
**Landscape radio button, WordPad Page
    Setup dialog box, 208**
**Large Icons option, sorting files and
    folders, 107**
left-handed mouse, 74
Line button, Paint utility, 231
**lines, drawing with Paint toolbox, 233–
    235**
**linking, OLE (Object Linking and
    Embedding), 288, 292–294**
links
    See also addresses
    Internet Explorer and, 338, 341, 350
listing fonts, 257–259
    troubleshooting, 271
log file for installing programs, 179–181
logging onto networks, 3
long filenames, 23–25, 101–105
    MS-DOS and, 104–105, 196
    networks and, 102
    root directory and, 102
    size of, 102
    special characters in, 102
**lost file fragments, ScanDisk (checking
    disks for damage), 140**

M

Magnify button, Paint utility, 230
mail. *See* Outlook Express (e-mail)
Mail list box, Internet Explorer, 345
**mail servers, ISPs (Internet Service
    Providers), 331**
**Make copies radio button, ScanDisk
    (checking disks for damage),
    140**
**margin settings, WordPad Page Setup
    dialog box, 208**
Media Player
    audio clips in documents, 149–151
    playing sounds, 148–149
    video files, 159–160
menu bar, Windows Explorer, 19–20
**menus and commands, Windows 98
    applications, 304–306**
**MIDI tab, Multimedia Properties dialog
    box, 167, 169**
**minus sign (–), Windows Explorer
    folders, 20**
modems, Internet Explorer and, 337
monitors
    color options, 53–55
    energy-saving feature, 65–66
    screen resolution, 51–53
mouse, 11–14
    customizing, 72–77
    dialog boxes and, 310–311
    dragging and dropping with, 28, 283–
        287
    left-handed, 74
    moving and copying text, 210–211
    right button, 13–14
    right-clicking to open Windows
        Explorer, 19–21
    selecting files and folders, 94

    selecting multiple items, 12–13
    single-click option, 75–76
    single-clicking and double-clicking,
        11–12
    single-clicking and double-clicking
        options, 8
    speed of double-clicking and pointers,
        72–73
    trails, 74–75
    triple-clicking to select paragraphs, 324
    Windows 98 applications and, 304–305
Mouse Properties dialog box
    double-click and pointer speed, 72–73
    trails, 74–75
moving
    See also dragging and dropping with
        mouse
    files and folders, 96–98
    Taskbar, 69–70
    WordPad text, 210–211
MS-DOS, 194–199
    installing programs and Windows
        comparison, 174–175
    long filenames and, 104–105
MS-DOS command prompt, 194–197
    file listings, 195
    font sizing, 196
    long filenames and, 196
    troubleshooting, 201
    TrueType fonts, 196
MS-DOS mode, 197–199
    Advanced Program Settings dialog
        box, 198
    caveat, 194
    CD-ROM drives and, 197
    Properties dialog box, 198–199
    Wolf.com, 197–199
multimedia, 145–172
    configuring for performance, 165–170

Index

P

S

W

IDG BOOKS WORLDWIDE, INC.
END-USER LICENSE AGREEMENT

Read This. You should carefully read these terms and conditions before opening the software packet(s) included with this book ("Book"). This is a license agreement ("Agreement") between you and IDG Books Worldwide, Inc. ("IDGB"). By opening the accompanying software packet(s), you acknowledge that you have read and accept the following terms and conditions. If you do not agree and do not want to be bound by such terms and conditions, promptly return the Book and the unopened software packet(s) to the place you obtained them for a full refund.

1. **License Grant.** IDGB grants to you (either an individual or entity) a nonexclusive license to use one copy of the enclosed software program(s) (collectively, the "Software") solely for your own personal or business purposes on a single computer (whether a standard computer or a workstation component of a multi-user network). The Software is in use on a computer when it is loaded into temporary memory (i.e., RAM) or installed into permanent memory (e.g., hard disk, CD-ROM or other storage device). IDGB reserves all rights not expressly granted herein.

2. **Ownership.** IDGB is the owner of all rights, titles, and interests, including copyright, in and to the compilation of the Software recorded on the CD-ROM. Copyright to the individual programs on the CD-ROM is owned by the author or other authorized copyright owner of each program. Ownership of the Software and all proprietary rights relating thereto remain with IDGB and its licensors.

3. **Restrictions on Use and Transfer.**

   (a) You may only (i) make one copy of the Software for backup or archival purposes, or (ii) transfer the Software to a single hard disk, provided that you keep the original for backup or archival purposes. You may not (i) rent or lease the Software, (ii) copy or reproduce the Software through a LAN or other network system or through any computer subscriber system or bulletin-board system, or (iii) modify, adapt, or create derivative works based on the Software.

   (b) You may not reverse engineer, decompile, or disassemble the Software. You may transfer the Software and user documentation on a permanent basis, provided that the transferee agrees to accept the terms and conditions of this Agreement and you retain no copies. If the Software is an update or has been updated, any transfer must include the most recent update and all prior versions.

4. **Restrictions on Use of Individual Programs.** You must follow the individual requirements and restrictions detailed for each individual program on the CD-ROM Installation Instructions page of this Book. These limitations are contained in the individual license agreements recorded on the CD-ROM. These restrictions include a requirement that after using the program for the period of time specified in its text, the user must pay a registration fee or discontinue use. By opening the Software packet(s), you will be agreeing to abide by the licenses and restrictions for these individual programs. None of the material on this disc or listed in this Book may ever be distributed, in original or modified form, for commercial purposes.

5. Limited Warranty.

   (a) IDGB warrants that the Software and CD-ROM are free from defects in materials and workmanship under normal use for a period of sixty (60) days from the date of purchase of this Book. If IDGB receives notification within the warranty period of defects in materials or workmanship, IDGB will replace the defective CD-ROM.

   (b) IDGB AND THE AUTHOR OF THE BOOK DISCLAIM ALL OTHER WARRANTIES, EXPRESS OR IMPLIED, INCLUDING WITHOUT LIMITATION IMPLIED WARRANTIES OF MERCHANTABILITY AND FITNESS FOR A PARTICULAR PURPOSE, WITH RESPECT TO THE SOFTWARE, THE PROGRAMS, THE SOURCE CODE CONTAINED THEREIN, AND/OR THE TECHNIQUES DESCRIBED IN THIS BOOK. IDGB DOES NOT WARRANT THAT THE FUNCTIONS CONTAINED IN THE SOFTWARE WILL MEET YOUR REQUIREMENTS OR THAT THE OPERATION OF THE SOFTWARE WILL BE ERROR FREE.

   (c) This limited warranty gives you specific legal rights, and you may have other rights that vary from jurisdiction to jurisdiction.

6. Remedies.

   (a) IDGB's entire liability and your exclusive remedy for defects in materials and workmanship shall be limited to replacement of the Software, which is returned to IDGB at the address set forth below with a copy of your receipt. This Limited Warranty is void if failure of the Software has resulted from accident, abuse, or misapplication. Any replacement Software will be warranted for the remainder of the original warranty period or thirty (30) days, whichever is longer.

   (b) In no event shall IDGB or the author be liable for any damages whatsoever (including without limitation damages for loss of business profits, business interruption, loss of business information, or any other pecuniary loss) arising out of the use of or inability to use the Book or the Software, even if IDGB has been advised of the possibility of such damages.

   (c) Because some jurisdictions do not allow the exclusion or limitation of liability for consequential or incidental damages, the above limitation or exclusion may not apply to you.

7. U.S. Government Restricted Rights. Use, duplication, or disclosure of the Software by the U.S. Government is subject to restrictions stated in paragraph (c) (1) (ii) of the Rights in Technical Data and Computer Software clause of DFARS 252.227-7013, and in subparagraphs (a) through (d) of the Commercial Computer—Restricted Rights clause at FAR 52.227-19, and in similar clauses in the NASA FAR supplement, when applicable.

8. General. This Agreement constitutes the entire understanding of the parties, and revokes and supersedes all prior agreements, oral or written, between them and may not be modified or amended except in a writing signed by both parties hereto which specifically refers to this Agreement. This Agreement shall take precedence over any other documents that may be in conflict herewith. If any one or more provisions contained in this Agreement are held by any court or tribunal to be invalid, illegal or otherwise unenforceable, each and every other provision shall remain in full force and effect.

CD-ROM Installation
Instructions

The CD-ROM includes the interactive *One Step at a Time On-Demand* software. This software coaches you through the exercises in the book while you work on a computer at your own pace.

The CD-ROM also includes 25 shareware and trial versions of software specially selected to introduce you to some great Windows programs.

Installing the software

INSTALLING THE ONE STEP AT A TIME ON-DEMAND INTERACTIVE SOFTWARE

The *One Step at a Time On-Demand* software can be installed on Windows 95, Windows 98, and Windows NT 4.0. To install the interactive software on your computer, follow these steps:

1 Place the *Windows 98 One Step at a Time* CD-ROM in your CD-ROM drive.

2 Launch Windows (if you haven't already).

3 Click the Start menu.

4 Select Run. The Run dialog box appears.

5 Type **D:\Setup.exe** (where D is your CD-ROM drive) in the Run dialog box.

6 Click OK to run the setup procedure. The On-Demand Installation dialog box appears.

7 Click Continue. The On-Demand Installation Options dialog box appears.

8 Click the Full/Network radio button (if this option is not already selected).

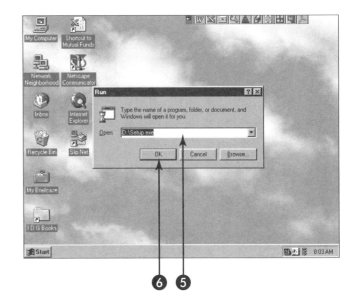

 NOTE *Full/Network installation requires 150MB of hard disk space. If you don't have enough hard disk space, click the Standard radio button to choose Standard installation. If you choose standard installation, you should always insert the CD-ROM when you start the software to hear sound.*

9 Click Next. The Determine Installation Drive and Directory dialog box appears.

10 Choose the default drive and directory that appears, or click Change to choose a different drive and directory.

11 Click Next. The Product Selection dialog box appears, which enables you to verify the software you want to install.

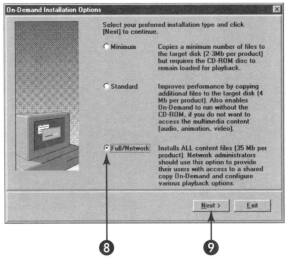

Copying exercise files

⑫ Click Finish to complete the installation. The On-Demand Installation dialog box displays the progress of the installation. After the installation, the Multiuser Pack Registration dialog box appears.

⑬ Enter information in the Multiuser Pack Registration dialog box.

⑭ Click OK. The On-Demand Installation dialog box appears.

⑮ Click OK to confirm the installation has been successfully completed.

Please see Appendix C, "What's on the CD-ROM," for information about running the *One Step at a Time On-Demand* interactive software.

■ Copying exercise files to your hard drive

Generally, your computer works more efficiently with files located on the hard drive rather than on a floppy disk or CD-ROM. To make your work in this book easier, copy the exercise files into a folder on your hard drive. You can then open and work with the files from that location when instructed to do so.

1 Double-click the My Computer icon on your desktop.

2 Double-click the hard drive (C:).

3 Select File ➢ New, and then choose Folder from the submenu that appears.

A new folder appears, with the name New Folder.

4 Type **One Step** to name the folder.

5 Press Enter.

6 Close the My Computer window.

7 Place the *Windows 98 One Step at a Time* CD-ROM into the CD-ROM drive.

8 Double-click the My Computer icon again. In the My Computer window, double-click the CD-ROM icon to open the drive where you inserted the CD-ROM.

9 Click the folder named Exercise Files.

10 Copy the selected folder by pressing Ctrl+C.

11 Close the CD-ROM window.

12 Double-click the My Computer icon on your desktop.

13 In the My Computer window, double-click the hard drive (C:).

14 Double-click the One Step folder.

15 Paste the Exercise Files folder into the One Step folder by pressing Ctrl+V. All of the exercise files are now located within this folder on your hard drive.

■ Using the exercise files

You need to make sure you have removed the Read-only attribute from any files you copy to the hard drive before you start using them. Otherwise, you will not be able to save changes to the files. To remove the Read-only attribute, open the One Step folder on your hard drive and press Ctrl+A to select all the files in the folder. From the File menu, select Properties. The Properties dialog box appears. Click the Read-only attribute to remove the check from the check box.

INSTALLING THE SHAREWARE AND TRIAL PROGRAMS ON THE CD-ROM

Each of the programs includes its own setup program, and each program is in its own folder. In most cases the setup program is called Setup.exe or Install.exe. If you don't find either one, take a look at !Readme.txt for further instructions.

To install the shareware programs, follow these steps:

1 Insert the *Windows 98 One Step at a Time* CD-ROM in your CD-ROM drive.

2 Click the Start button.

3 Select Programs ➢ Windows Explorer.

4 Select the Shareware folder on the CD-ROM.